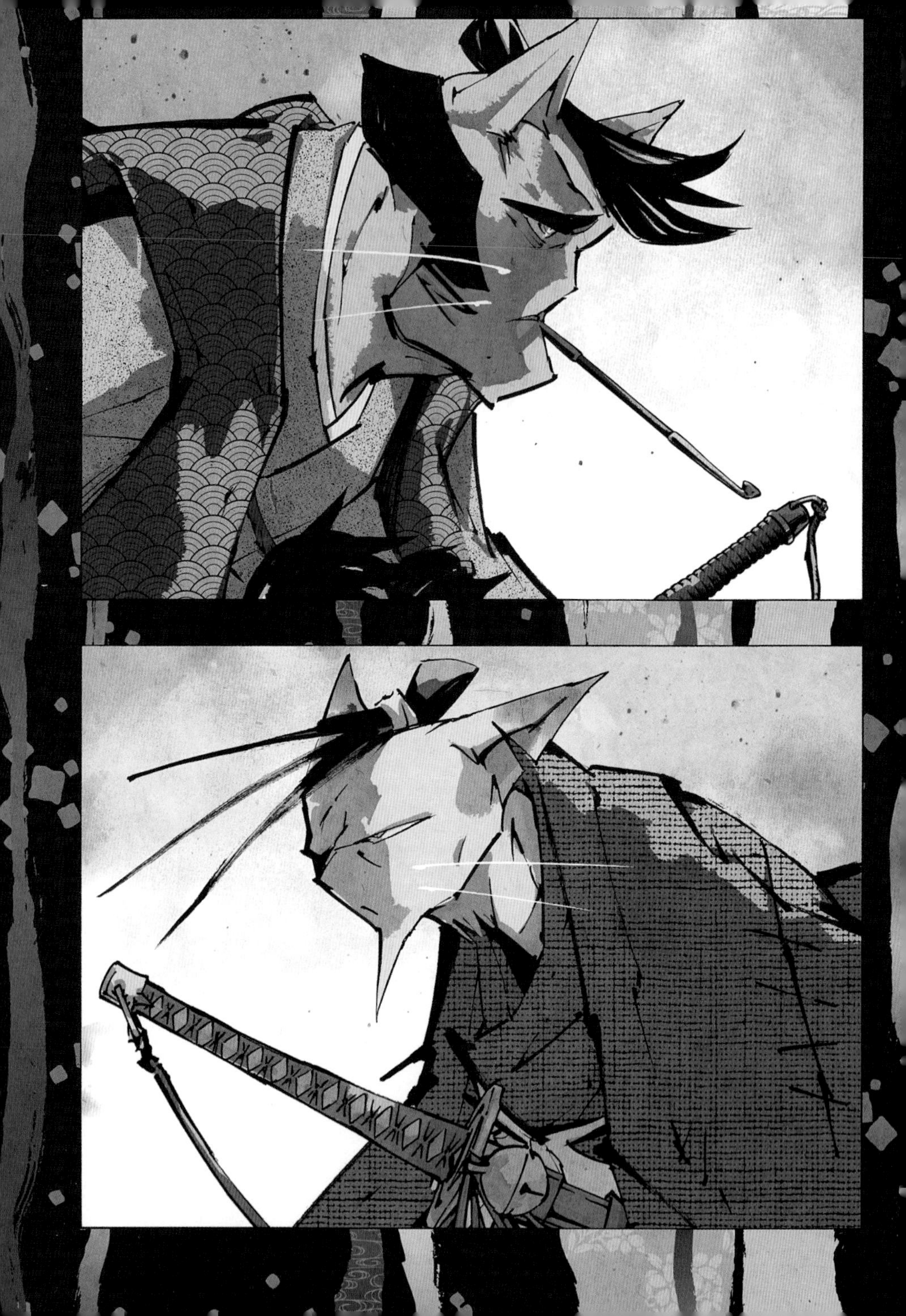

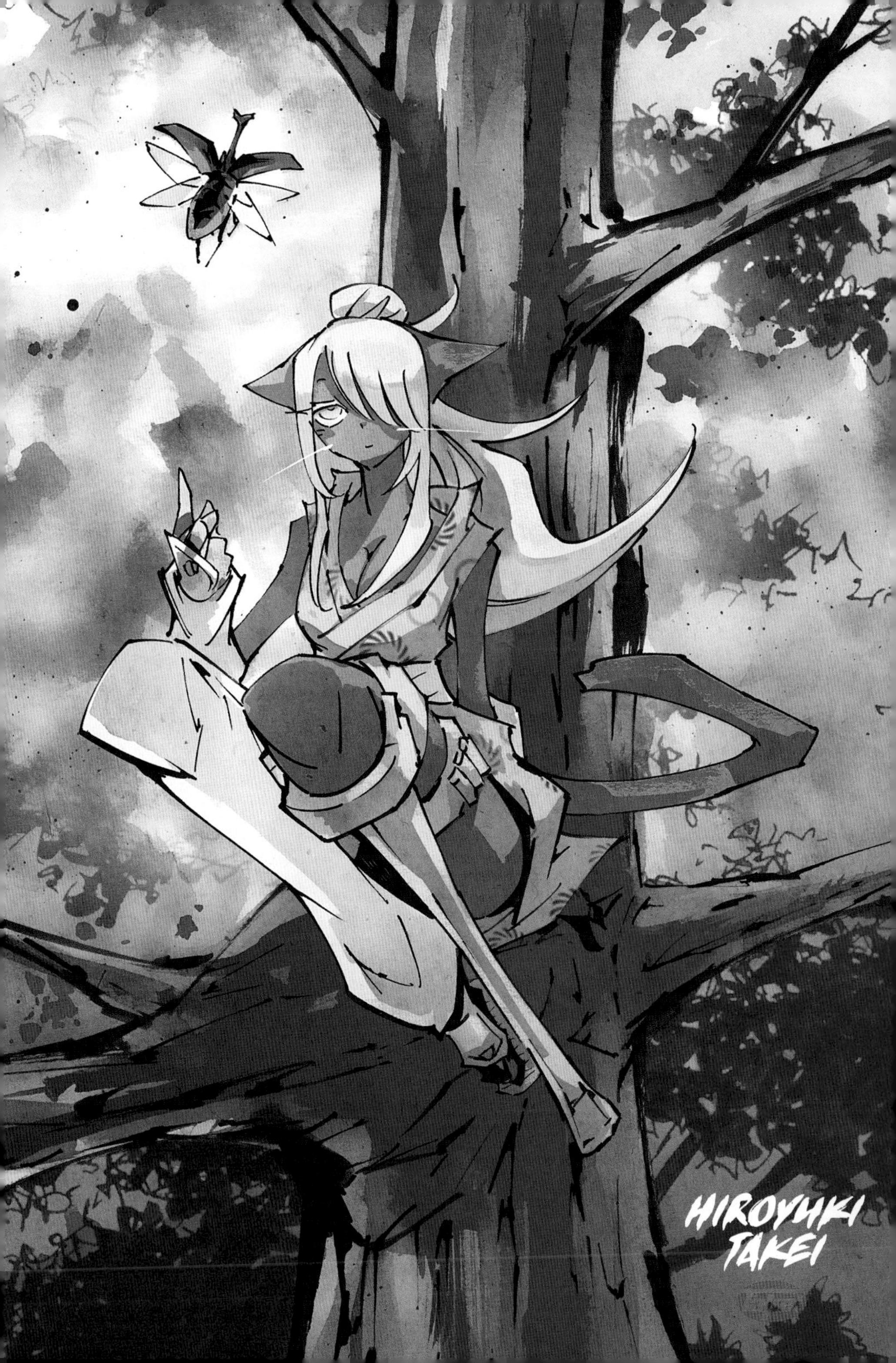
HIROYUKI
TAKEI

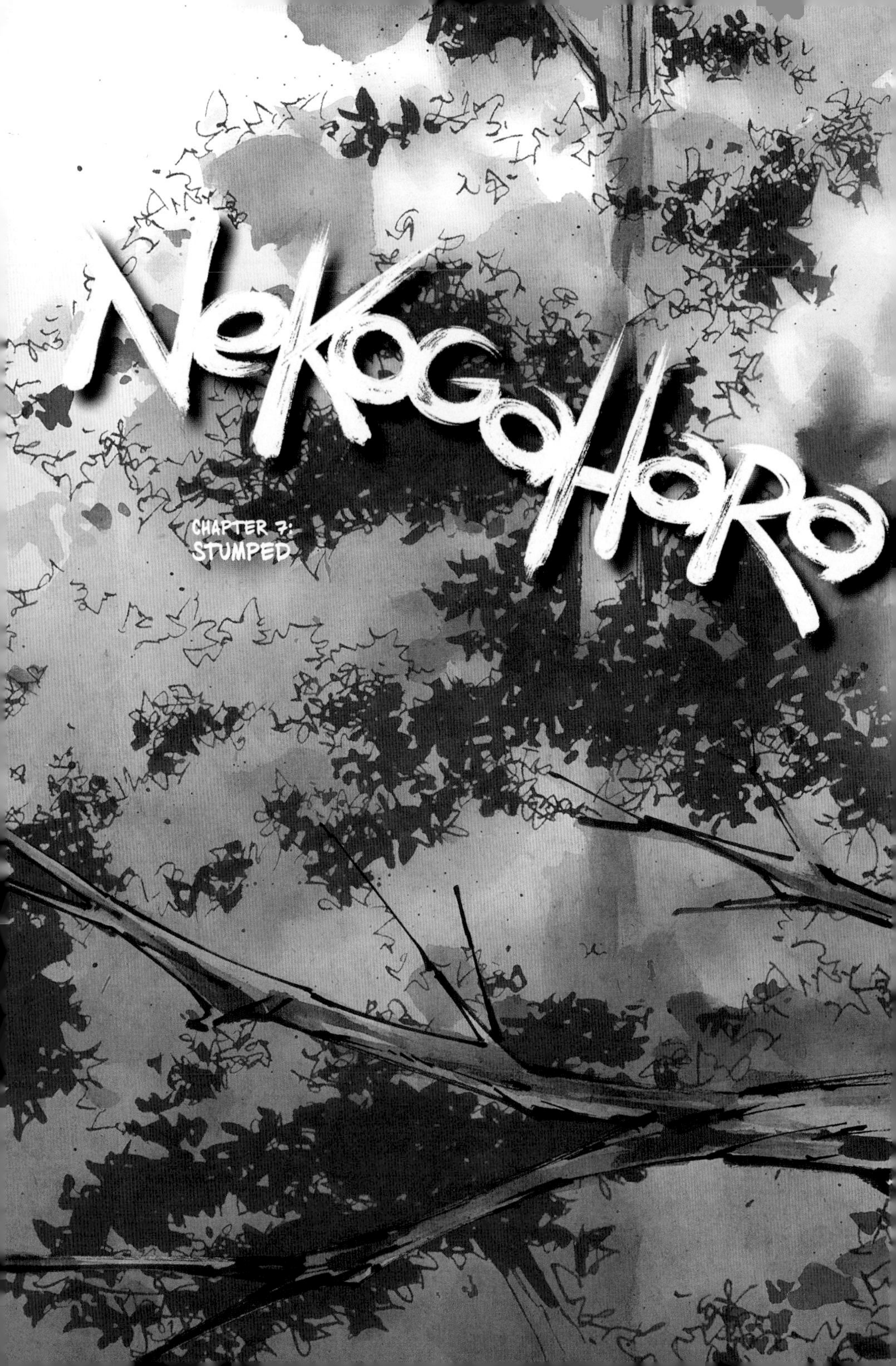
NEKOGAHARA
CHAPTER 7:
STUMPED

NEKOGAHARA VOLUME TWO CONTENTS

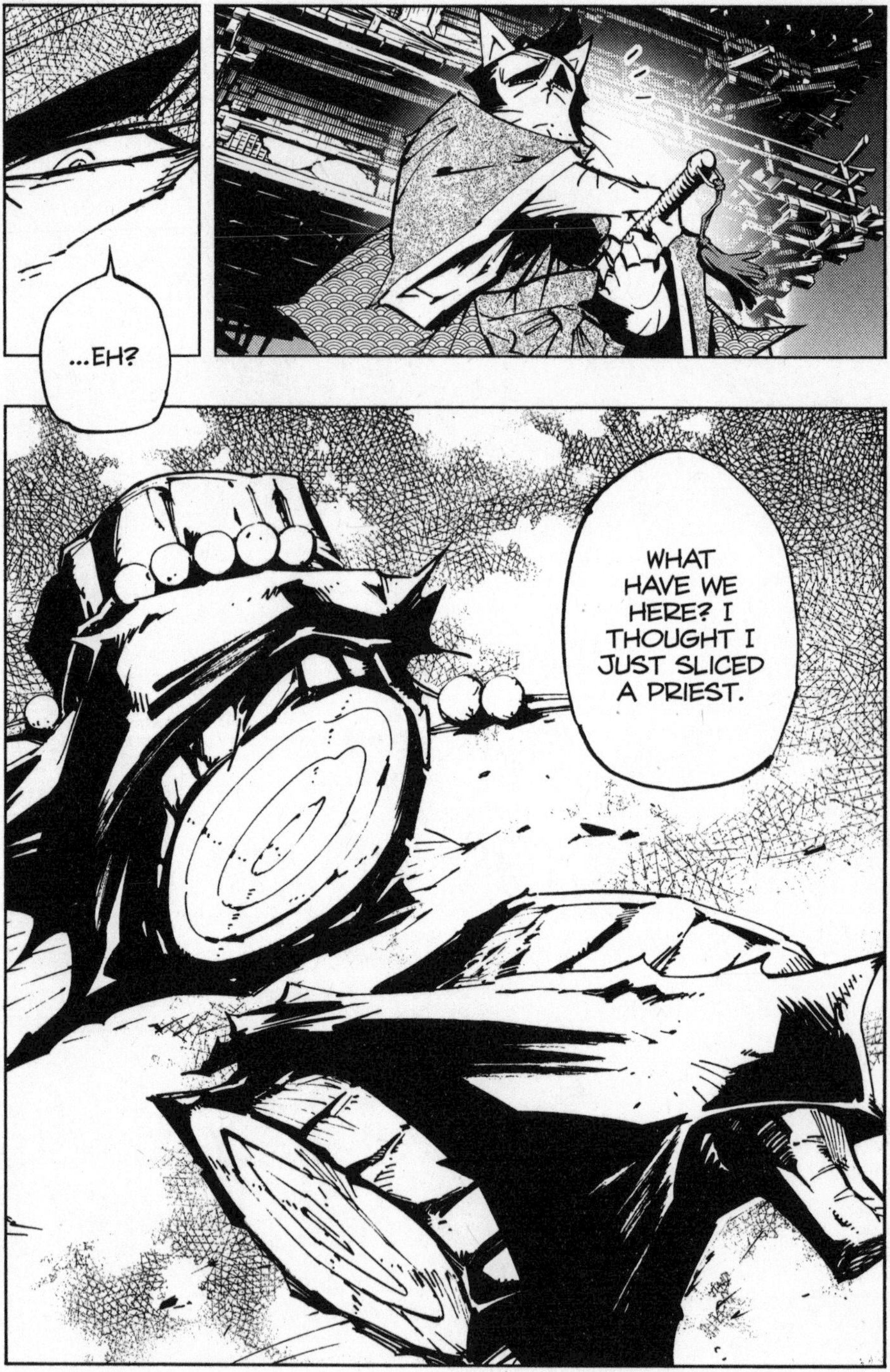
...EH?
WHAT HAVE WE HERE? I THOUGHT I JUST SLICED A PRIEST.

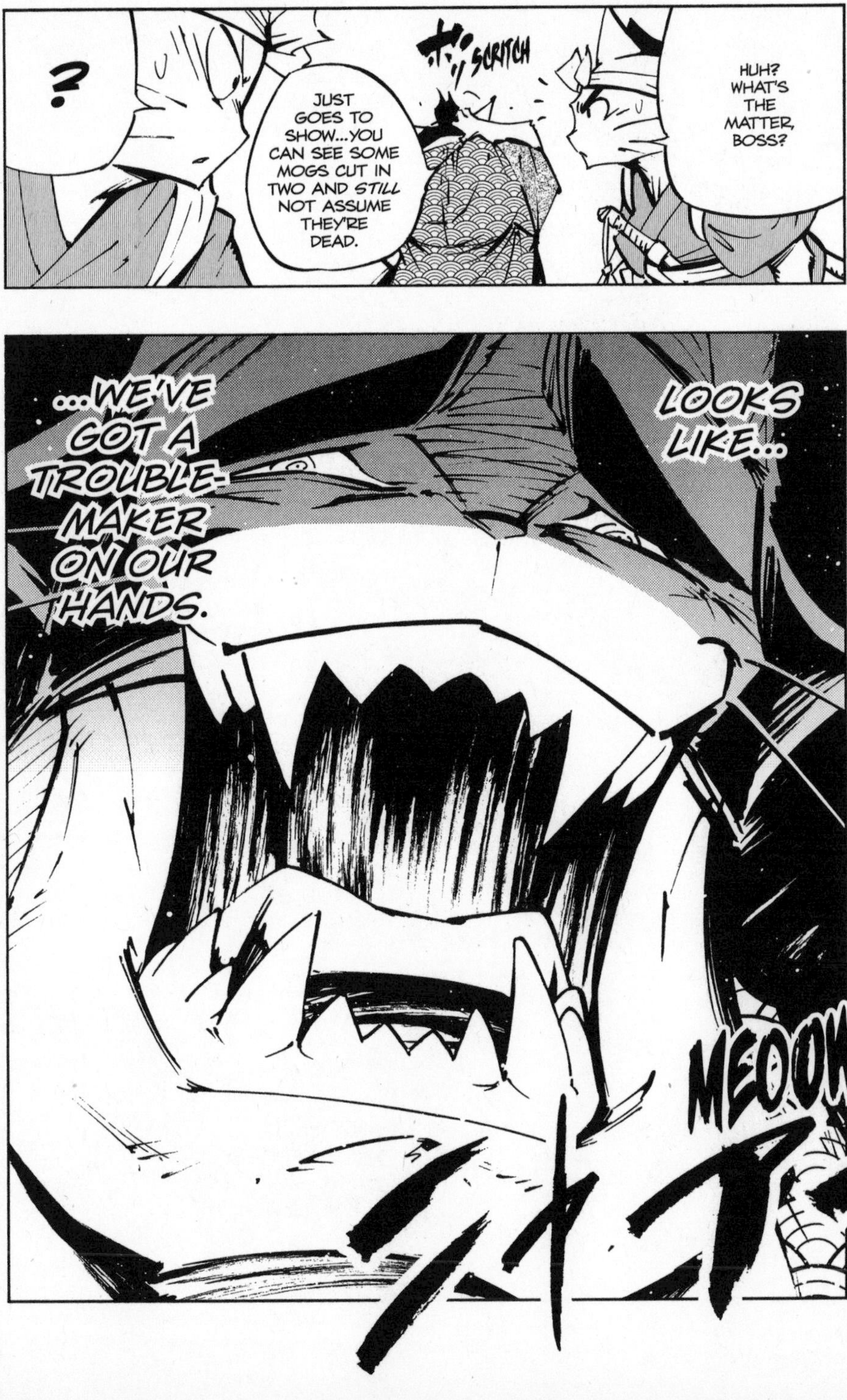
HUH? WHAT'S THE MATTER, BOSS?
SCRITCH
JUST GOES TO SHOW...YOU CAN SEE SOME MOGS CUT IN TWO AND *STILL* NOT ASSUME THEY'RE DEAD.
?
LOOKS LIKE...
...WE'VE GOT A TROUBLE-MAKER ON OUR HANDS.
MEOOW

猫ヶ原

ネコガハラ

NEKOGAHARA

CHAPTER 7: STUMPED

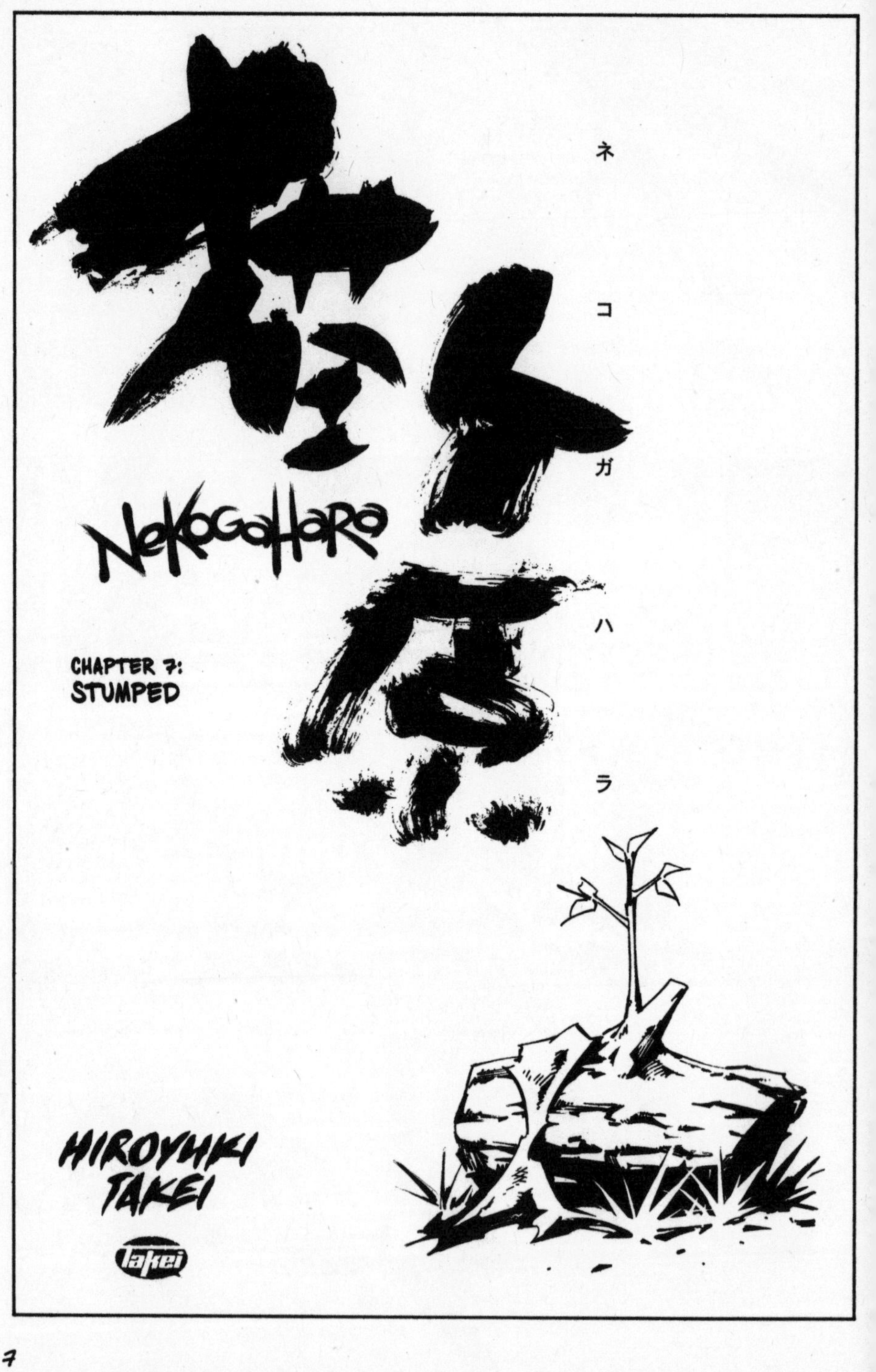

HIROYUKI TAKEI

Takei

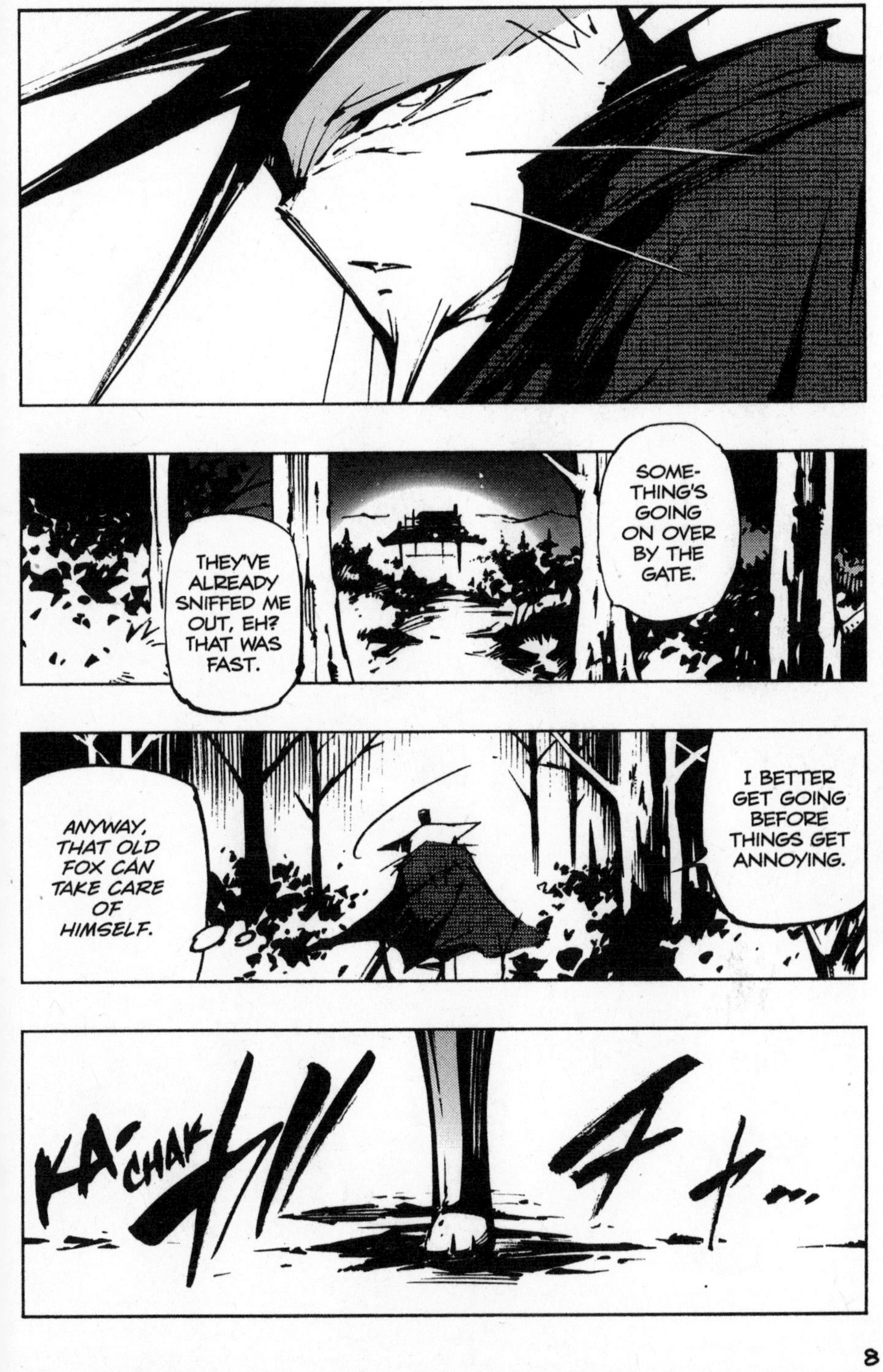
SOME-THING'S GOING ON OVER BY THE GATE.
THEY'VE ALREADY SNIFFED ME OUT, EH? THAT WAS FAST.
I BETTER GET GOING BEFORE THINGS GET ANNOYING.
ANYWAY, THAT OLD FOX CAN TAKE CARE OF HIMSELF.
KA-CHAK

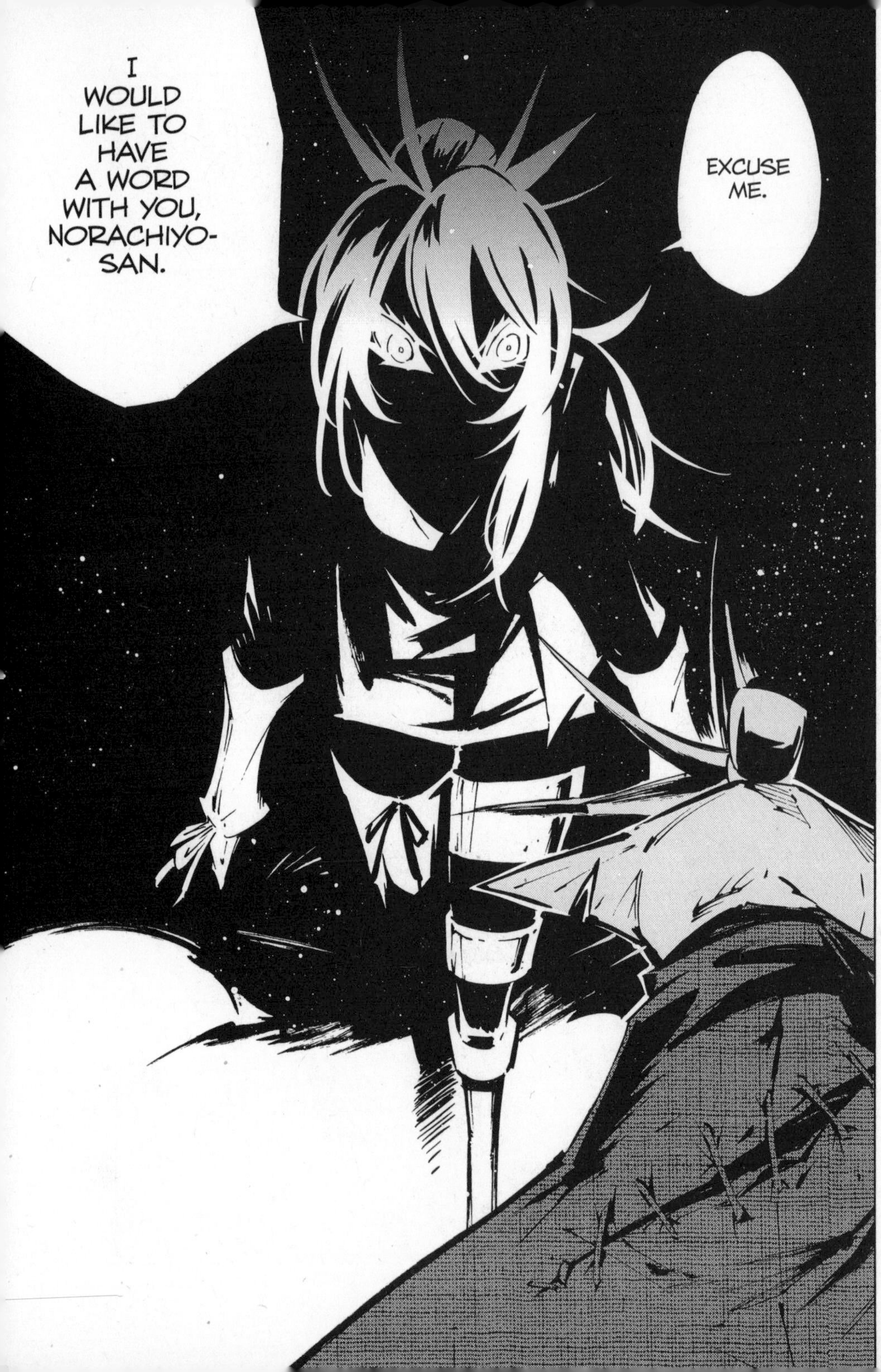
EXCUSE ME.
I WOULD LIKE TO HAVE A WORD WITH YOU, NORACHIYO-SAN.

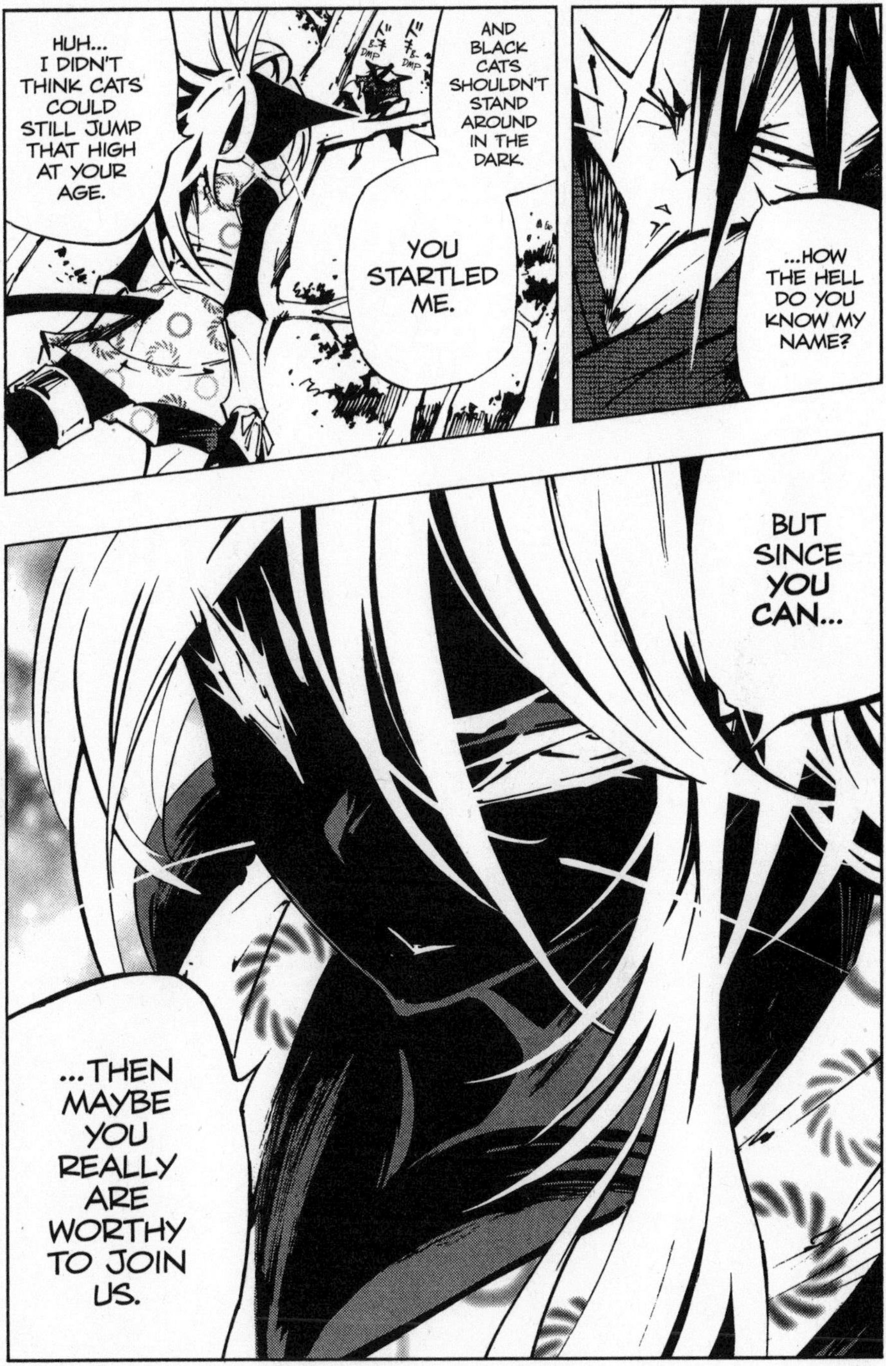
...HOW THE HELL DO YOU KNOW MY NAME?
AND BLACK CATS SHOULDN'T STAND AROUND IN THE DARK.
HUH... I DIDN'T THINK CATS COULD STILL JUMP THAT HIGH AT YOUR AGE.
YOU STARTLED ME.
BUT SINCE YOU CAN...
...THEN MAYBE YOU REALLY ARE WORTHY TO JOIN US.

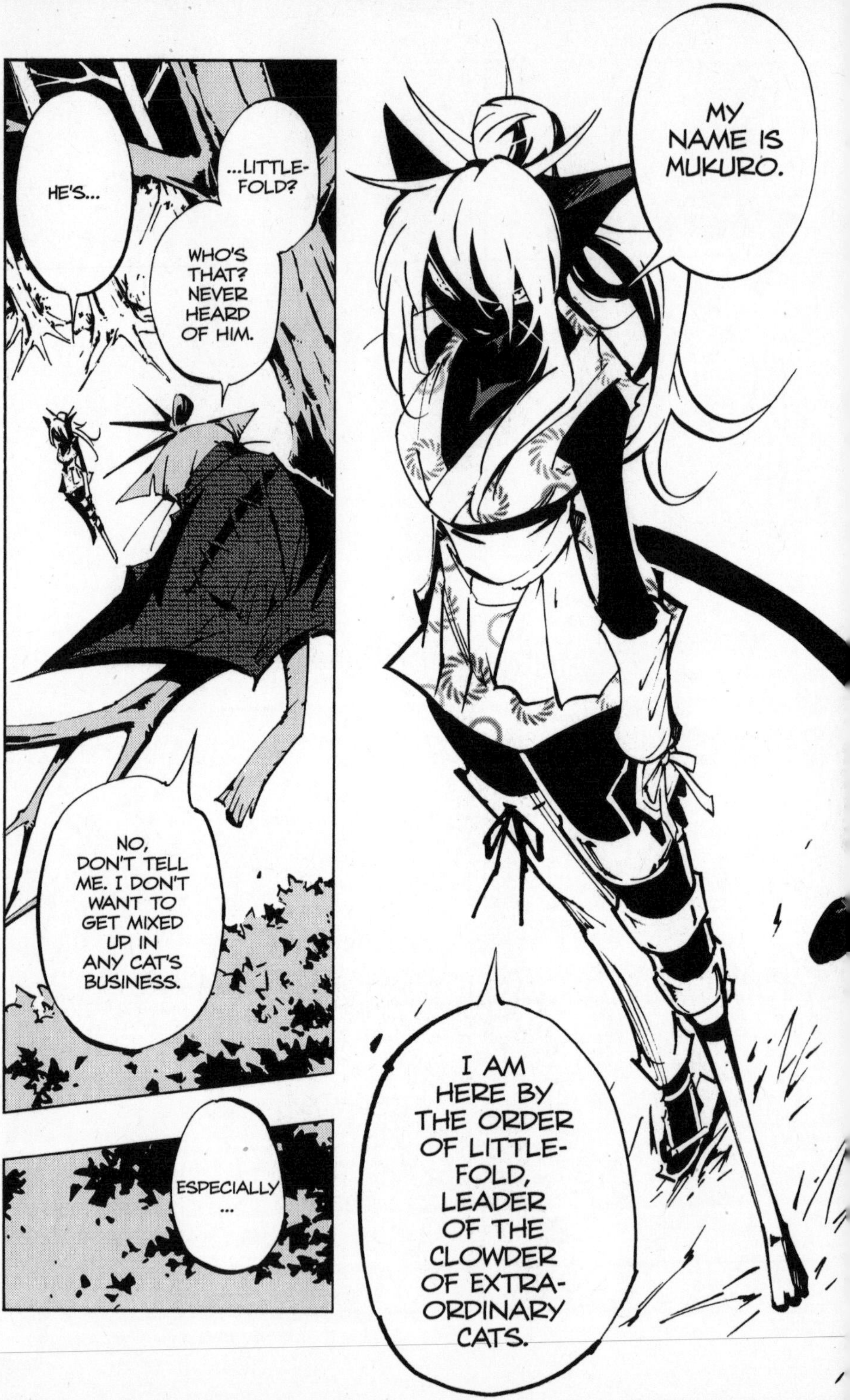

MY NAME IS MUKURO.
I AM HERE BY THE ORDER OF LITTLE-FOLD, LEADER OF THE CLOWDER OF EXTRA-ORDINARY CATS.
...LITTLE-FOLD?
WHO'S THAT? NEVER HEARD OF HIM.
HE'S...
NO, DON'T TELL ME. I DON'T WANT TO GET MIXED UP IN ANY CAT'S BUSINESS.
ESPECIALLY ...

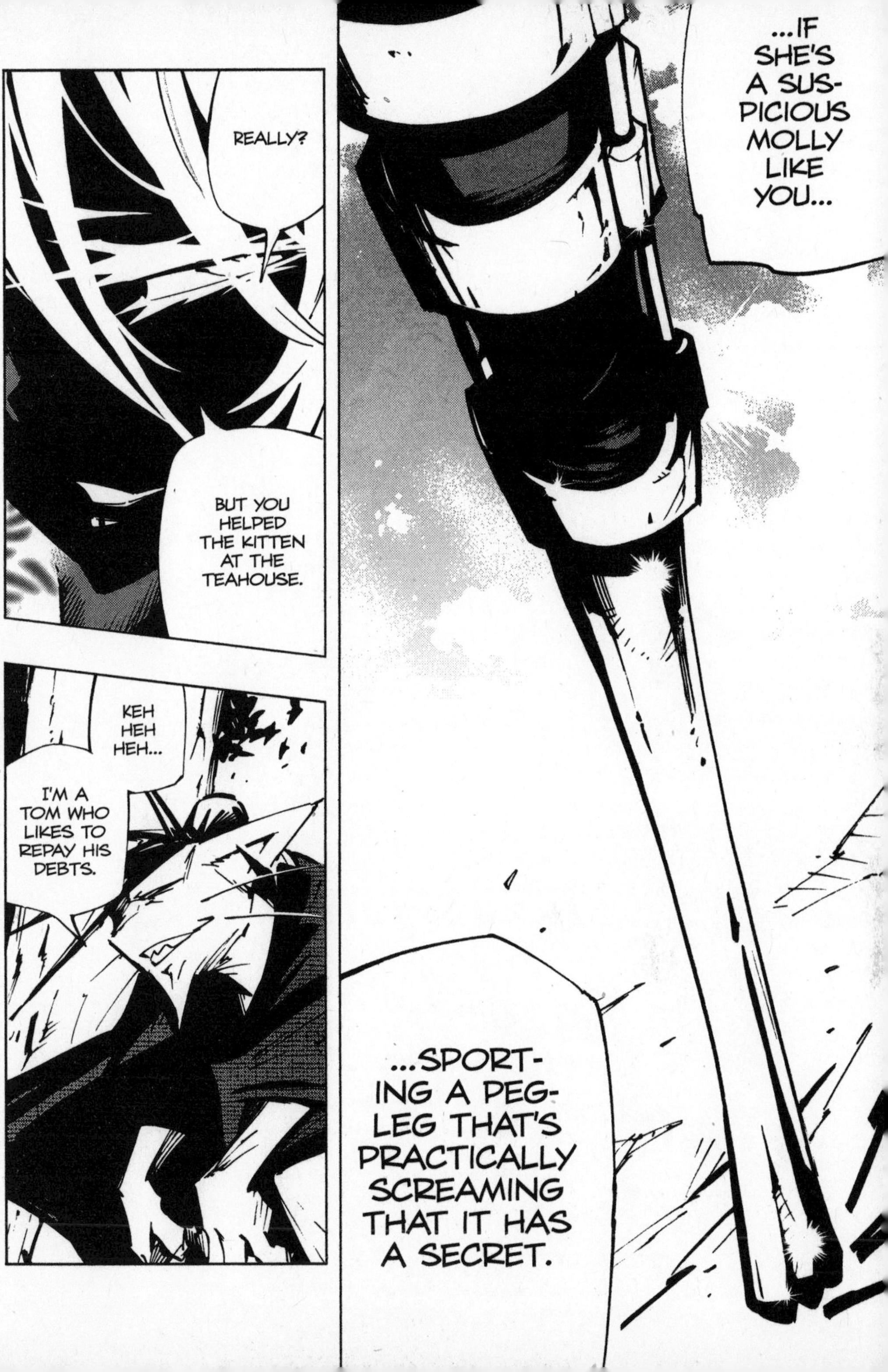
...IF SHE'S A SUS-PICIOUS MOLLY LIKE YOU...
...SPORT-ING A PEG-LEG THAT'S PRACTICALLY SCREAMING THAT IT HAS A SECRET.
REALLY?
BUT YOU HELPED THE KITTEN AT THE TEAHOUSE.
KEH HEH HEH...
I'M A TOM WHO LIKES TO REPAY HIS DEBTS.

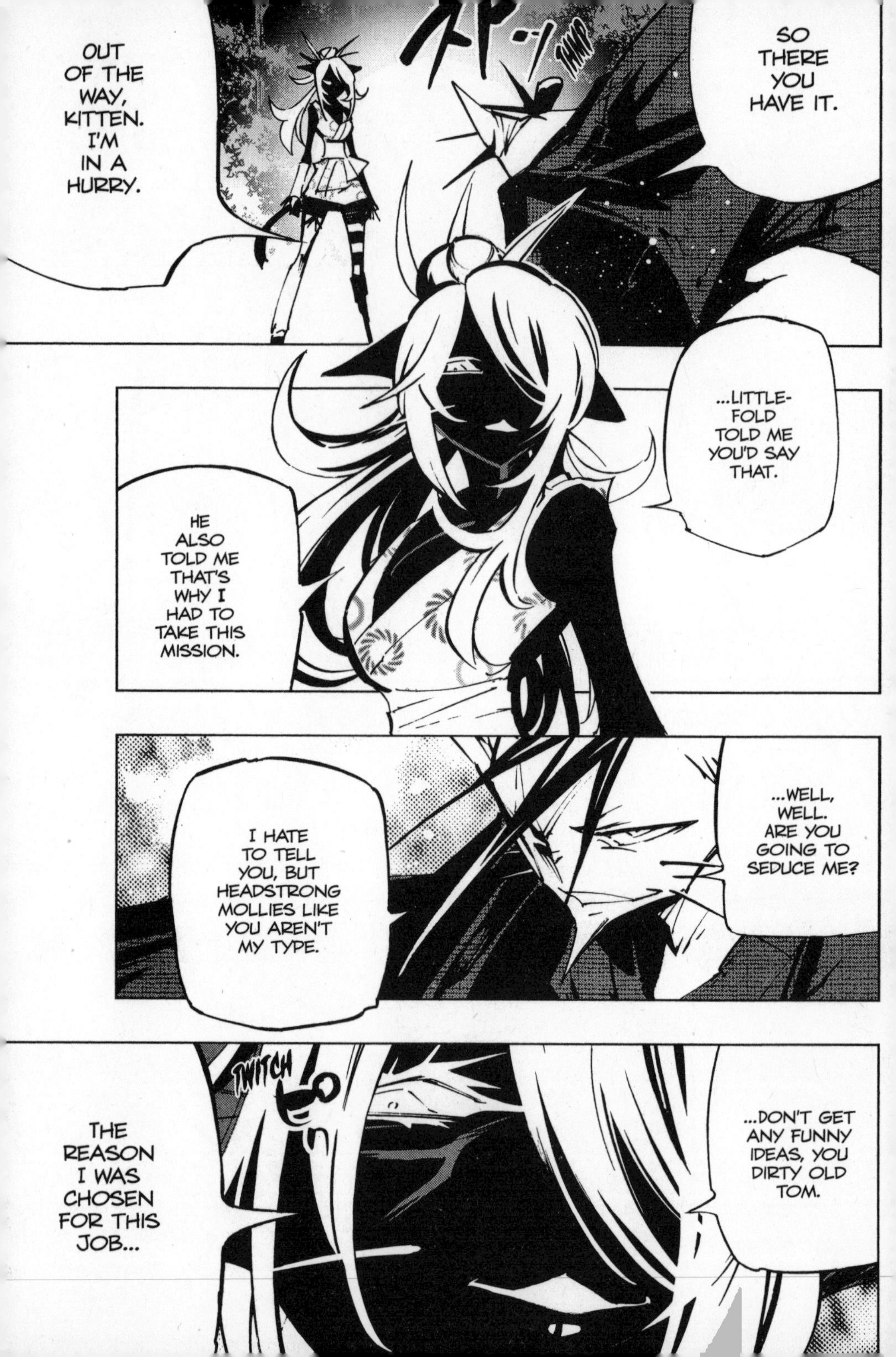
SO THERE YOU HAVE IT.
THMP
OUT OF THE WAY, KITTEN. I'M IN A HURRY.
...LITTLE-FOLD TOLD ME YOU'D SAY THAT.
HE ALSO TOLD ME THAT'S WHY I HAD TO TAKE THIS MISSION.
...WELL, WELL. ARE YOU GOING TO SEDUCE ME?
I HATE TO TELL YOU, BUT HEADSTRONG MOLLIES LIKE YOU AREN'T MY TYPE.
...DON'T GET ANY FUNNY IDEAS, YOU DIRTY OLD TOM.
TWITCH
THE REASON I WAS CHOSEN FOR THIS JOB...

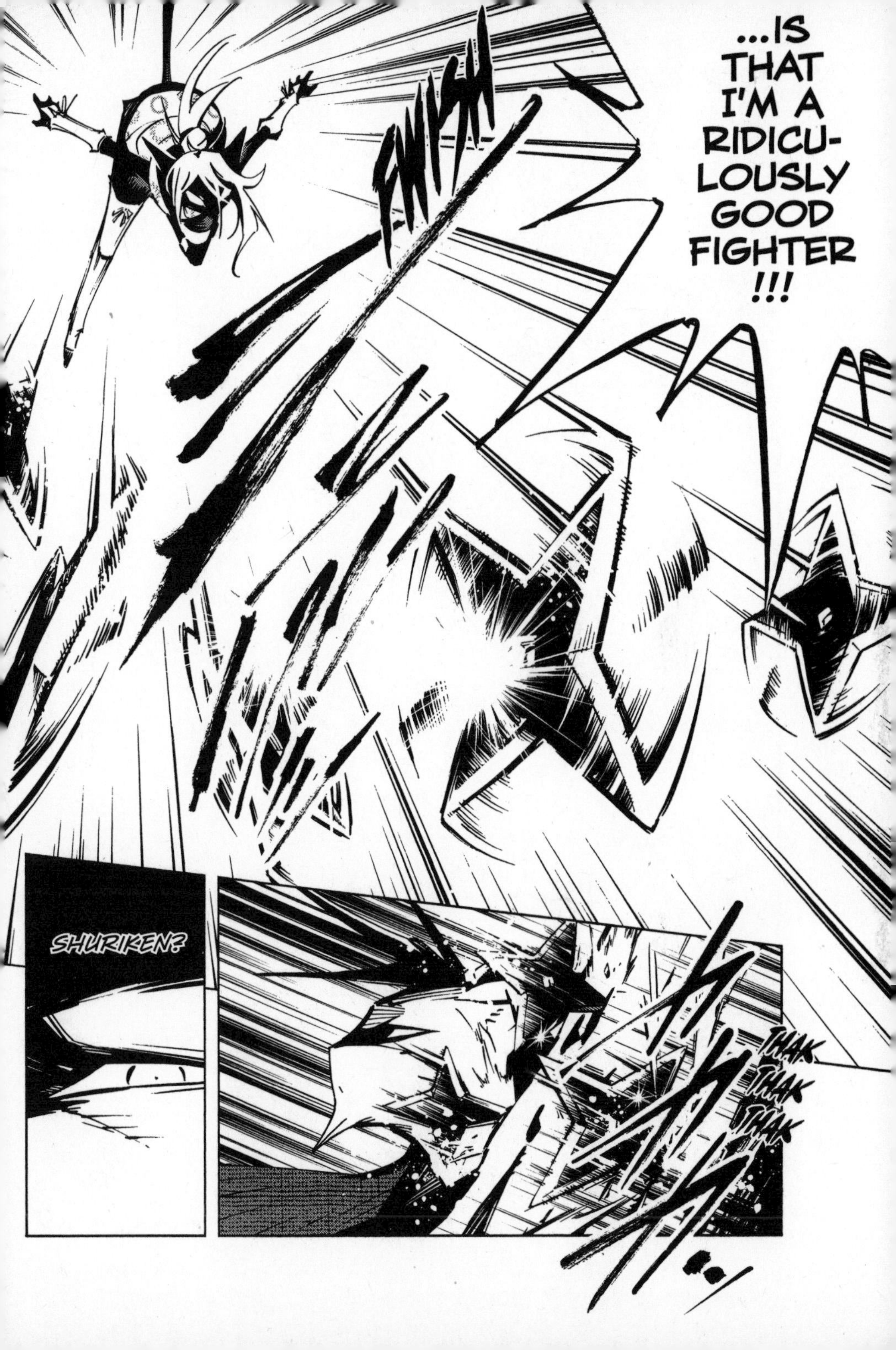
...IS THAT I'M A RIDICU-LOUSLY GOOD FIGHTER!!!
FWISH
THAK THAK THAK
SHURIKEN?

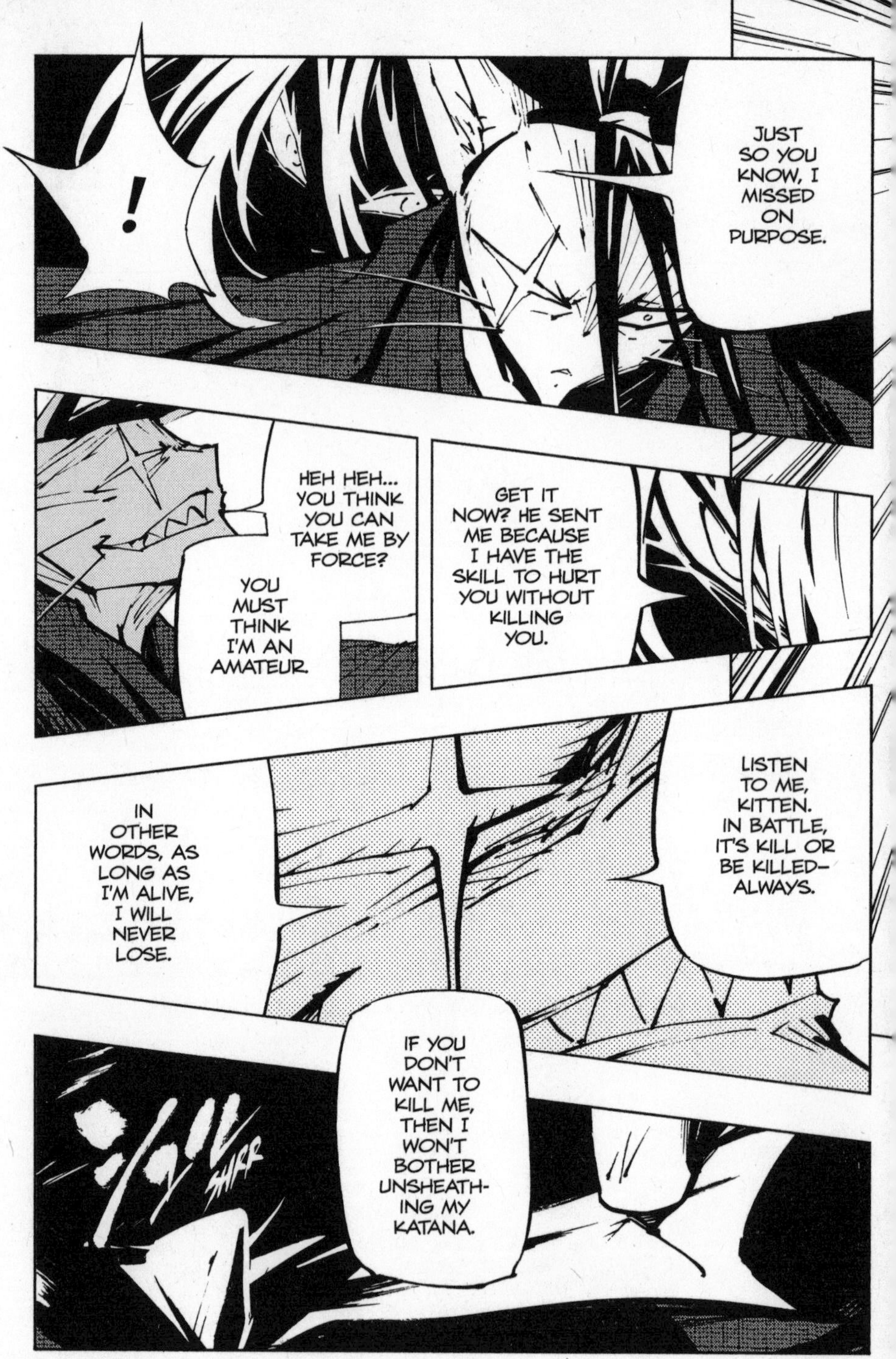
JUST SO YOU KNOW, I MISSED ON PURPOSE.
!
GET IT NOW? HE SENT ME BECAUSE I HAVE THE SKILL TO HURT YOU WITHOUT KILLING YOU.
HEH HEH... YOU THINK YOU CAN TAKE ME BY FORCE?
YOU MUST THINK I'M AN AMATEUR.
LISTEN TO ME, KITTEN. IN BATTLE, IT'S KILL OR BE KILLED—ALWAYS.
IN OTHER WORDS, AS LONG AS I'M ALIVE, I WILL NEVER LOSE.
IF YOU DON'T WANT TO KILL ME, THEN I WON'T BOTHER UNSHEATHING MY KATANA.
SHFF

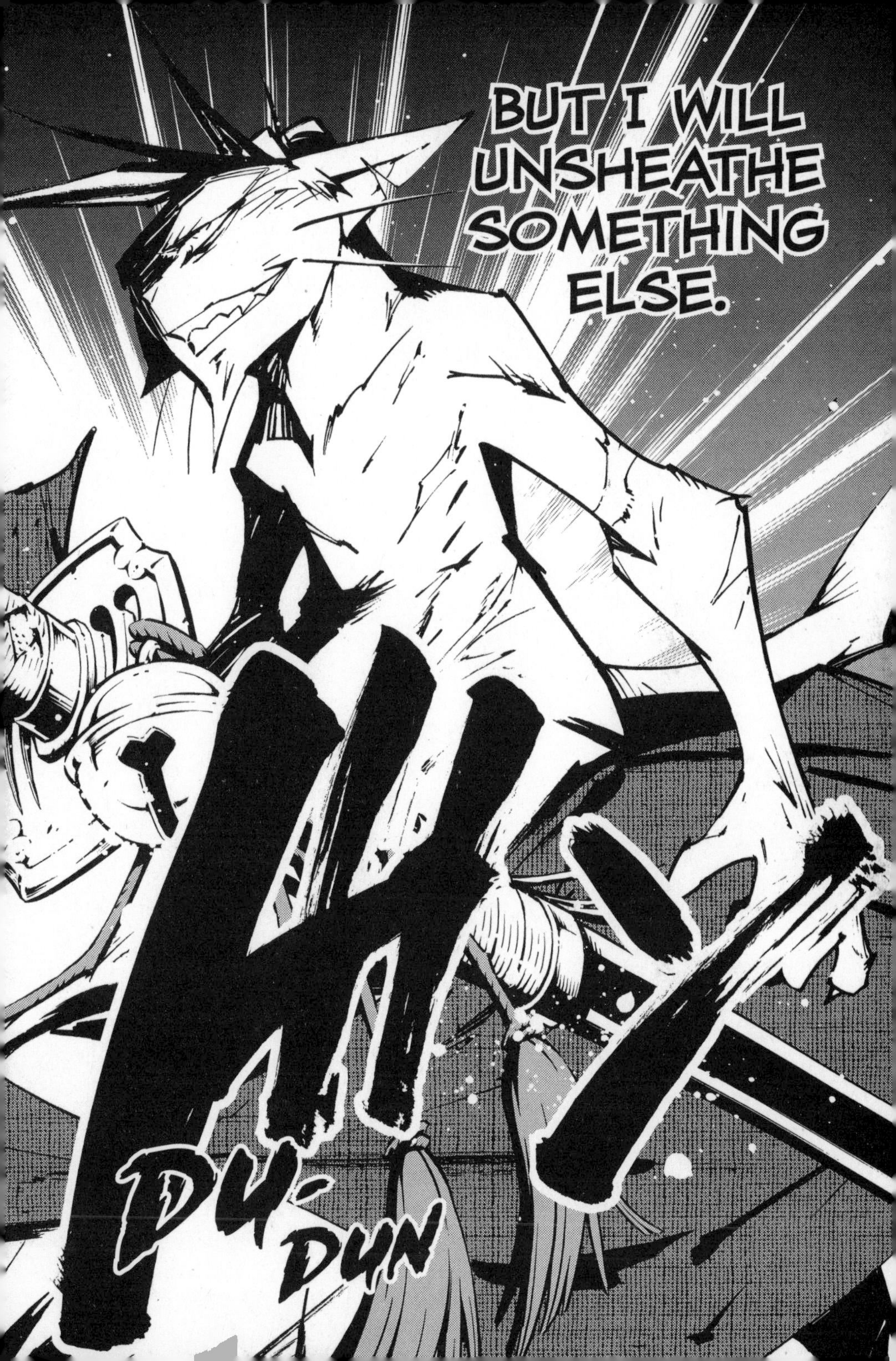
BUT I WILL UNSHEATHE SOMETHING ELSE.
DU-DUN

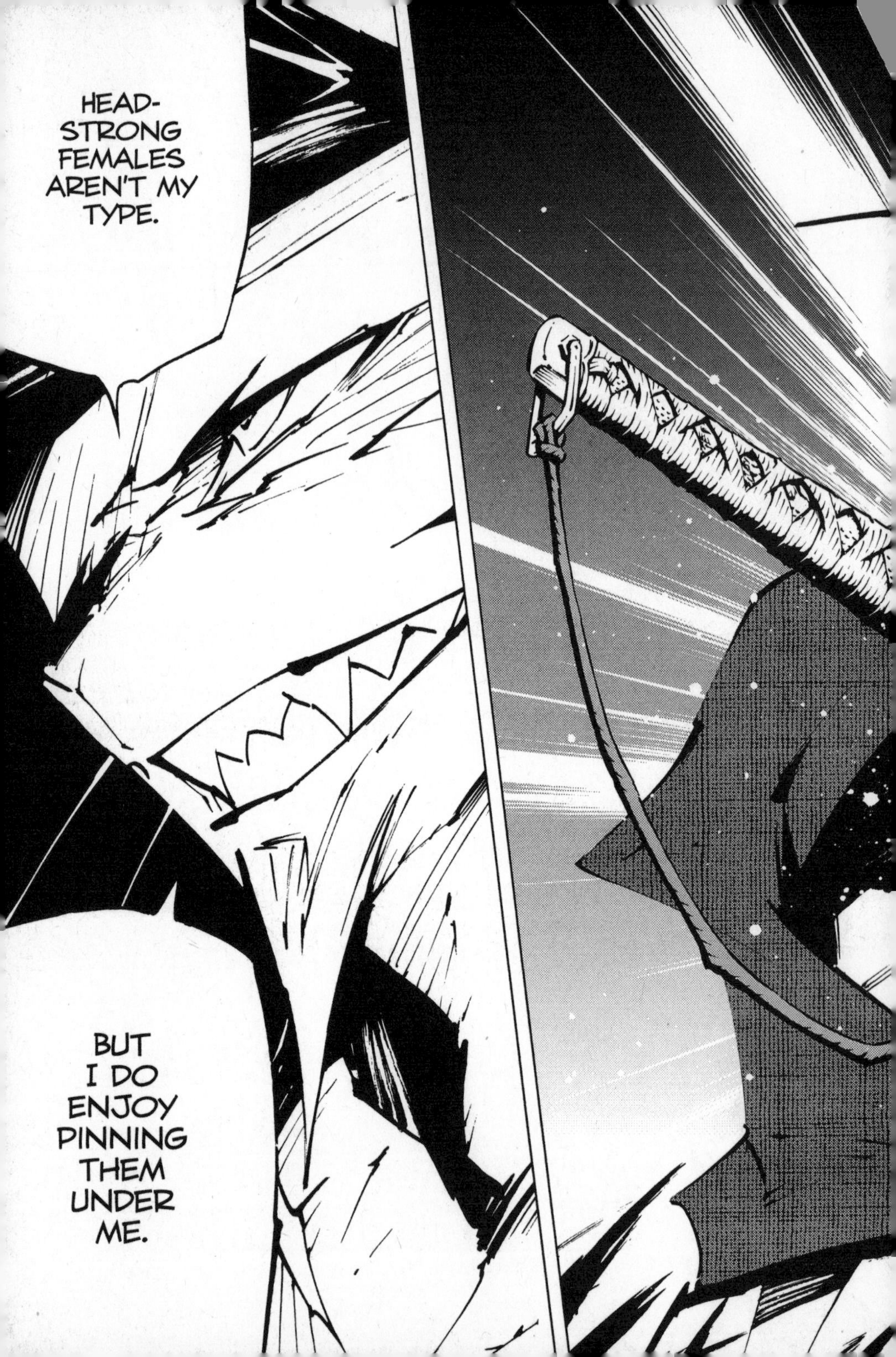
HEAD-STRONG FEMALES AREN'T MY TYPE.
BUT I DO ENJOY PINNING THEM UNDER ME.

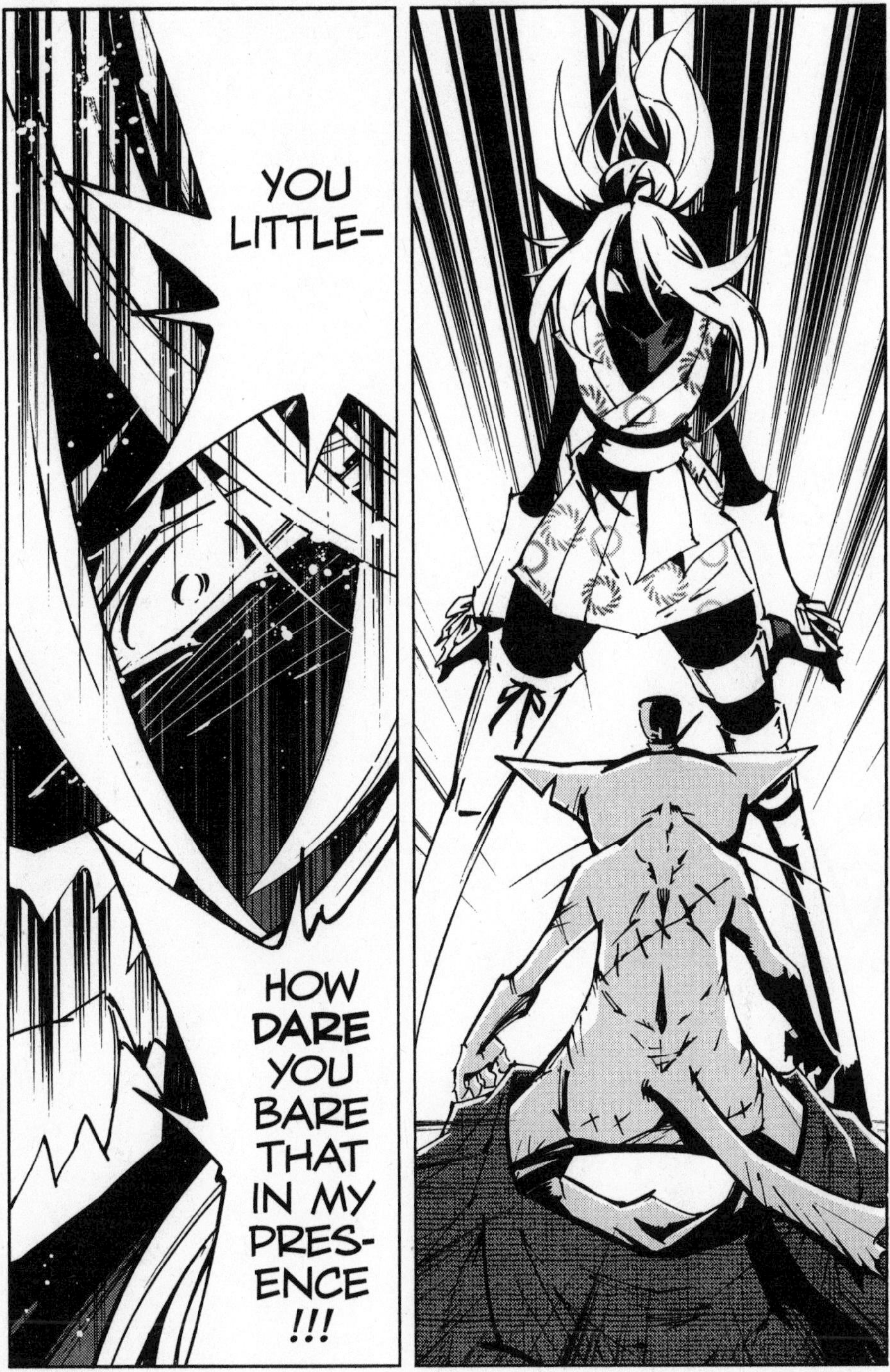
YOU LITTLE-
HOW DARE YOU BARE THAT IN MY PRESENCE!!!

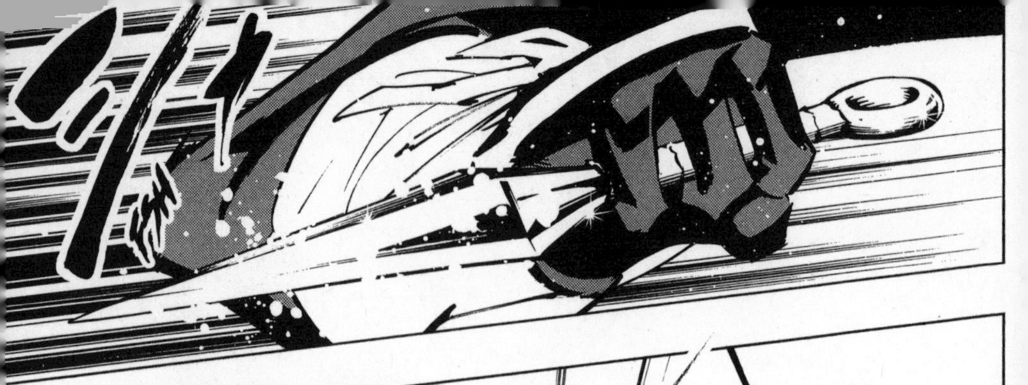
FSH
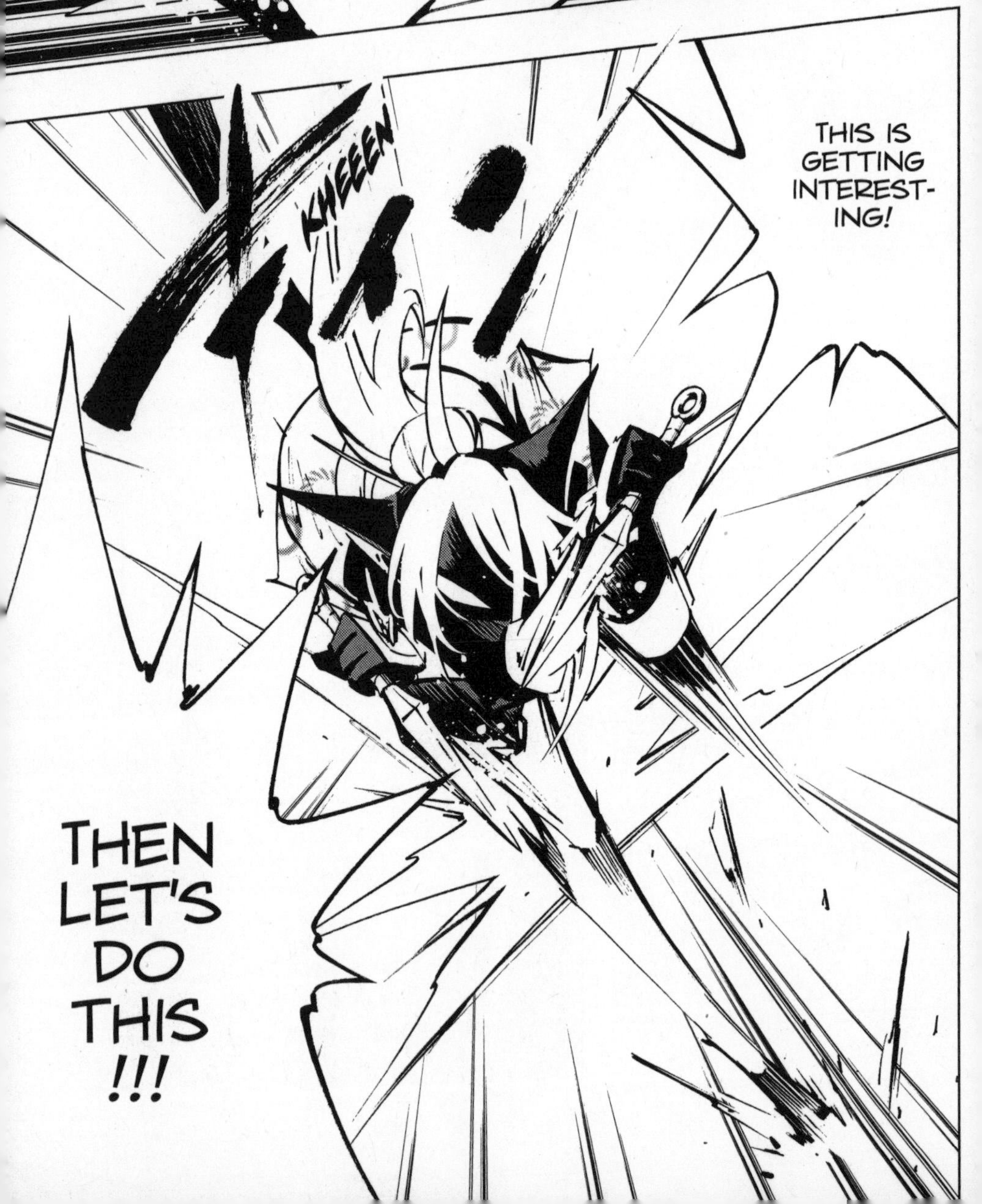
KHEEEN
THIS IS GETTING INTEREST-ING!
THEN LET'S DO THIS!!!

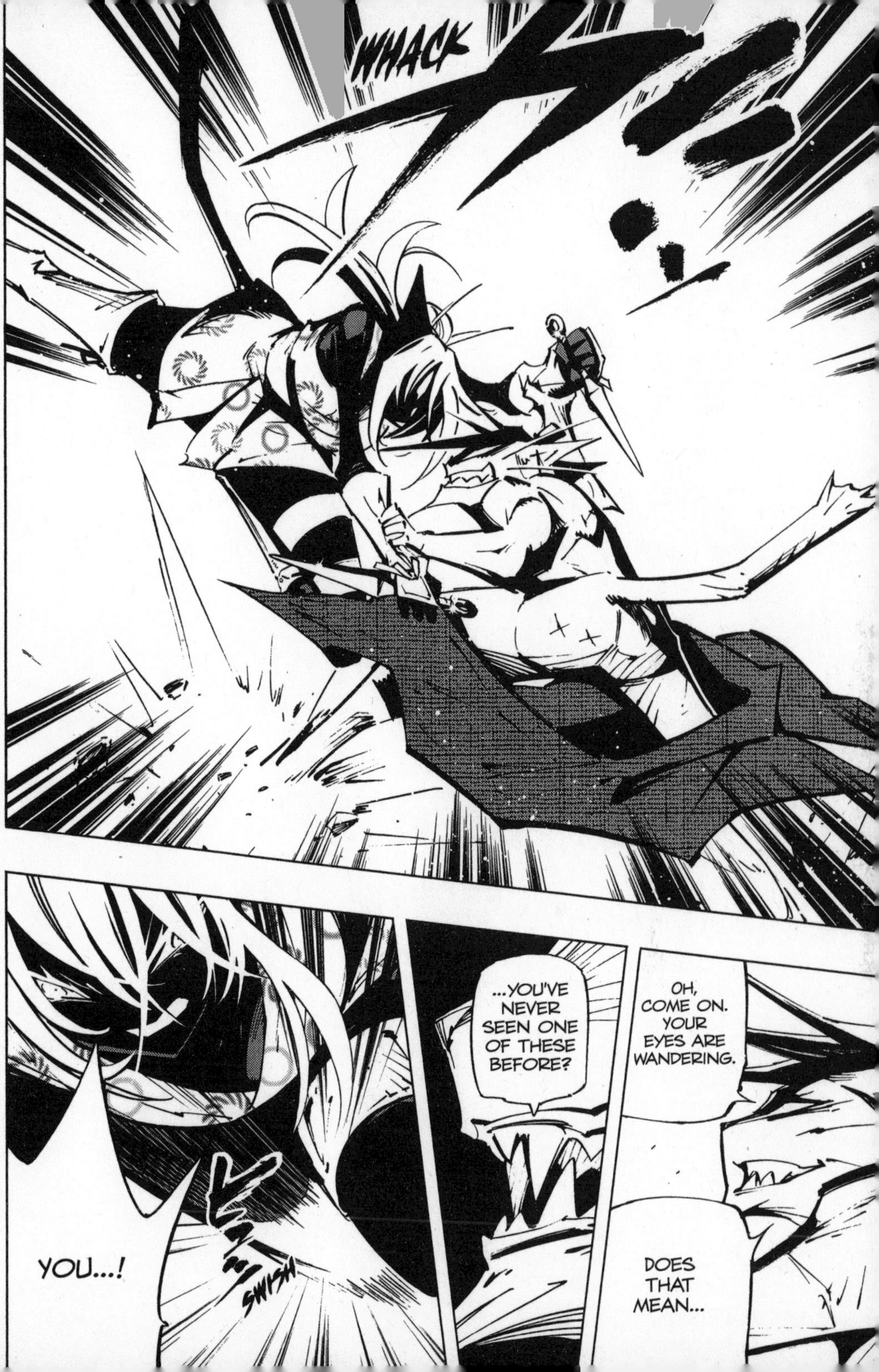
WHACK
OH, COME ON. YOUR EYES ARE WANDERING.
DOES THAT MEAN...
...YOU'VE NEVER SEEN ONE OF THESE BEFORE?
SWISH
YOU...!

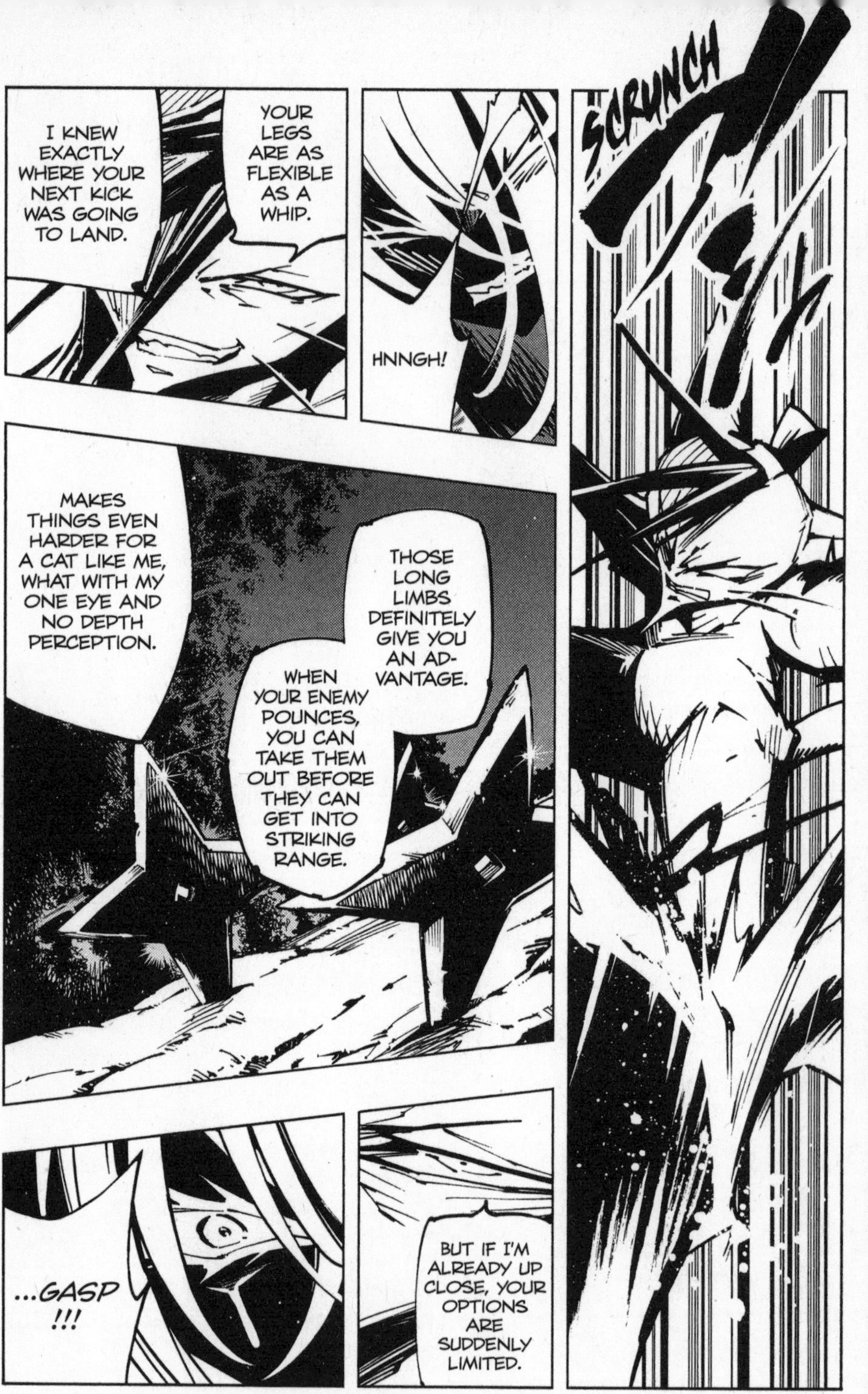
SCRUNCH
HNNGH!
YOUR LEGS ARE AS FLEXIBLE AS A WHIP.
I KNEW EXACTLY WHERE YOUR NEXT KICK WAS GOING TO LAND.
THOSE LONG LIMBS DEFINITELY GIVE YOU AN AD-VANTAGE.
WHEN YOUR ENEMY POUNCES, YOU CAN TAKE THEM OUT BEFORE THEY CAN GET INTO STRIKING RANGE.
MAKES THINGS EVEN HARDER FOR A CAT LIKE ME, WHAT WITH MY ONE EYE AND NO DEPTH PERCEPTION.
BUT IF I'M ALREADY UP CLOSE, YOUR OPTIONS ARE SUDDENLY LIMITED.
...GASP !!!

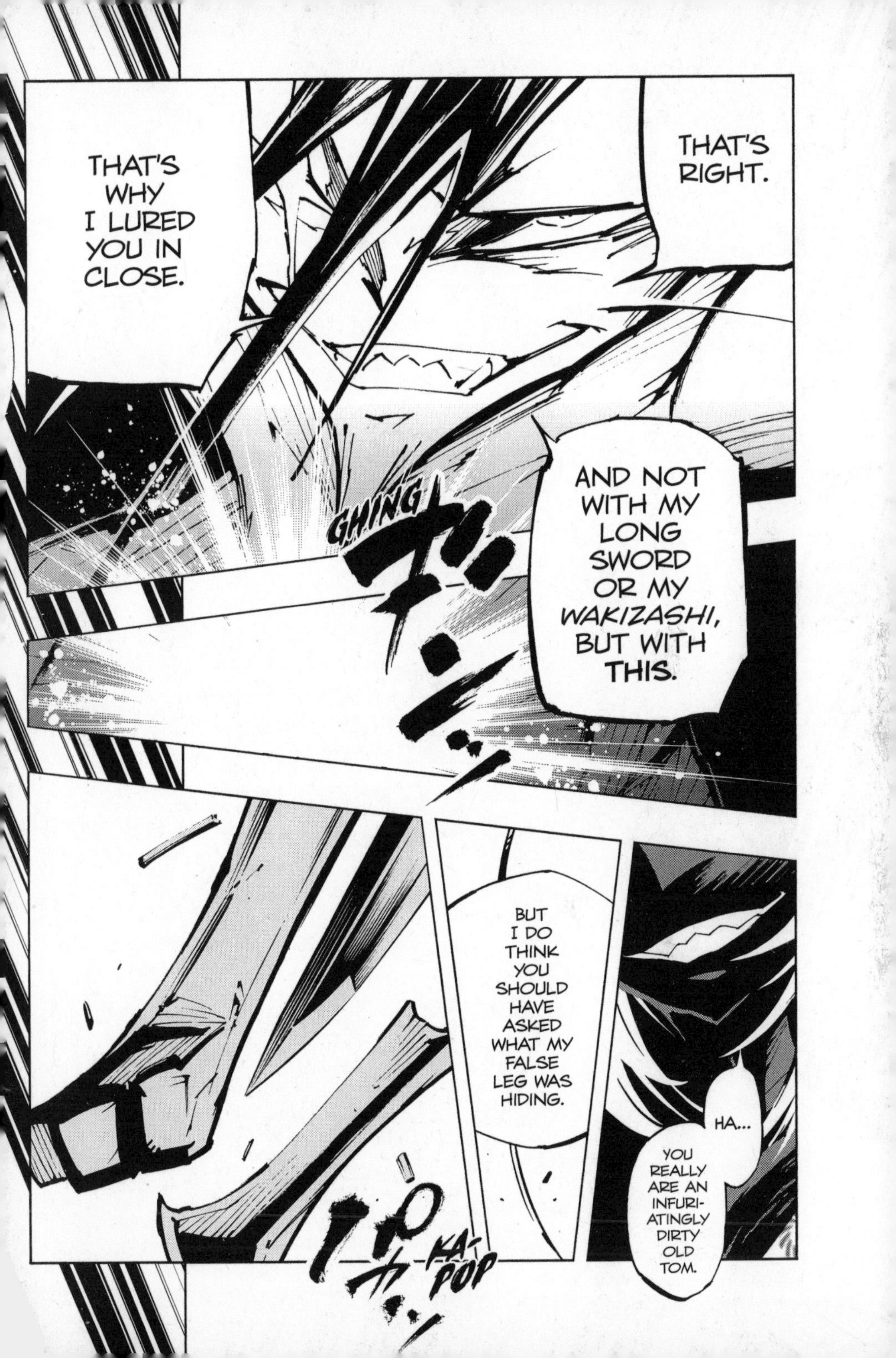
THAT'S RIGHT.
THAT'S WHY I LURED YOU IN CLOSE.
GHING
AND NOT WITH MY LONG SWORD OR MY *WAKIZASHI*, BUT WITH **THIS.**
HA...
YOU REALLY ARE AN INFURI-ATINGLY DIRTY OLD TOM.
BUT I DO THINK YOU SHOULD HAVE ASKED WHAT MY FALSE LEG WAS HIDING.
KA-POP

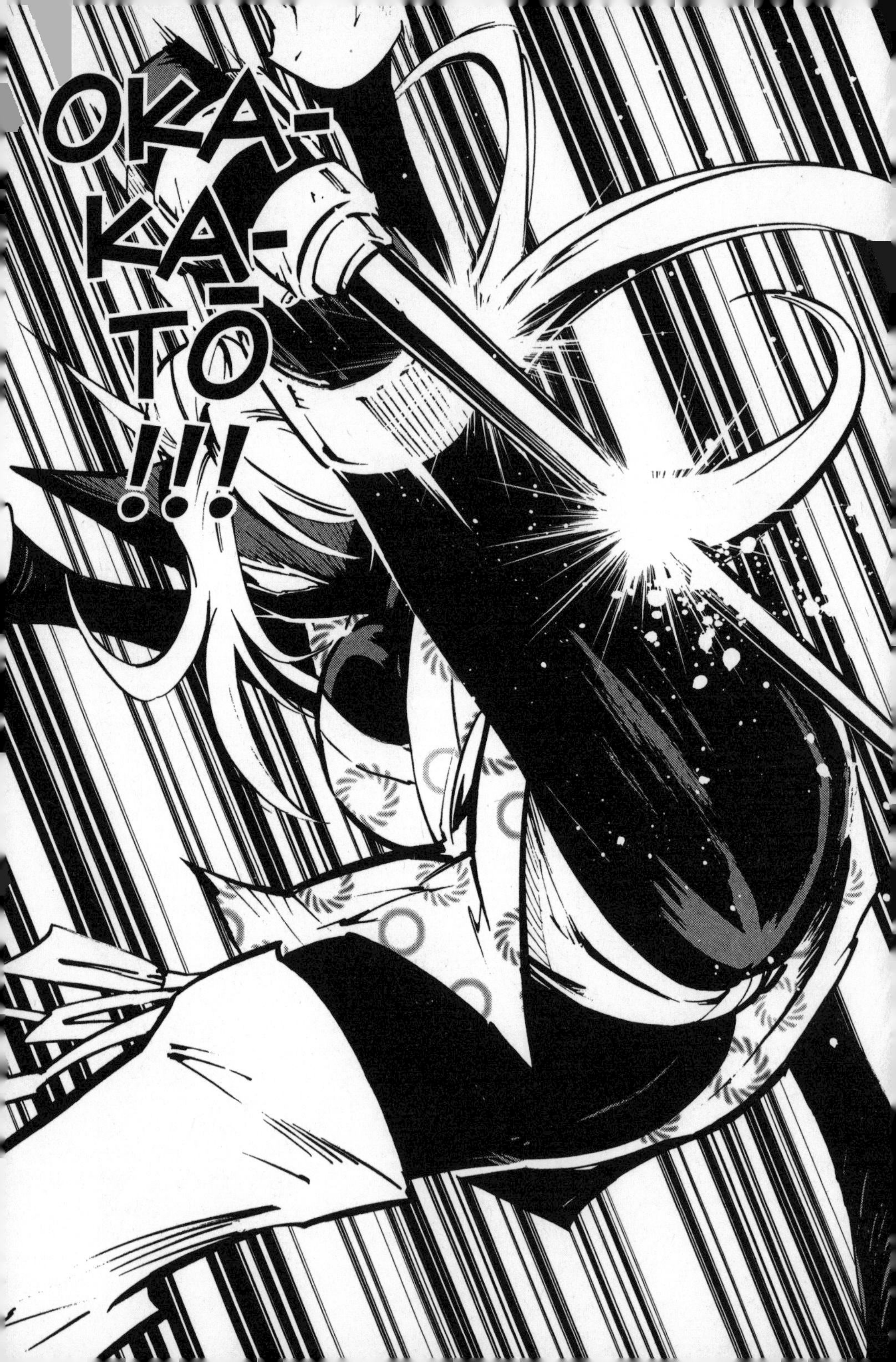
OKA-KA-TŌ!!!

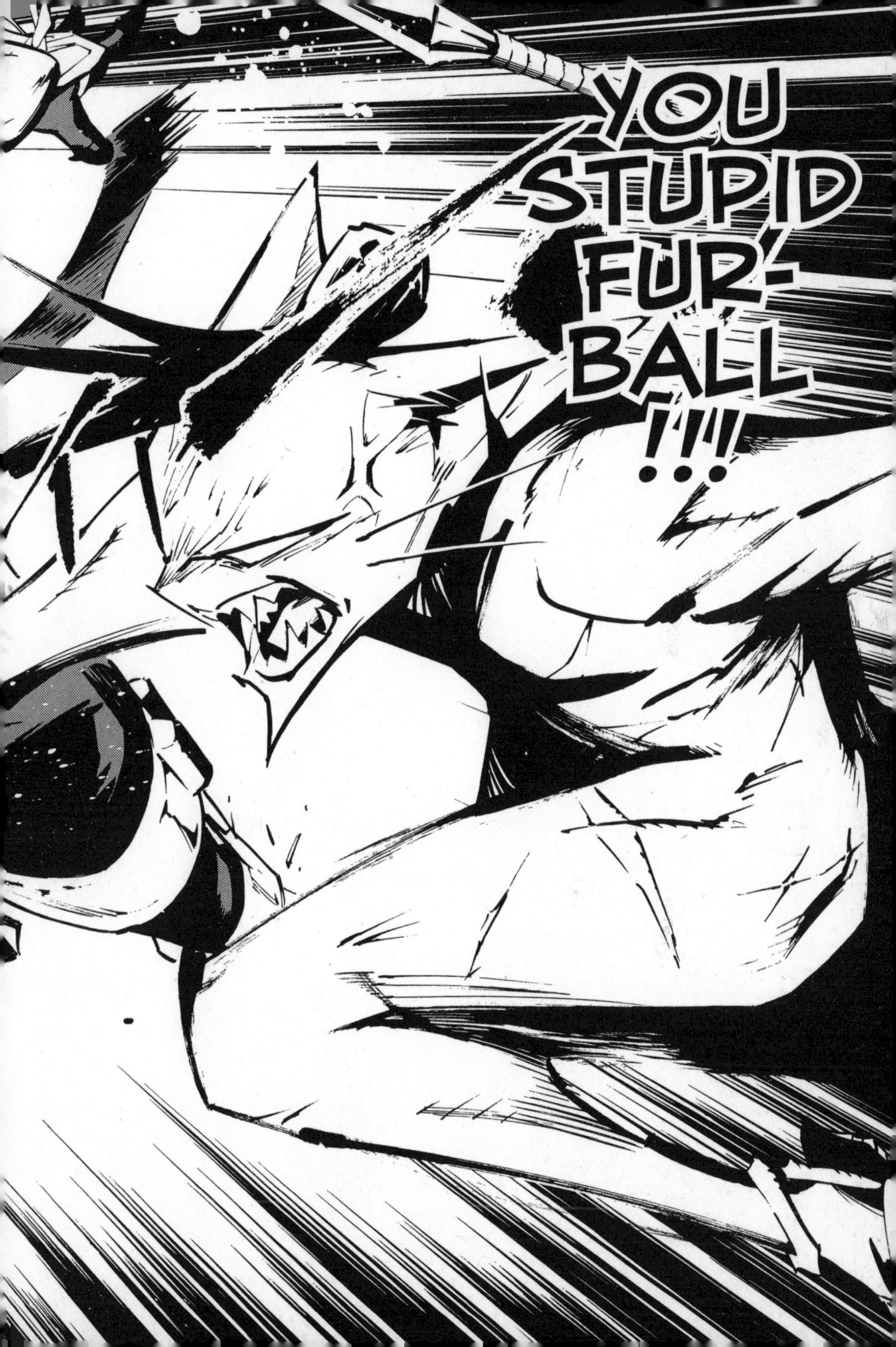
YOU STUPID FUR-BALL!!!

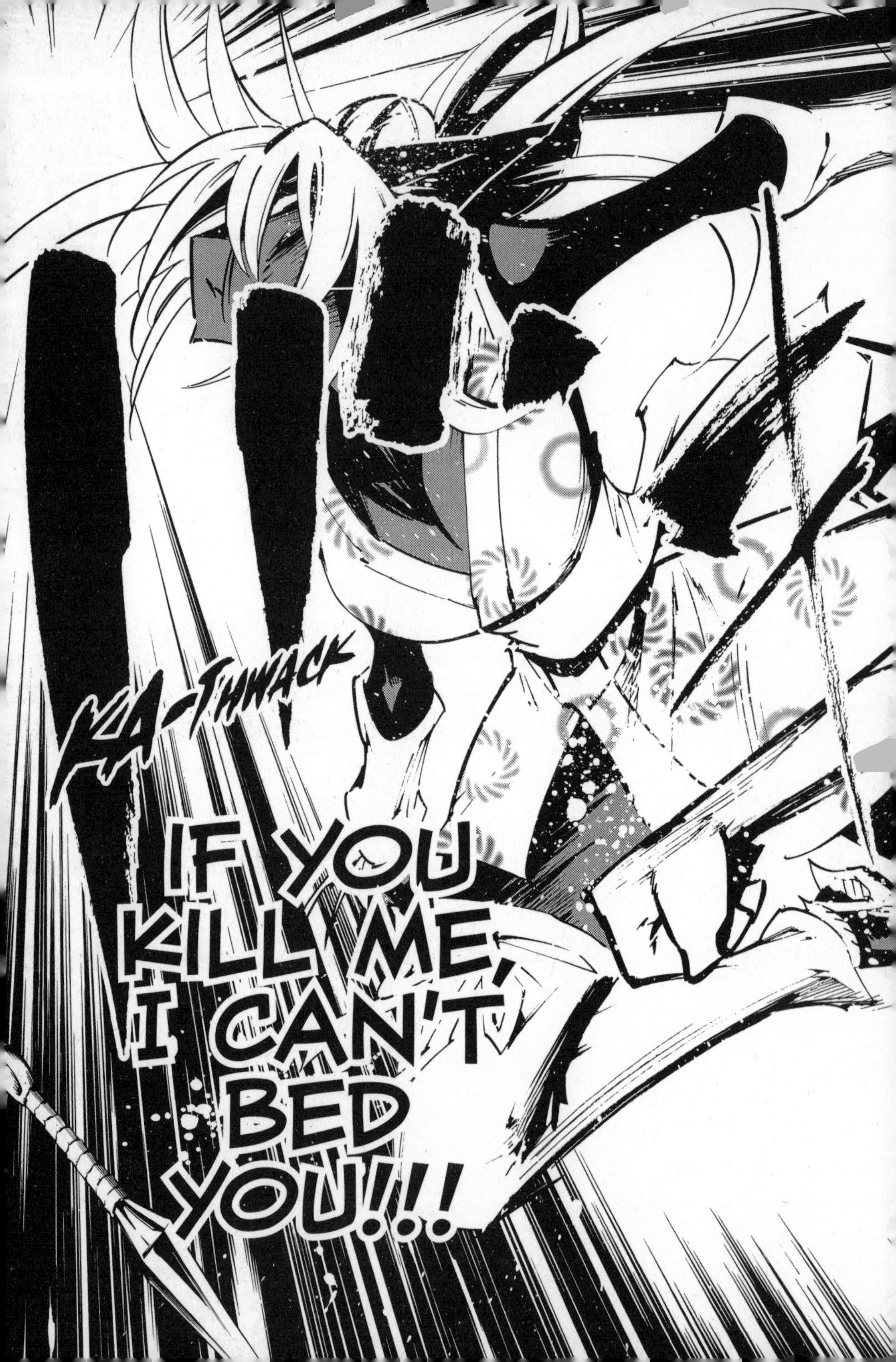
KA-THWACK
IF YOU KILL ME, I CAN'T BED YOU!!!

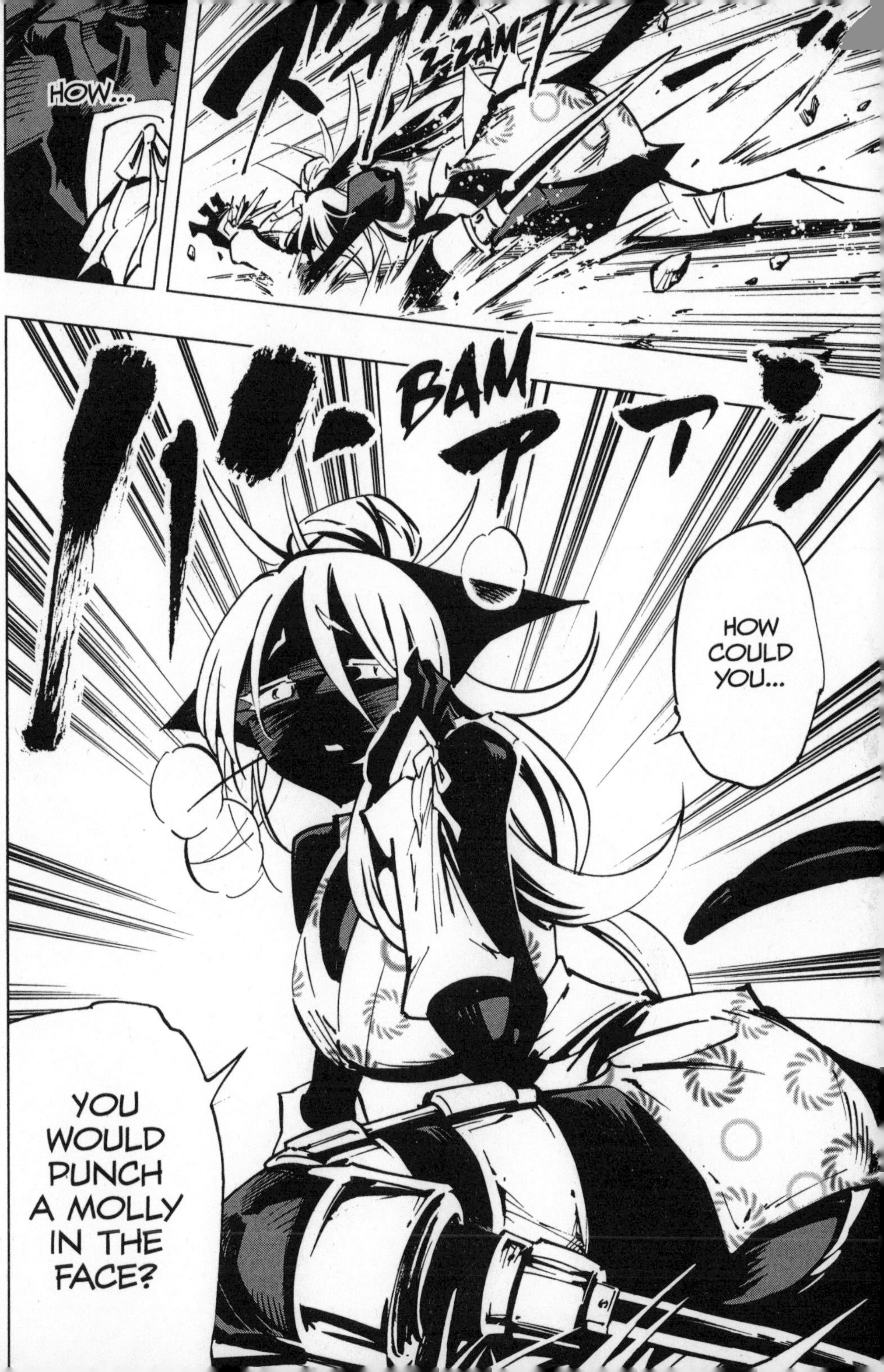
Z-ZAM
HOW...
BAM
HOW COULD YOU...
YOU WOULD PUNCH A MOLLY IN THE FACE?

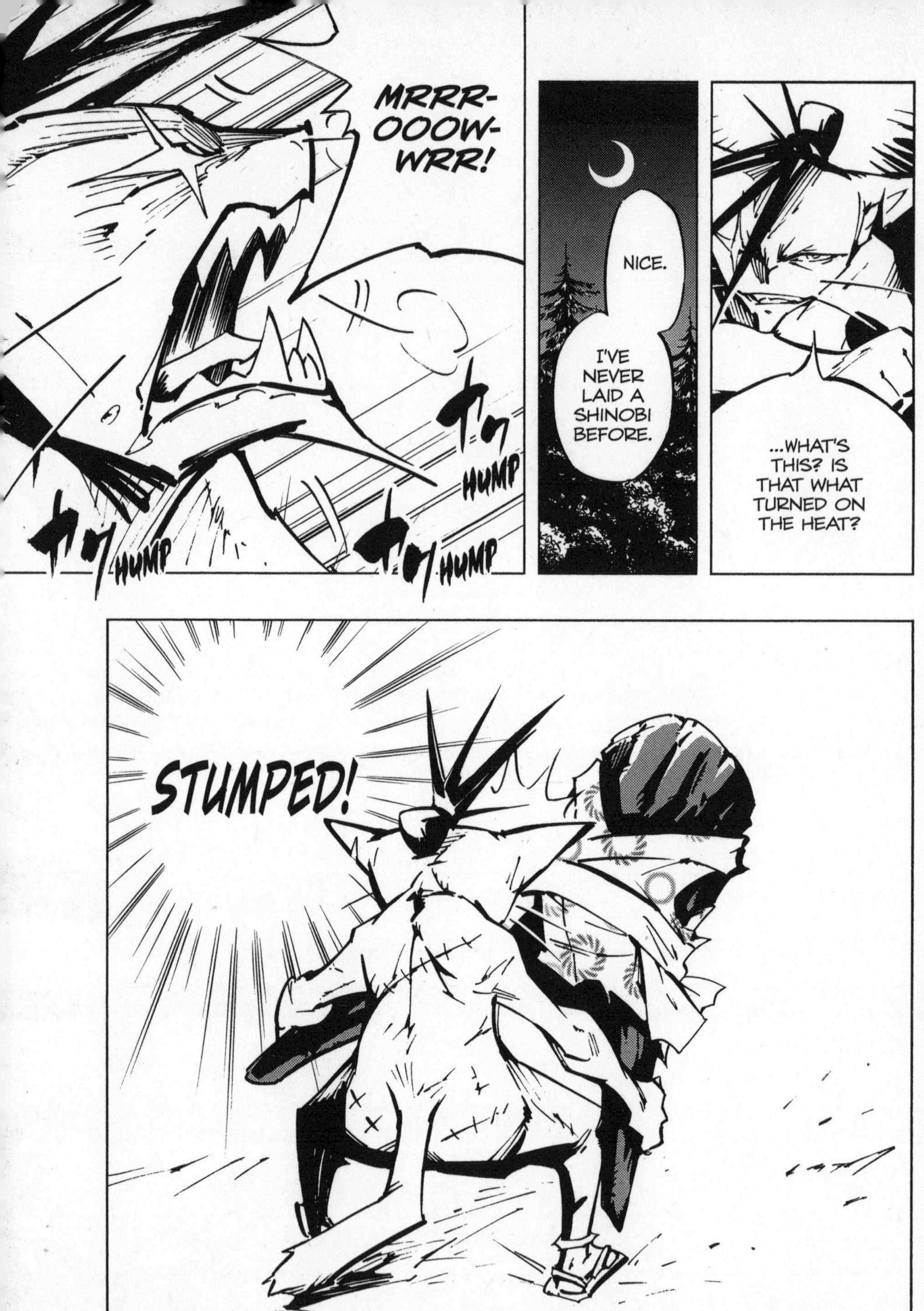
...WHAT'S THIS? IS THAT WHAT TURNED ON THE HEAT?
NICE.
I'VE NEVER LAID A SHINOBI BEFORE.
MRRR-OOOW-WRR!
HUMP
HUMP
HUMP
STUMPED!

猫ヶ原

ネコガハラ

NeKoGaHara

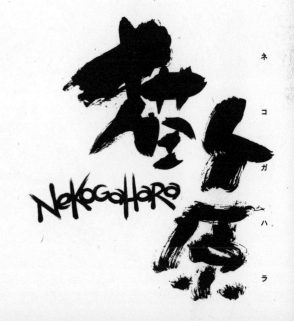

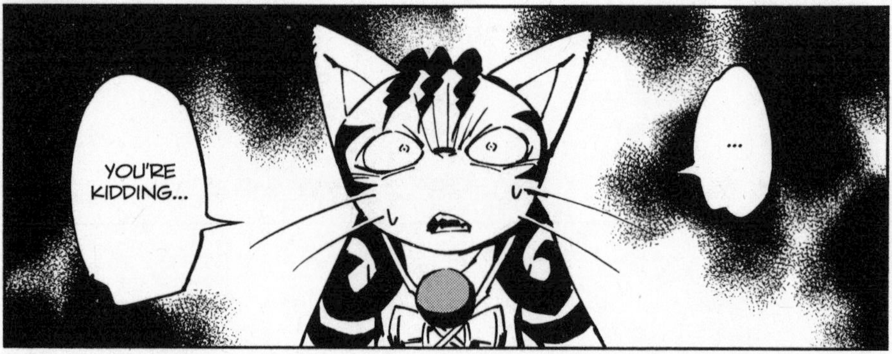
...
YOU'RE KIDDING...

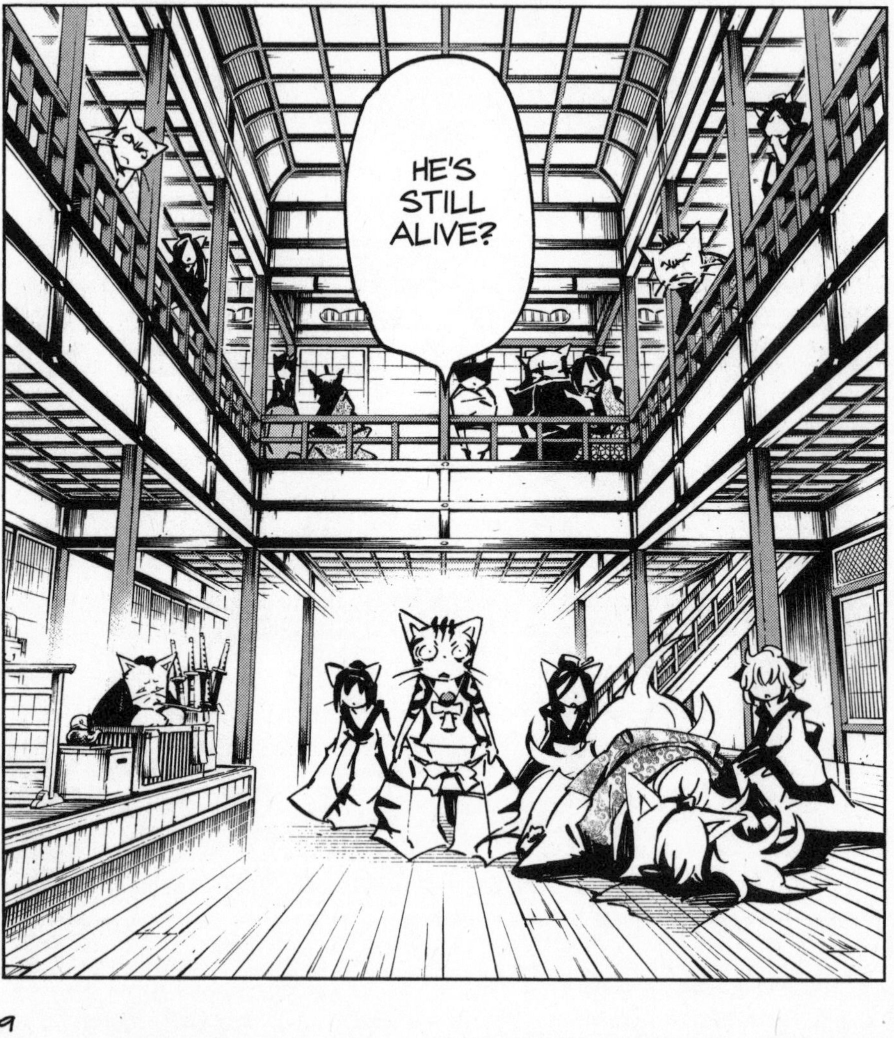
HE'S STILL ALIVE?

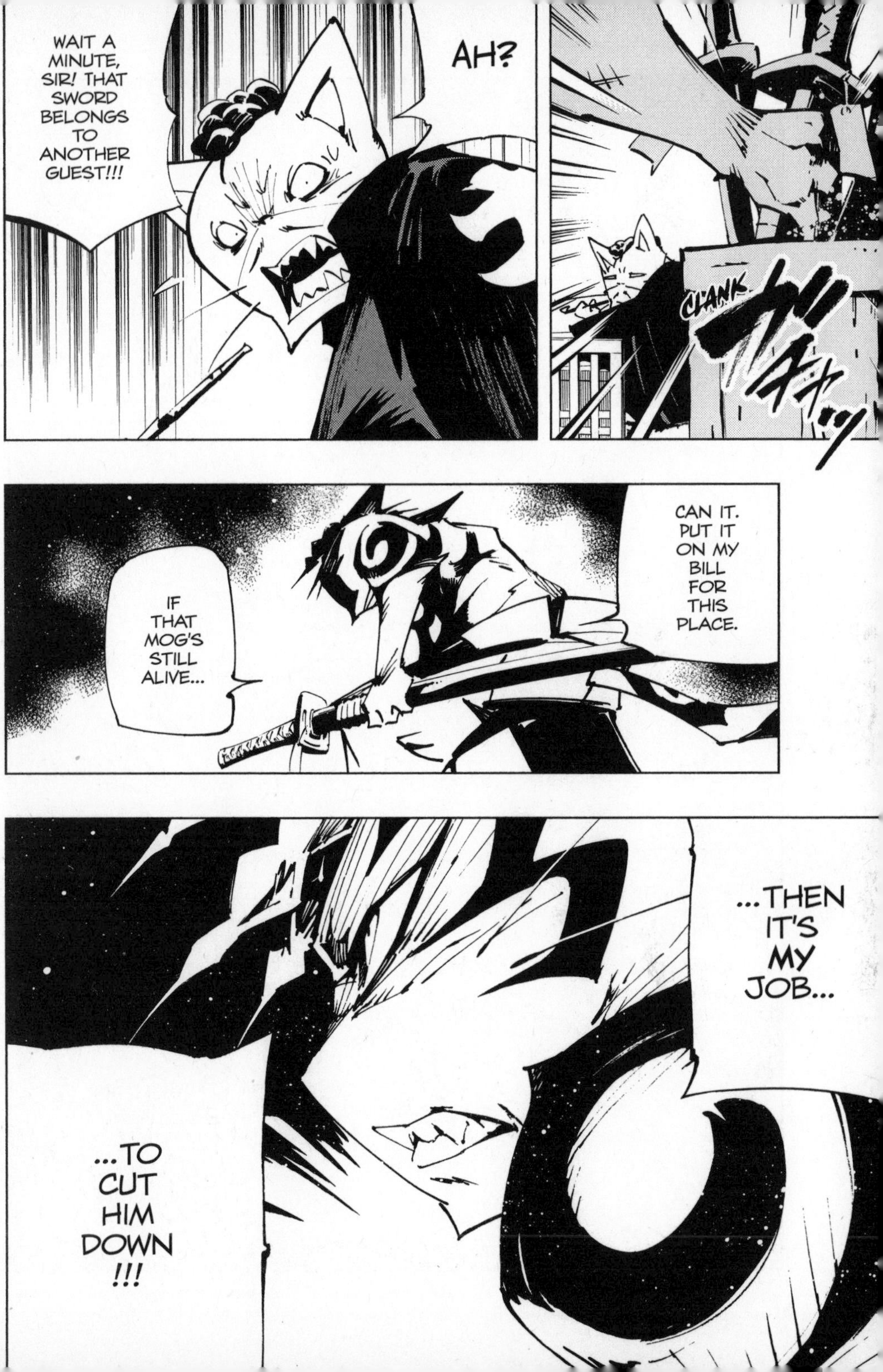
CLANK
ガタッ
AH?
WAIT A MINUTE, SIR! THAT SWORD BELONGS TO ANOTHER GUEST!!!
CAN IT. PUT IT ON MY BILL FOR THIS PLACE.
IF THAT MOG'S STILL ALIVE...
...THEN IT'S MY JOB...
...TO CUT HIM DOWN!!!

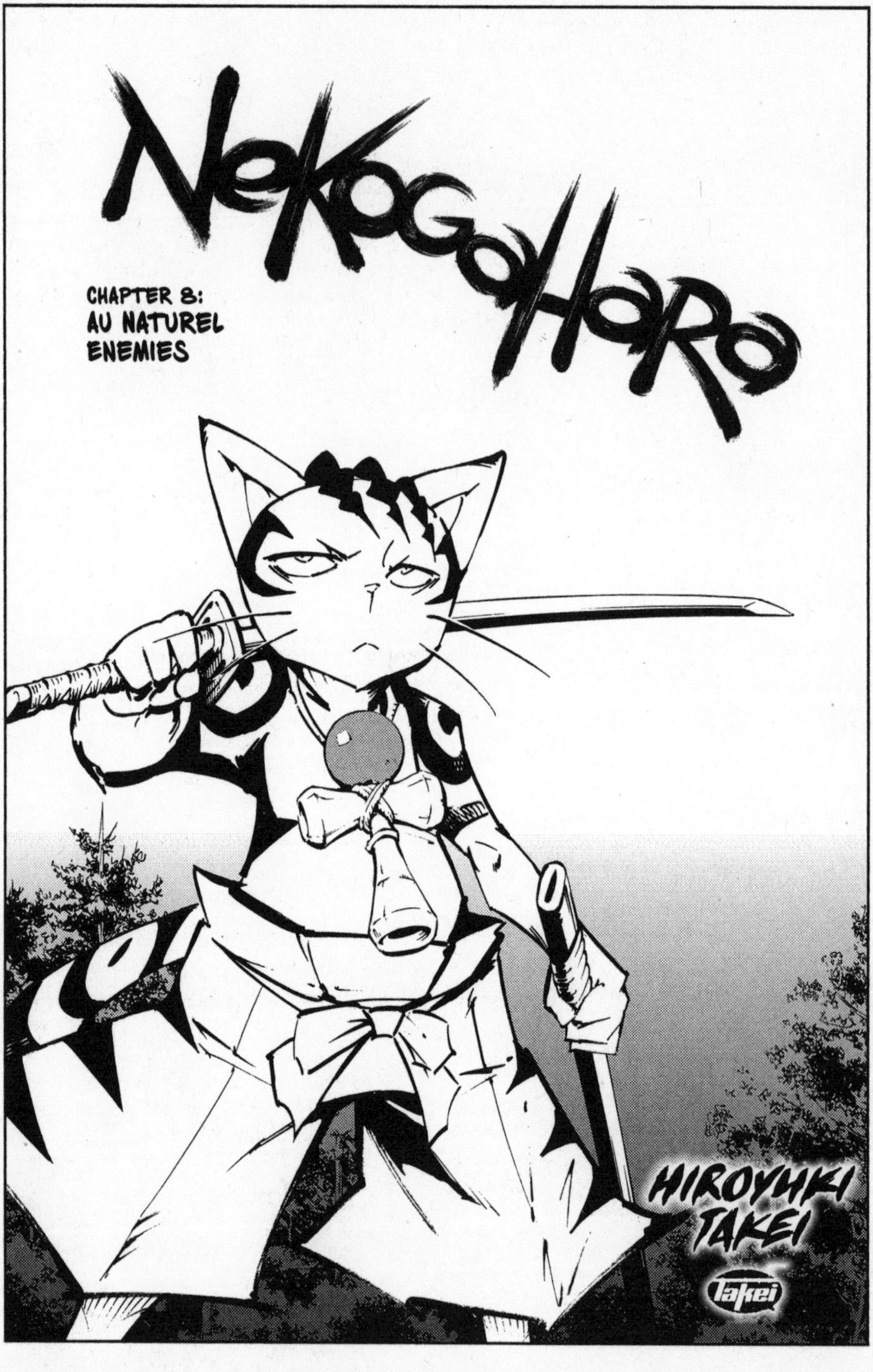
NEKOGAHARA
CHAPTER 8:
AU NATUREL
ENEMIES
HIROYUKI
TAKEI
Takei

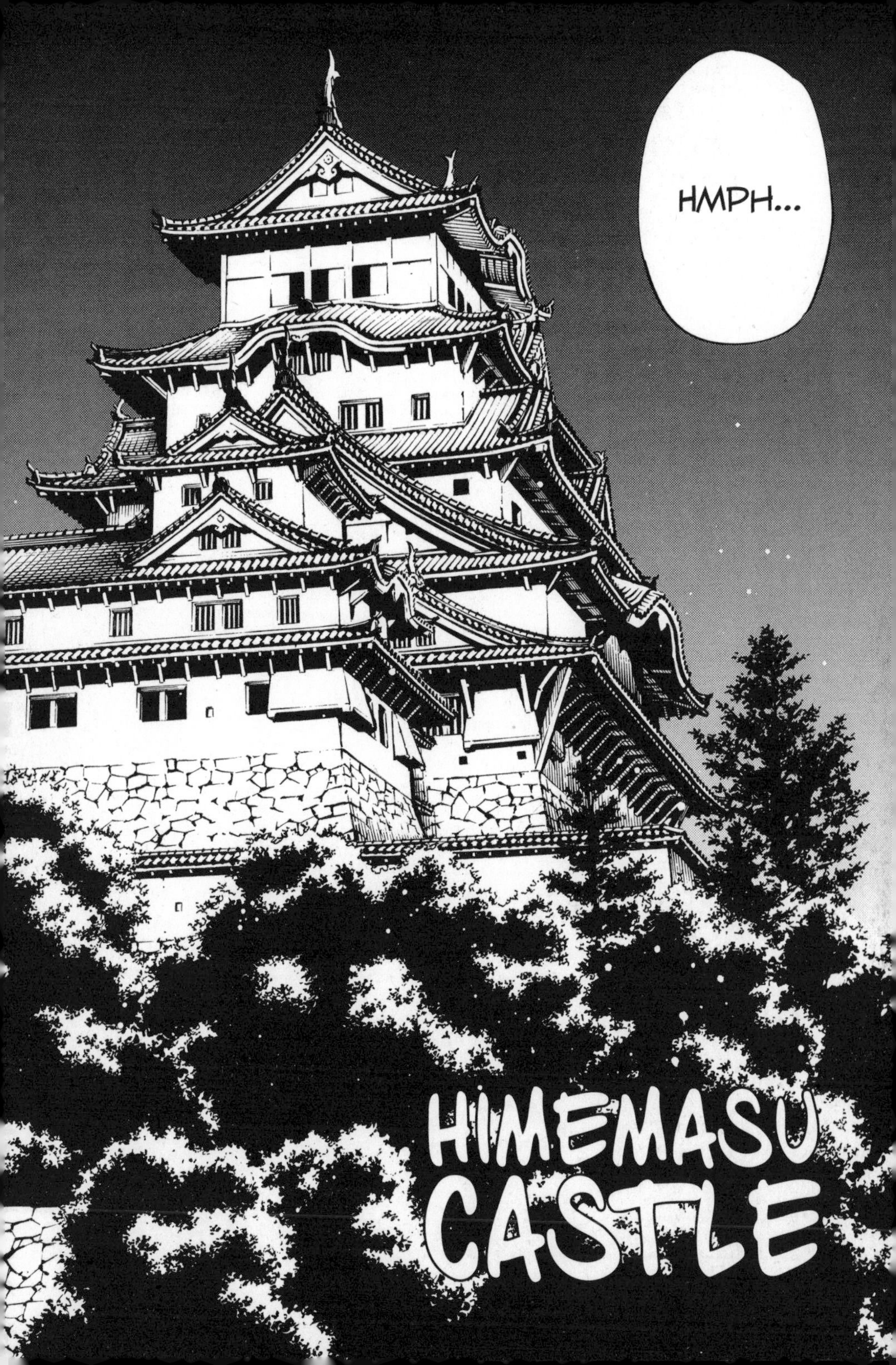
HMPH...
HIMEMASU CASTLE

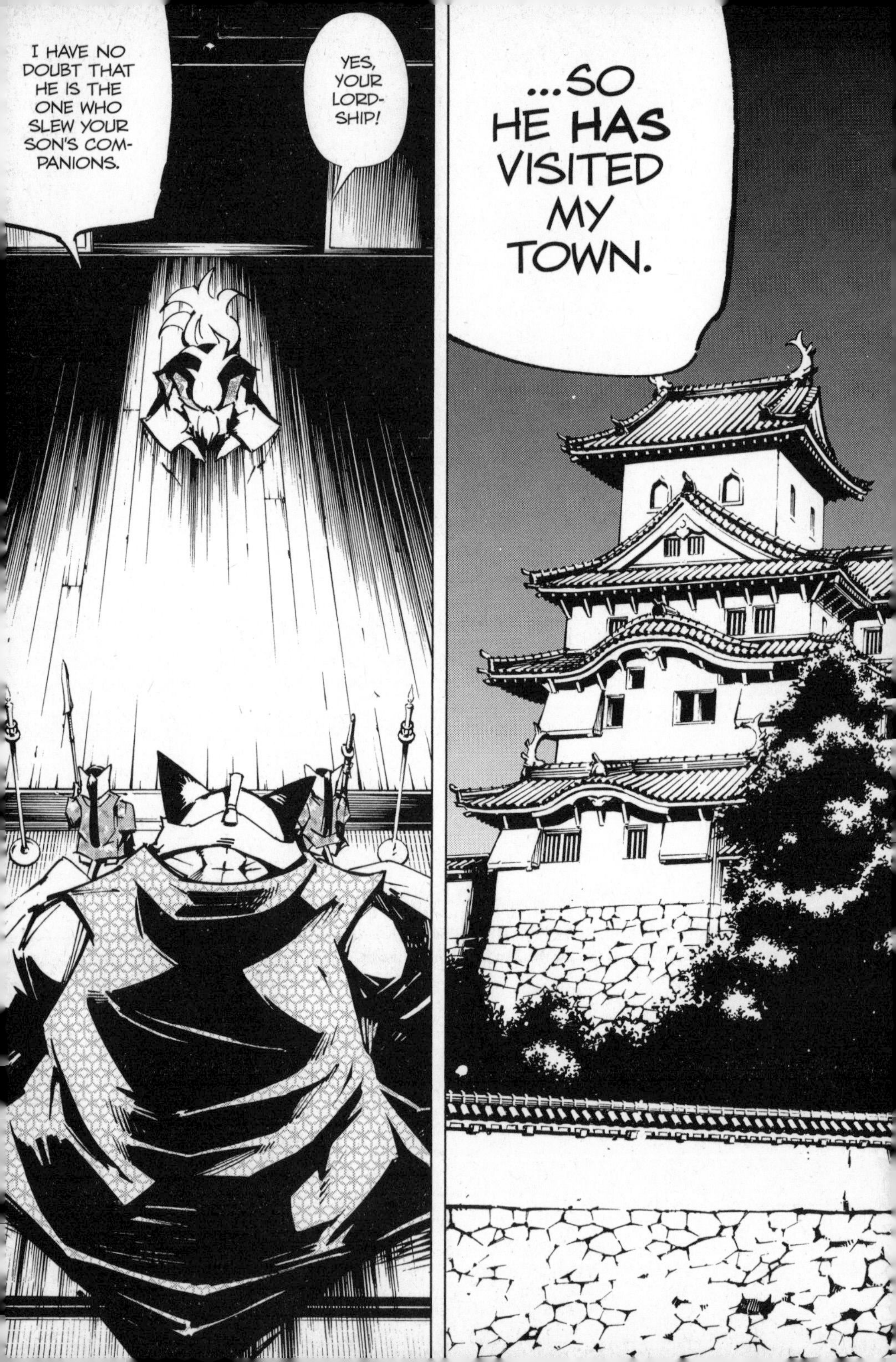
...SO HE HAS VISITED MY TOWN.
YES, YOUR LORDSHIP!
I HAVE NO DOUBT THAT HE IS THE ONE WHO SLEW YOUR SON'S COMPANIONS.

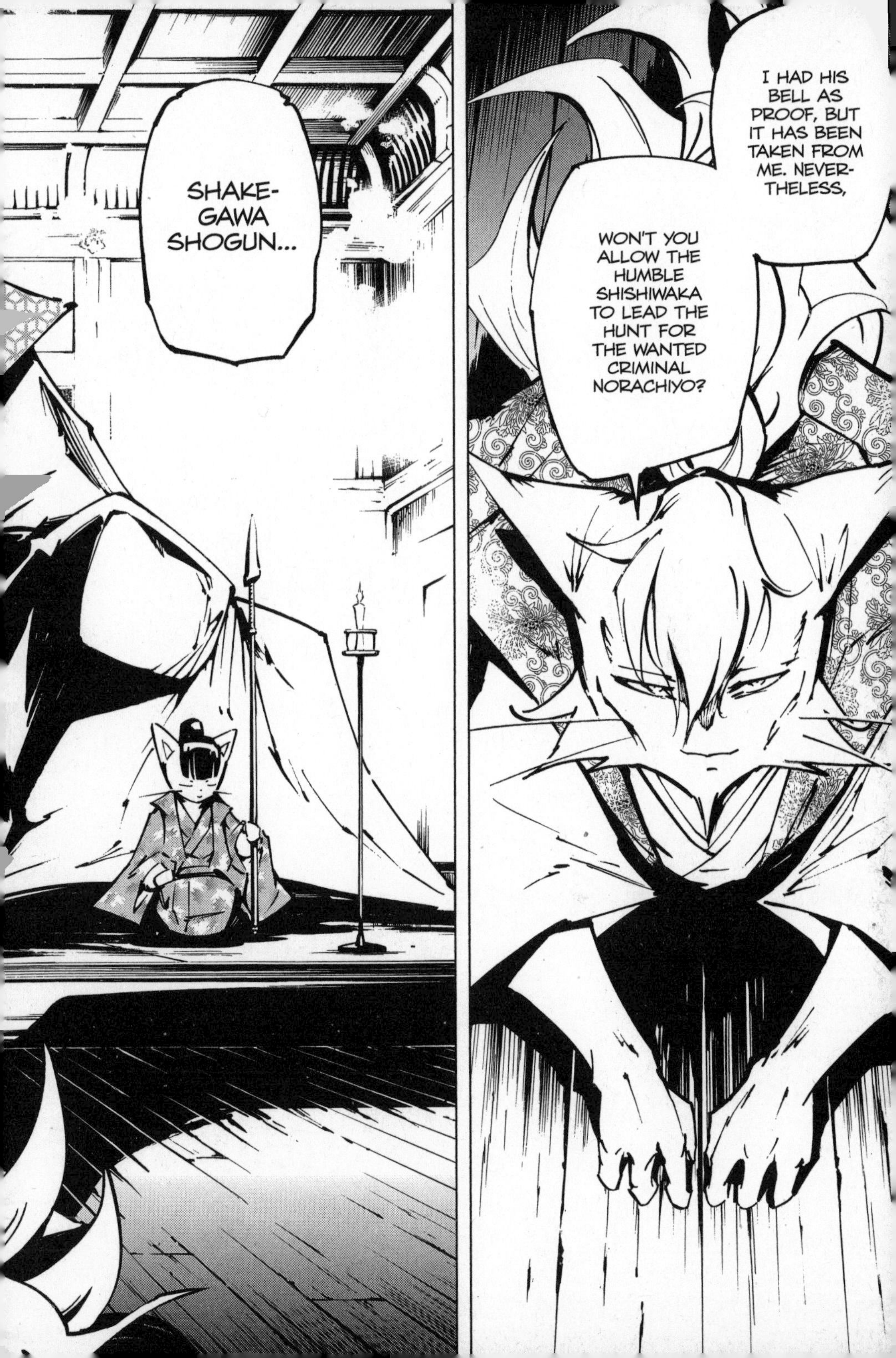
I HAD HIS BELL AS PROOF, BUT IT HAS BEEN TAKEN FROM ME. NEVER-THELESS,
WON'T YOU ALLOW THE HUMBLE SHISHIWAKA TO LEAD THE HUNT FOR THE WANTED CRIMINAL NORACHIYO?
SHAKE-GAWA SHOGUN...

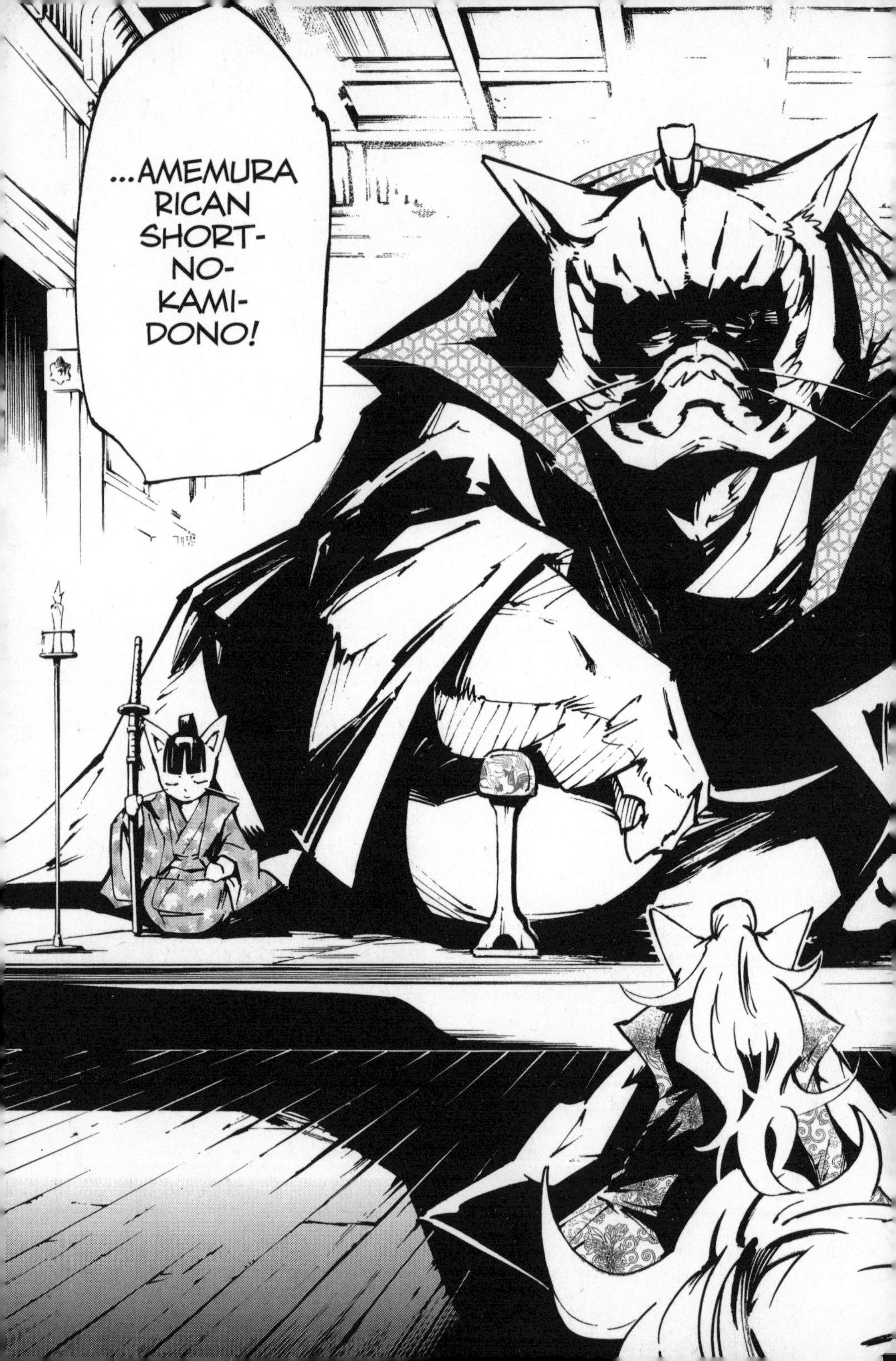
...AMEMURA RICAN SHORT-NO-KAMI-DONO!

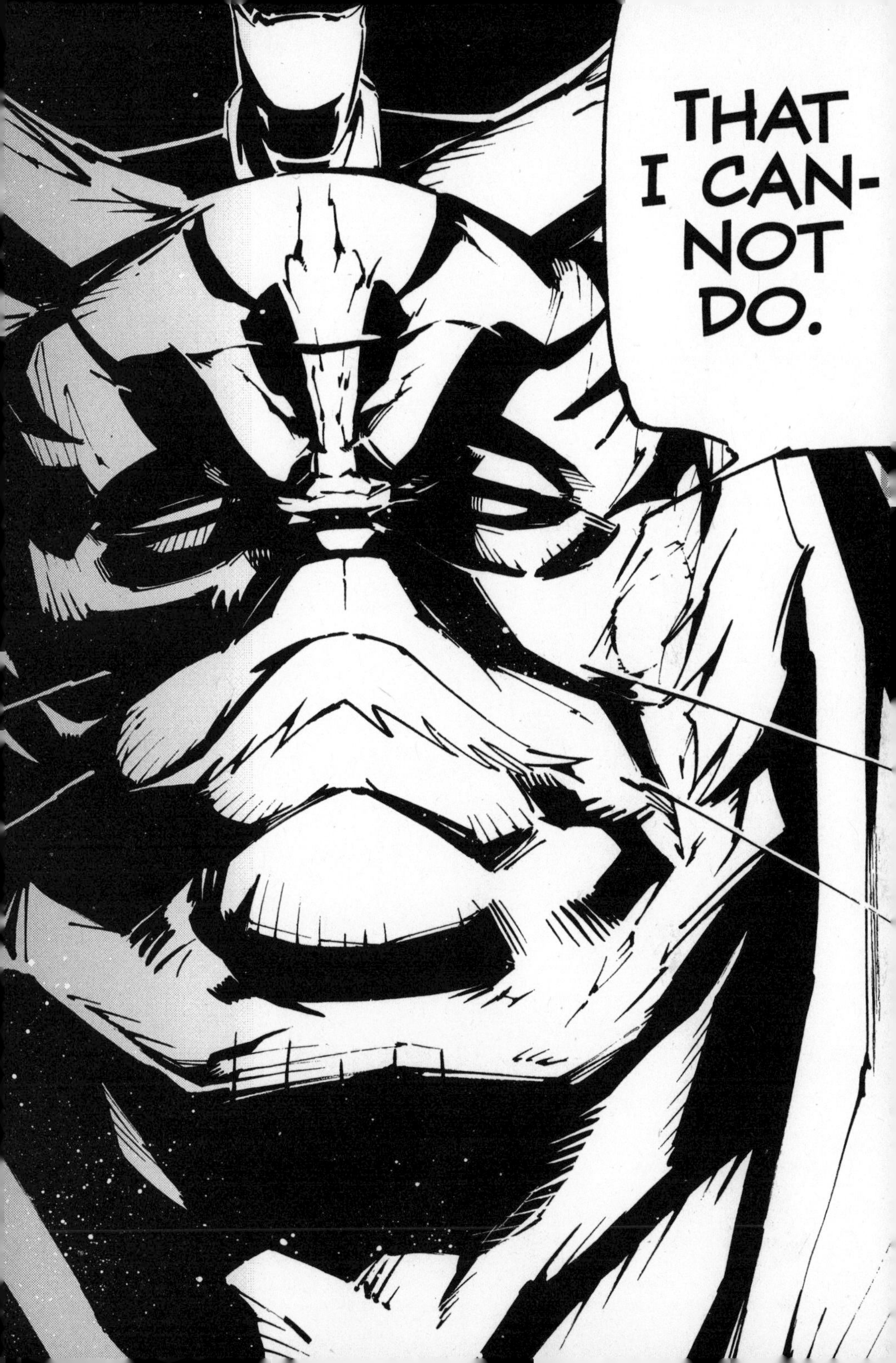
THAT I CAN-NOT DO.

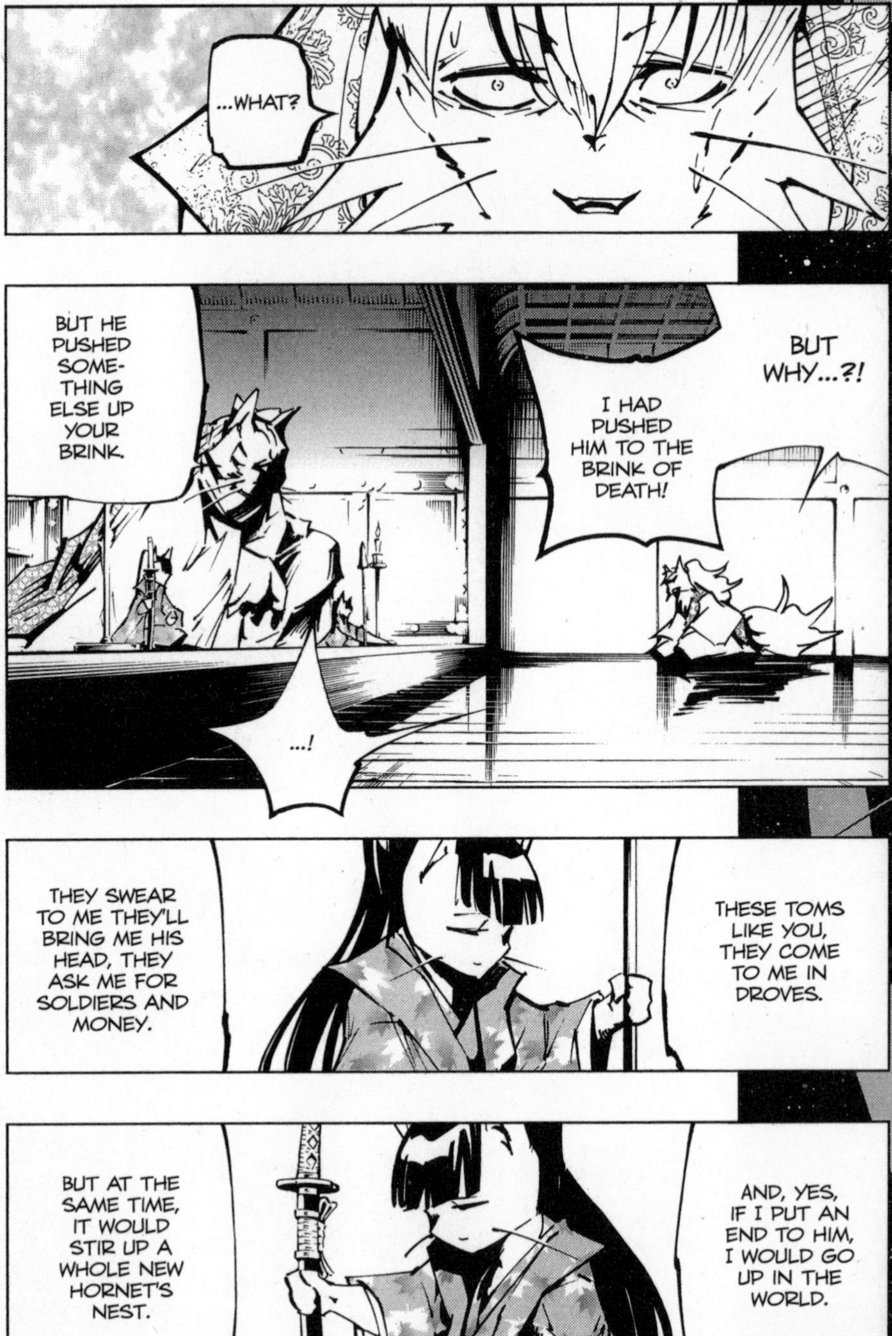
...WHAT?
BUT WHY...?!
I HAD PUSHED HIM TO THE BRINK OF DEATH!
BUT HE PUSHED SOMETHING ELSE UP YOUR BRINK.
...!
THESE TOMS LIKE YOU, THEY COME TO ME IN DROVES.
THEY SWEAR TO ME THEY'LL BRING ME HIS HEAD, THEY ASK ME FOR SOLDIERS AND MONEY.
AND, YES, IF I PUT AN END TO HIM, I WOULD GO UP IN THE WORLD.
BUT AT THE SAME TIME, IT WOULD STIR UP A WHOLE NEW HORNET'S NEST.

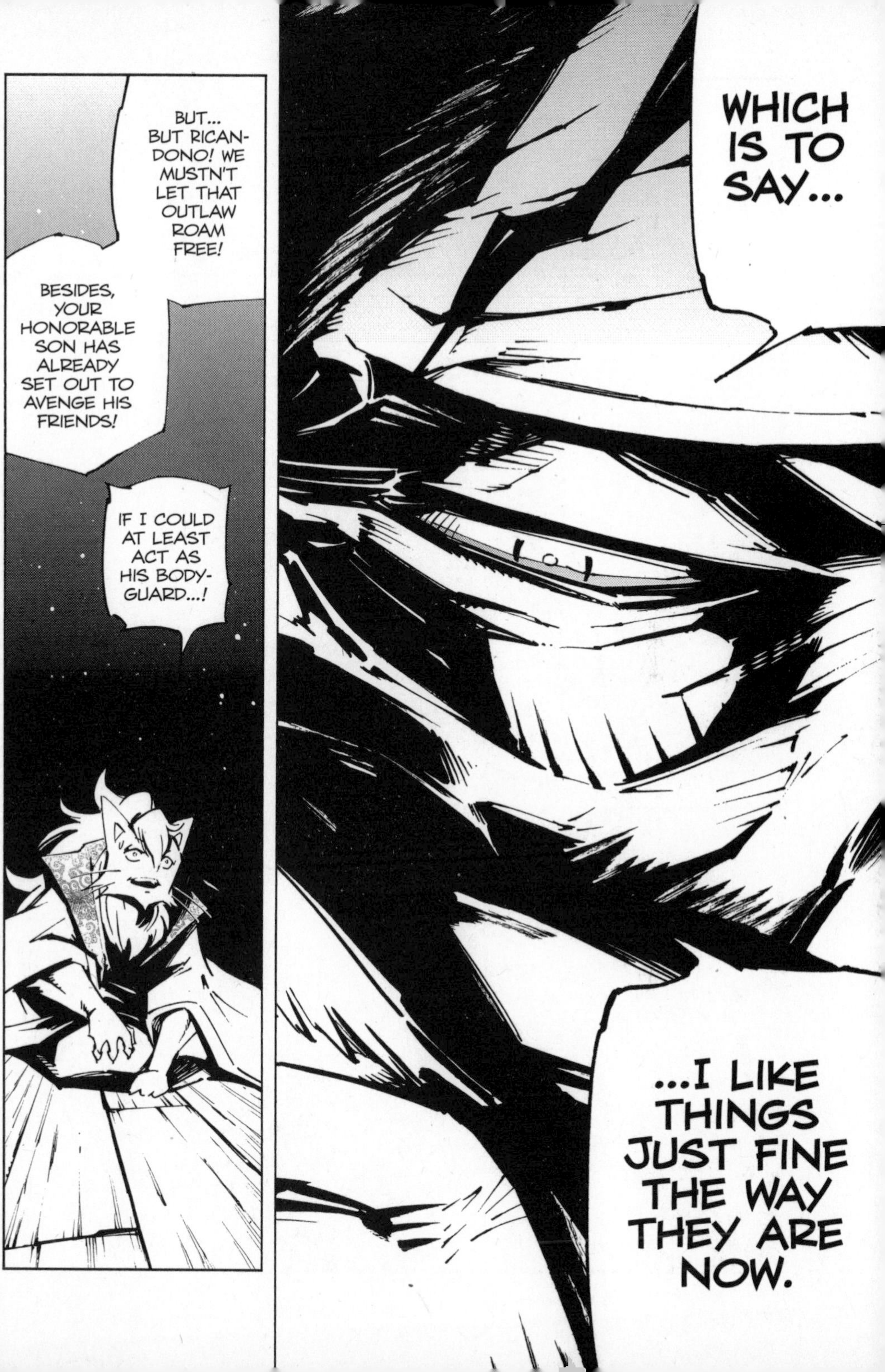
WHICH IS TO SAY...
...I LIKE THINGS JUST FINE THE WAY THEY ARE NOW.
BUT... BUT RICAN-DONO! WE MUSTN'T LET THAT OUTLAW ROAM FREE!
BESIDES, YOUR HONORABLE SON HAS ALREADY SET OUT TO AVENGE HIS FRIENDS!
IF I COULD AT LEAST ACT AS HIS BODY-GUARD...!

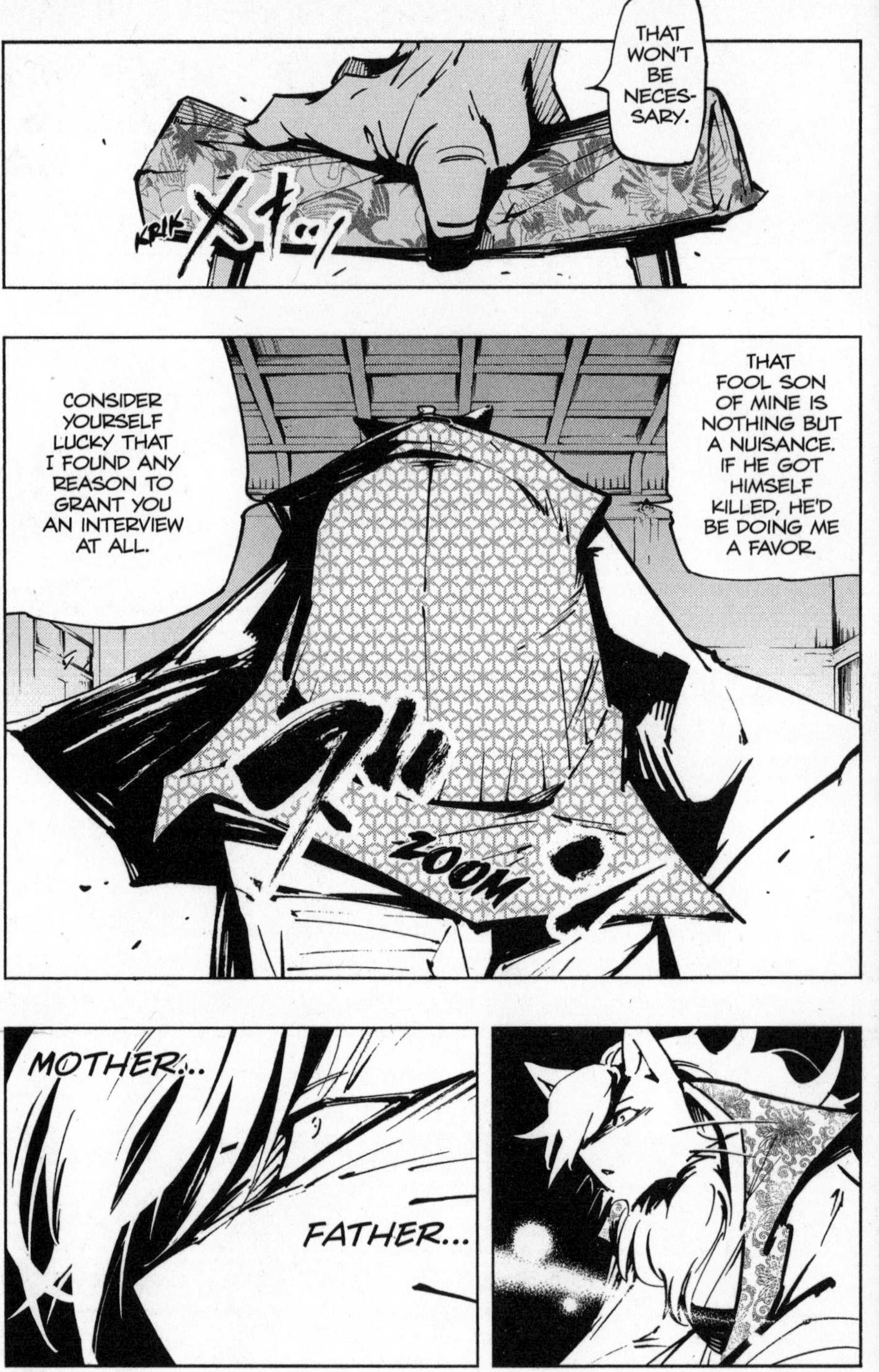
THAT WON'T BE NECES-SARY.
KRIK
THAT FOOL SON OF MINE IS NOTHING BUT A NUISANCE. IF HE GOT HIMSELF KILLED, HE'D BE DOING ME A FAVOR.
CONSIDER YOURSELF LUCKY THAT I FOUND ANY REASON TO GRANT YOU AN INTERVIEW AT ALL.
ZOOM
MOTHER...
FATHER...

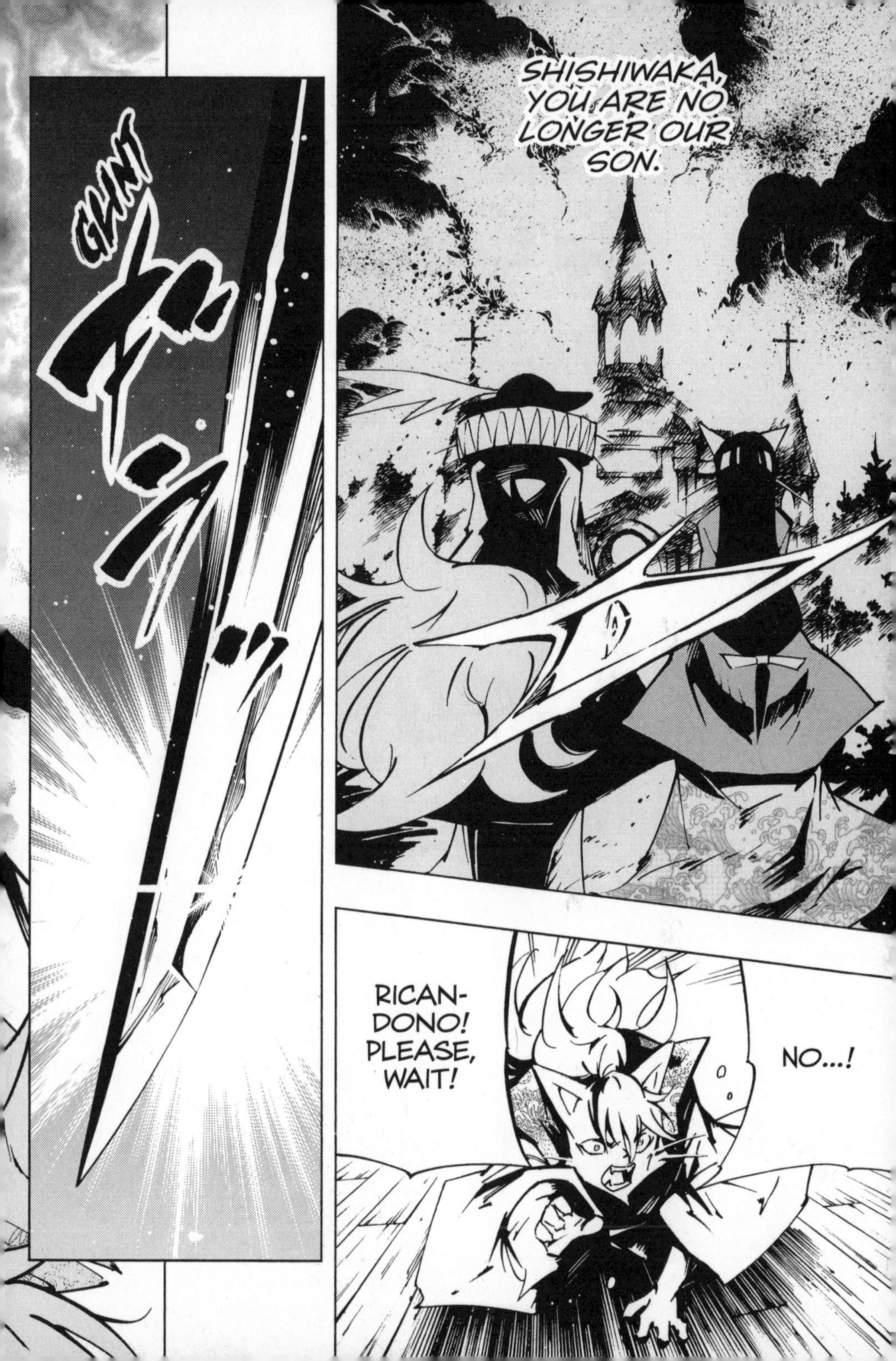
SHISHIWAKA, YOU ARE NO LONGER OUR SON.
NO...!
RICAN-DONO! PLEASE, WAIT!
GLINT

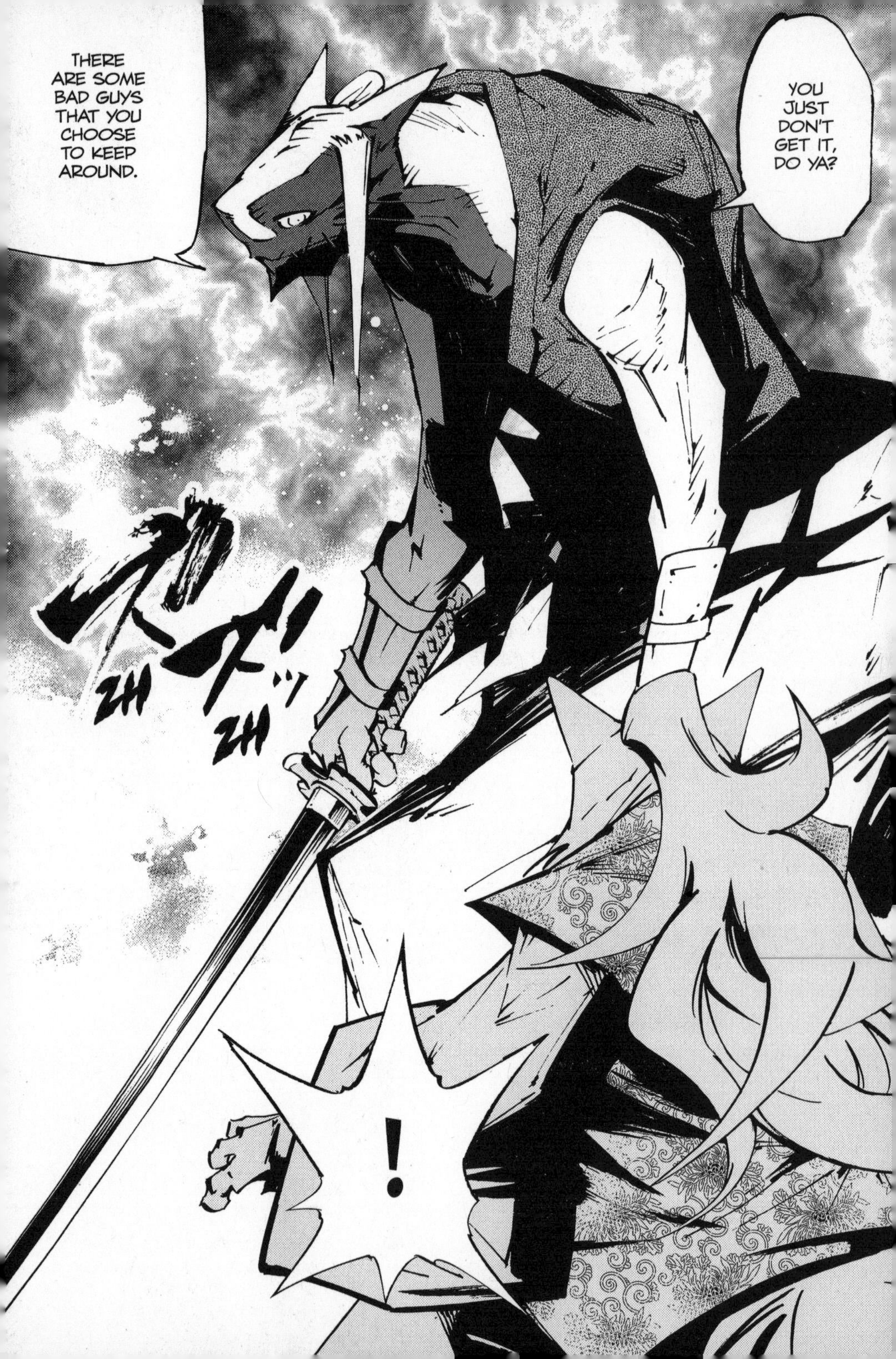
YOU JUST DON'T GET IT, DO YA?
THERE ARE SOME BAD GUYS THAT YOU CHOOSE TO KEEP AROUND.
ZH
ZH
!

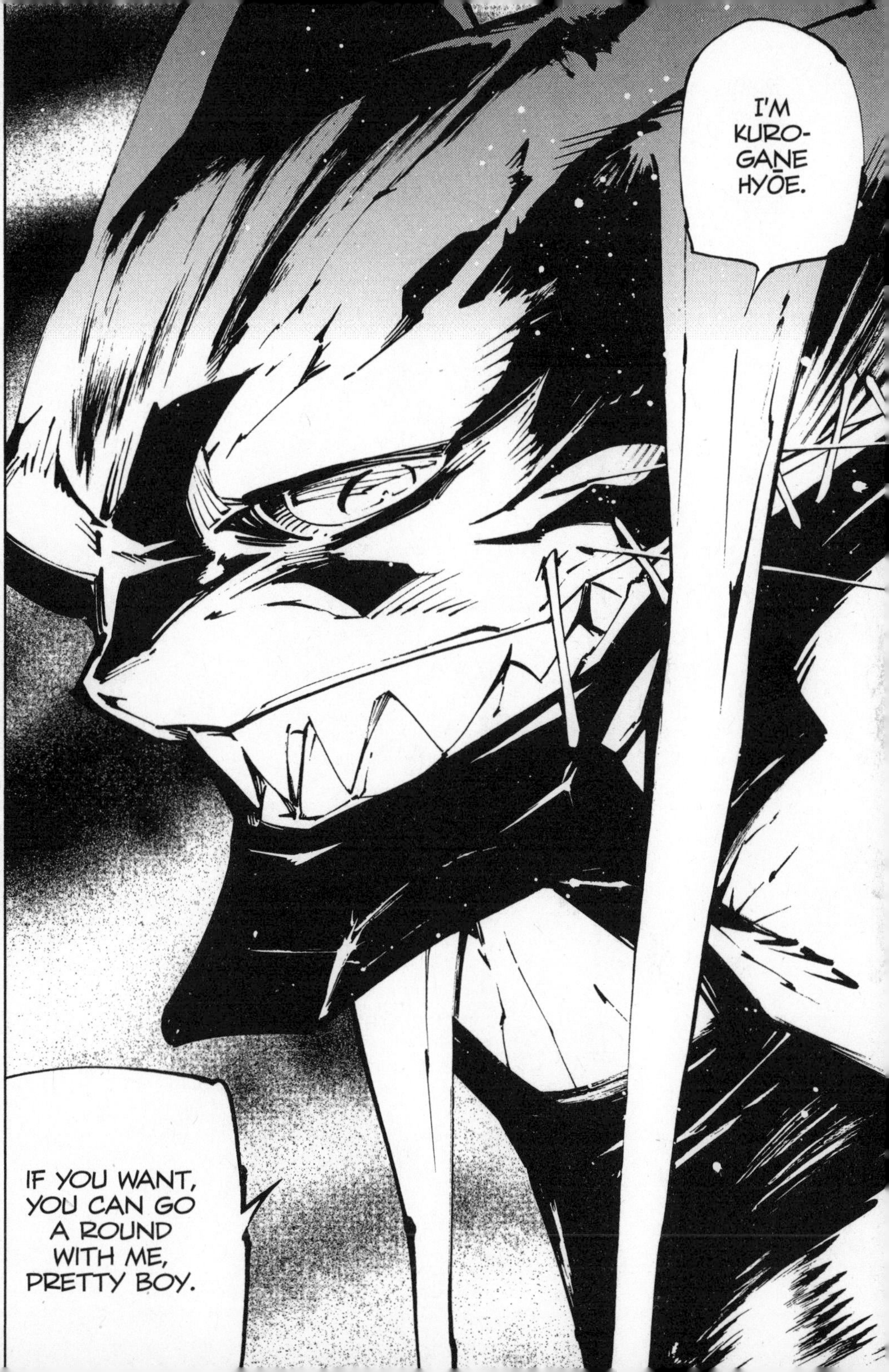
I'M KURO-GANE HYŌE.
IF YOU WANT, YOU CAN GO A ROUND WITH ME, PRETTY BOY.

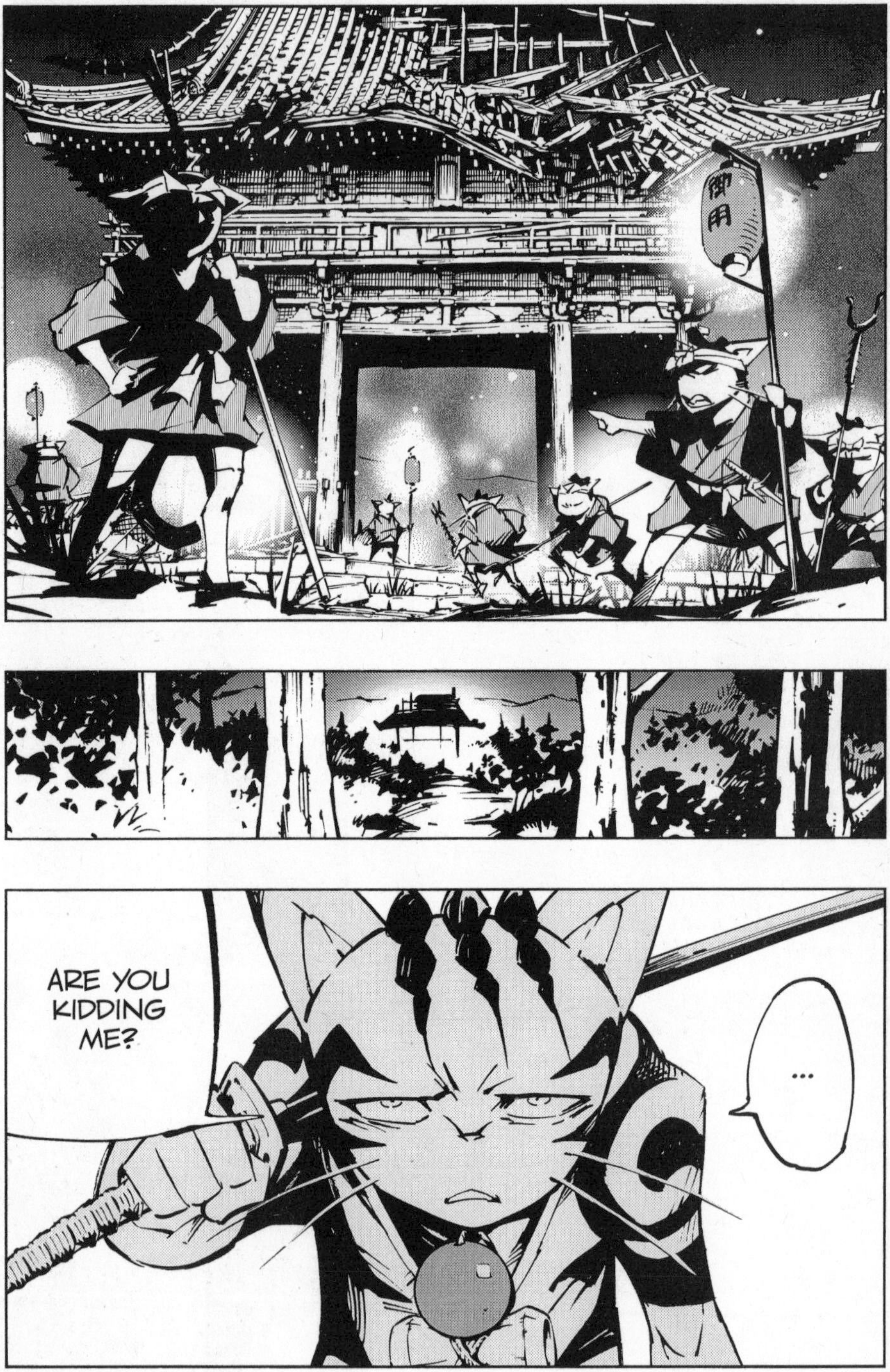
LANTERN: POLICE
ARE YOU KIDDING ME?
...

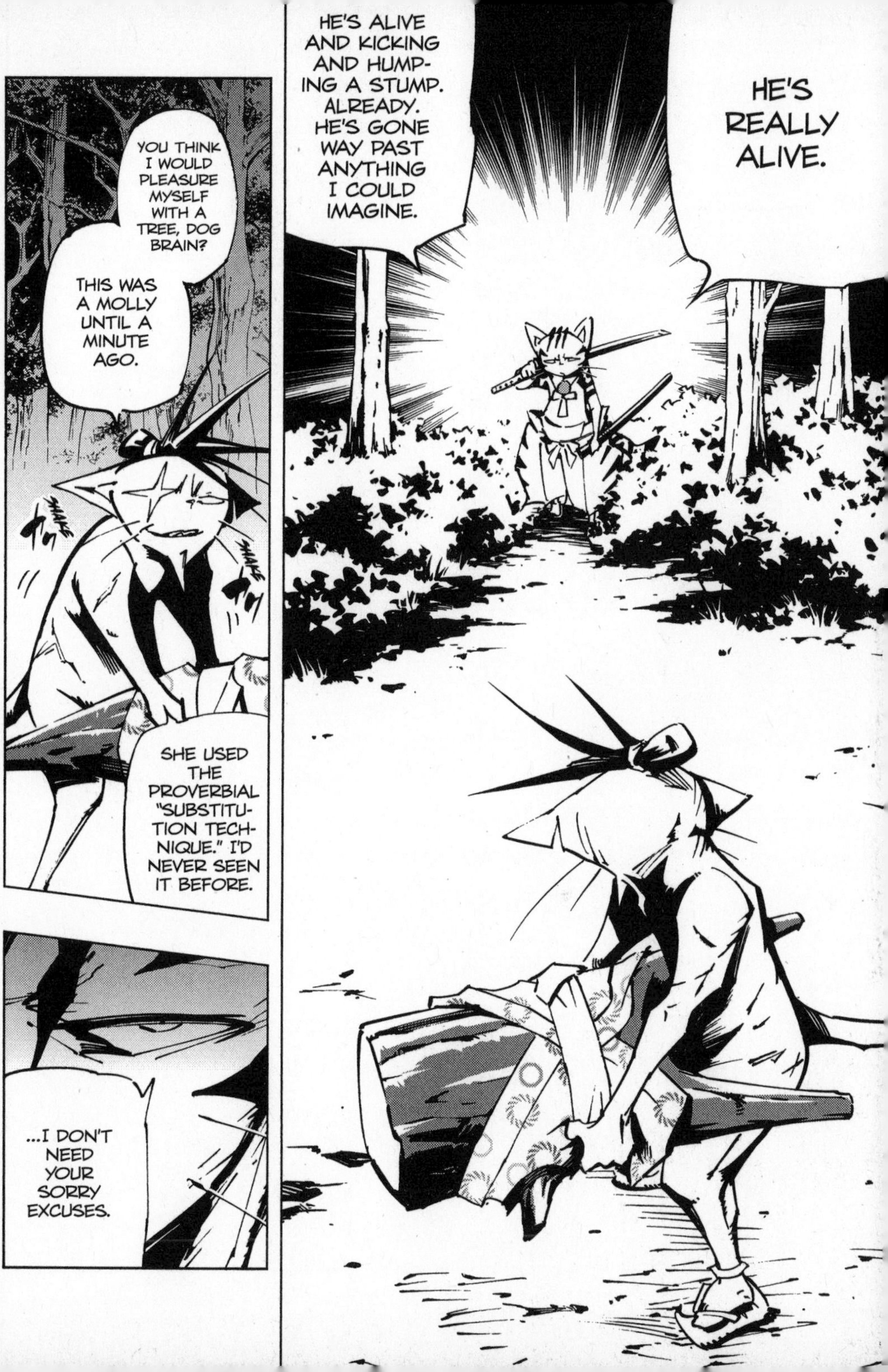
HE'S REALLY ALIVE.
HE'S ALIVE AND KICKING AND HUMPING A STUMP. ALREADY. HE'S GONE WAY PAST ANYTHING I COULD IMAGINE.
YOU THINK I WOULD PLEASURE MYSELF WITH A TREE, DOG BRAIN?
THIS WAS A MOLLY UNTIL A MINUTE AGO.
SHAKE
SHAKE
SHE USED THE PROVERBIAL "SUBSTITUTION TECHNIQUE." I'D NEVER SEEN IT BEFORE.
...I DON'T NEED YOUR SORRY EXCUSES.

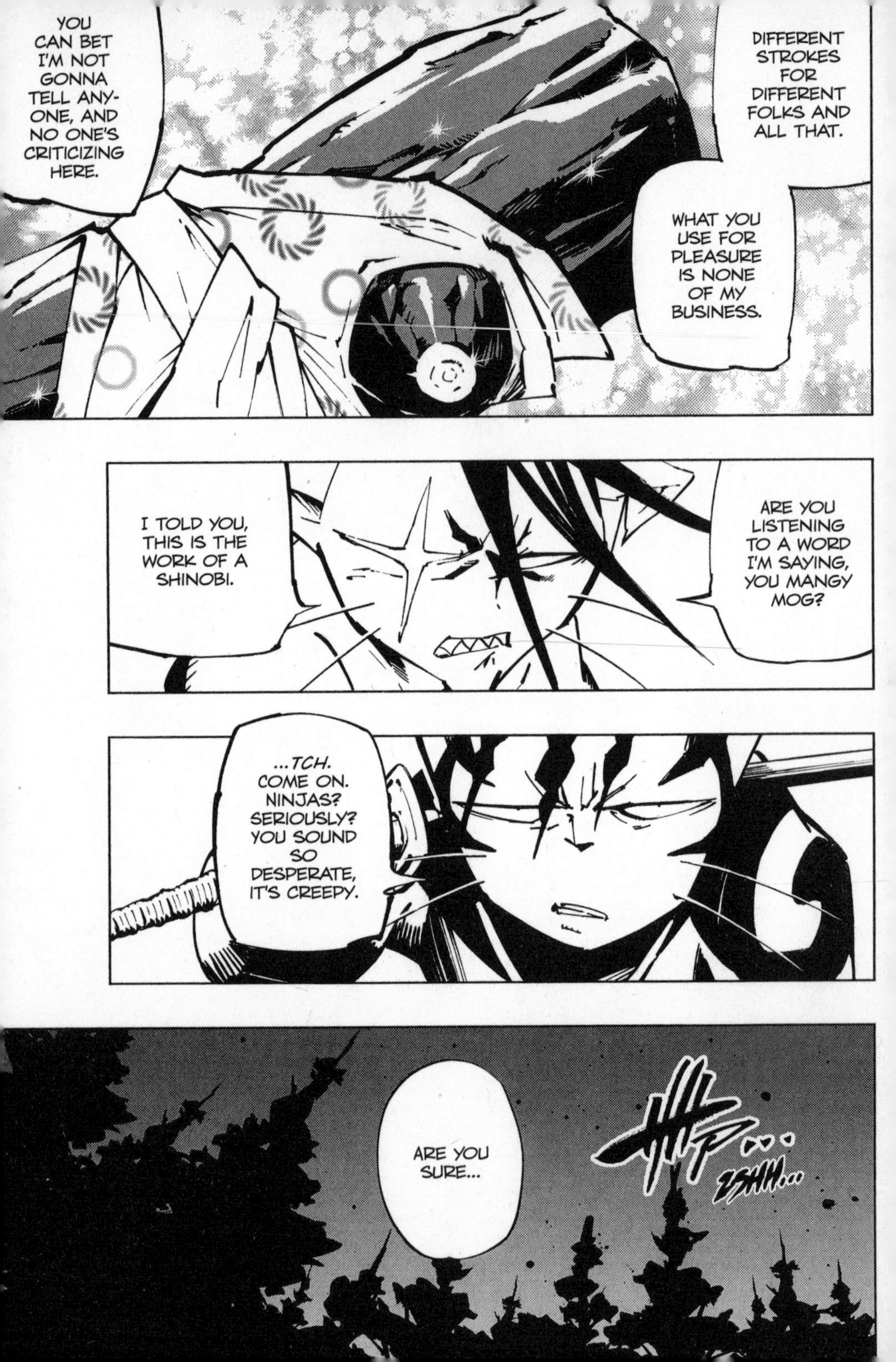
DIFFERENT STROKES FOR DIFFERENT FOLKS AND ALL THAT.
WHAT YOU USE FOR PLEASURE IS NONE OF MY BUSINESS.
YOU CAN BET I'M NOT GONNA TELL ANY-ONE, AND NO ONE'S CRITICIZING HERE.
ARE YOU LISTENING TO A WORD I'M SAYING, YOU MANGY MOG?
I TOLD YOU, THIS IS THE WORK OF A SHINOBI.
...TCH. COME ON. NINJAS? SERIOUSLY? YOU SOUND SO DESPERATE, IT'S CREEPY.
ZSHH...
ARE YOU SURE...

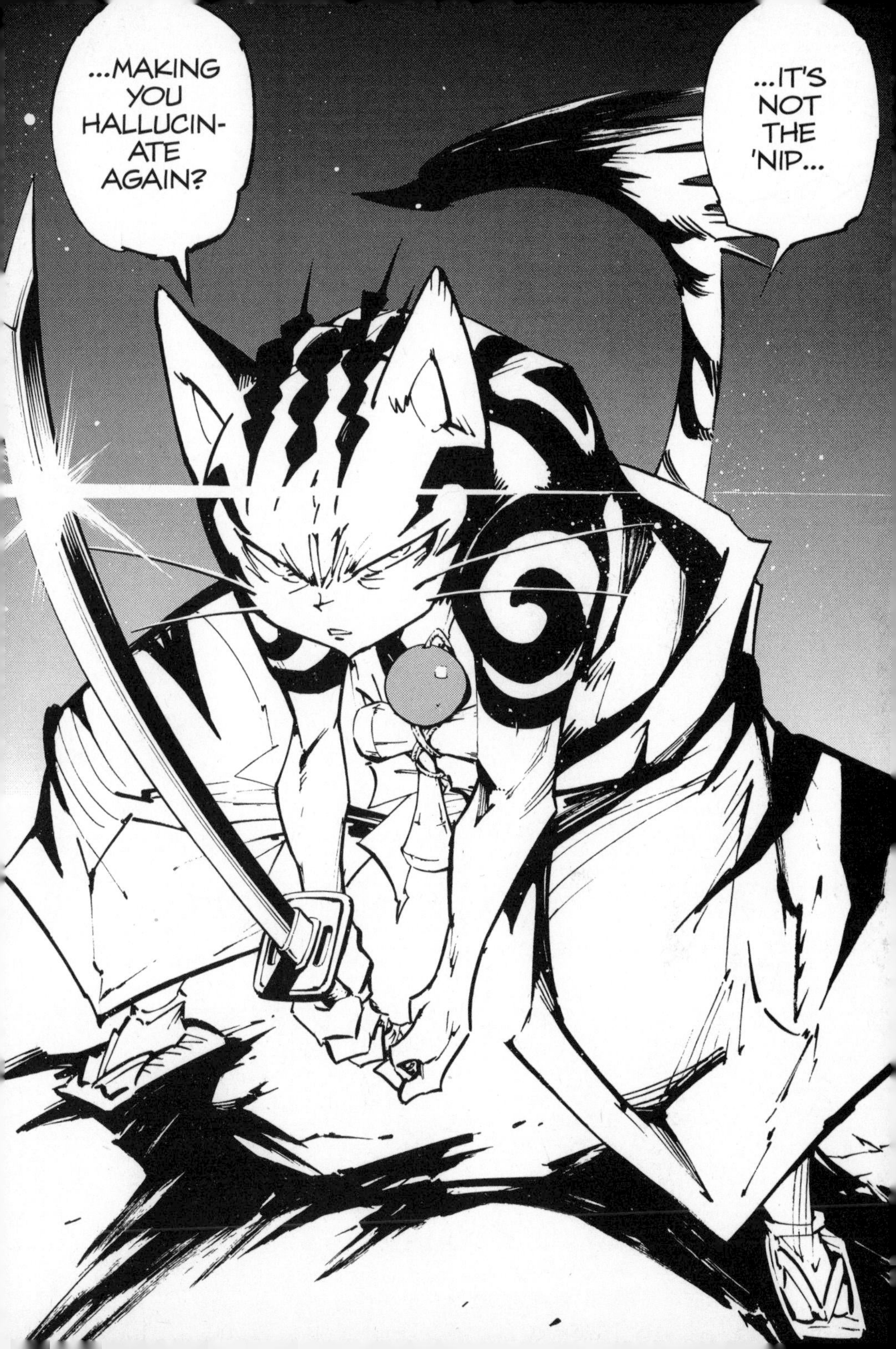
...IT'S NOT THE 'NIP...
...MAKING YOU HALLUCINATE AGAIN?

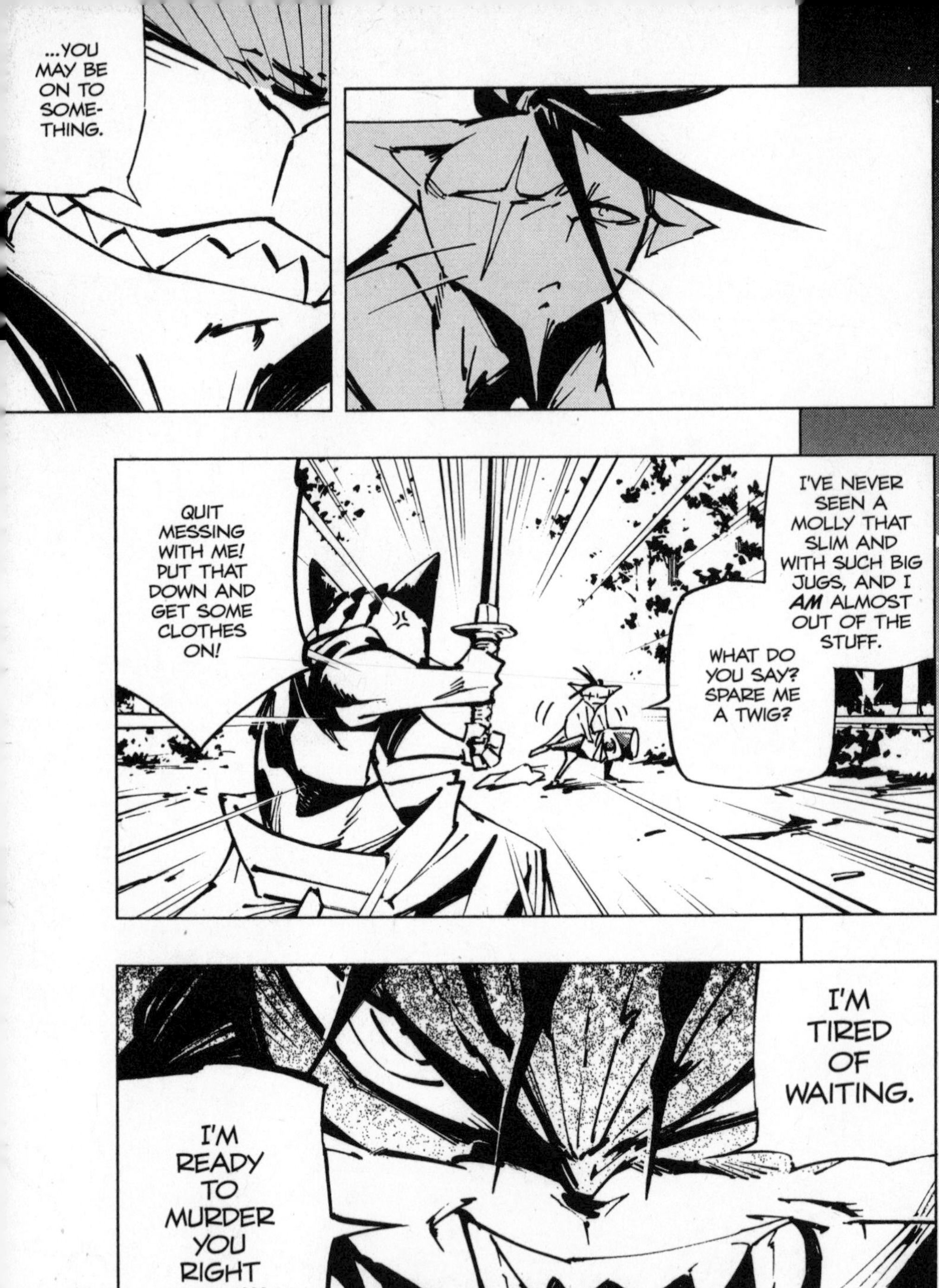
...YOU MAY BE ON TO SOME-THING.
I'VE NEVER SEEN A MOLLY THAT SLIM AND WITH SUCH BIG JUGS, AND I *AM* ALMOST OUT OF THE STUFF.
WHAT DO YOU SAY? SPARE ME A TWIG?
QUIT MESSING WITH ME! PUT THAT DOWN AND GET SOME CLOTHES ON!
I'M TIRED OF WAITING.
I'M READY TO MURDER YOU RIGHT NOW!!!

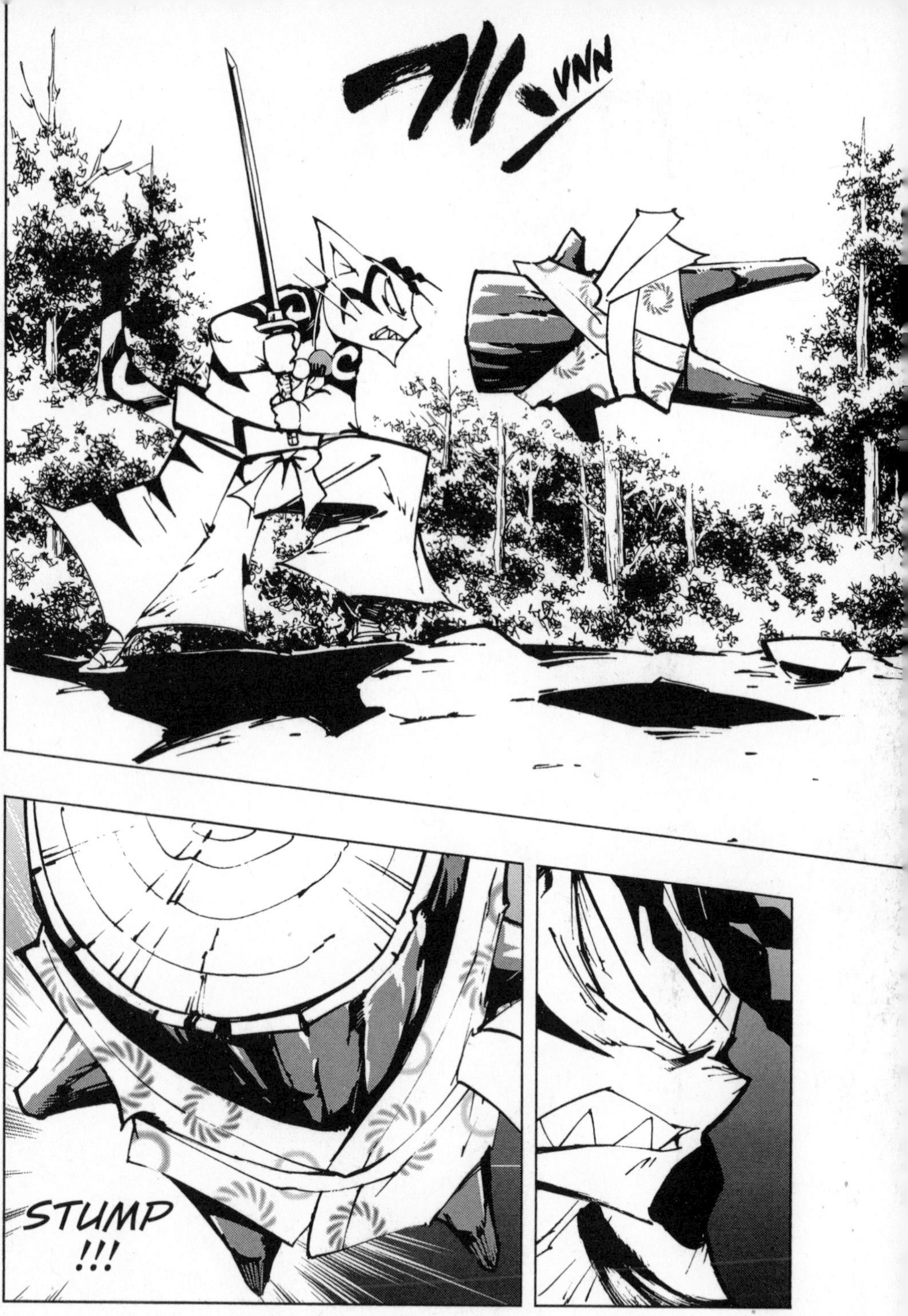
VNN
STUMP
!!!

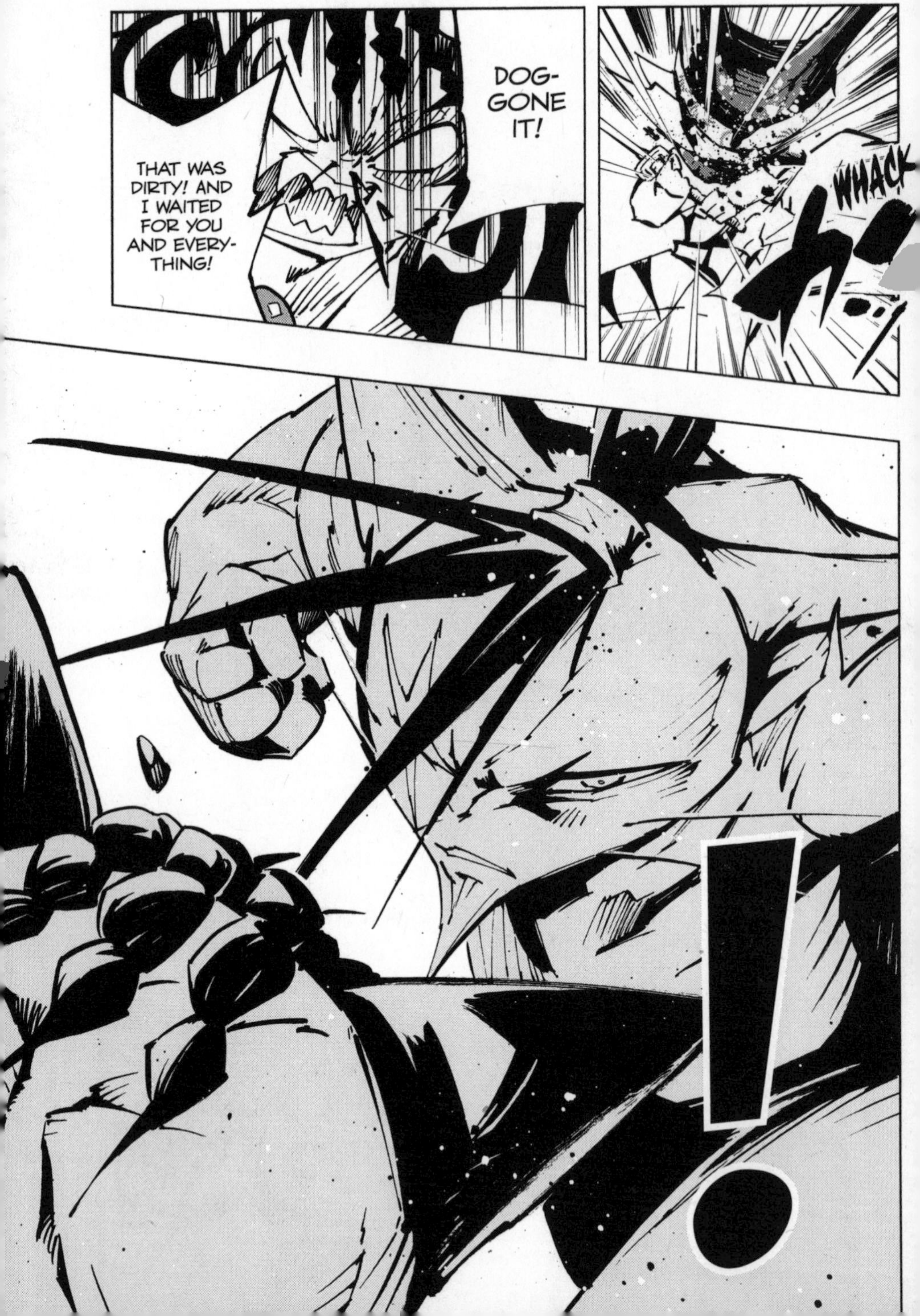
WHACK
DOG-GONE IT!
THAT WAS DIRTY! AND I WAITED FOR YOU AND EVERYTHING!

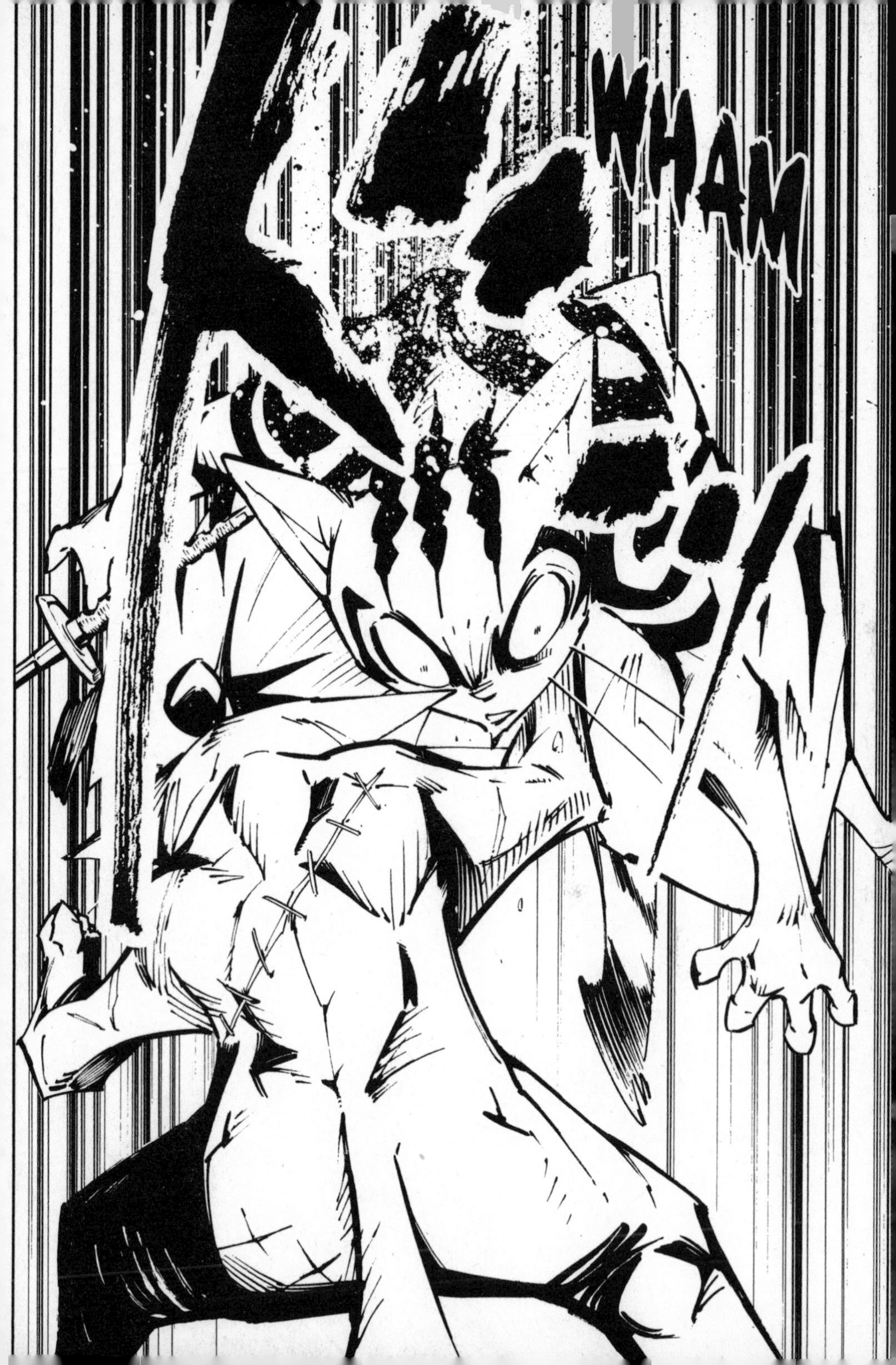
WHAM

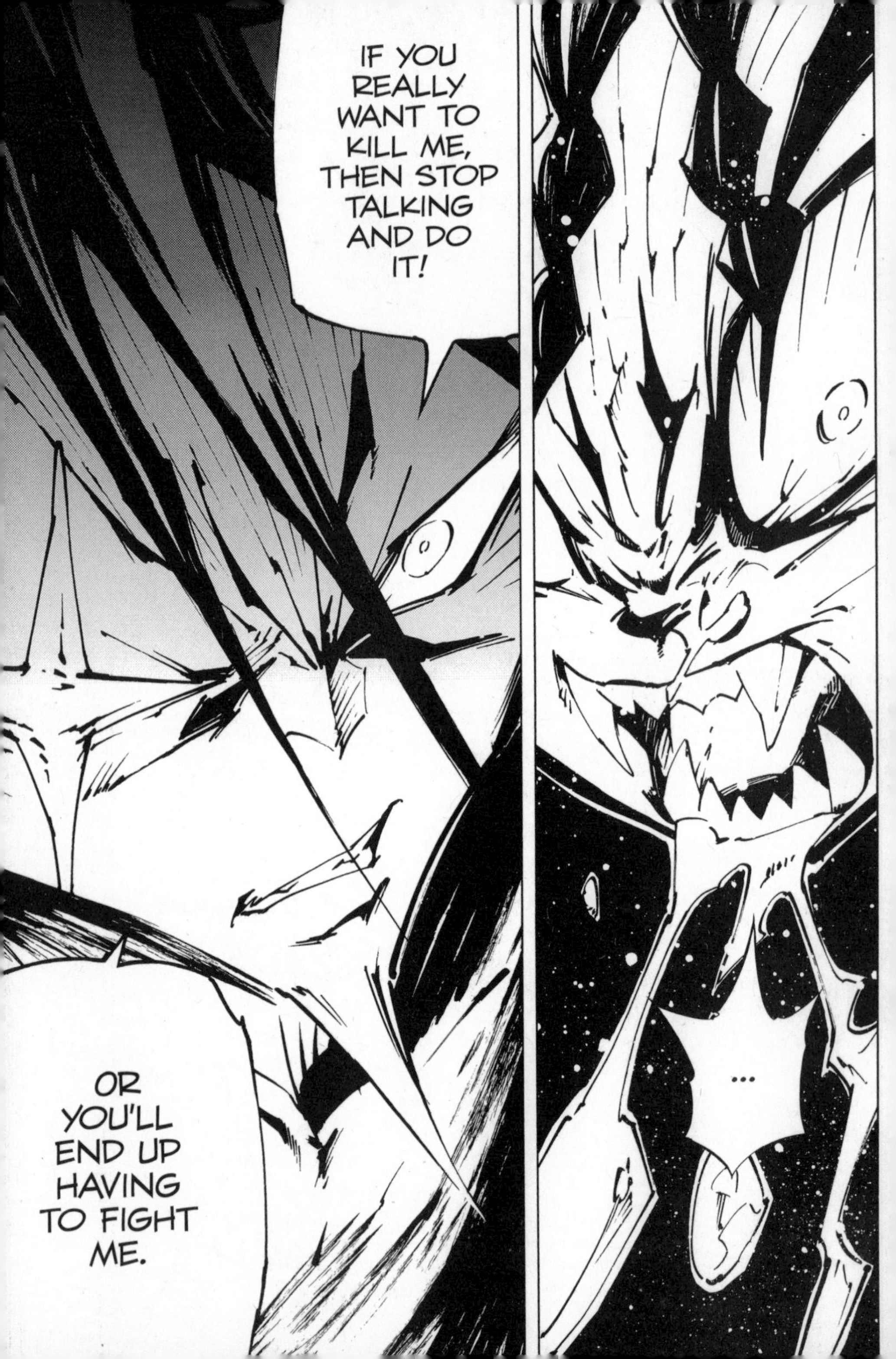
...
IF YOU REALLY WANT TO KILL ME, THEN STOP TALKING AND DO IT!
OR YOU'LL END UP HAVING TO FIGHT ME.

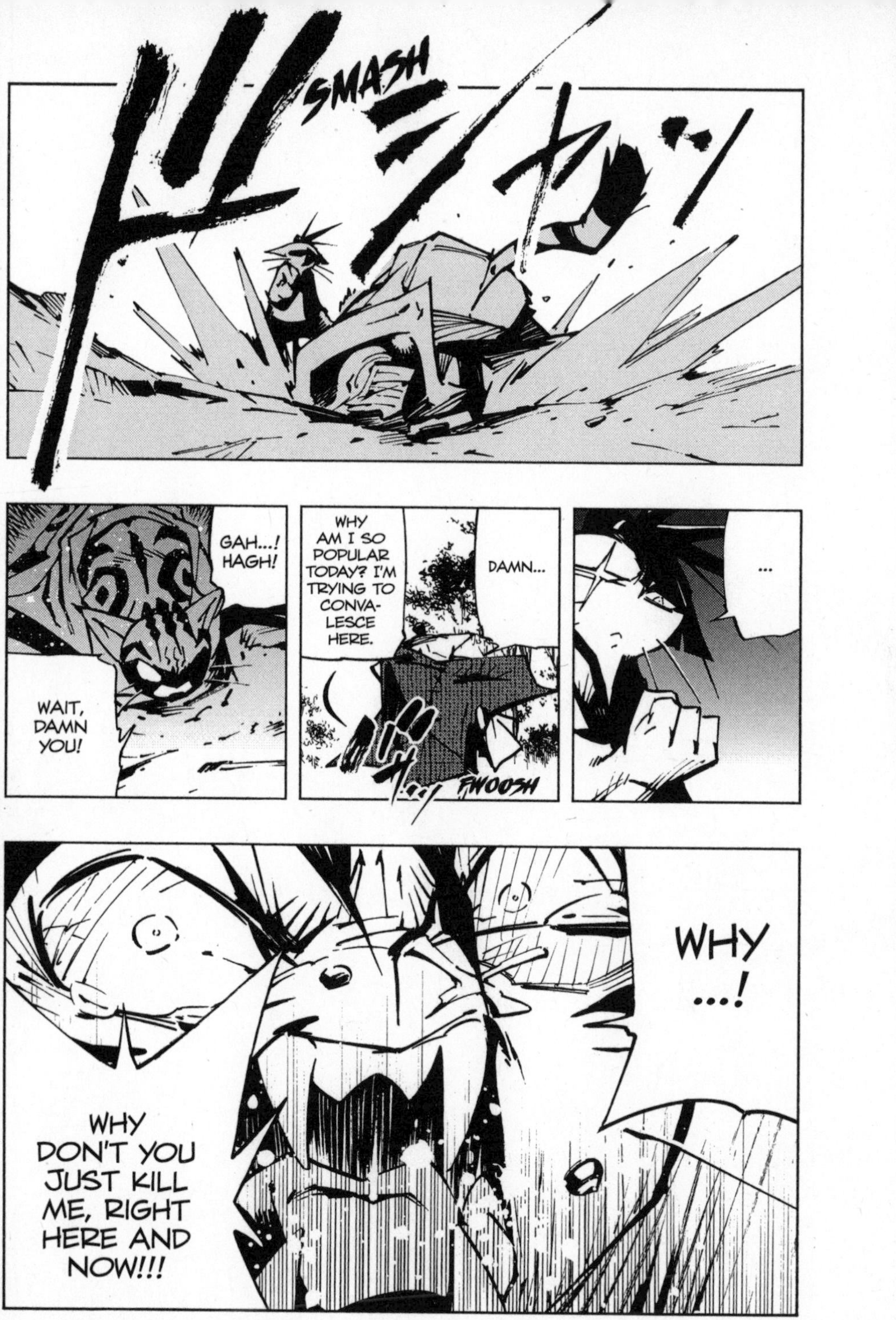
SMASH
...
DAMN...
WHY AM I SO POPULAR TODAY? I'M TRYING TO CONVALESCE HERE.
FWOOSH
GAH...! HAGH!
WAIT, DAMN YOU!
WHY ...!
WHY DON'T YOU JUST KILL ME, RIGHT HERE AND NOW!!!

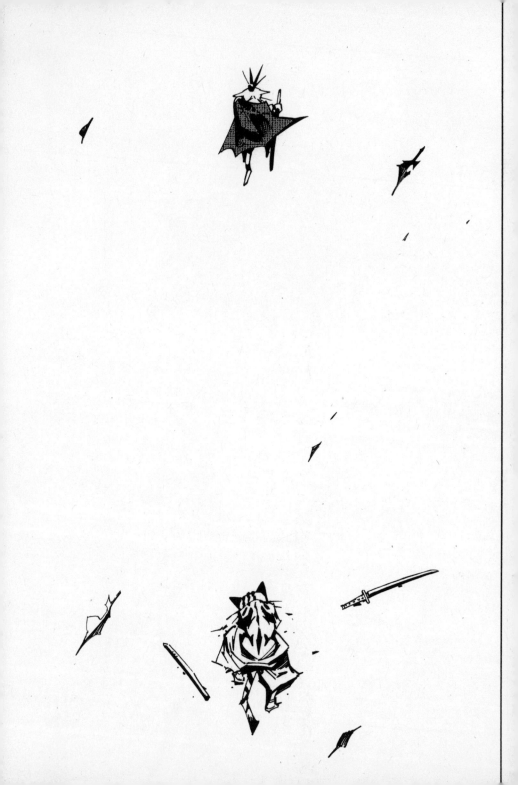

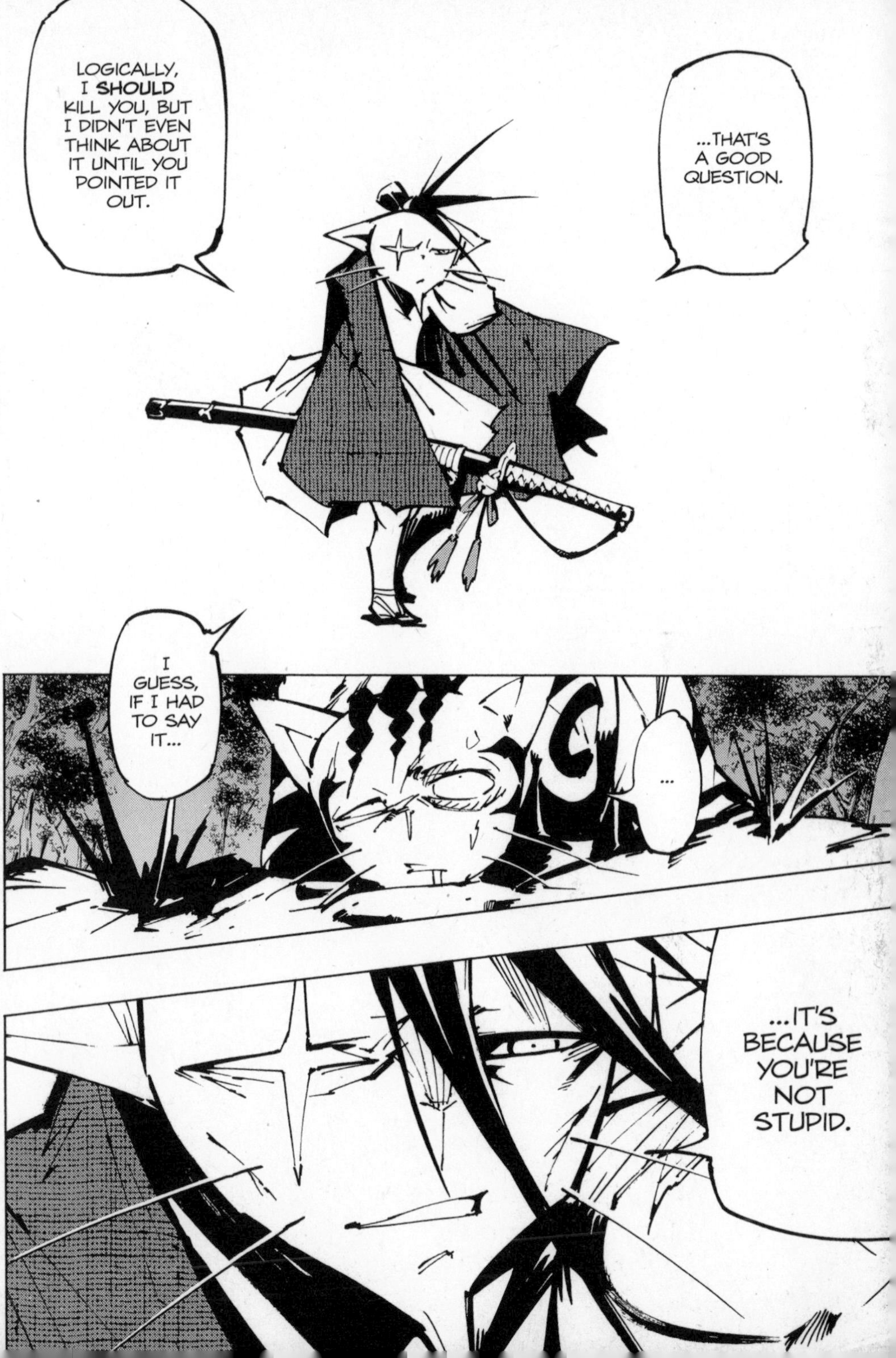
...THAT'S A GOOD QUESTION.
LOGICALLY, I **SHOULD** KILL YOU, BUT I DIDN'T EVEN THINK ABOUT IT UNTIL YOU POINTED IT OUT.
...
I GUESS, IF I HAD TO SAY IT...
...IT'S BECAUSE YOU'RE NOT STUPID.

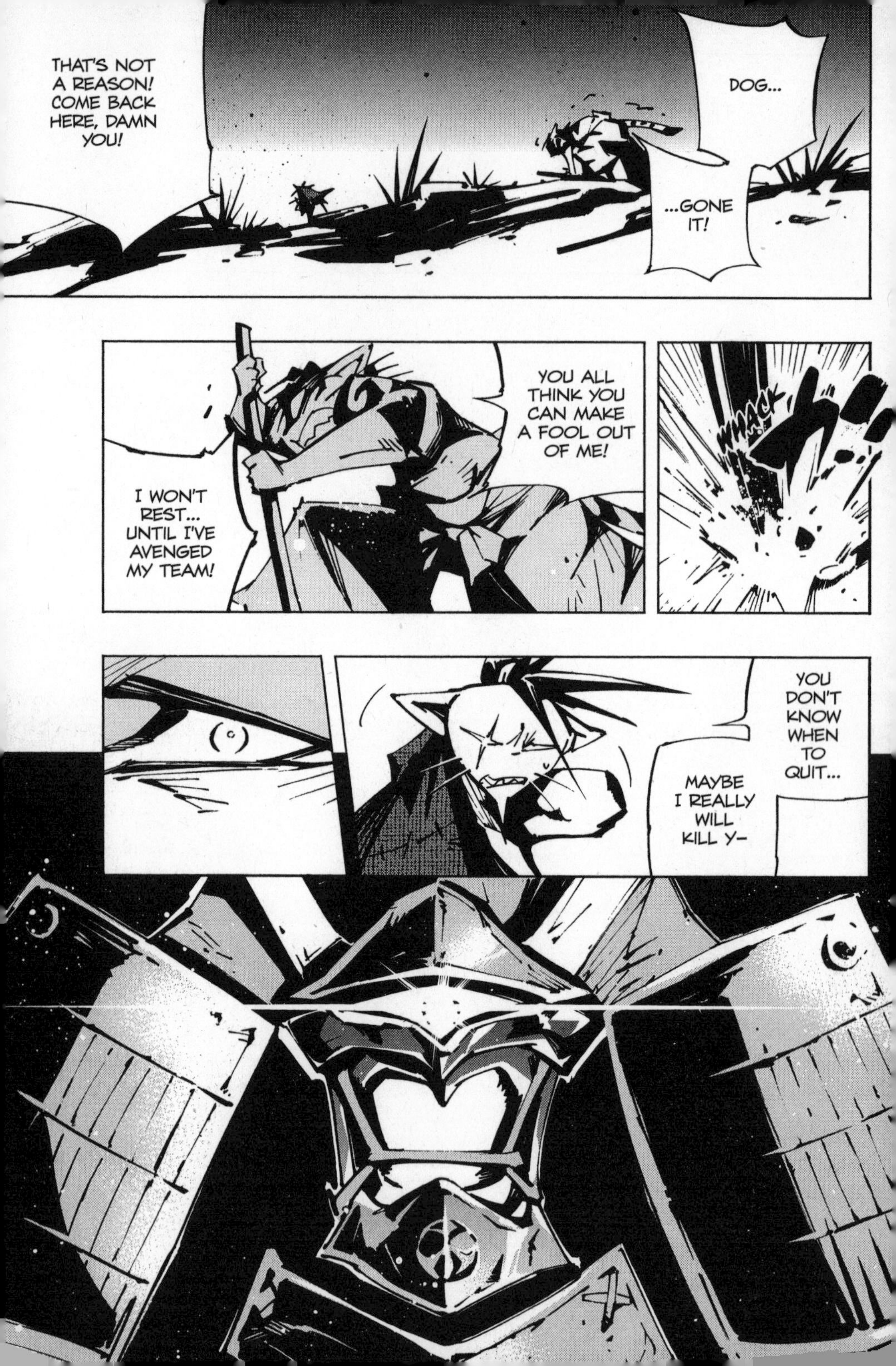
DOG...
...GONE IT!
THAT'S NOT A REASON! COME BACK HERE, DAMN YOU!
WHACK
YOU ALL THINK YOU CAN MAKE A FOOL OUT OF ME!
I WON'T REST... UNTIL I'VE AVENGED MY TEAM!
YOU DON'T KNOW WHEN TO QUIT...
MAYBE I REALLY WILL KILL Y-

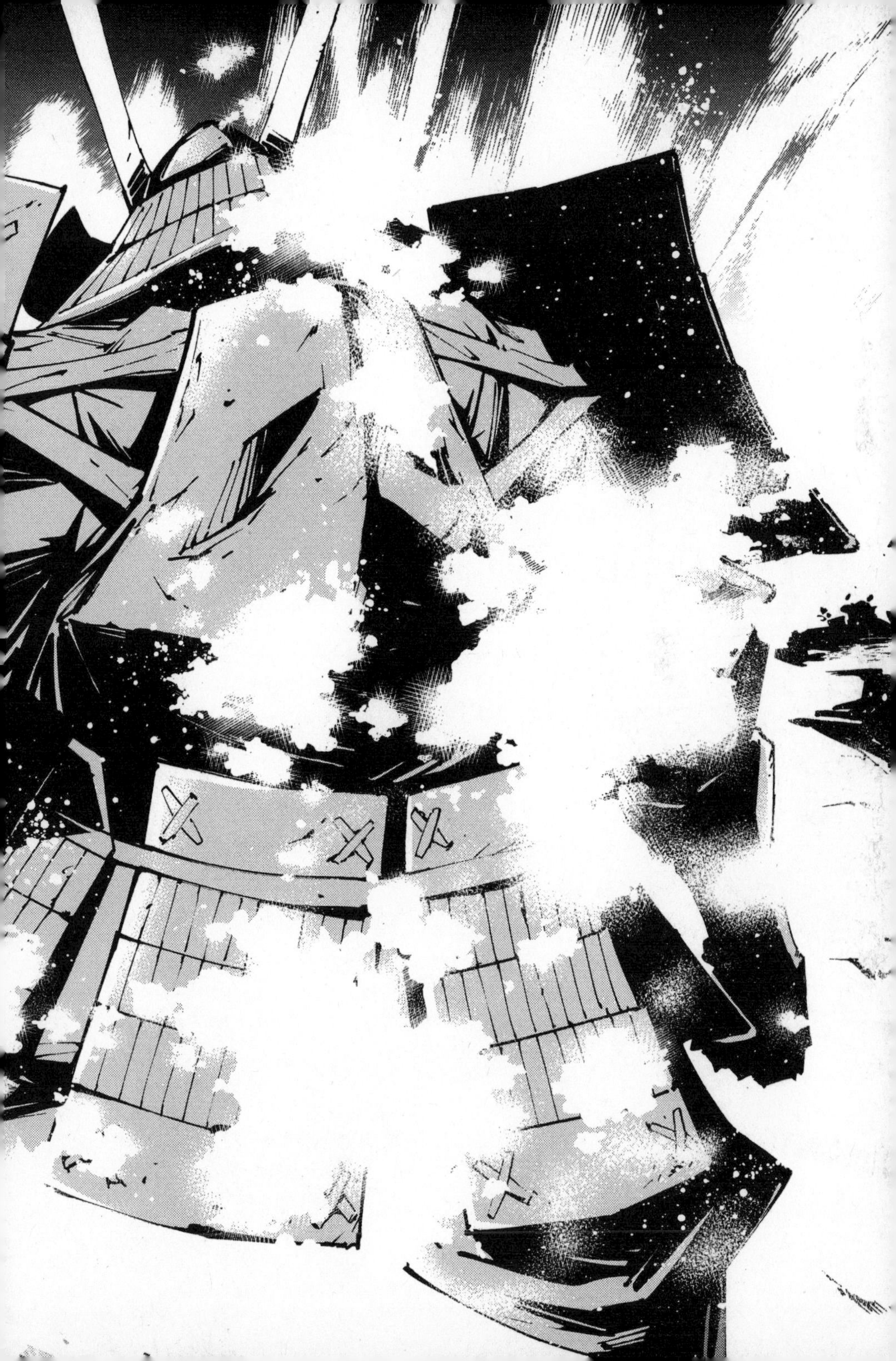

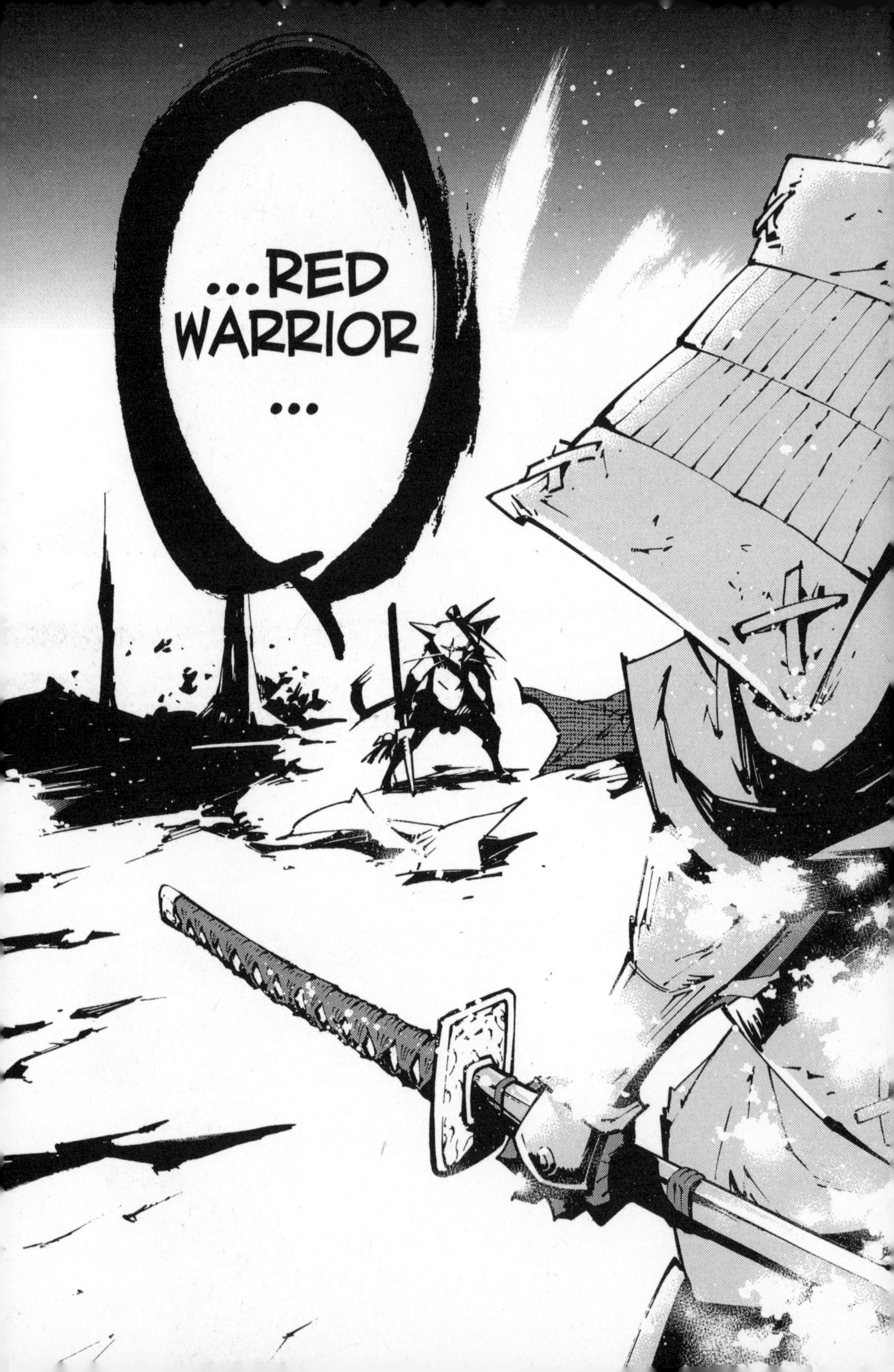
...RED WARRIOR ...

猫ヶ原

NeKoGaHara

ネコガハラ

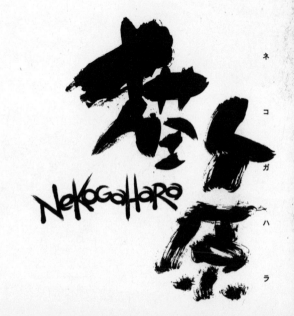

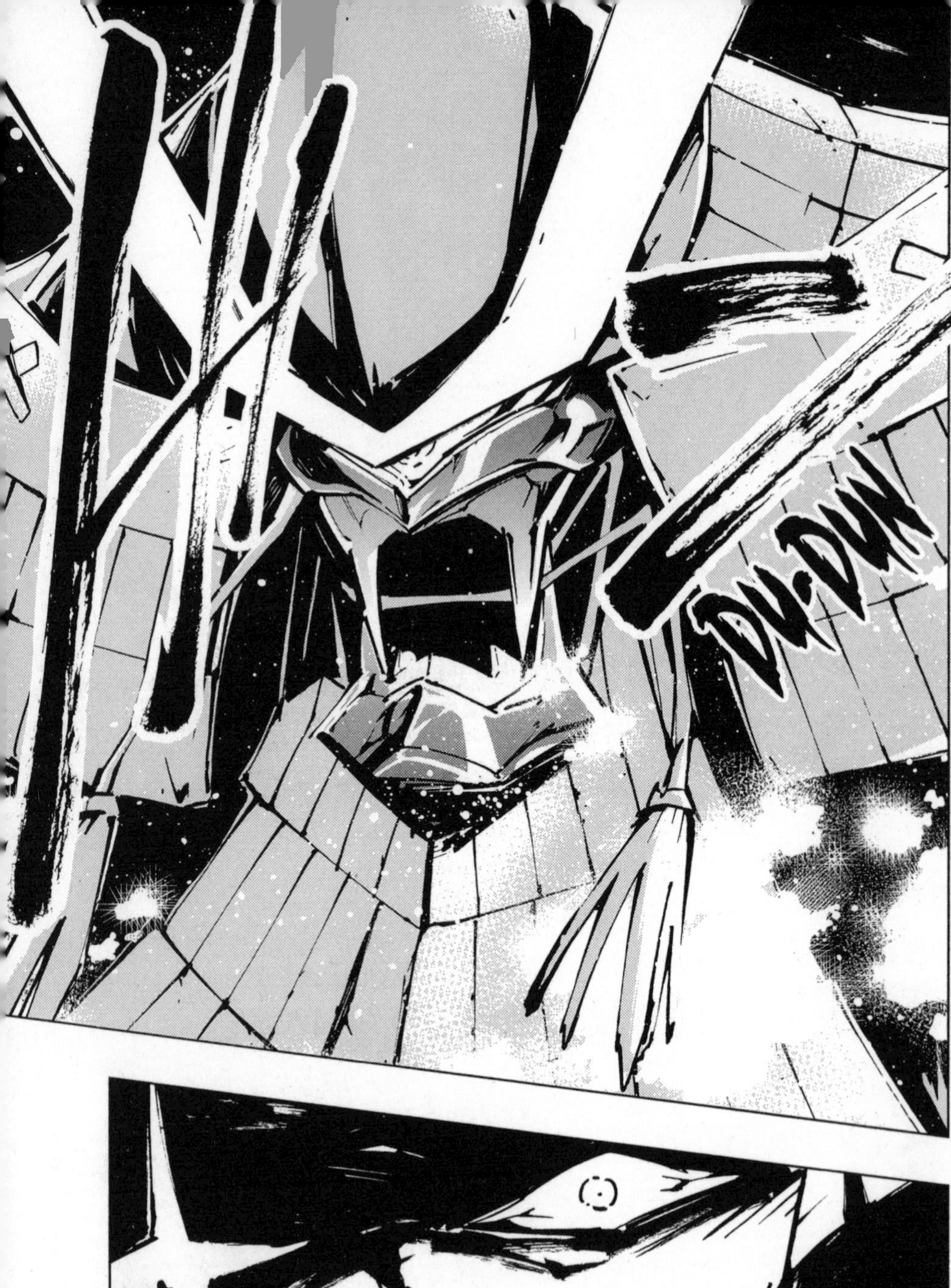
DU-DUN

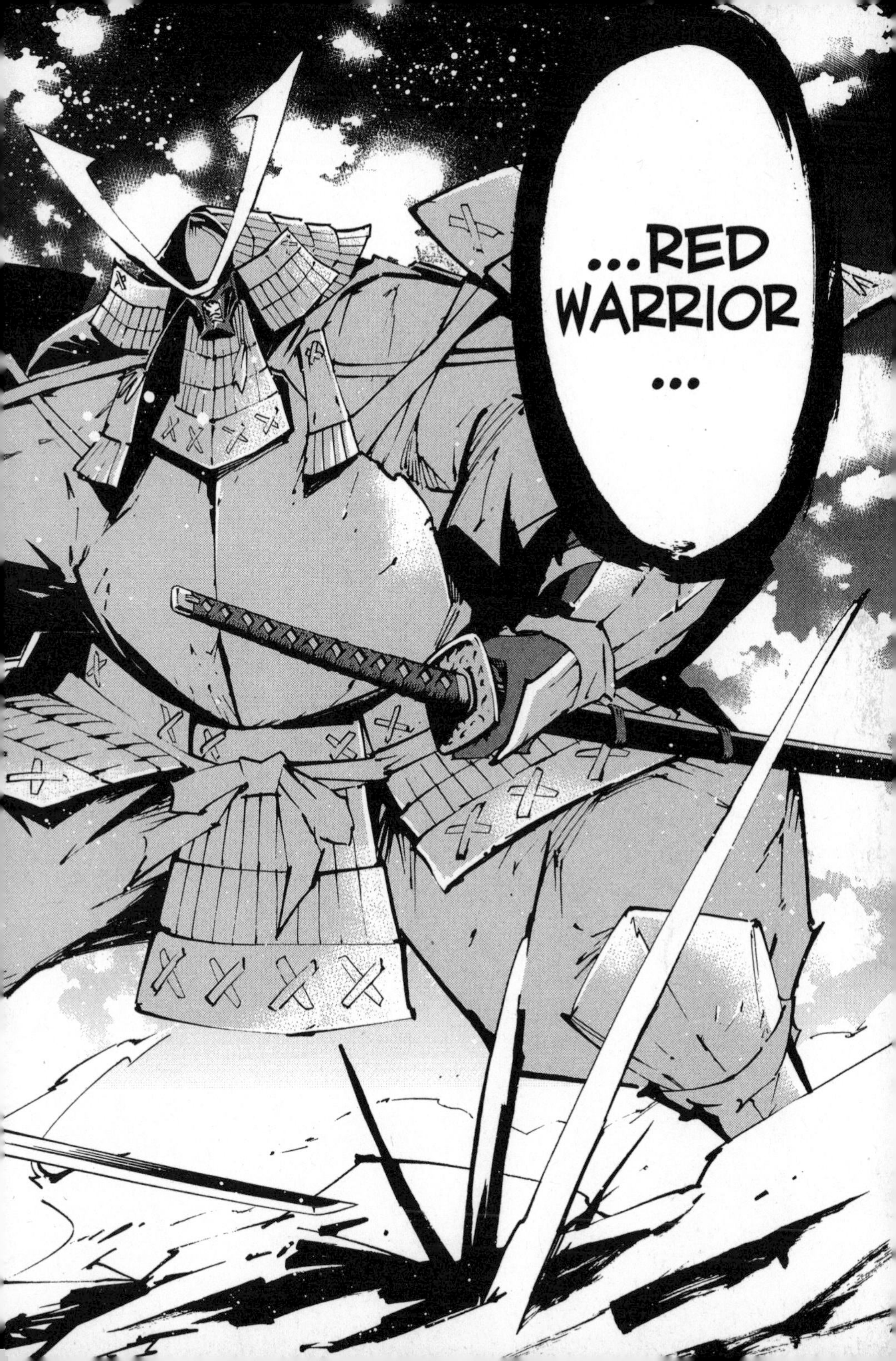
...RED WARRIOR ...

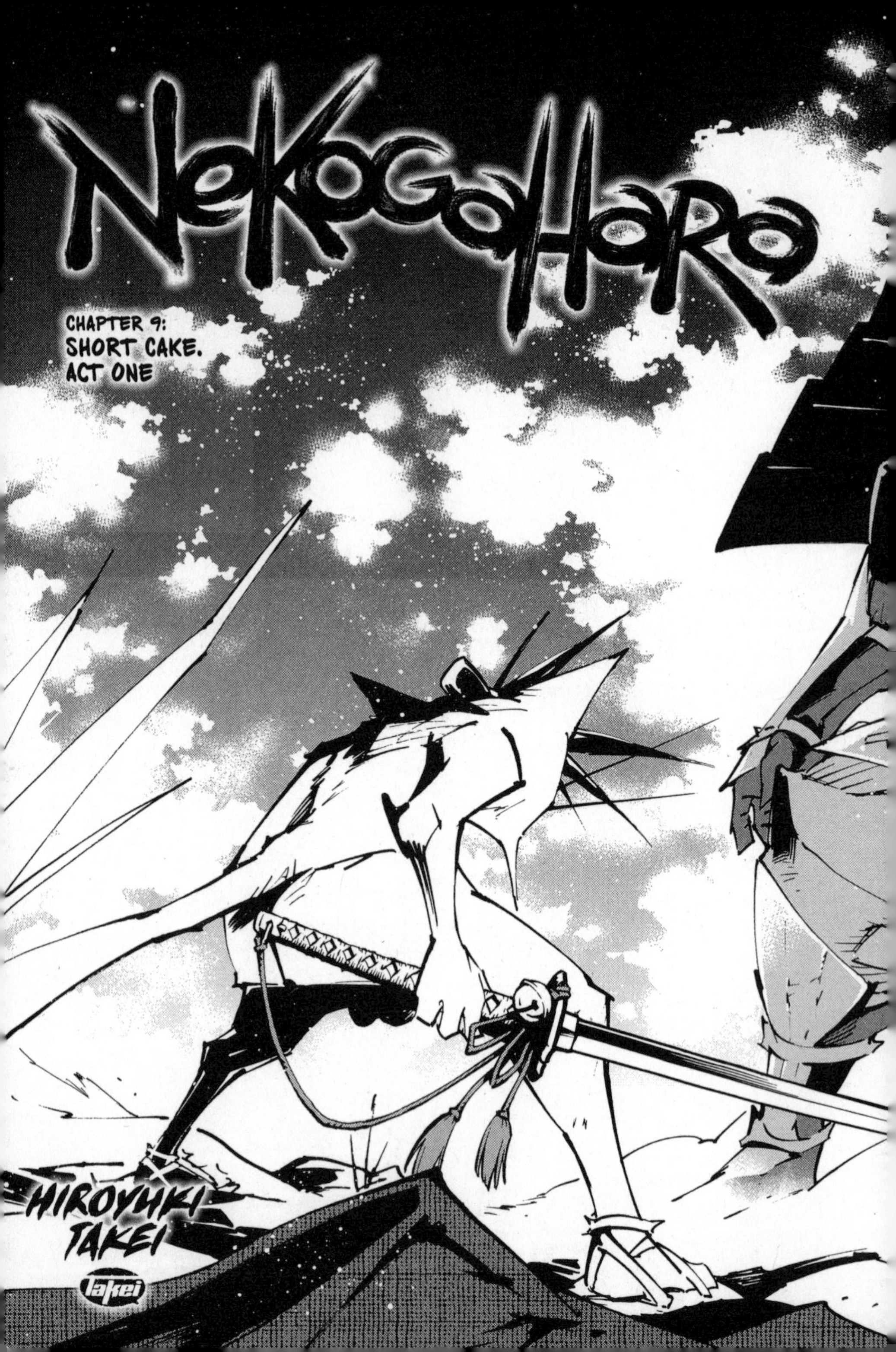
NekoGaHara
CHAPTER 9:
SHORT CAKE.
ACT ONE
HIROYUKI
TAKEI

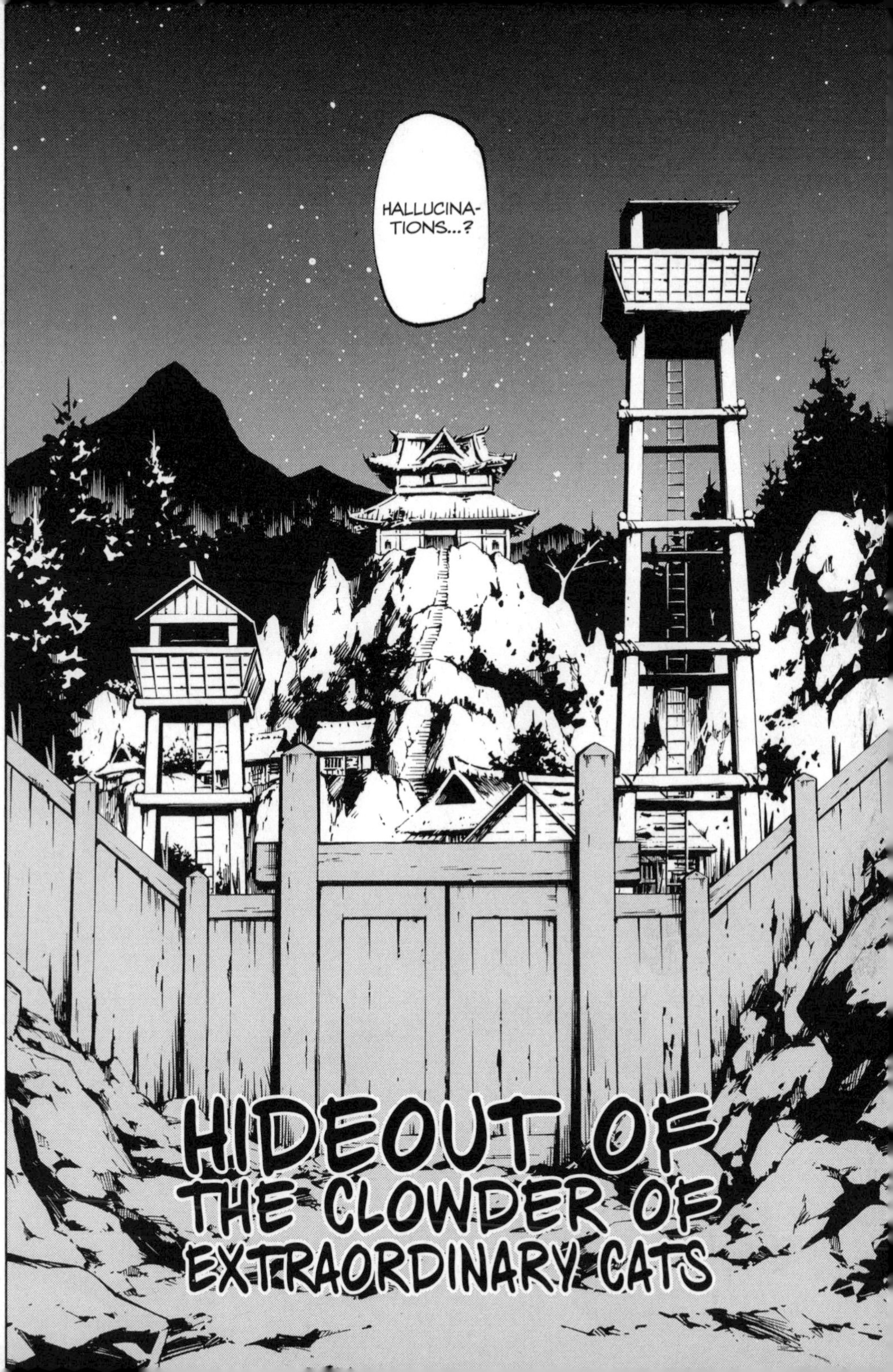
HALLUCINA-
TIONS...?
HIDEOUT OF
THE CLOWDER OF
EXTRAORDINARY CATS

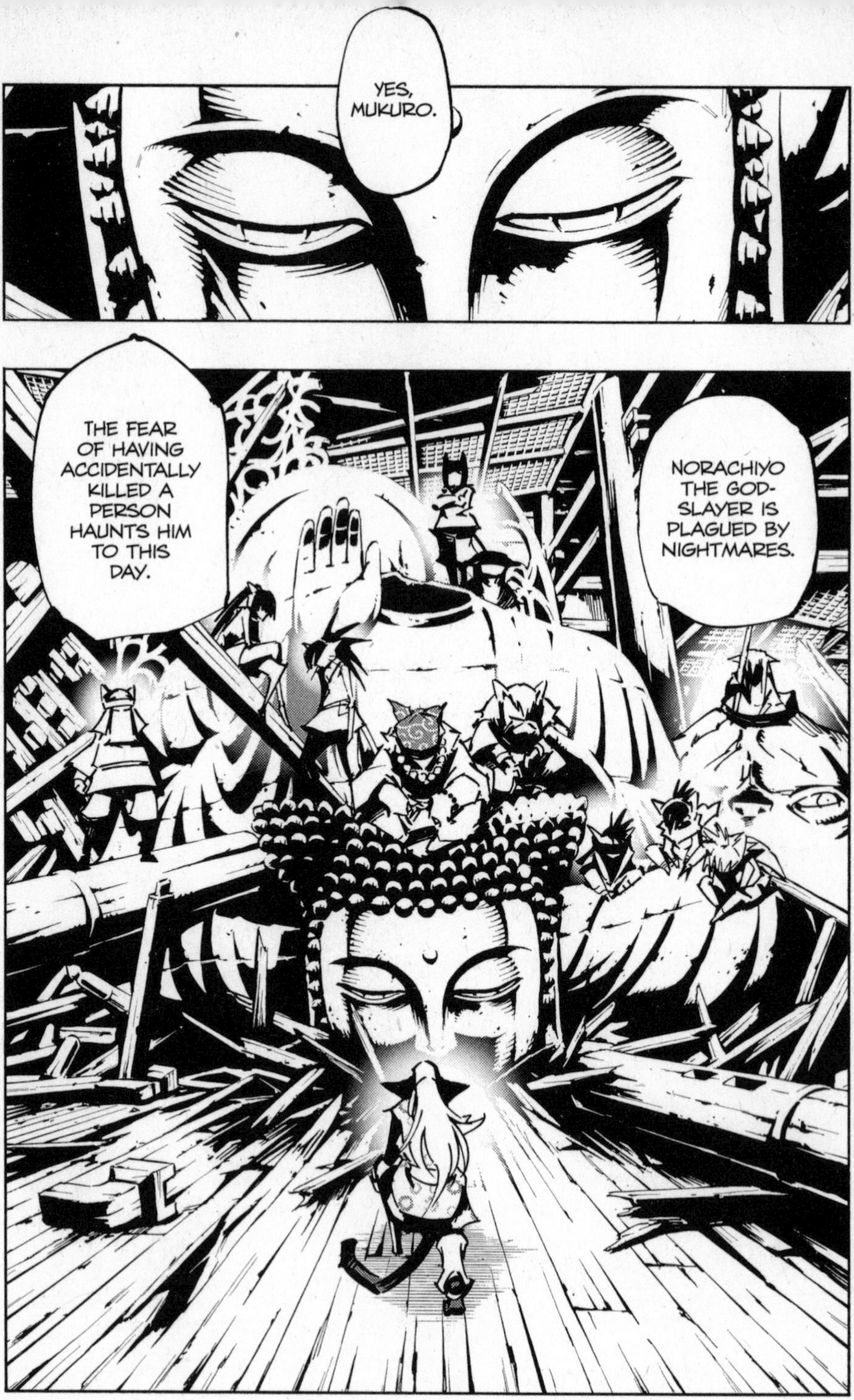
YES, MUKURO.
NORACHIYO THE GOD-SLAYER IS PLAGUED BY NIGHTMARES.
THE FEAR OF HAVING ACCIDENTALLY KILLED A PERSON HAUNTS HIM TO THIS DAY.

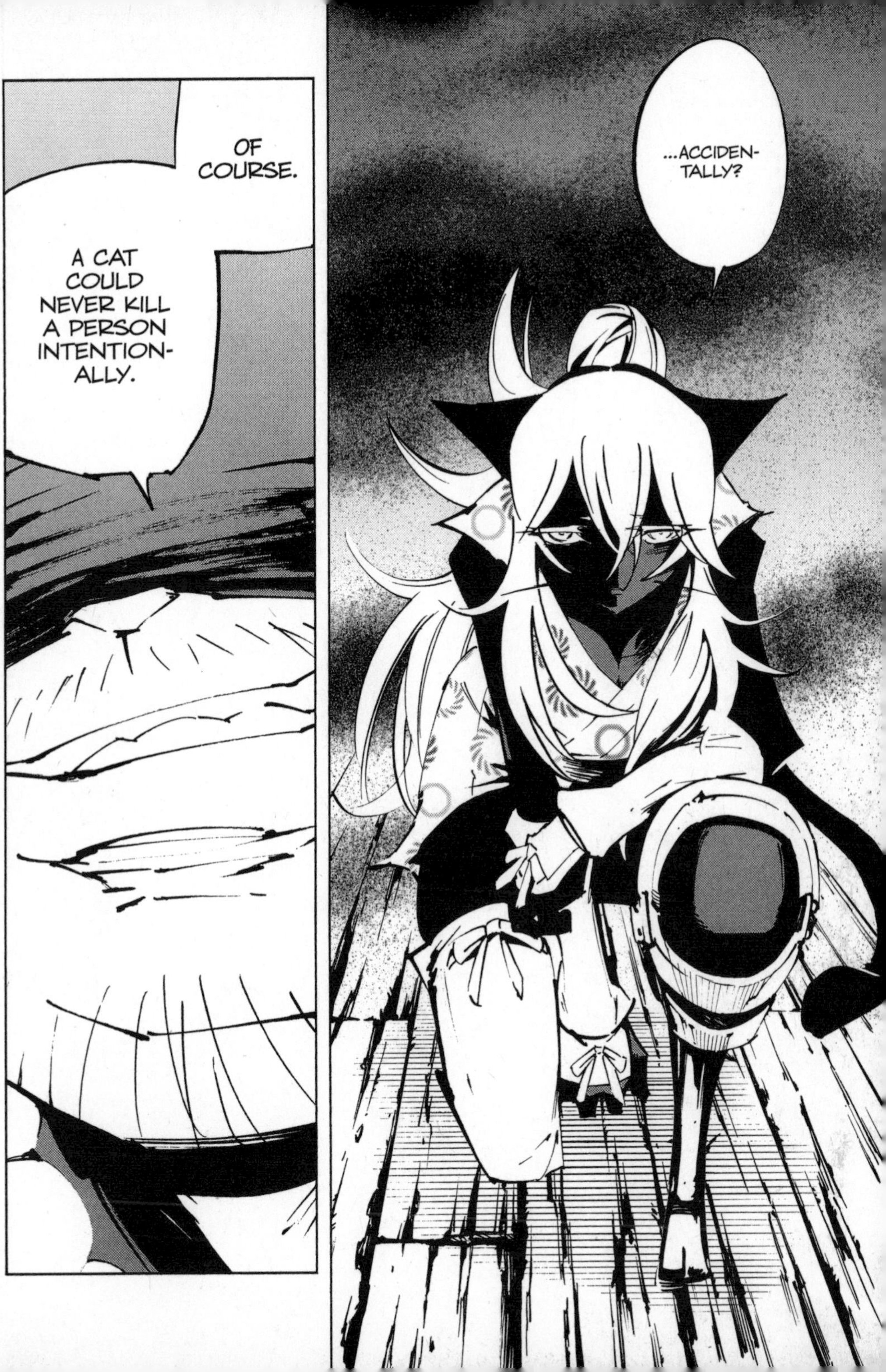
...ACCIDEN-TALLY?
OF COURSE.
A CAT COULD NEVER KILL A PERSON INTENTION-ALLY.

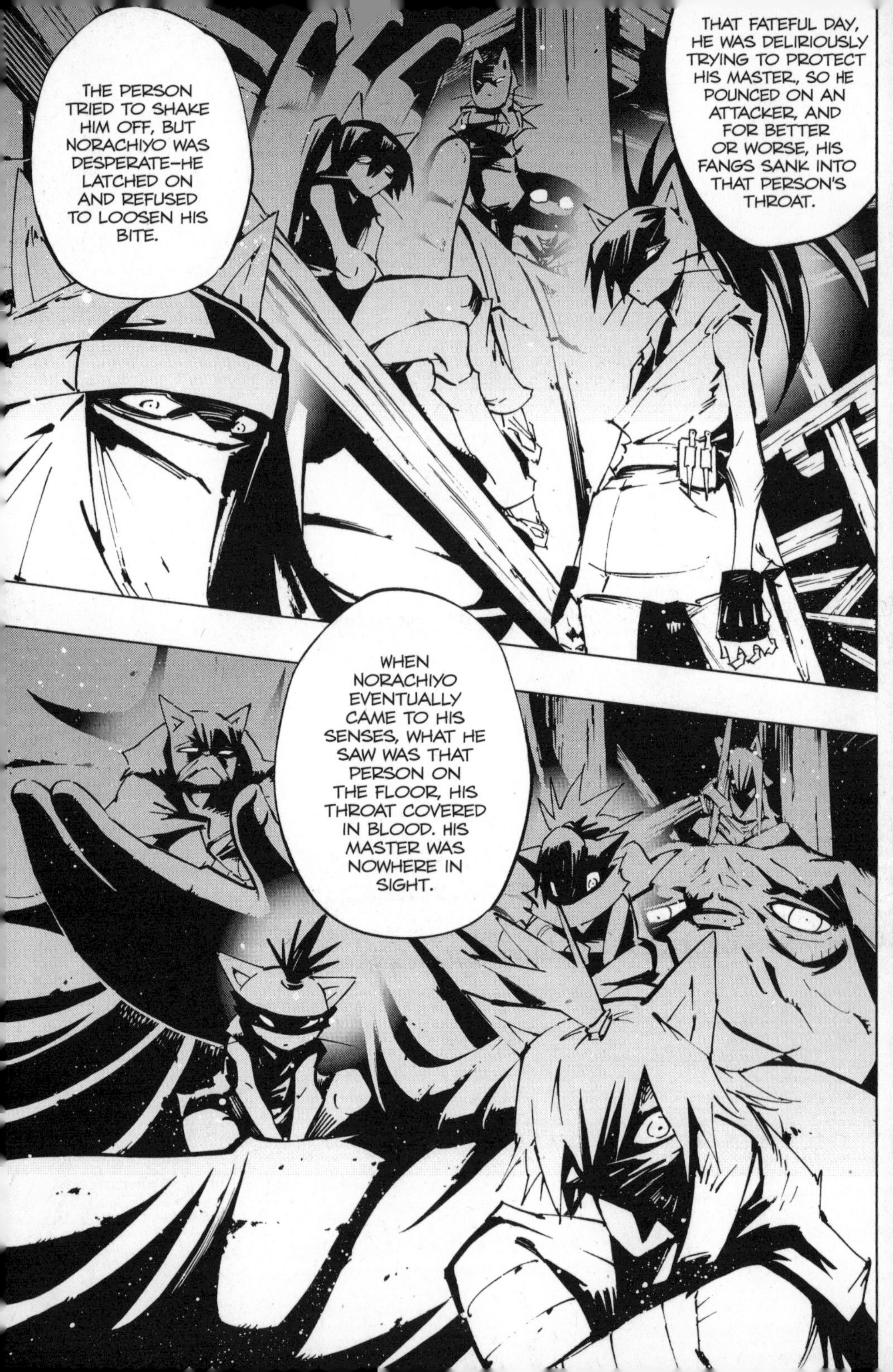
THAT FATEFUL DAY, HE WAS DELIRIOUSLY TRYING TO PROTECT HIS MASTER., SO HE POUNCED ON AN ATTACKER, AND FOR BETTER OR WORSE, HIS FANGS SANK INTO THAT PERSON'S THROAT.
THE PERSON TRIED TO SHAKE HIM OFF, BUT NORACHIYO WAS DESPERATE—HE LATCHED ON AND REFUSED TO LOOSEN HIS BITE.
WHEN NORACHIYO EVENTUALLY CAME TO HIS SENSES, WHAT HE SAW WAS THAT PERSON ON THE FLOOR, HIS THROAT COVERED IN BLOOD. HIS MASTER WAS NOWHERE IN SIGHT.

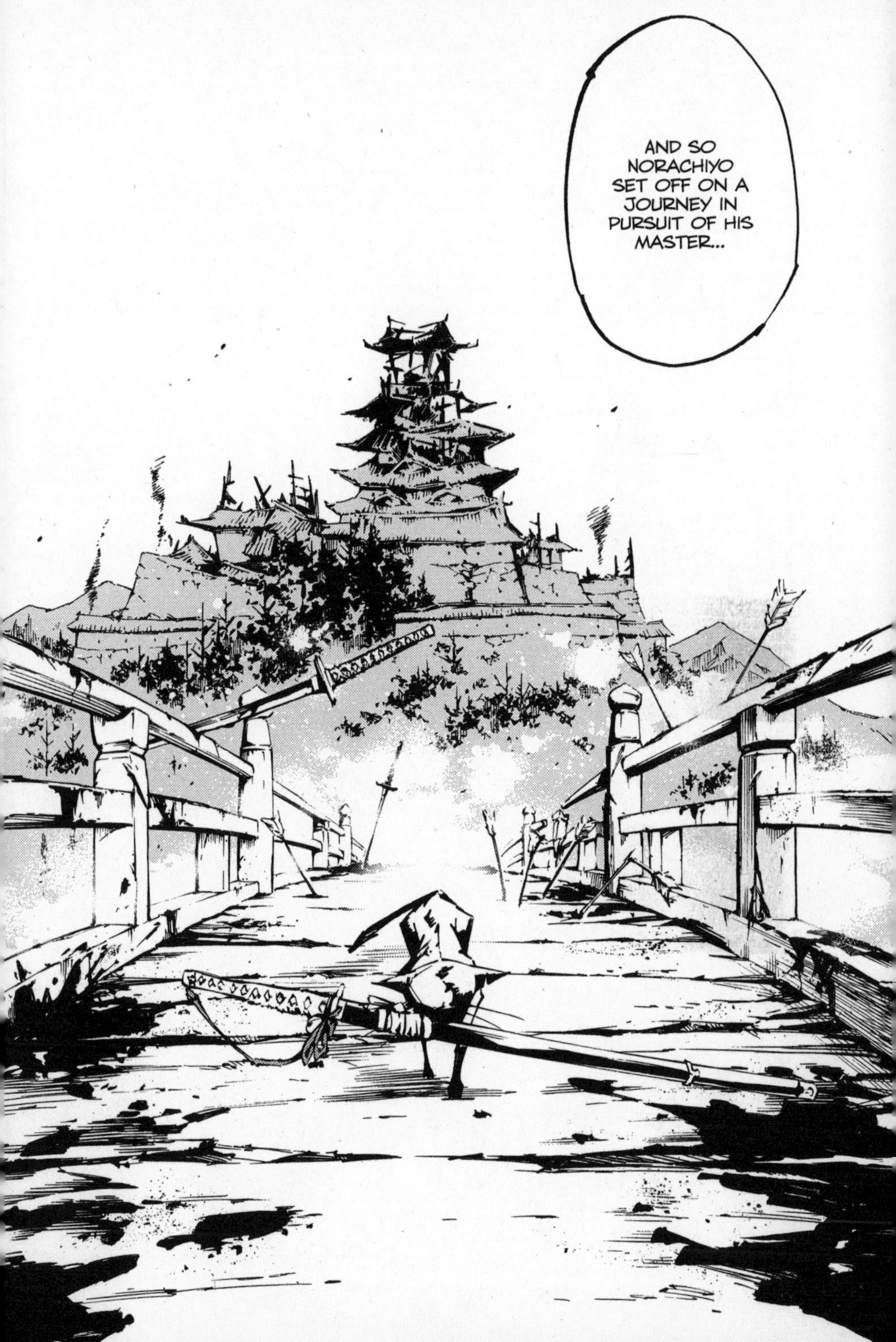
AND SO NORACHIYO SET OFF ON A JOURNEY IN PURSUIT OF HIS MASTER...

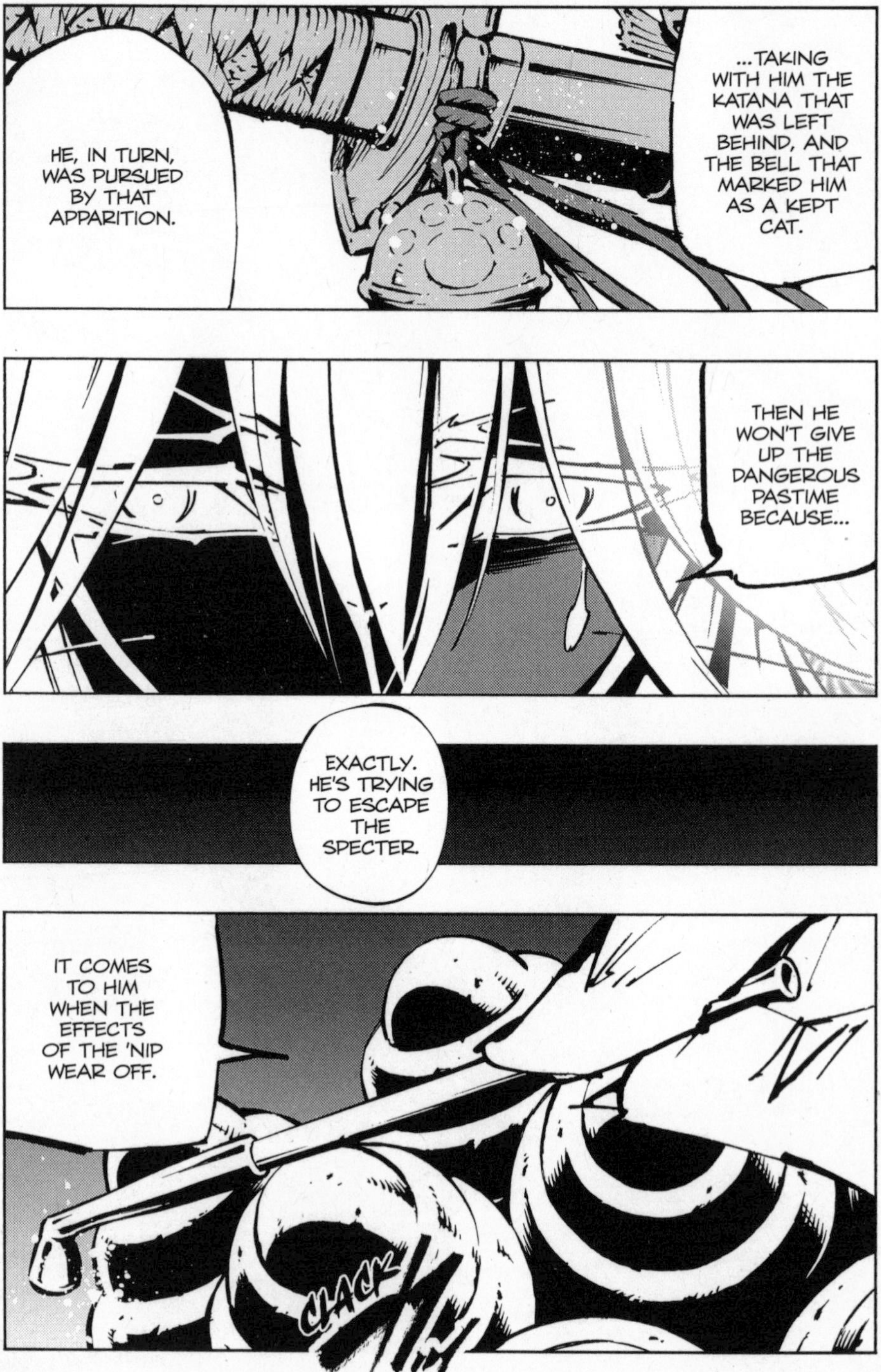
...TAKING WITH HIM THE KATANA THAT WAS LEFT BEHIND, AND THE BELL THAT MARKED HIM AS A KEPT CAT.
HE, IN TURN, WAS PURSUED BY THAT APPARITION.
THEN HE WON'T GIVE UP THE DANGEROUS PASTIME BECAUSE...
EXACTLY. HE'S TRYING TO ESCAPE THE SPECTER.
IT COMES TO HIM WHEN THE EFFECTS OF THE 'NIP WEAR OFF.
CLACK

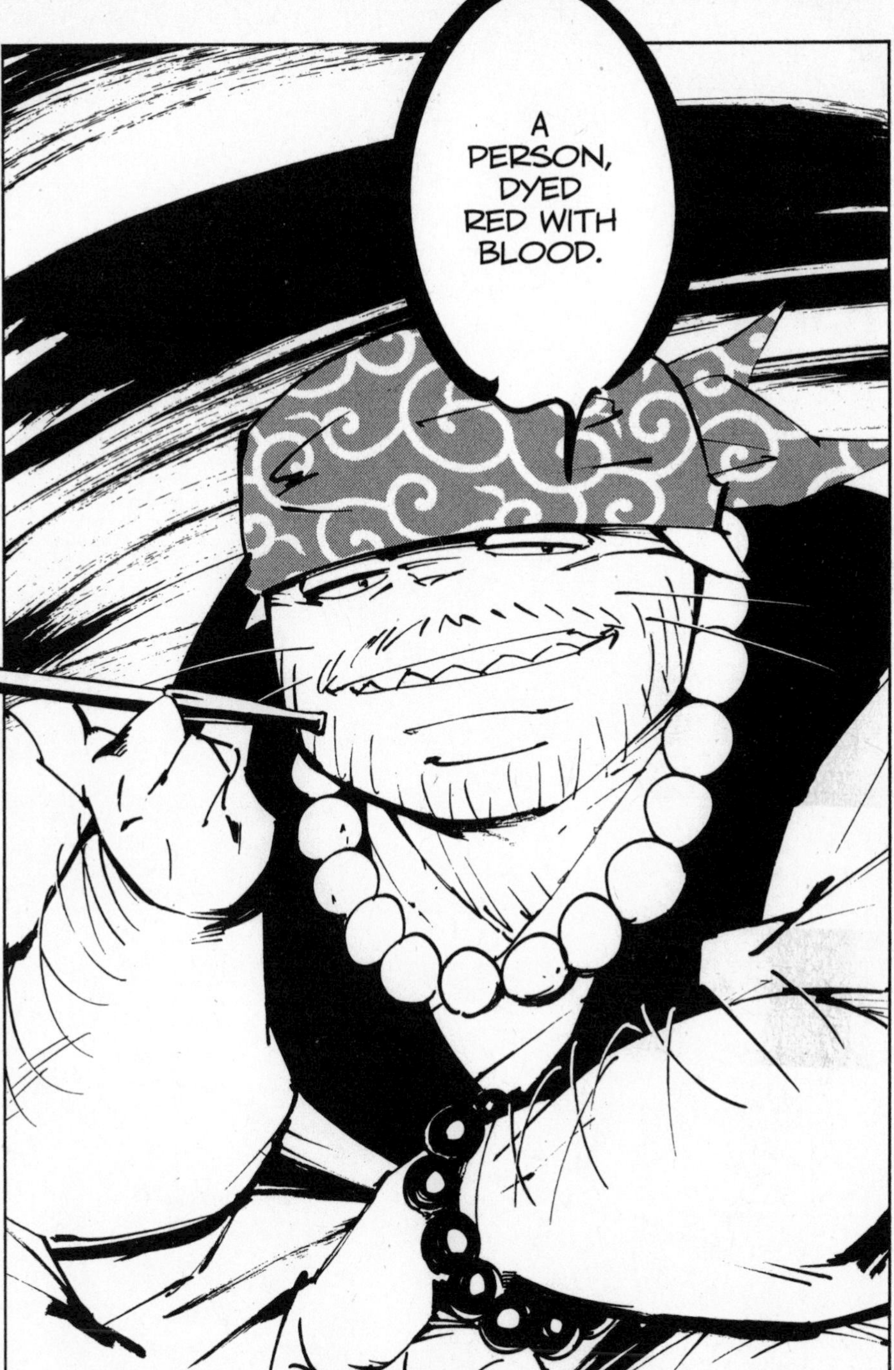
A PERSON, DYED RED WITH BLOOD.

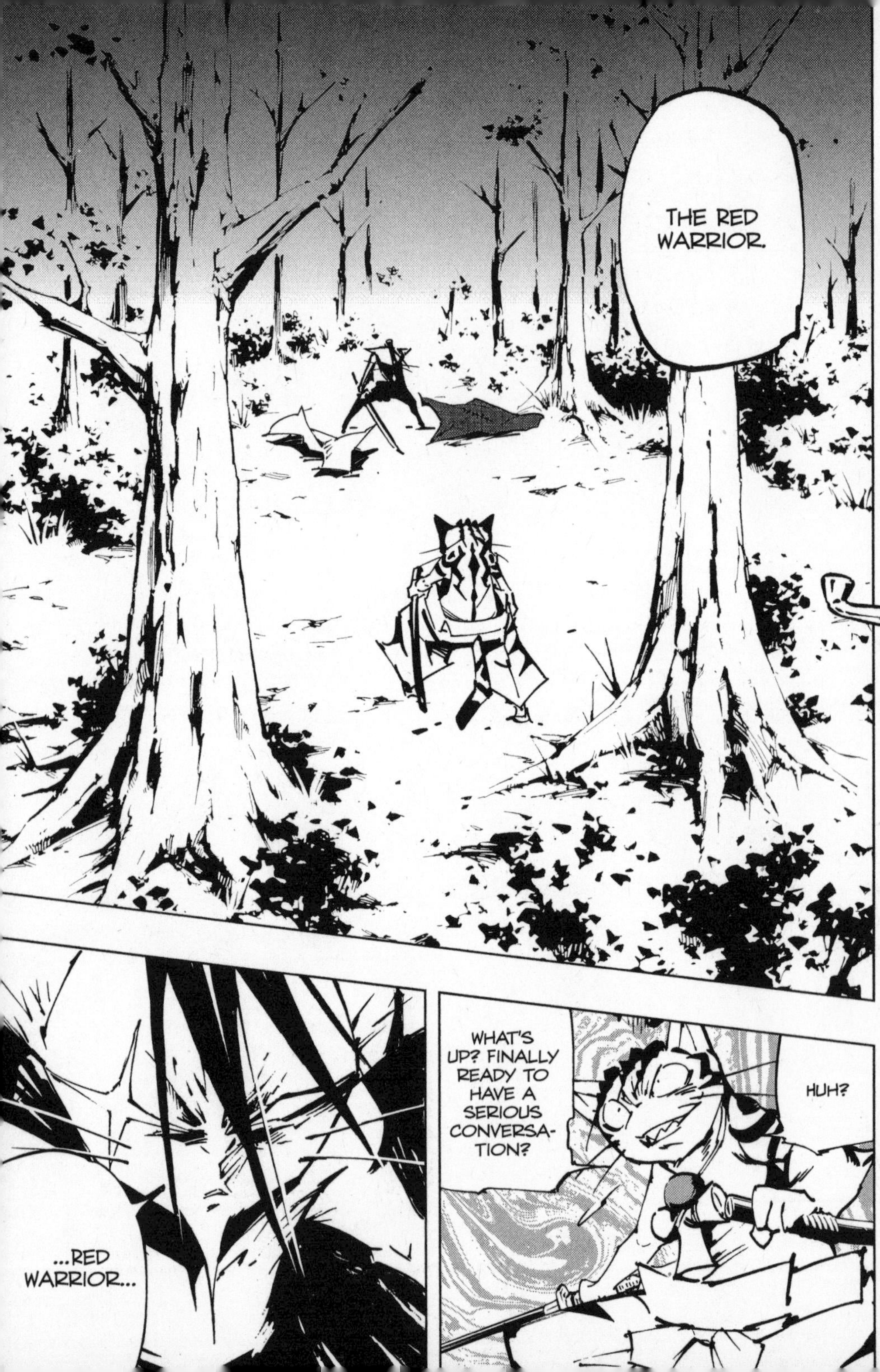
THE RED WARRIOR.
HUH?
WHAT'S UP? FINALLY READY TO HAVE A SERIOUS CONVERSATION?
...RED WARRIOR...

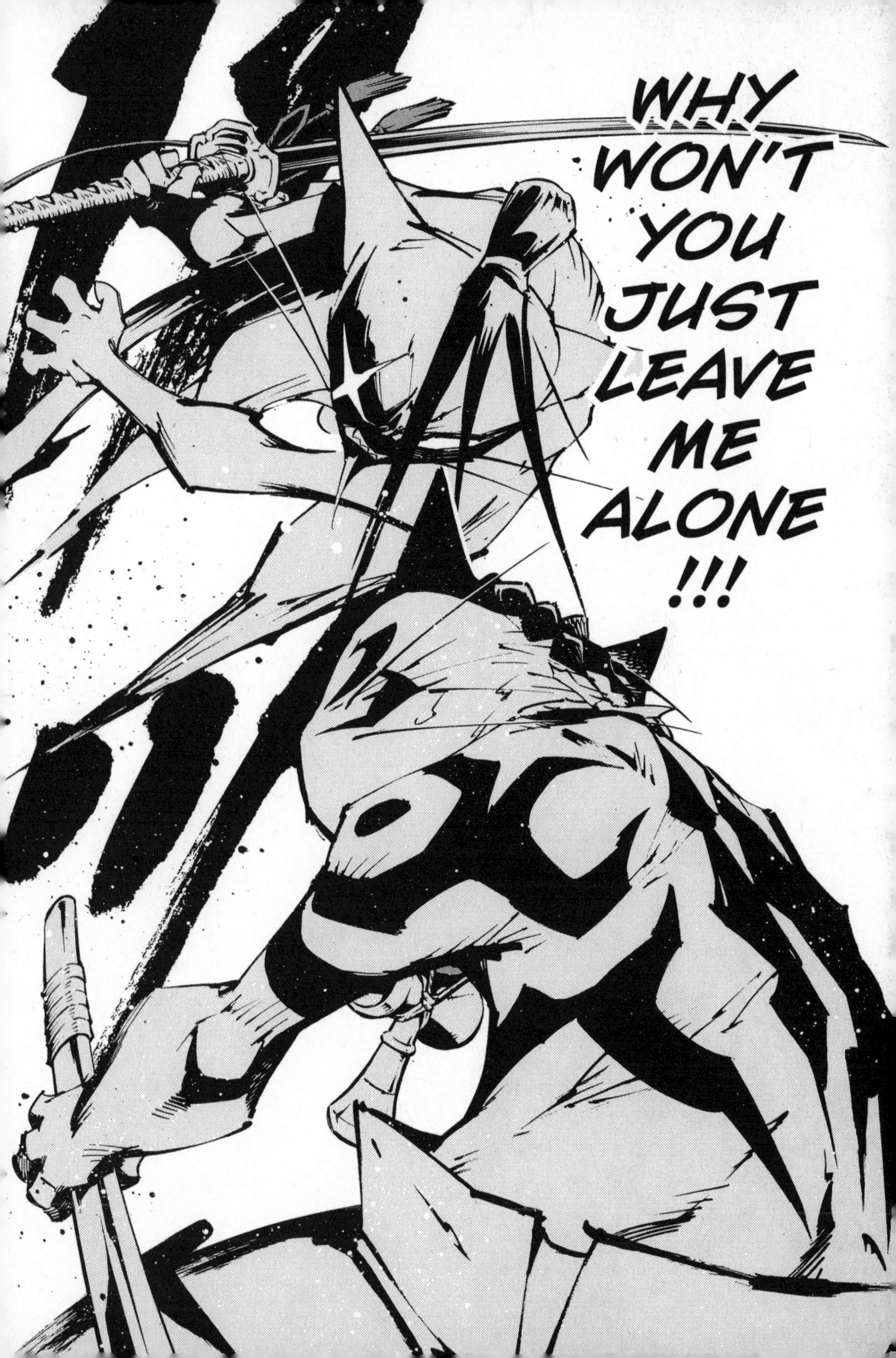
WHY WON'T YOU JUST LEAVE ME ALONE !!!

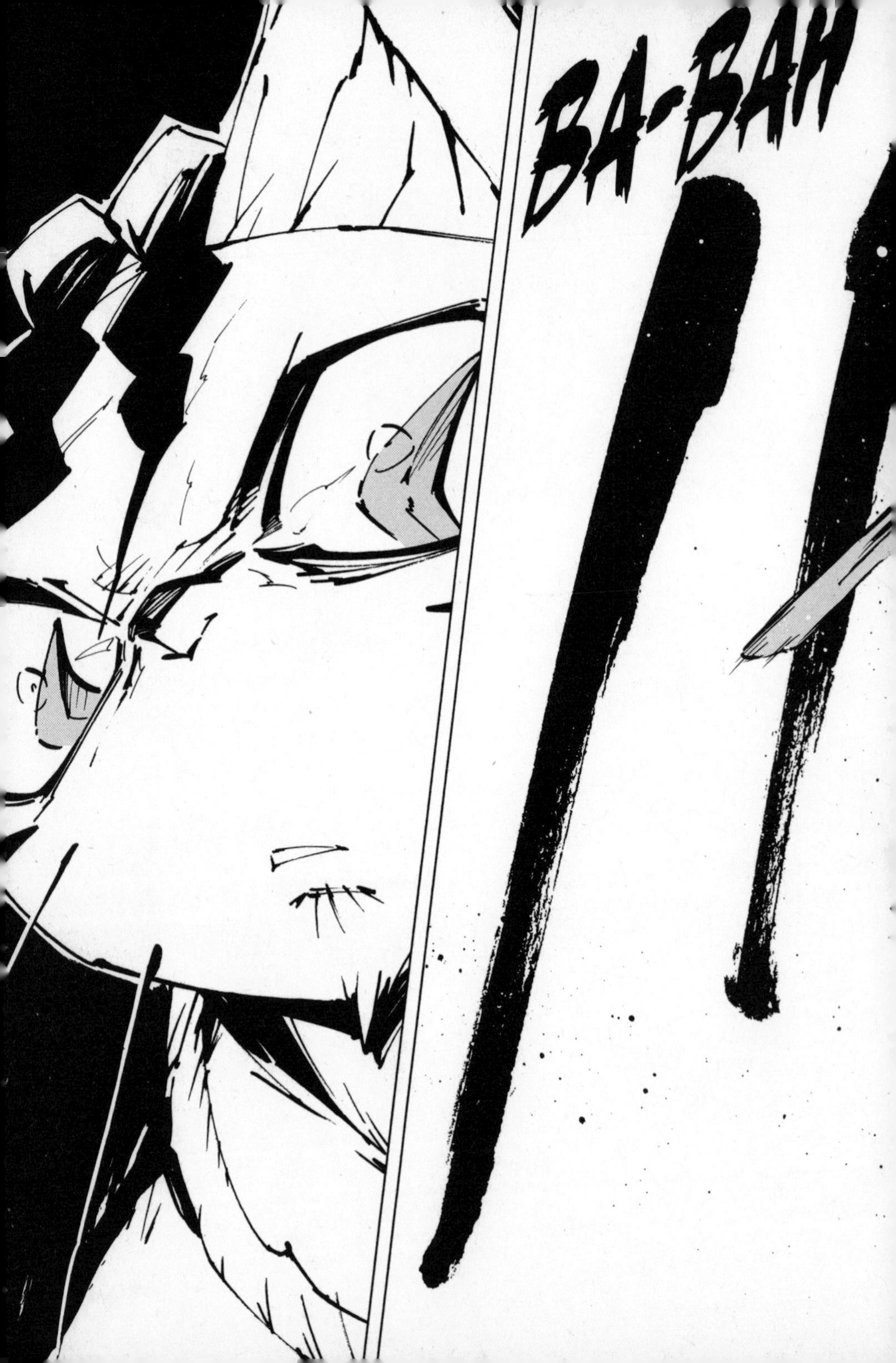
BA-BAH

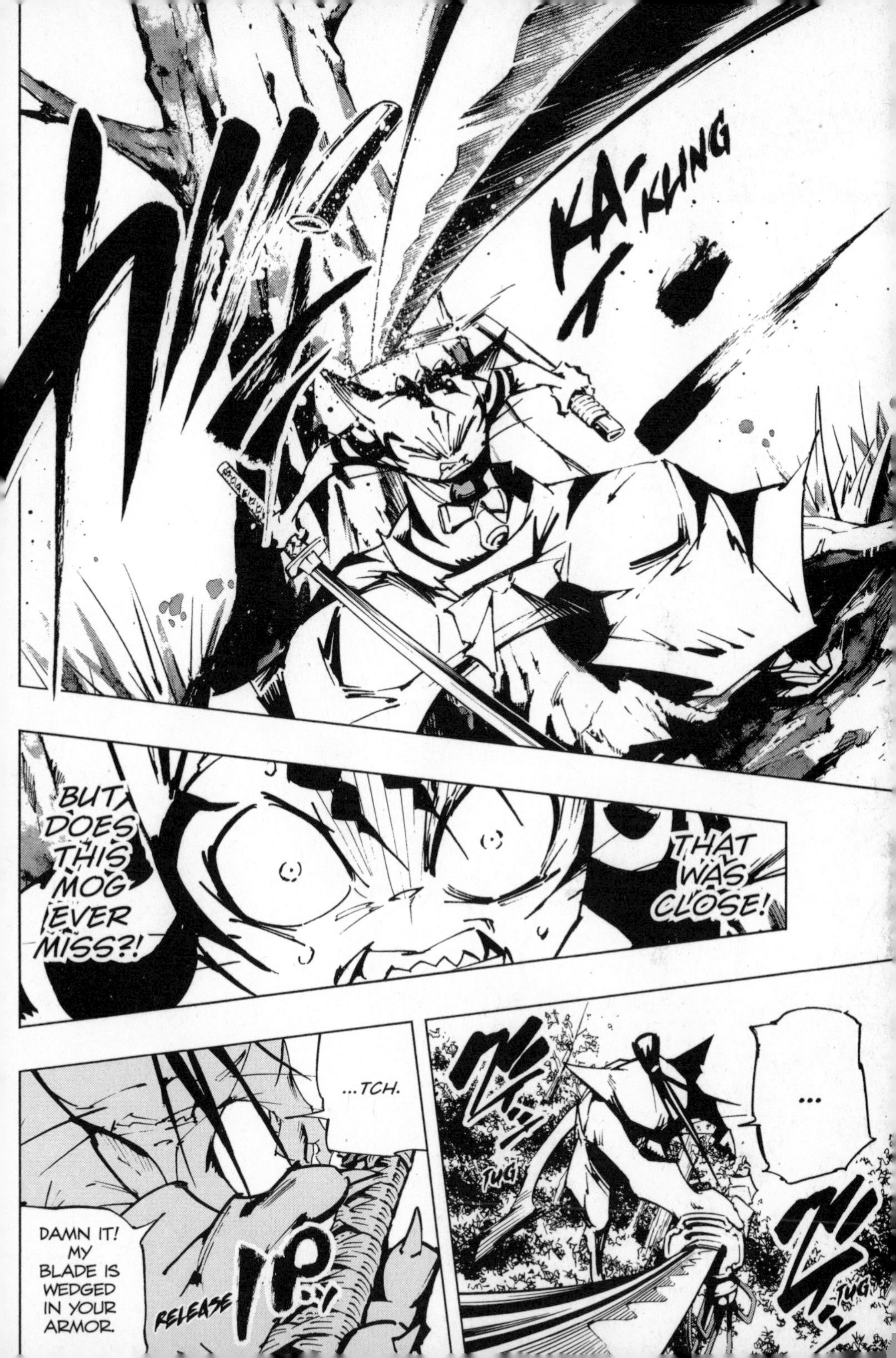
KA-KLING
THAT WAS CLOSE!
BUT DOES THIS MOG EVER MISS?!
...
TUG
TUG
...TCH.
DAMN IT! MY BLADE IS WEDGED IN YOUR ARMOR.
RELEASE

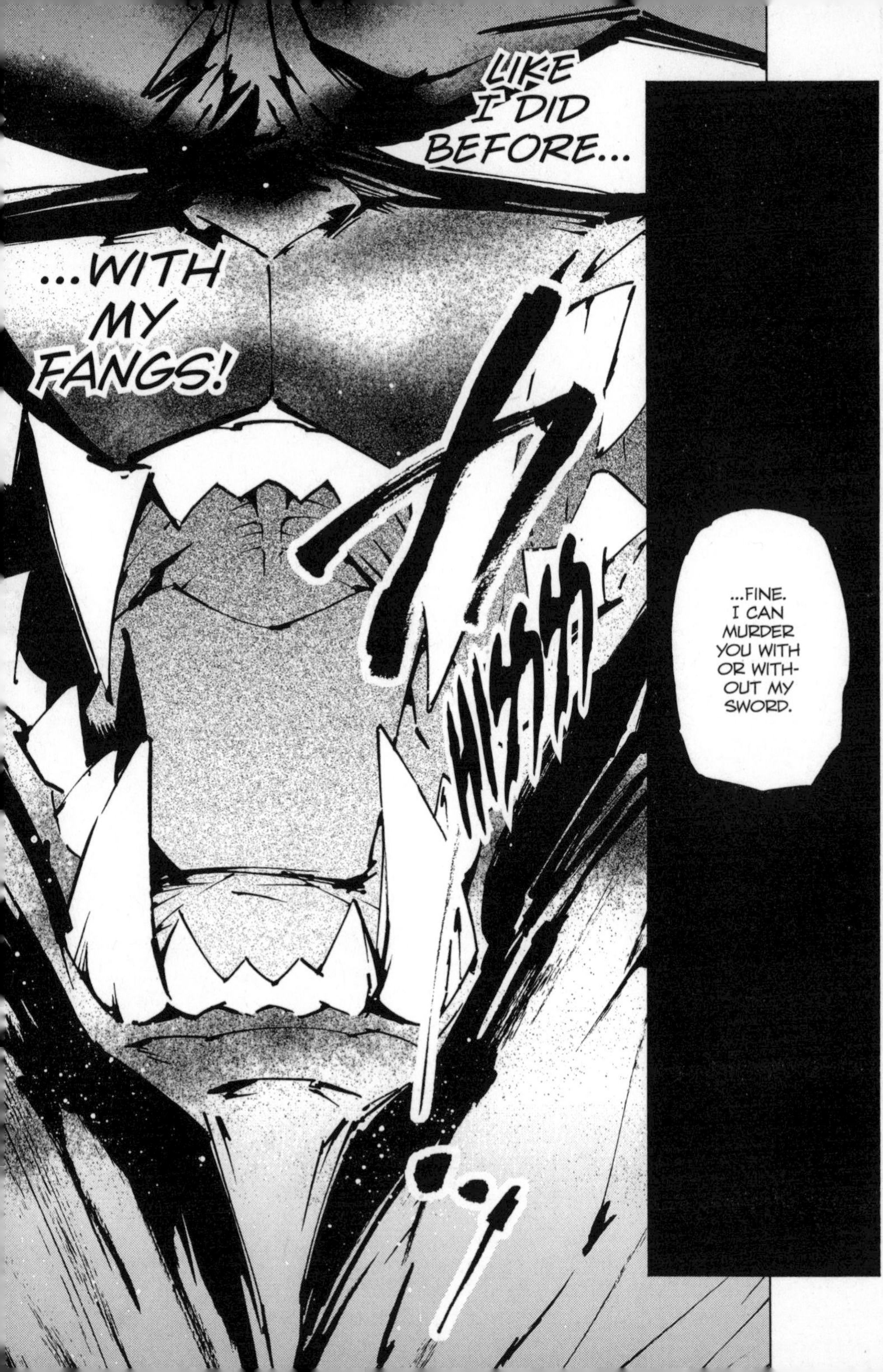
...FINE. I CAN MURDER YOU WITH OR WITH-OUT MY SWORD.
LIKE I DID BEFORE...
...WITH MY FANGS!
HISSS

猫ヶ原

ネコガハラ

NEKOGAHARA

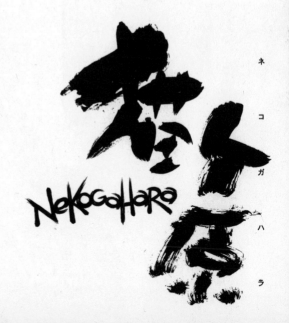

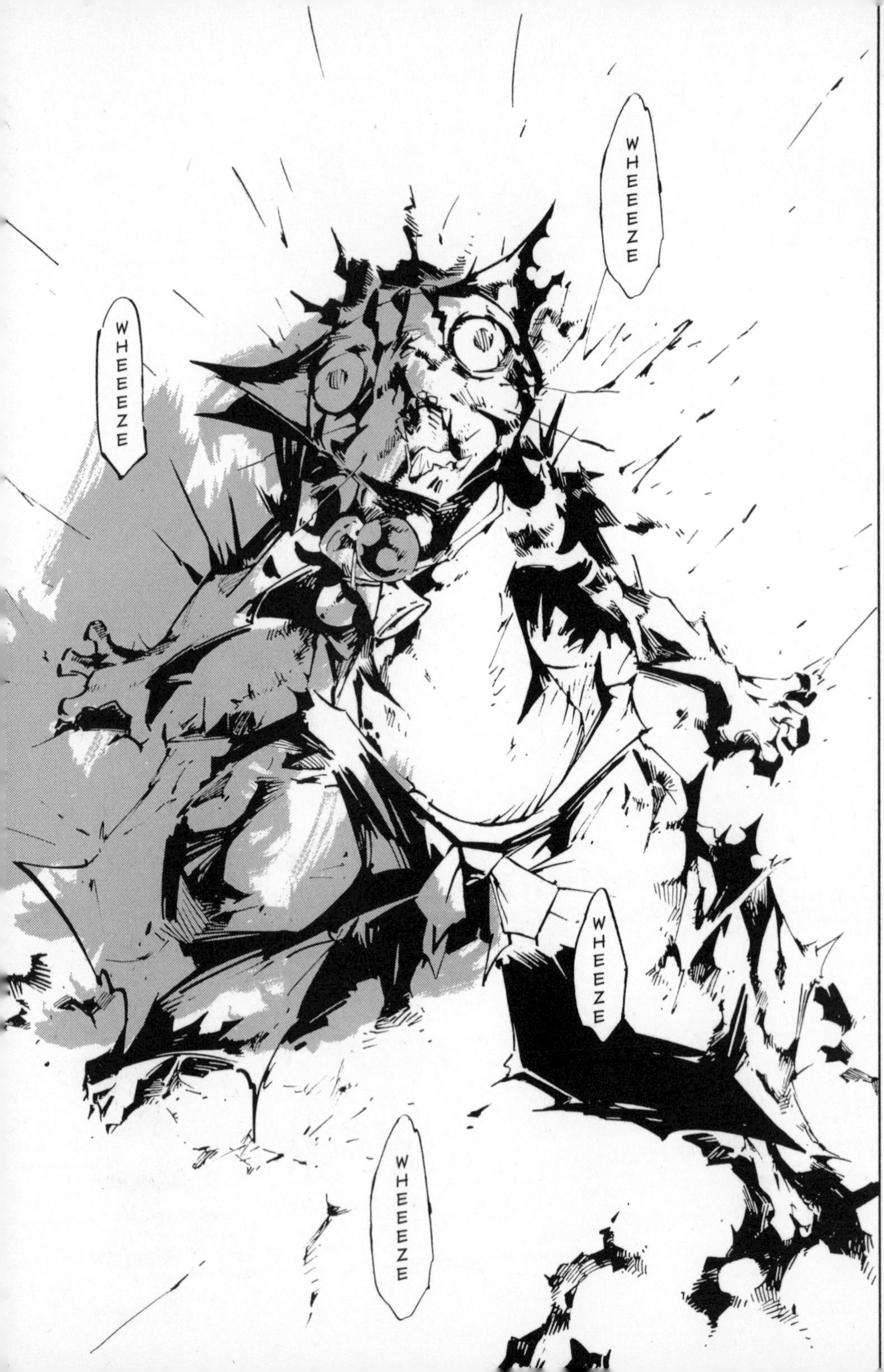
WHEEEZE
WHEEEZE
WHEEZE
WHEEEZE

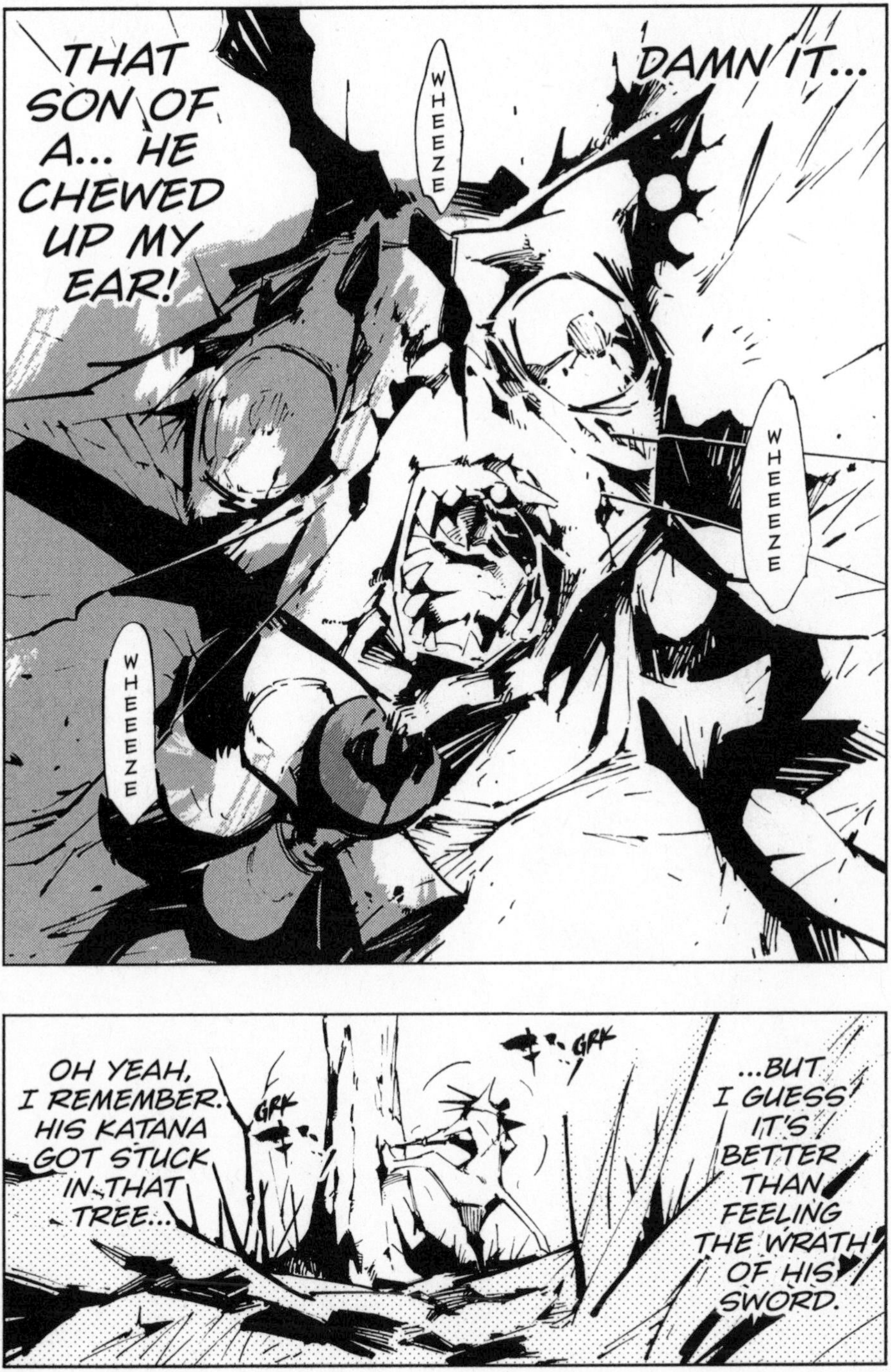
DAMN IT...
WHEEZE
THAT SON OF A... HE CHEWED UP MY EAR!
WHEEEZE
WHEEEZE
...BUT I GUESS IT'S BETTER THAN FEELING THE WRATH OF HIS SWORD.
GRK
GRK
OH YEAH, I REMEMBER. HIS KATANA GOT STUCK IN THAT TREE...

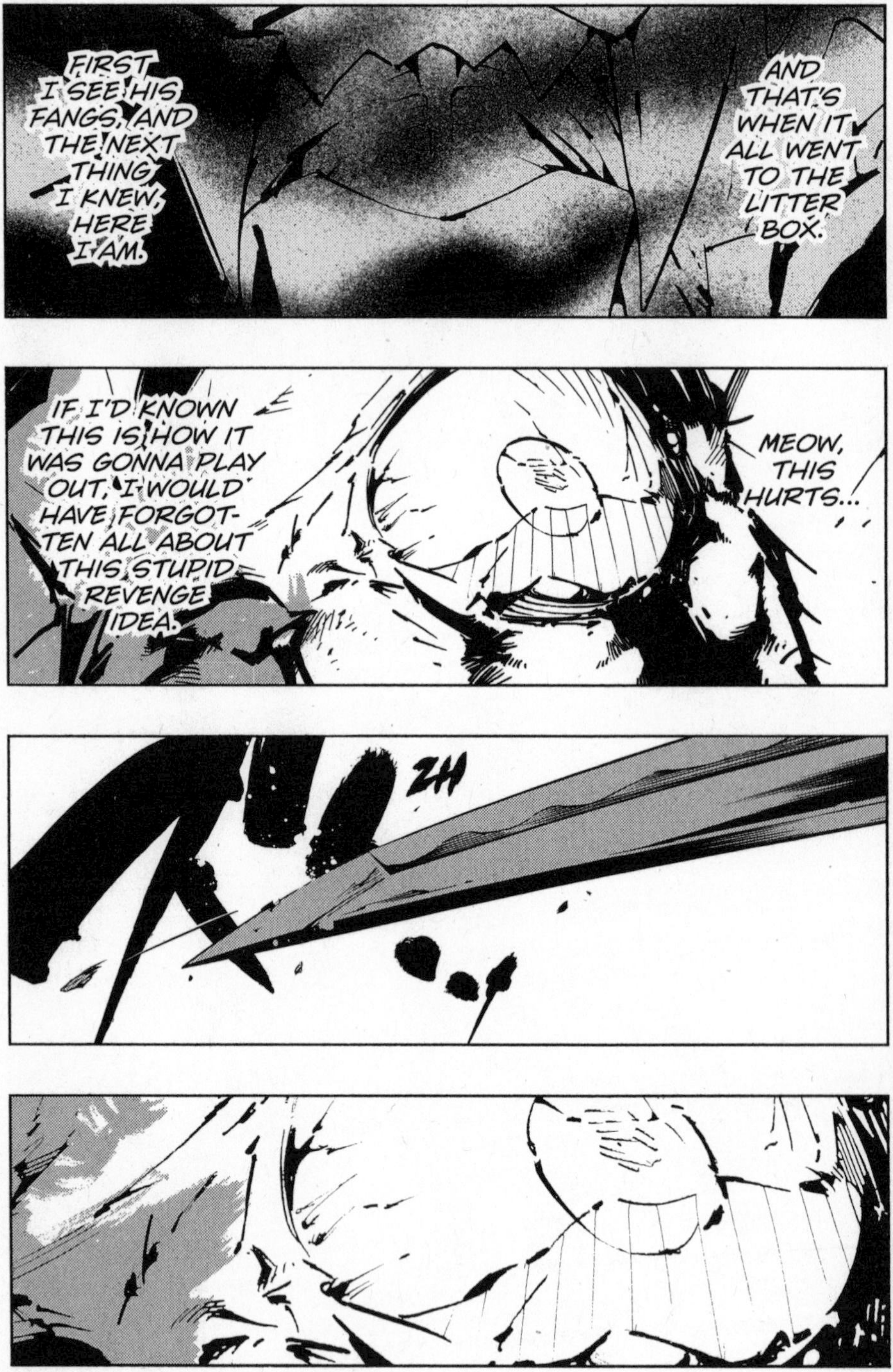
AND THAT'S WHEN IT ALL WENT TO THE LITTER BOX.
FIRST I SEE HIS FANGS, AND THE NEXT THING I KNEW, HERE I AM.
MEOW, THIS HURTS...
IF I'D KNOWN THIS IS HOW IT WAS GONNA PLAY OUT, I WOULD HAVE FORGOTTEN ALL ABOUT THIS STUPID REVENGE IDEA.
ZH

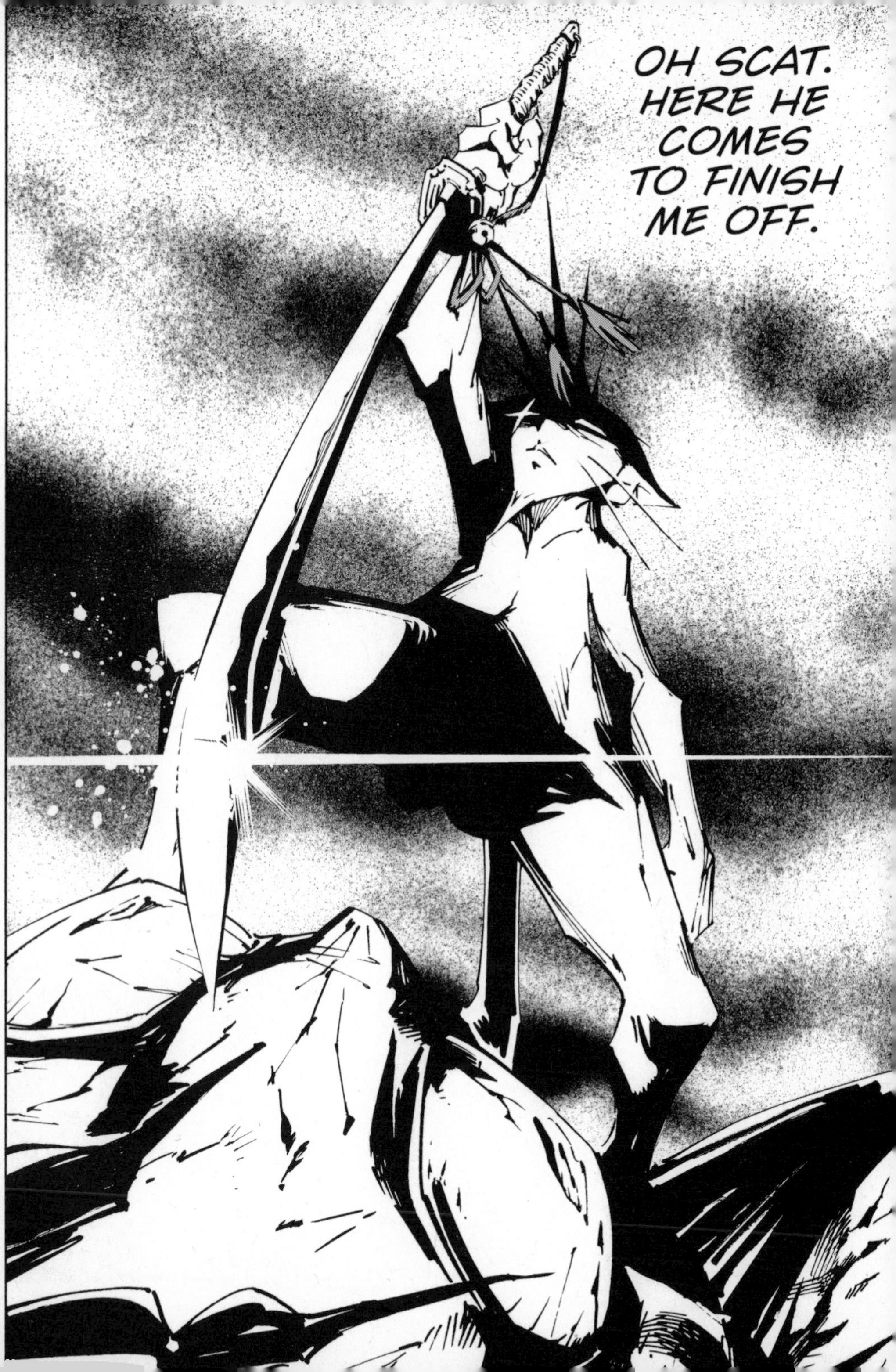
OH SCAT. HERE HE COMES TO FINISH ME OFF.

BUT COME ON... HOW CAN THIS OLD TOM BE SO TOUGH?

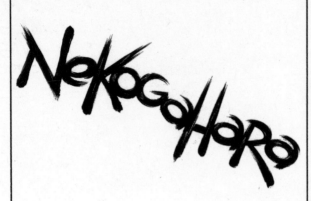

NekoGaHara

HIROYUKI TAKEI

Takei

CHAPTER 10: SHORT CAKE. ACT TWO

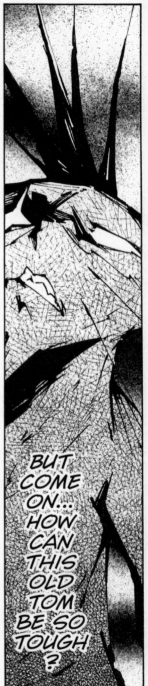

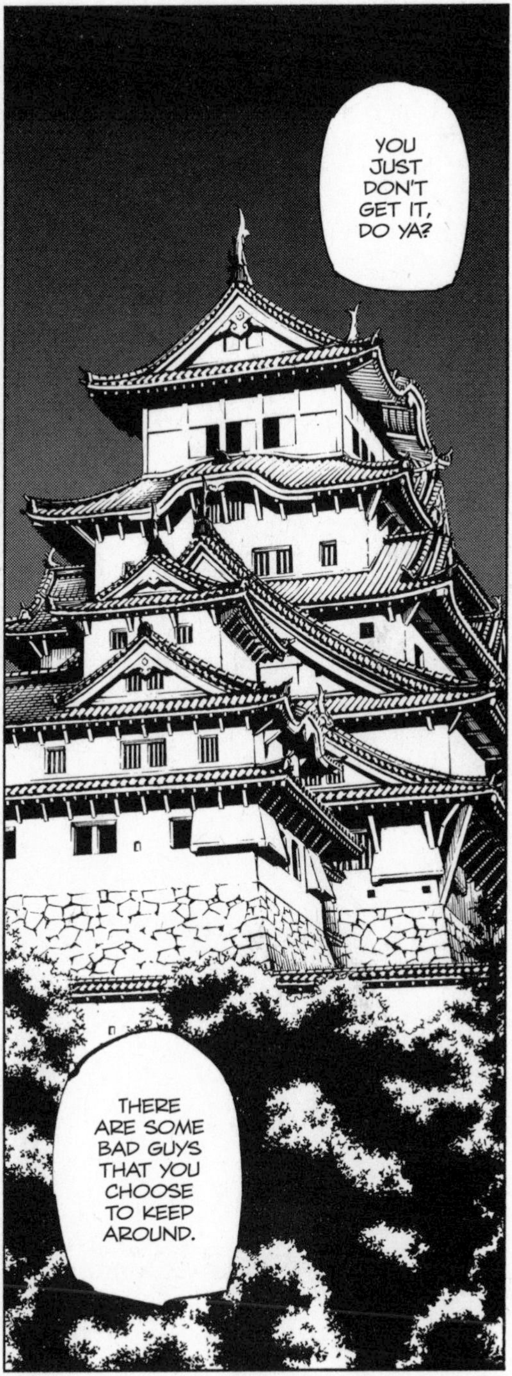
YOU JUST DON'T GET IT, DO YA?
THERE ARE SOME BAD GUYS THAT YOU CHOOSE TO KEEP AROUND.

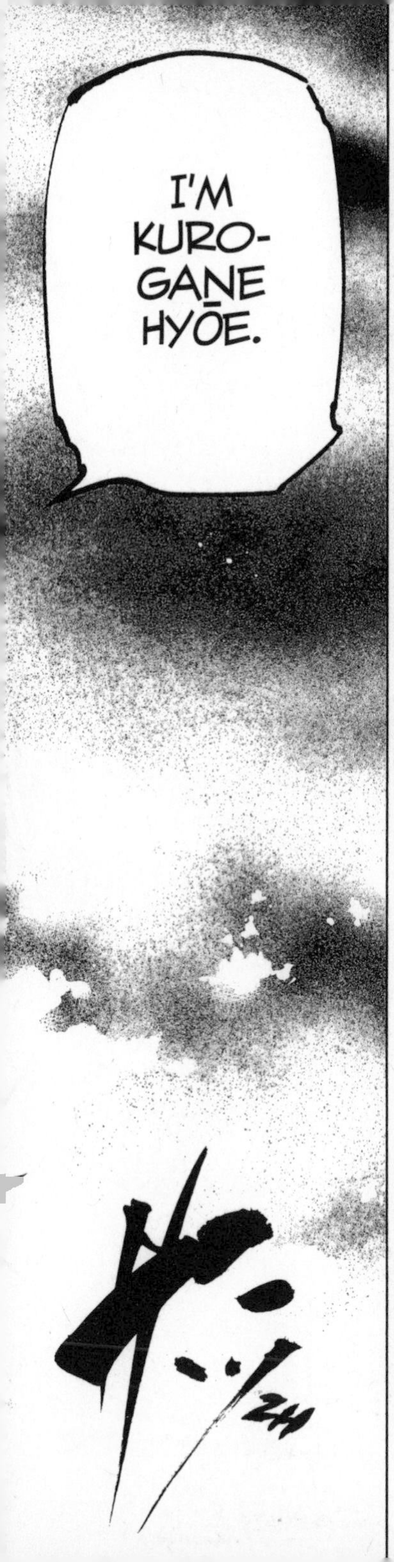
I'M KURO-GANE HYŌE.
ZH

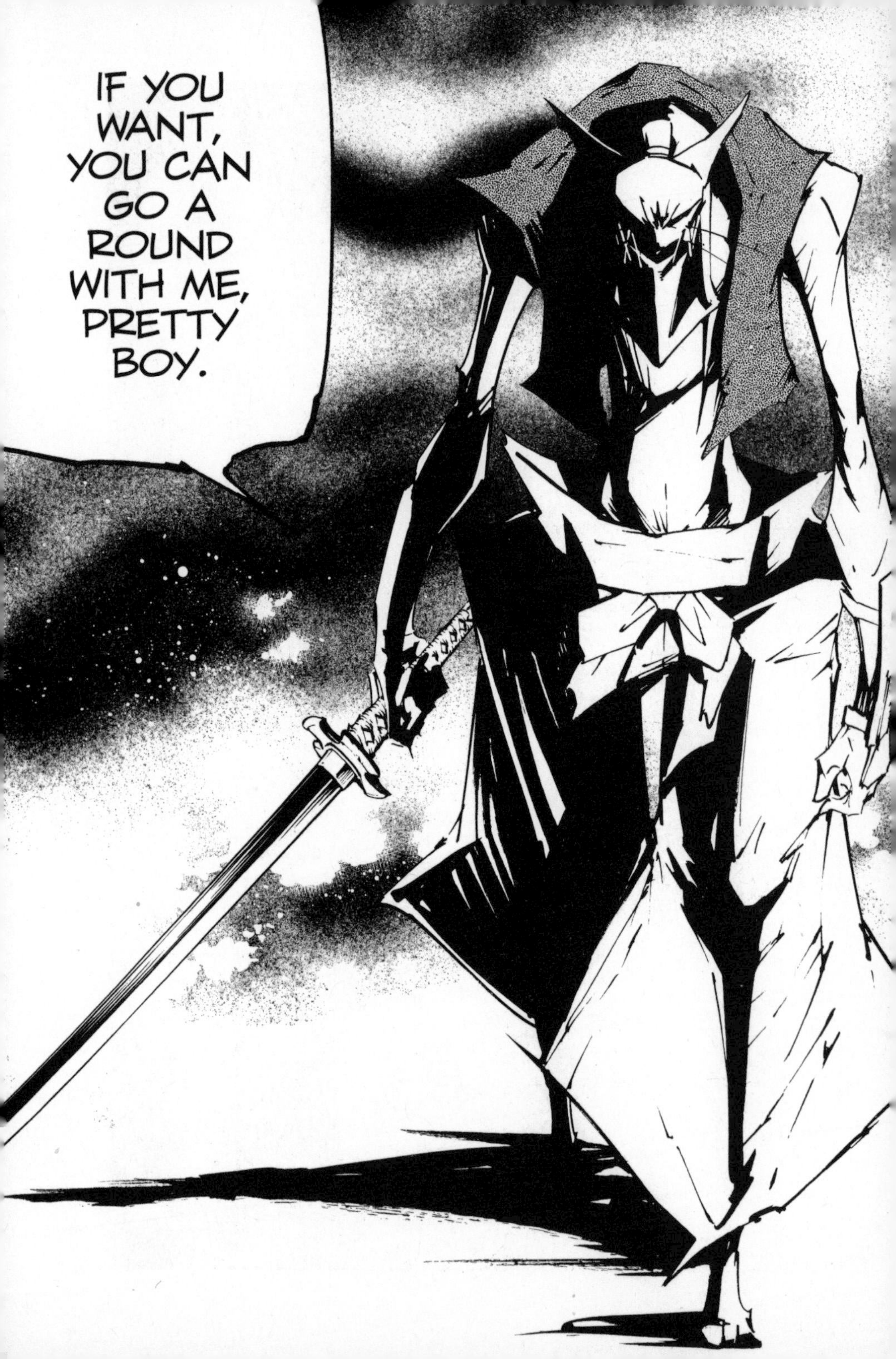
IF YOU WANT, YOU CAN GO A ROUND WITH ME, PRETTY BOY.

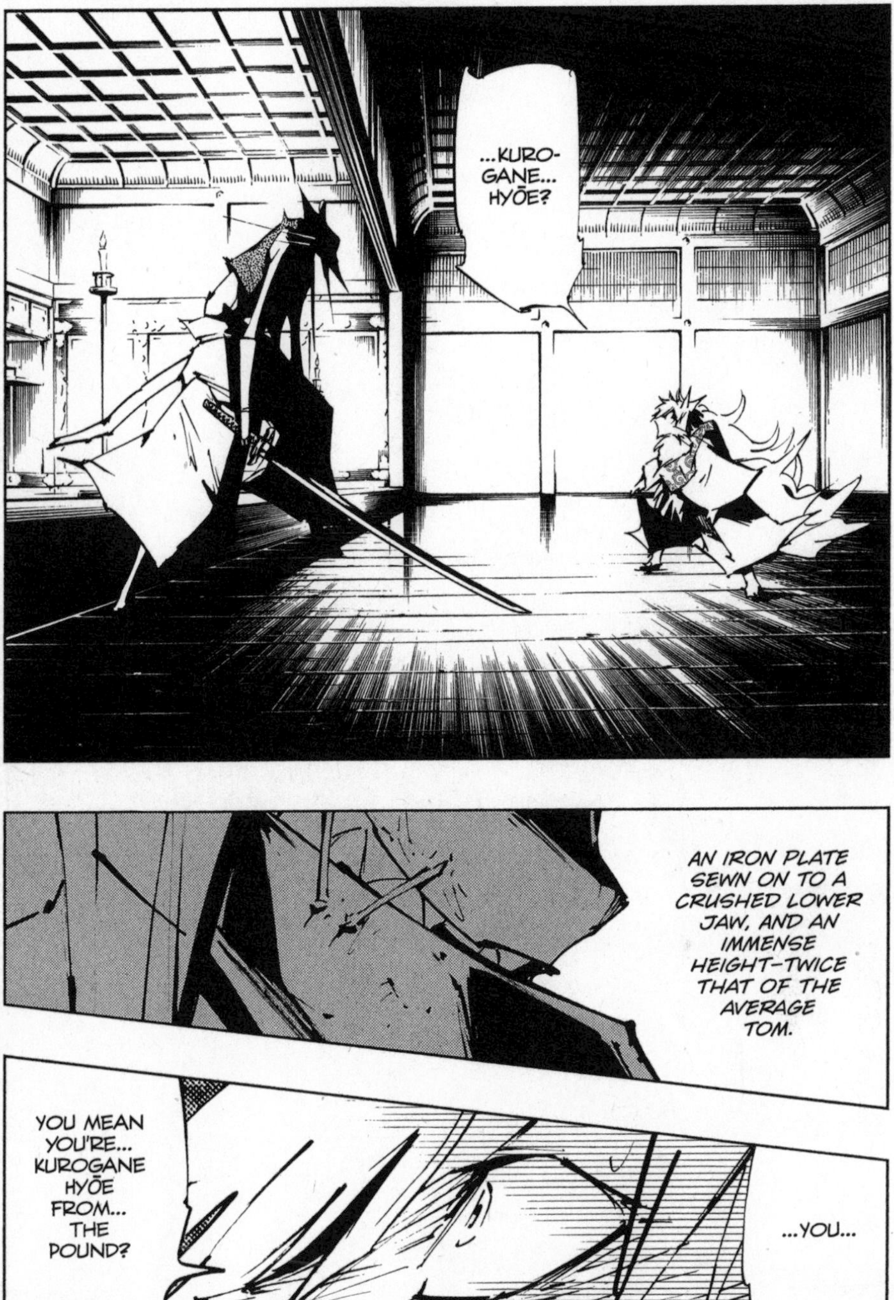

...KURO-GANE... HYŌE?
AN IRON PLATE SEWN ON TO A CRUSHED LOWER JAW, AND AN IMMENSE HEIGHT–TWICE THAT OF THE AVERAGE TOM.
...YOU...
YOU MEAN YOU'RE... KUROGANE HYŌE FROM... THE POUND?

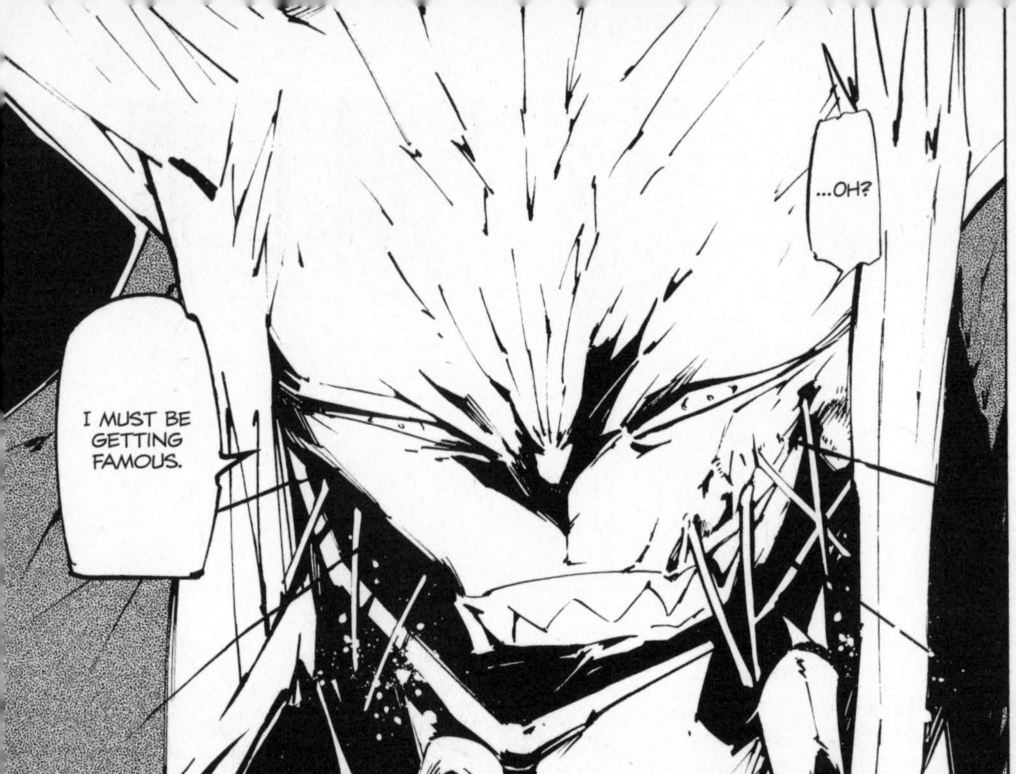
...OH?
I MUST BE GETTING FAMOUS.
KRIK
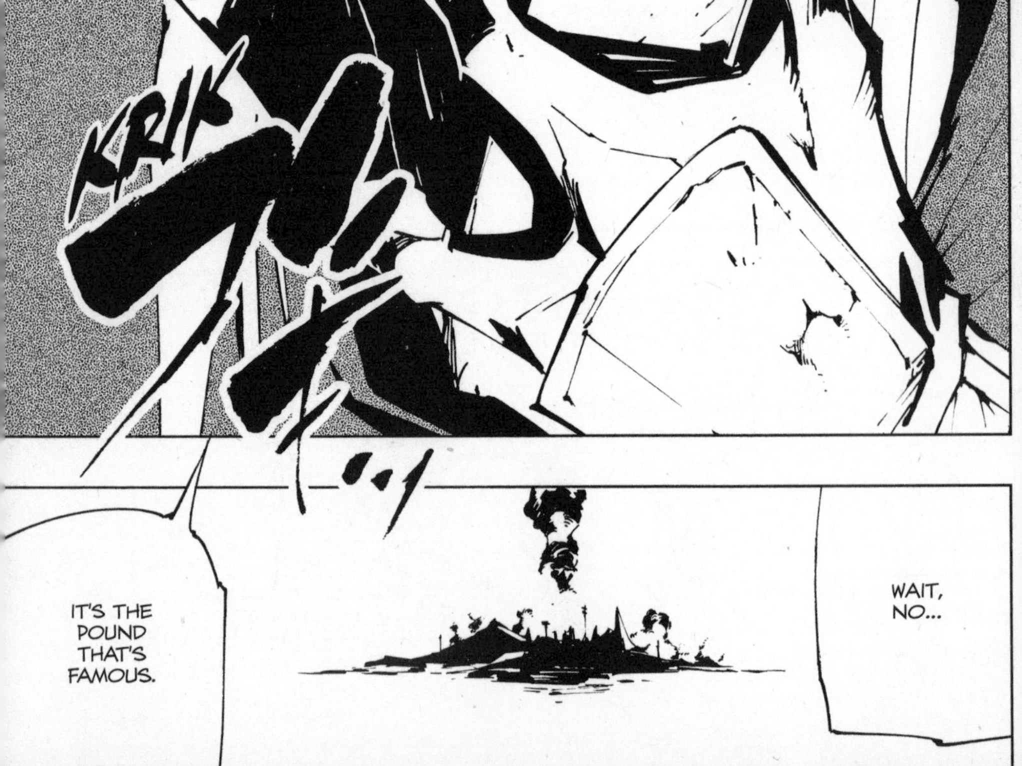
WAIT, NO...
IT'S THE POUND THAT'S FAMOUS.

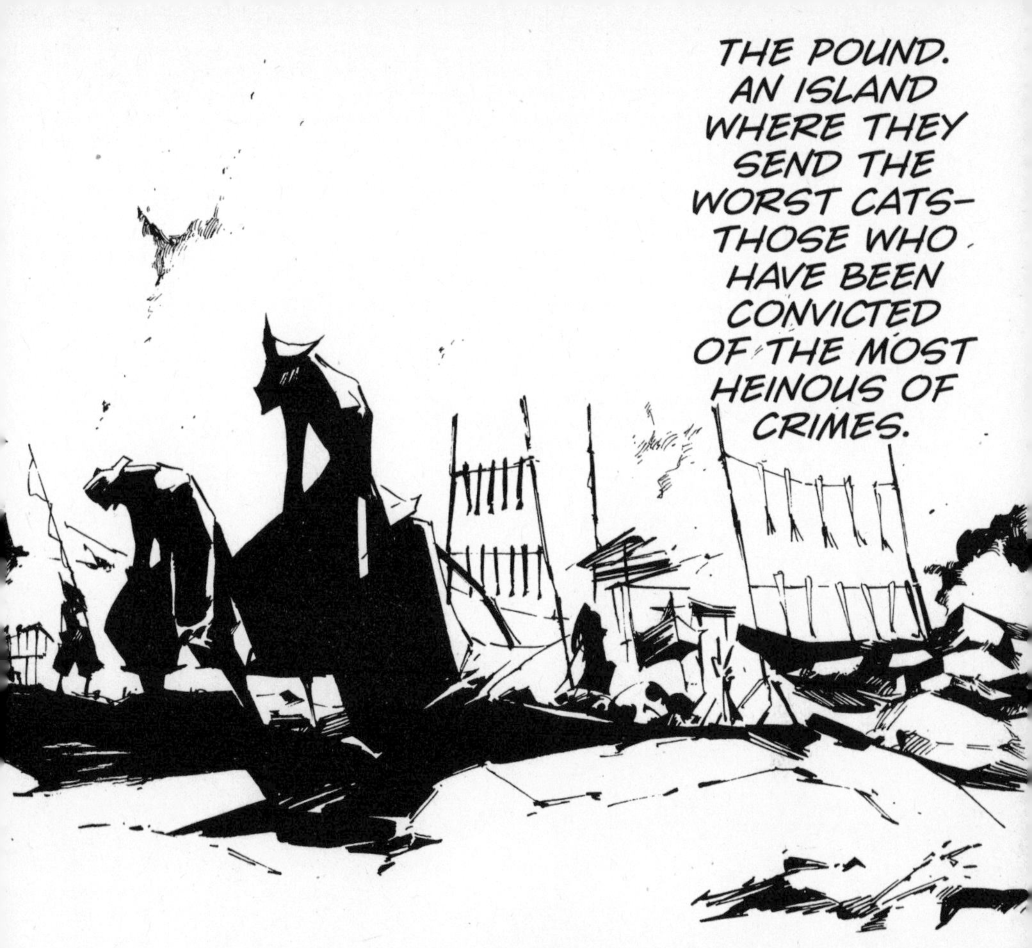
THE POUND. AN ISLAND WHERE THEY SEND THE WORST CATS-THOSE WHO HAVE BEEN CONVICTED OF THE MOST HEINOUS OF CRIMES.
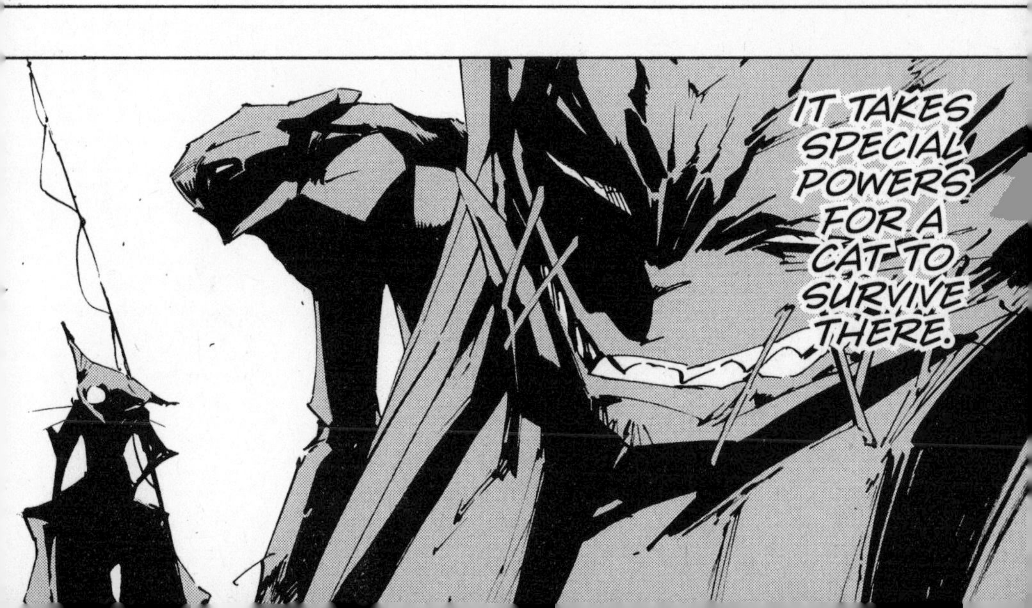
IT TAKES SPECIAL POWERS FOR A CAT TO SURVIVE THERE.

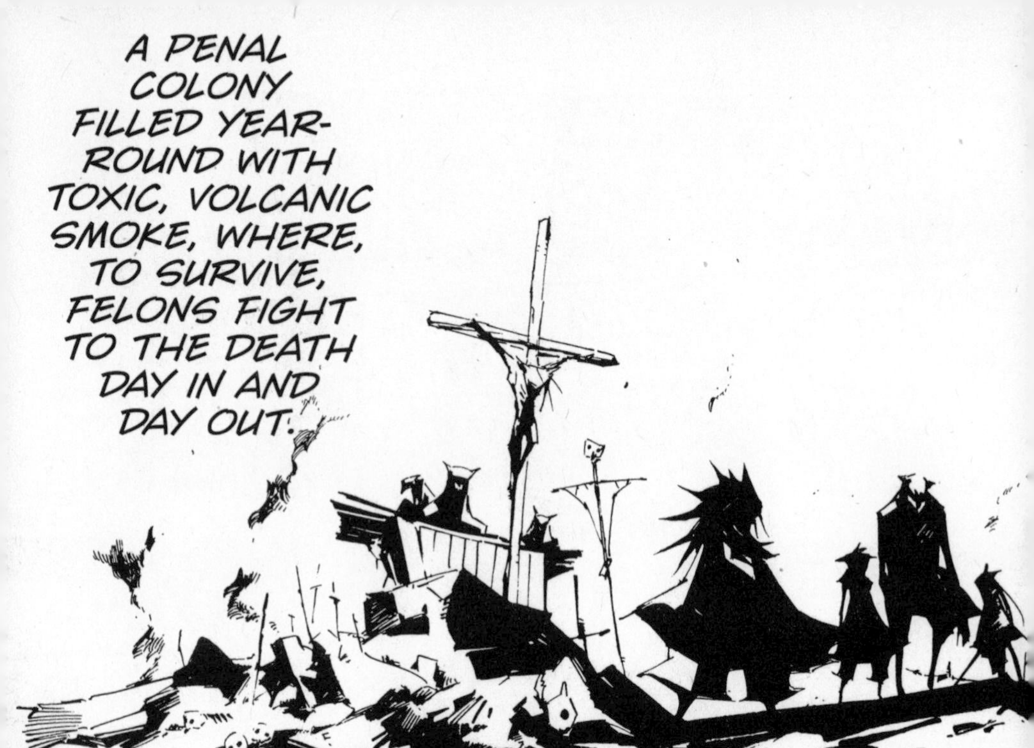
A PENAL COLONY FILLED YEAR-ROUND WITH TOXIC, VOLCANIC SMOKE, WHERE, TO SURVIVE, FELONS FIGHT TO THE DEATH DAY IN AND DAY OUT.
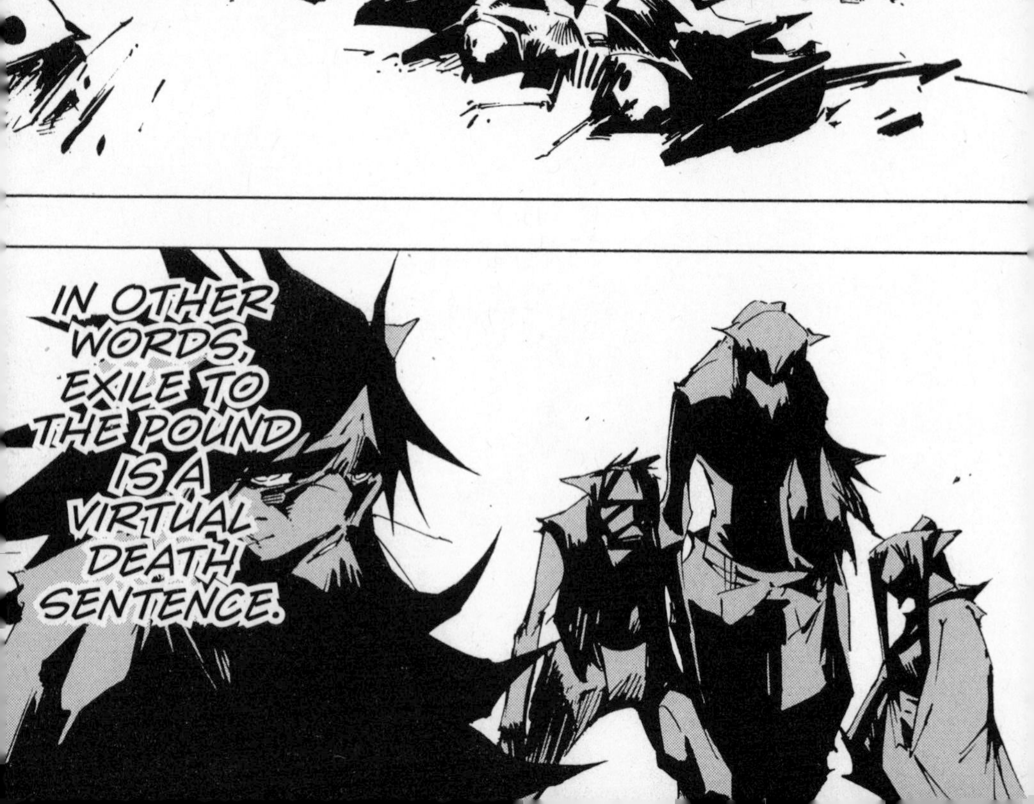
IN OTHER WORDS, EXILE TO THE POUND IS A VIRTUAL DEATH SENTENCE.

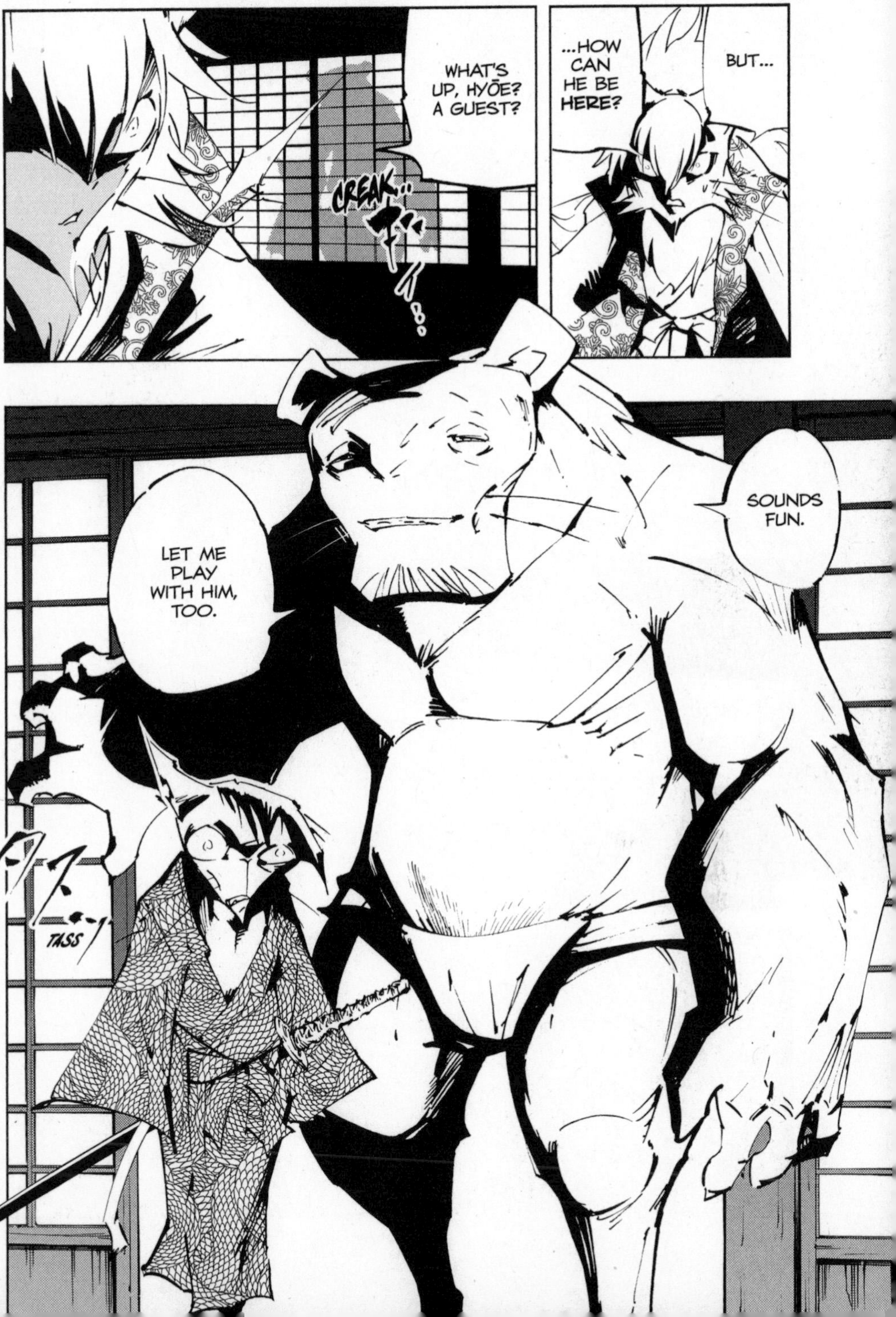
BUT...
...HOW CAN HE BE HERE?
WHAT'S UP, HYŌE? A GUEST?
CREAK..
SOUNDS FUN.
LET ME PLAY WITH HIM, TOO.
TASS

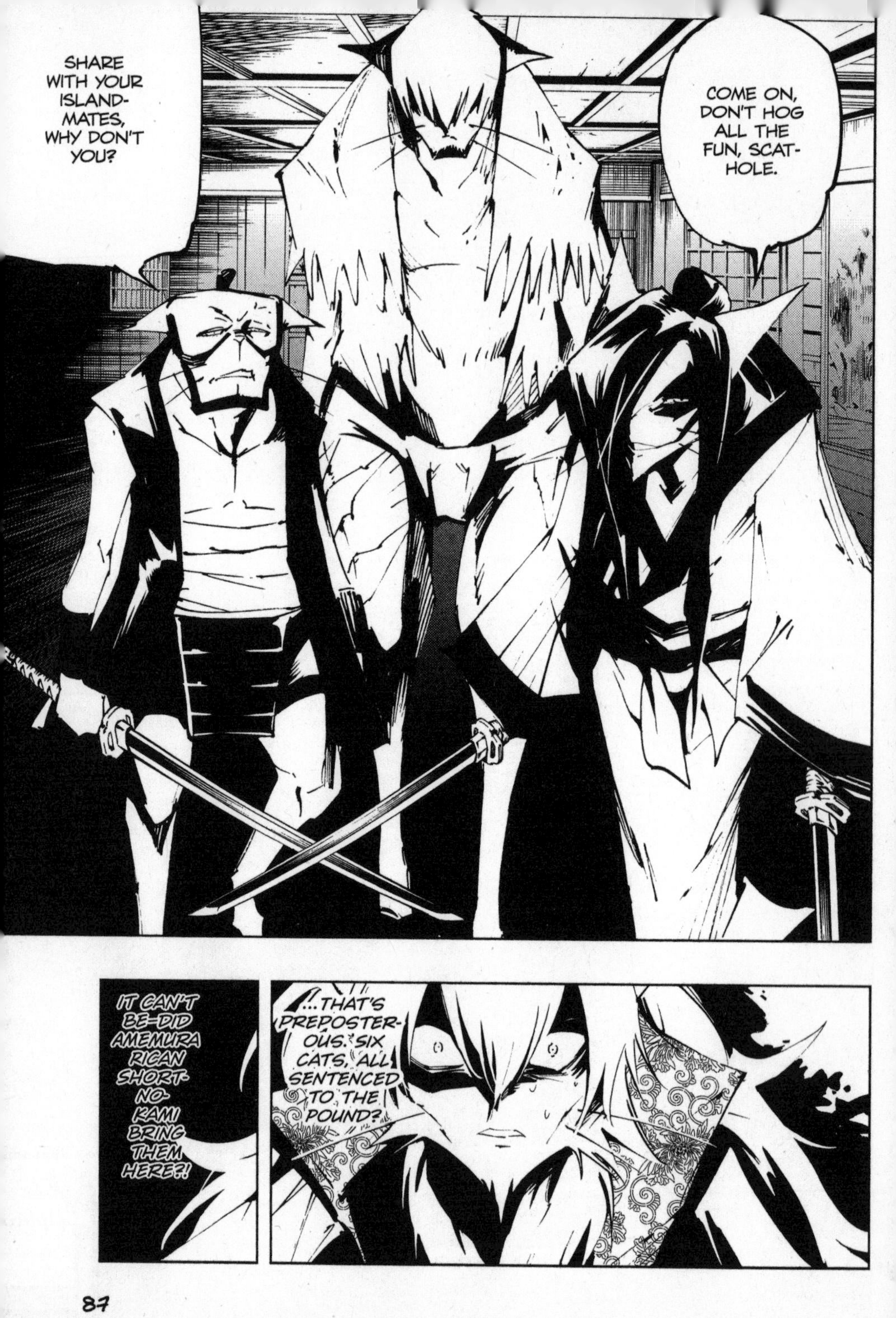
COME ON, DON'T HOG ALL THE FUN, SCAT-HOLE.
SHARE WITH YOUR ISLAND-MATES, WHY DON'T YOU?
...THAT'S PREPOSTER-OUS. SIX CATS, ALL SENTENCED TO THE POUND?
IT CAN'T BE—DID AMEMURA RICAN SHORT-NO-KAMI BRING THEM HERE?!

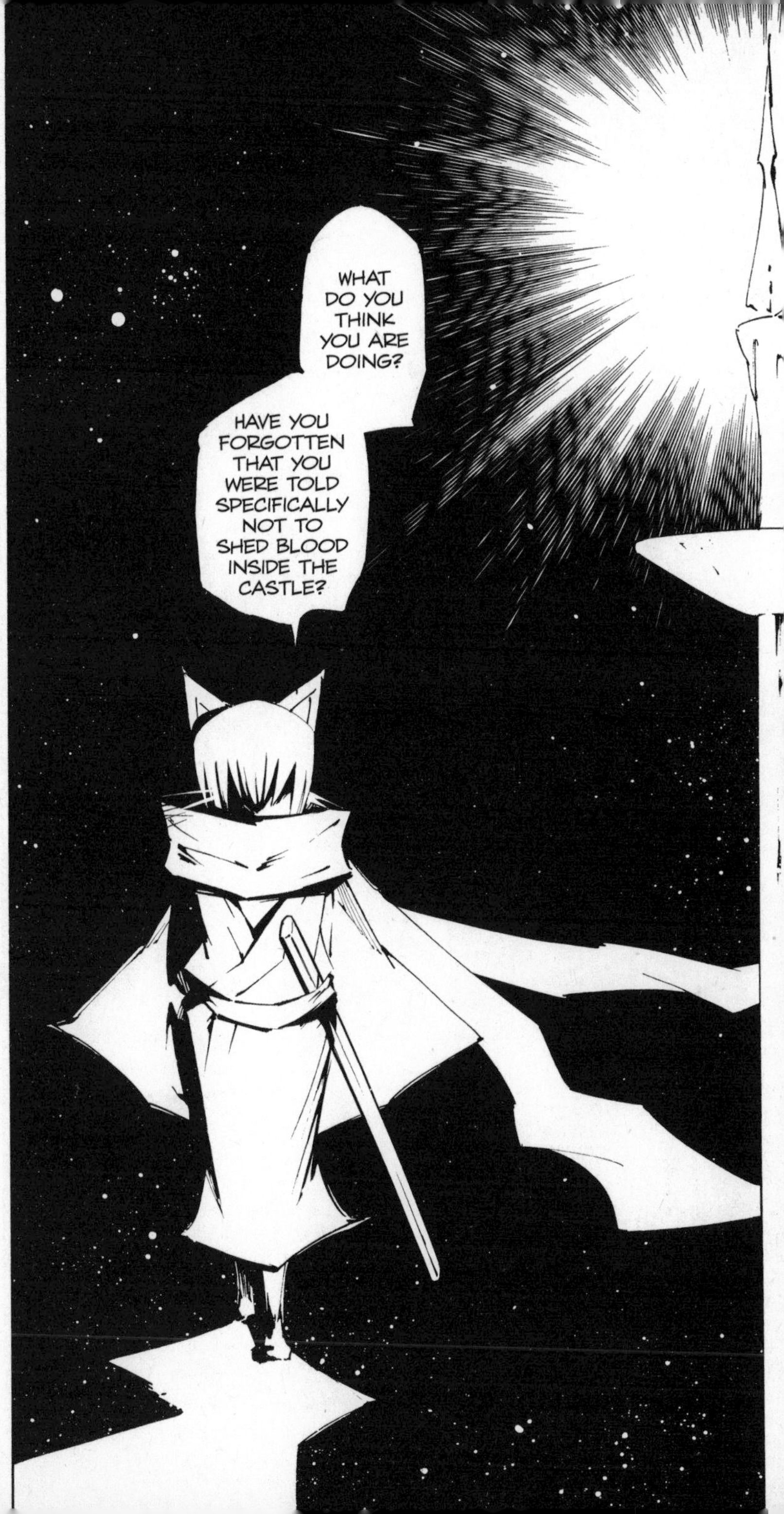
WHAT DO YOU THINK YOU ARE DOING?
HAVE YOU FORGOTTEN THAT YOU WERE TOLD SPECIFICALLY NOT TO SHED BLOOD INSIDE THE CASTLE?

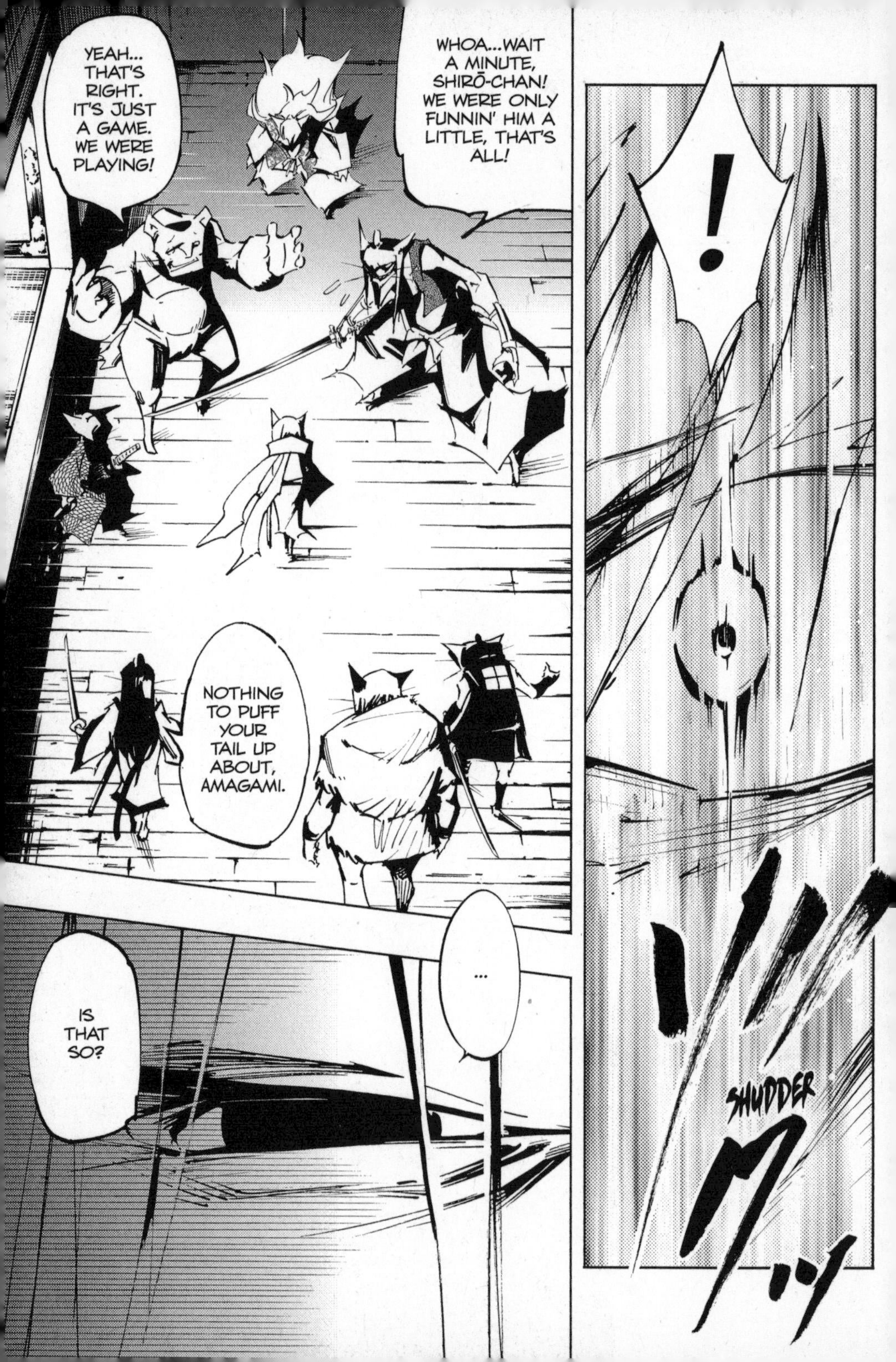
!
SHUDDER
WHOA...WAIT A MINUTE, SHIRŌ-CHAN! WE WERE ONLY FUNNIN' HIM A LITTLE, THAT'S ALL!
YEAH... THAT'S RIGHT. IT'S JUST A GAME. WE WERE PLAYING!
NOTHING TO PUFF YOUR TAIL UP ABOUT, AMAGAMI.
...
IS THAT SO?

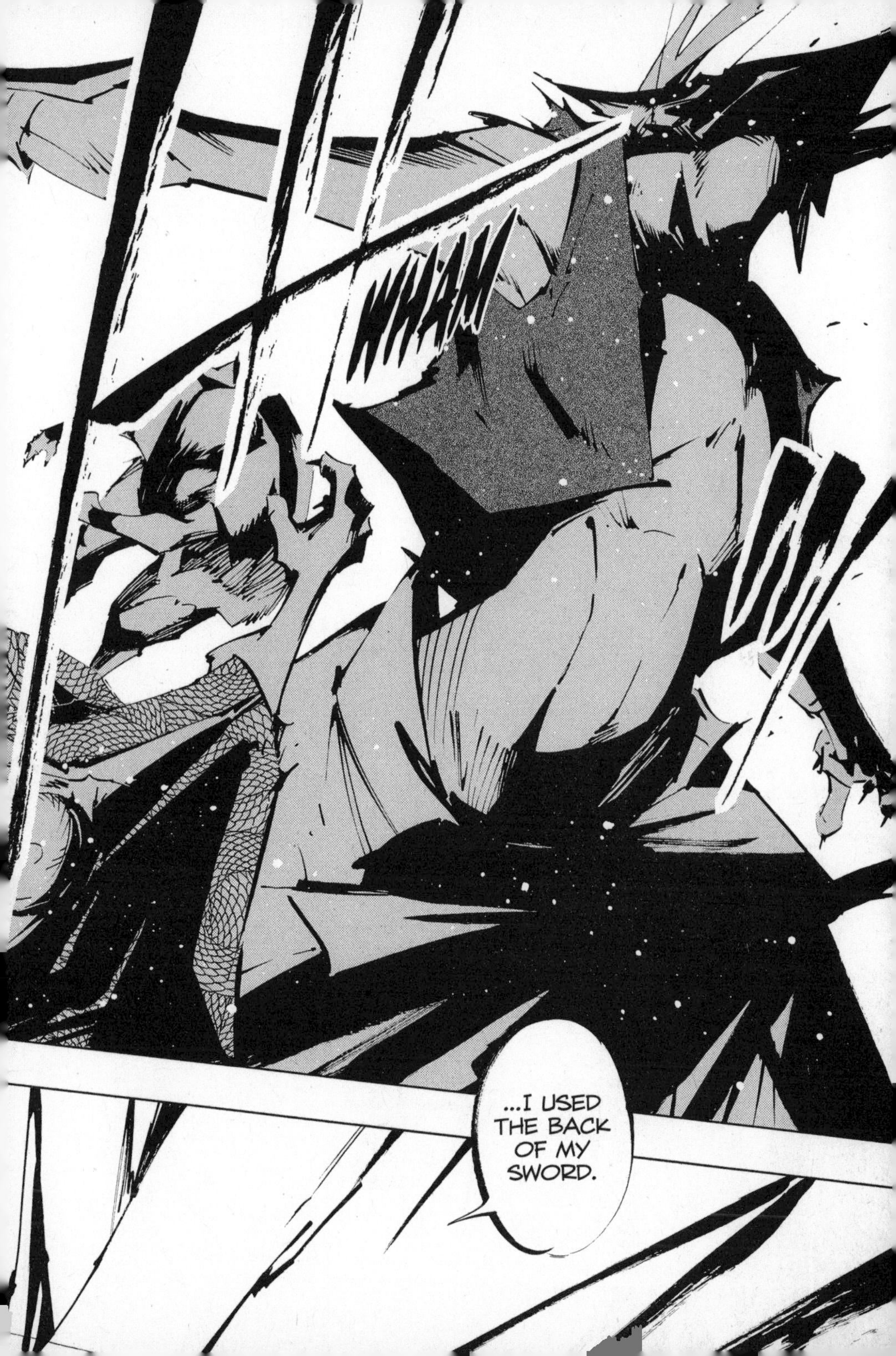
WHAM
...I USED THE BACK OF MY SWORD.

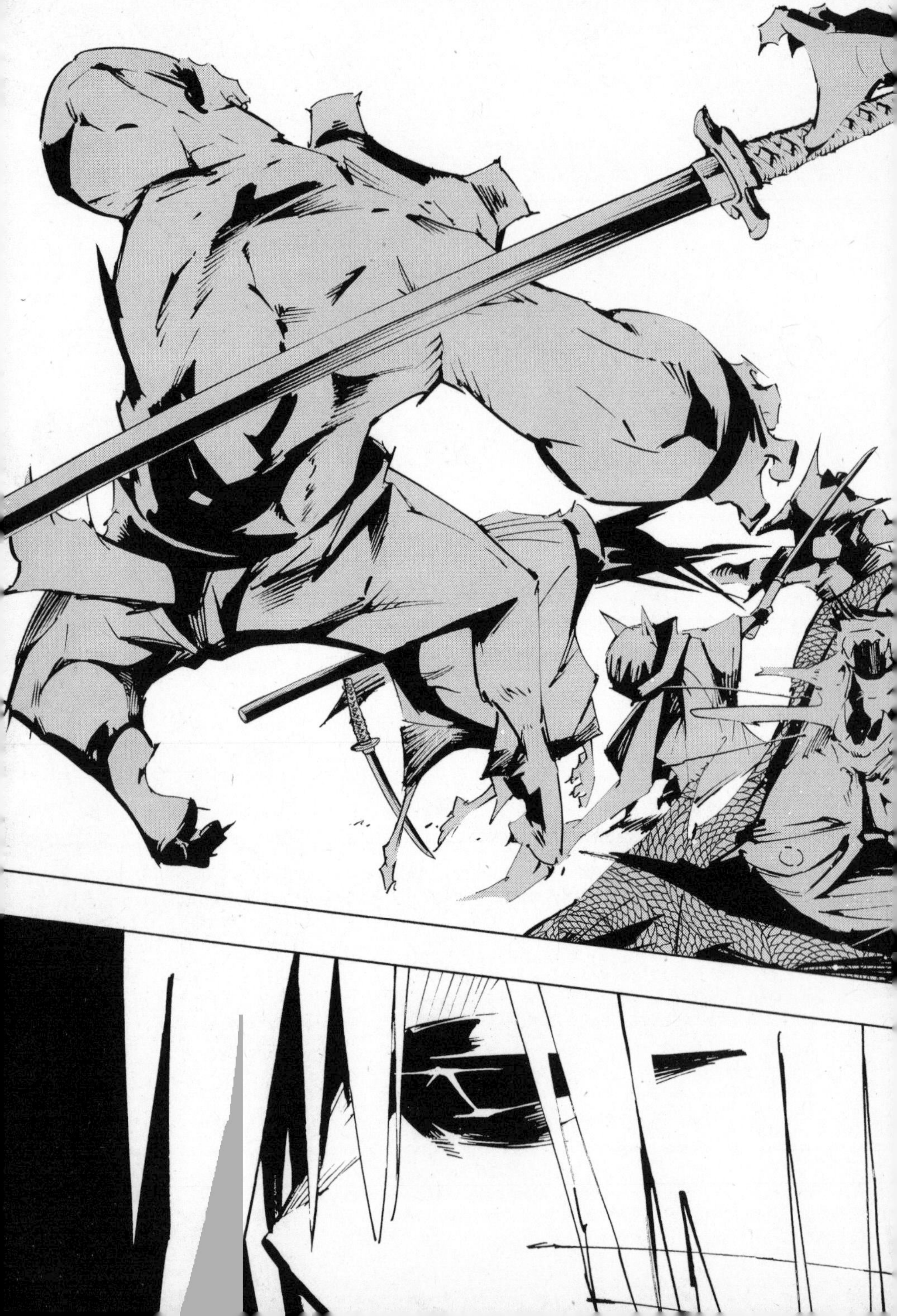

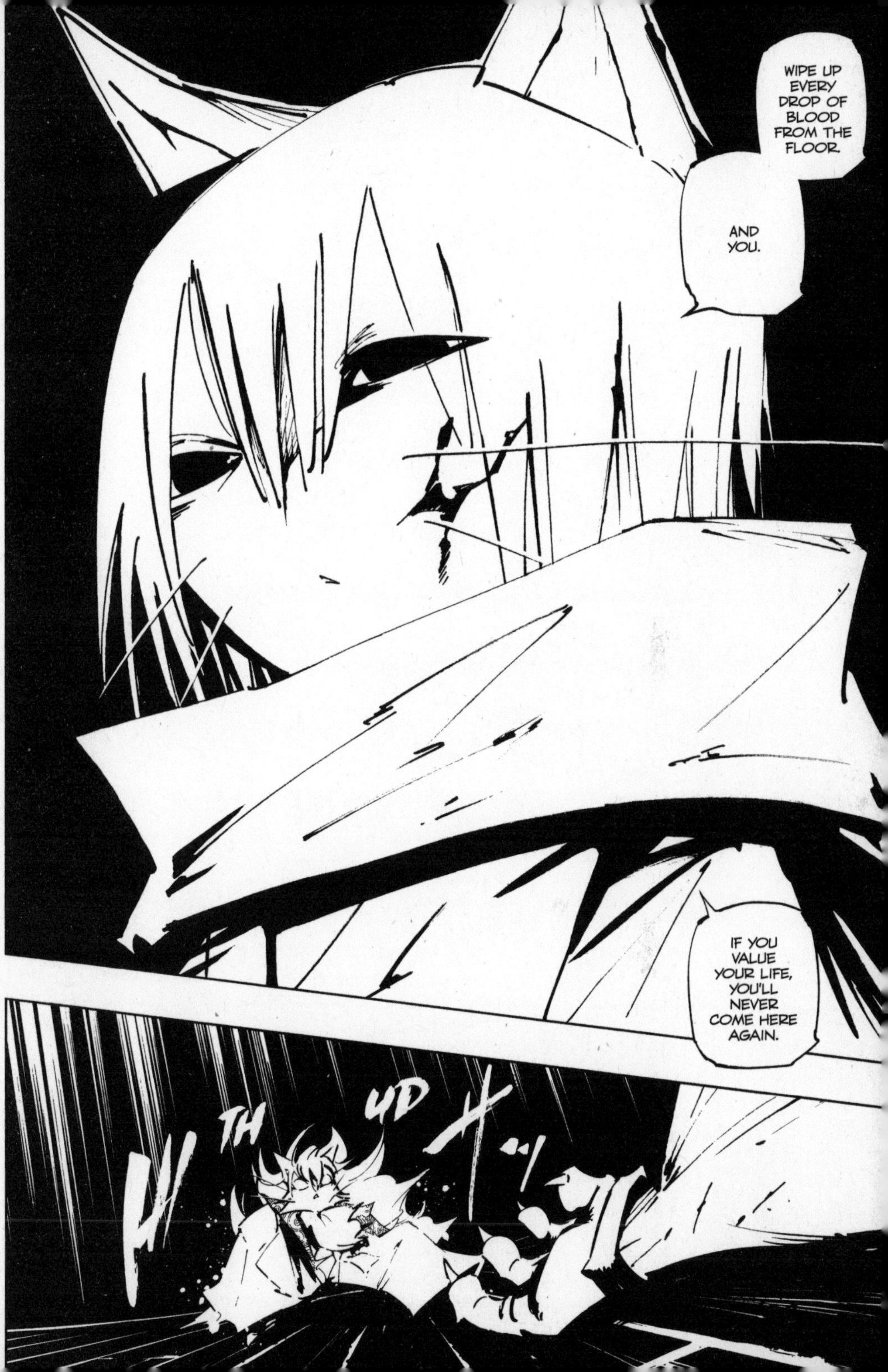
WIPE UP EVERY DROP OF BLOOD FROM THE FLOOR.
AND YOU.
IF YOU VALUE YOUR LIFE, YOU'LL NEVER COME HERE AGAIN.
THUD

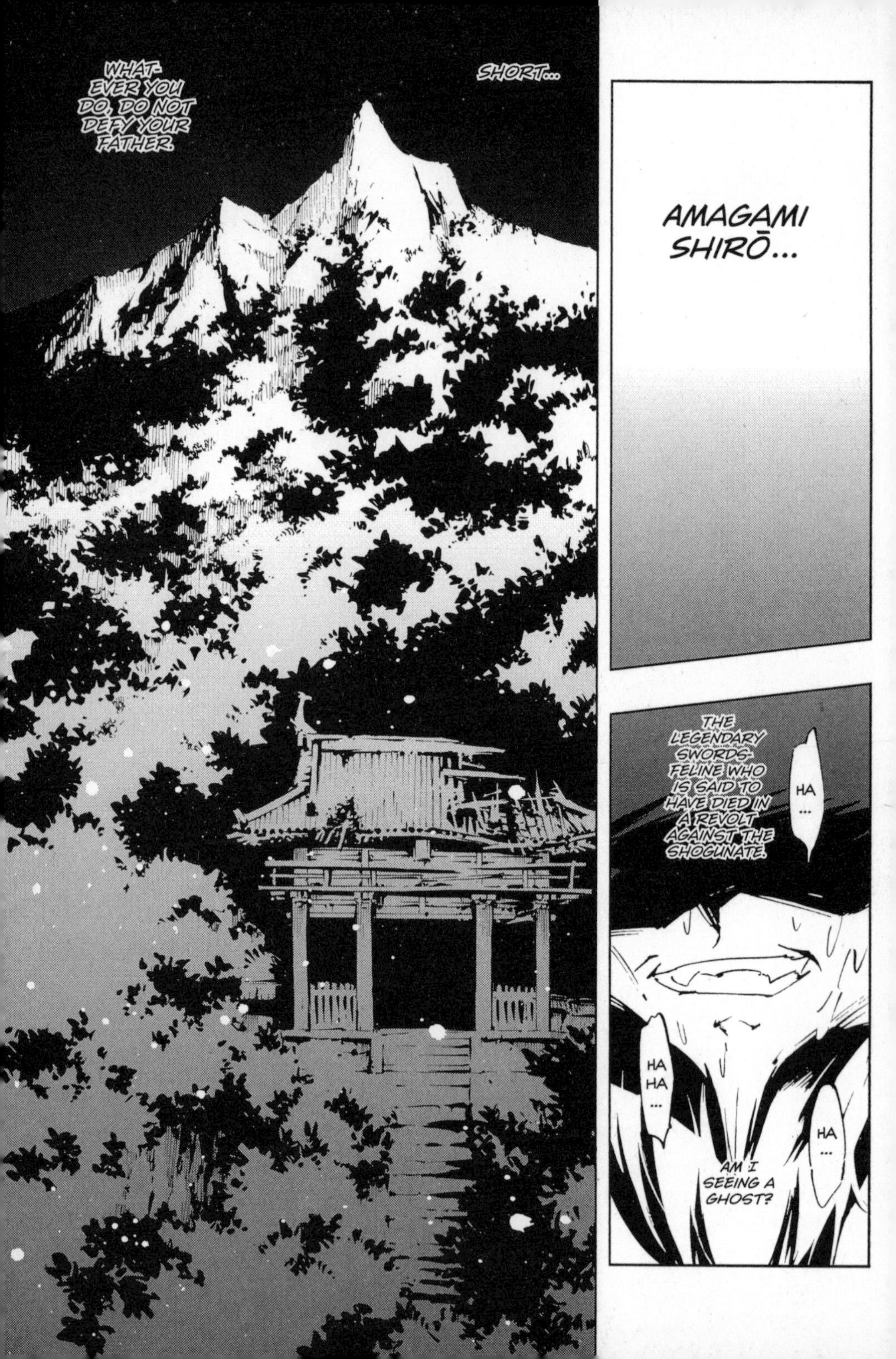
AMAGAMI SHIRŌ...
HA ...
THE LEGENDARY SWORDS-FELINE WHO IS SAID TO HAVE DIED IN A REVOLT AGAINST THE SHOGUNATE.
HA HA ...
HA ...
AM I SEEING A GHOST?
SHORT...
WHAT-EVER YOU DO, DO NOT DEFY YOUR FATHER.

猫ヶ原

ネコガハラ

NeKoGaHaRa

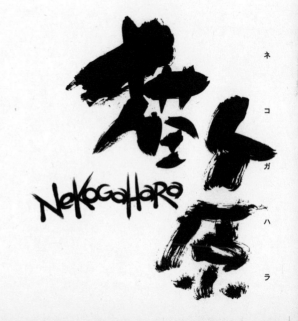

THE
WORLD
IS
ROTTEN
WITH
TOUGH
GUYS.

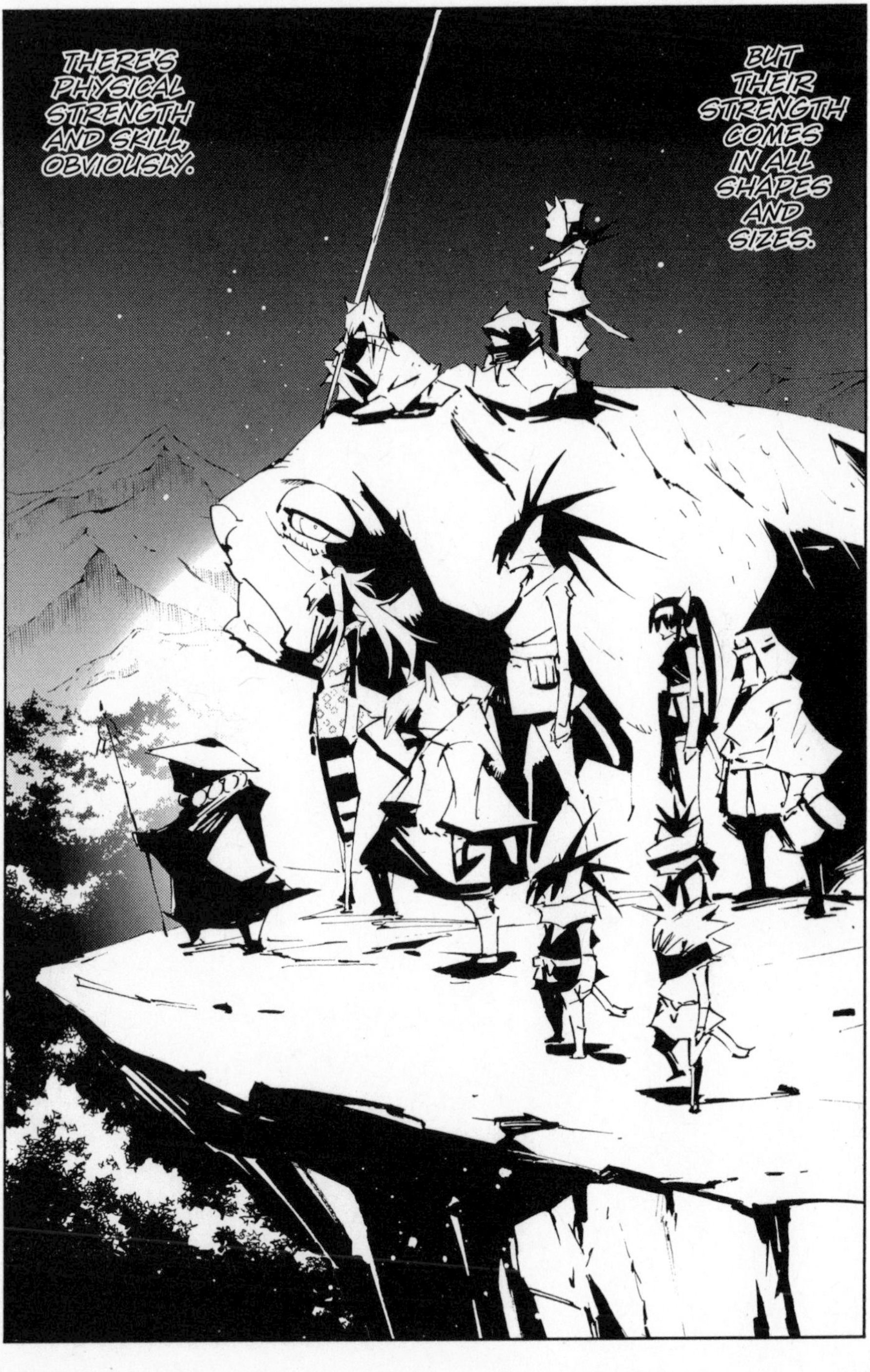
BUT THEIR STRENGTH COMES IN ALL SHAPES AND SIZES.
THERE'S PHYSICAL STRENGTH AND SKILL, OBVIOUSLY.

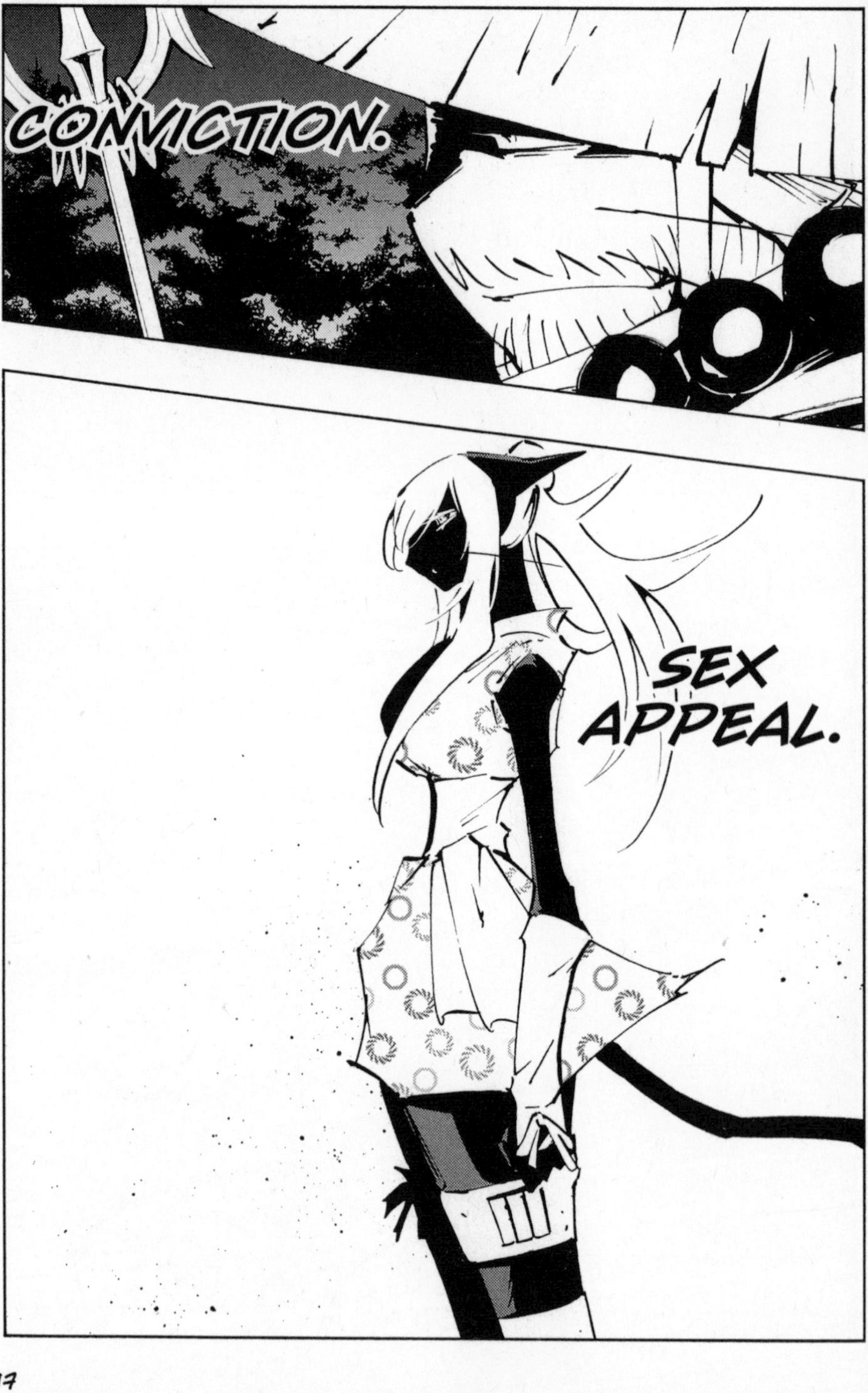
CONVICTION.
SEX APPEAL.

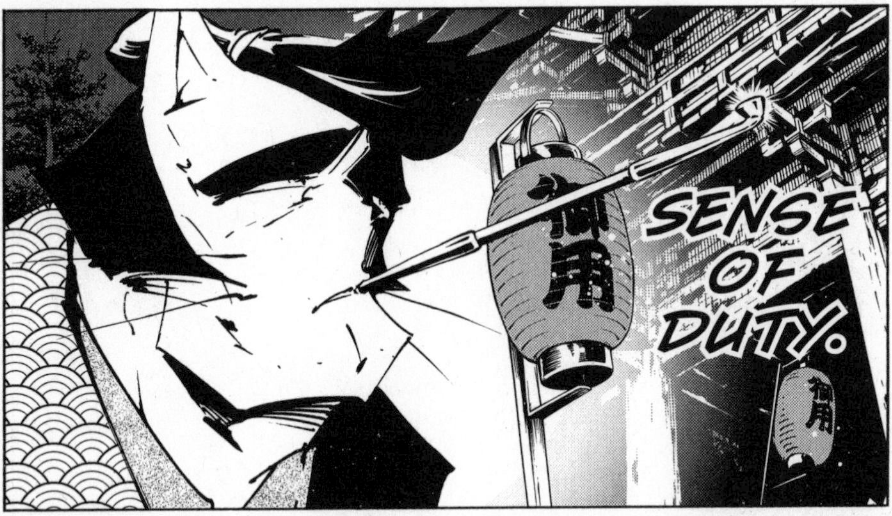
御用
SENSE OF DUTY.

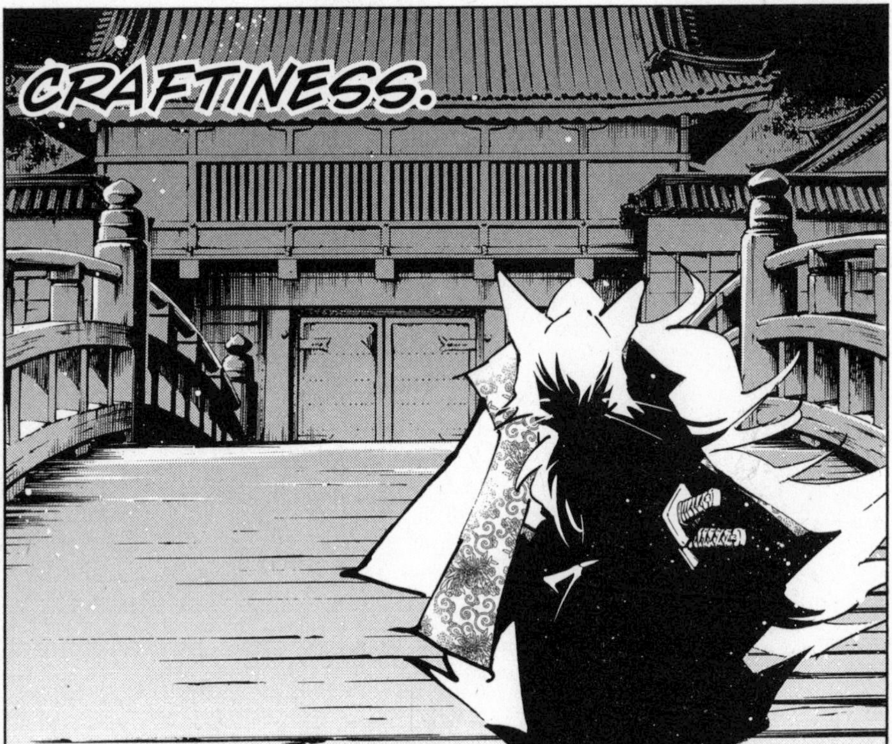
CRAFTINESS.

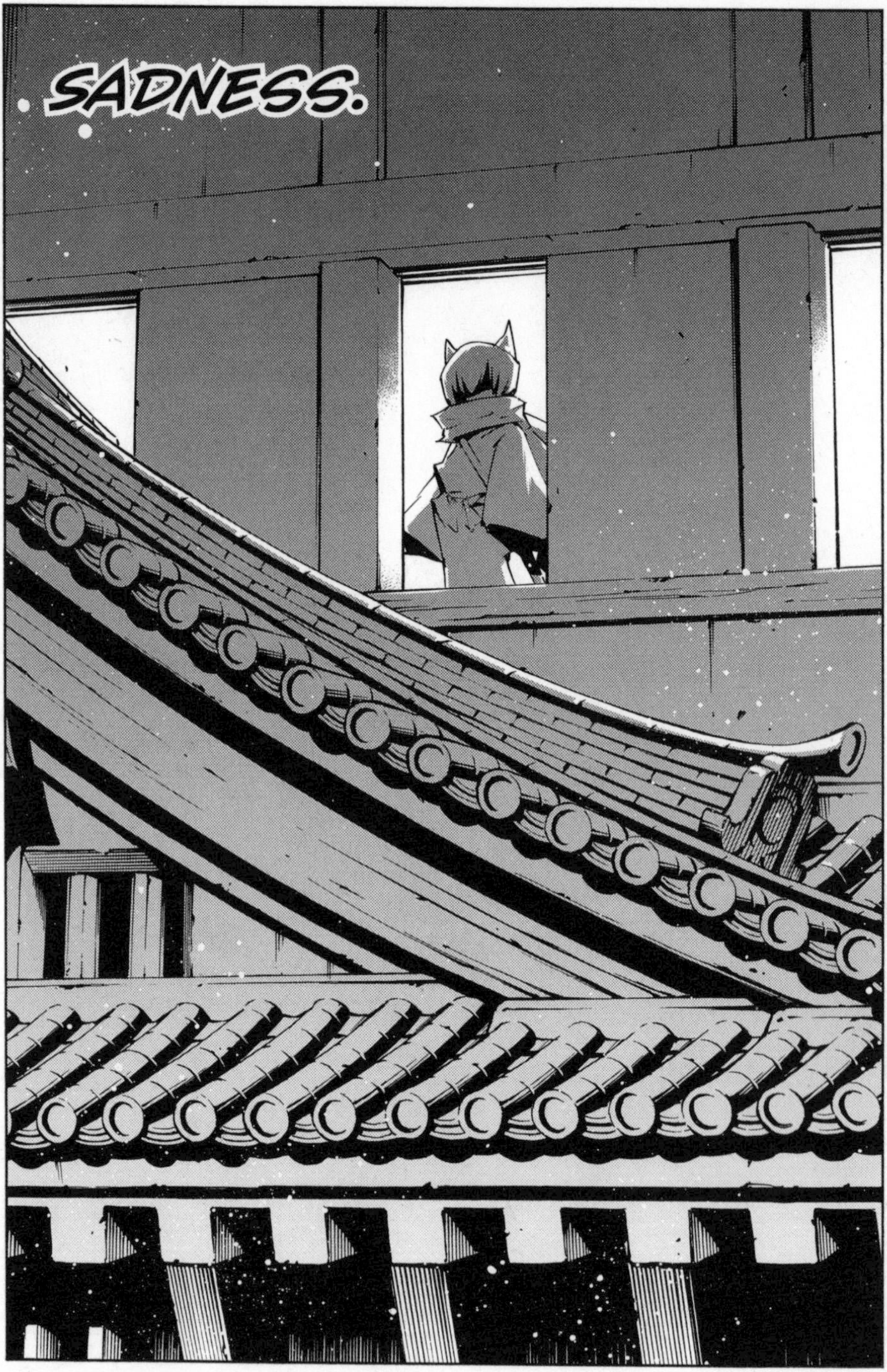
SADNESS.

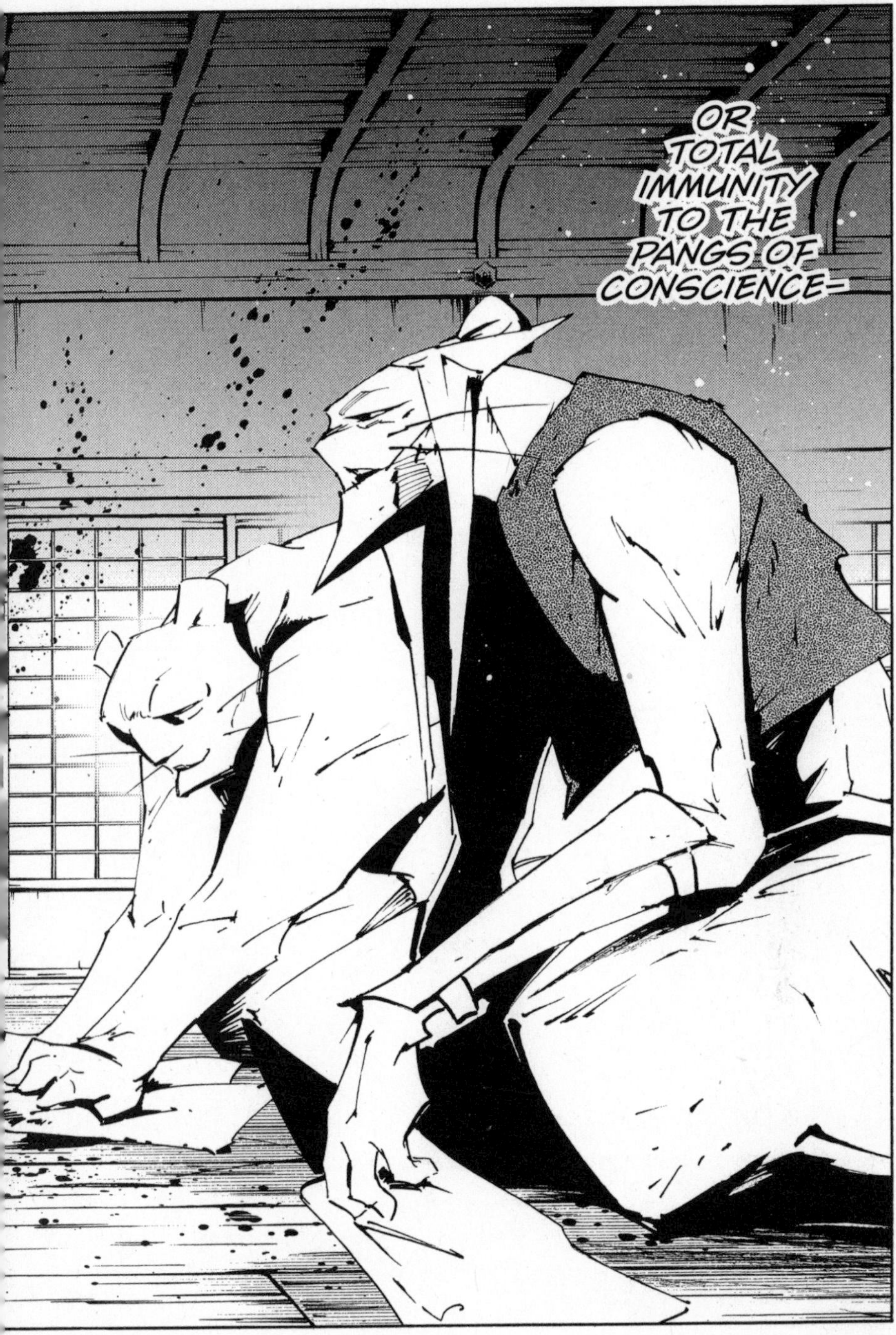
OR TOTAL IMMUNITY TO THE PANGS OF CONSCIENCE-

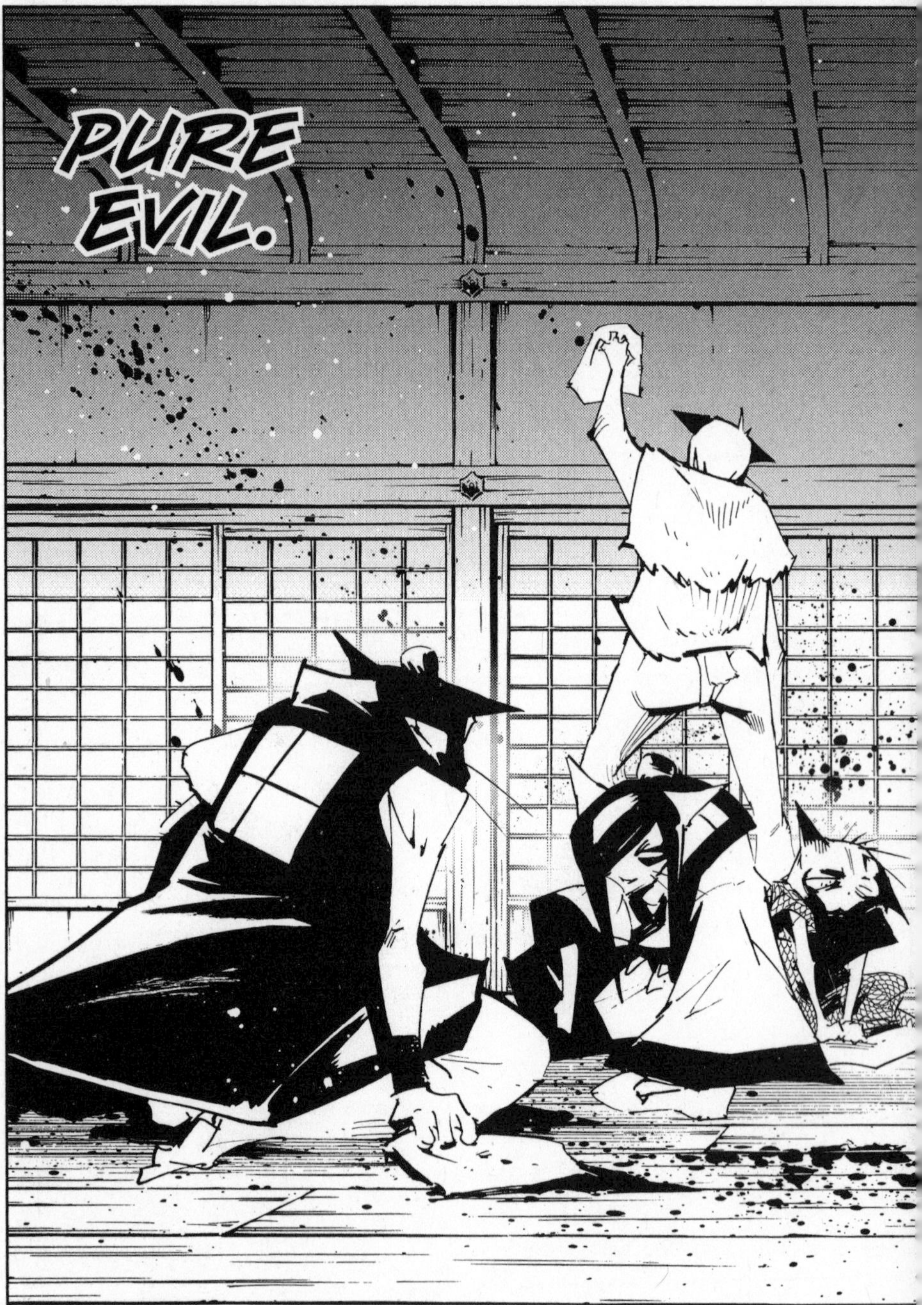
PURE EVIL.

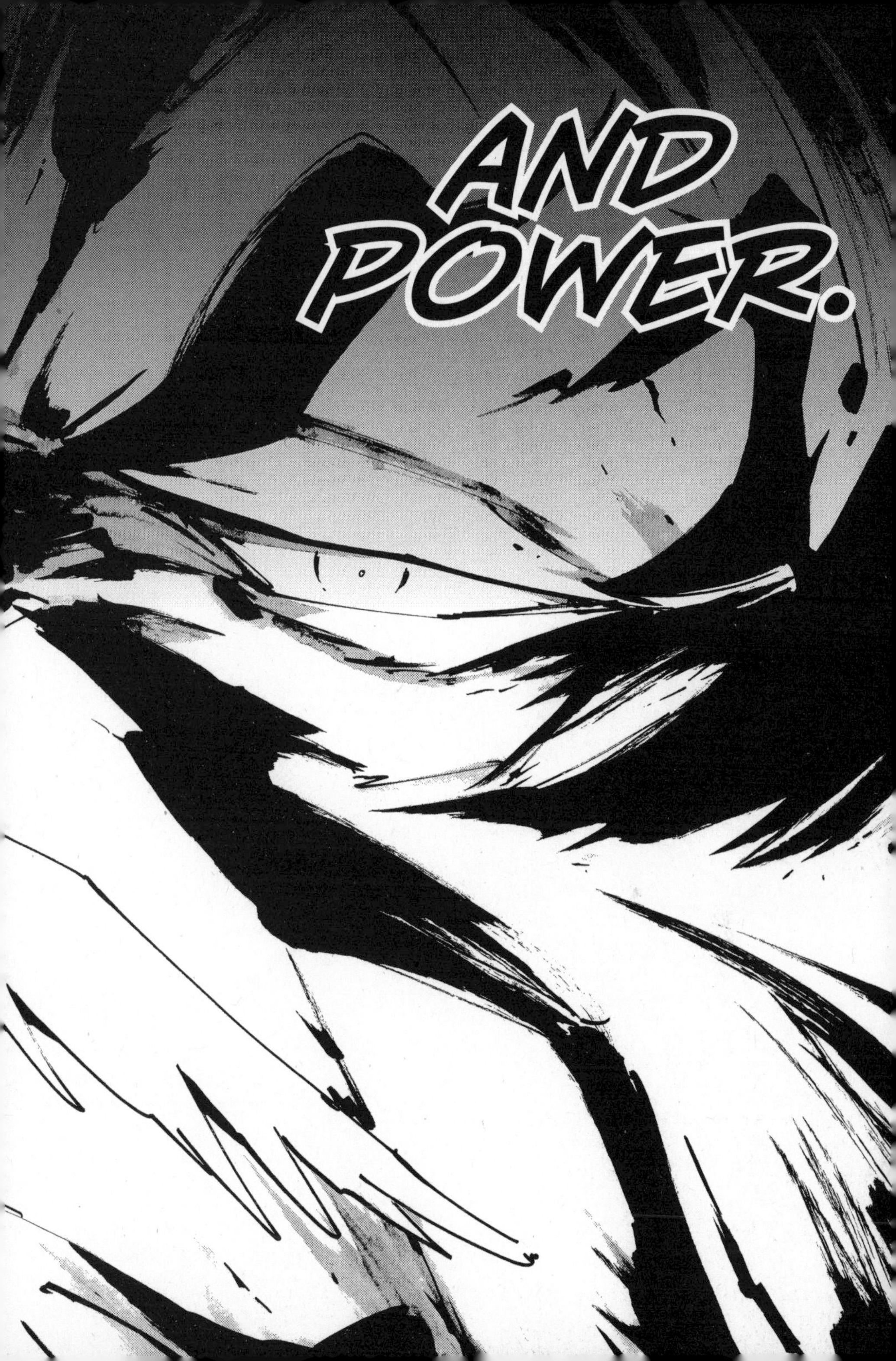
AND POWER.

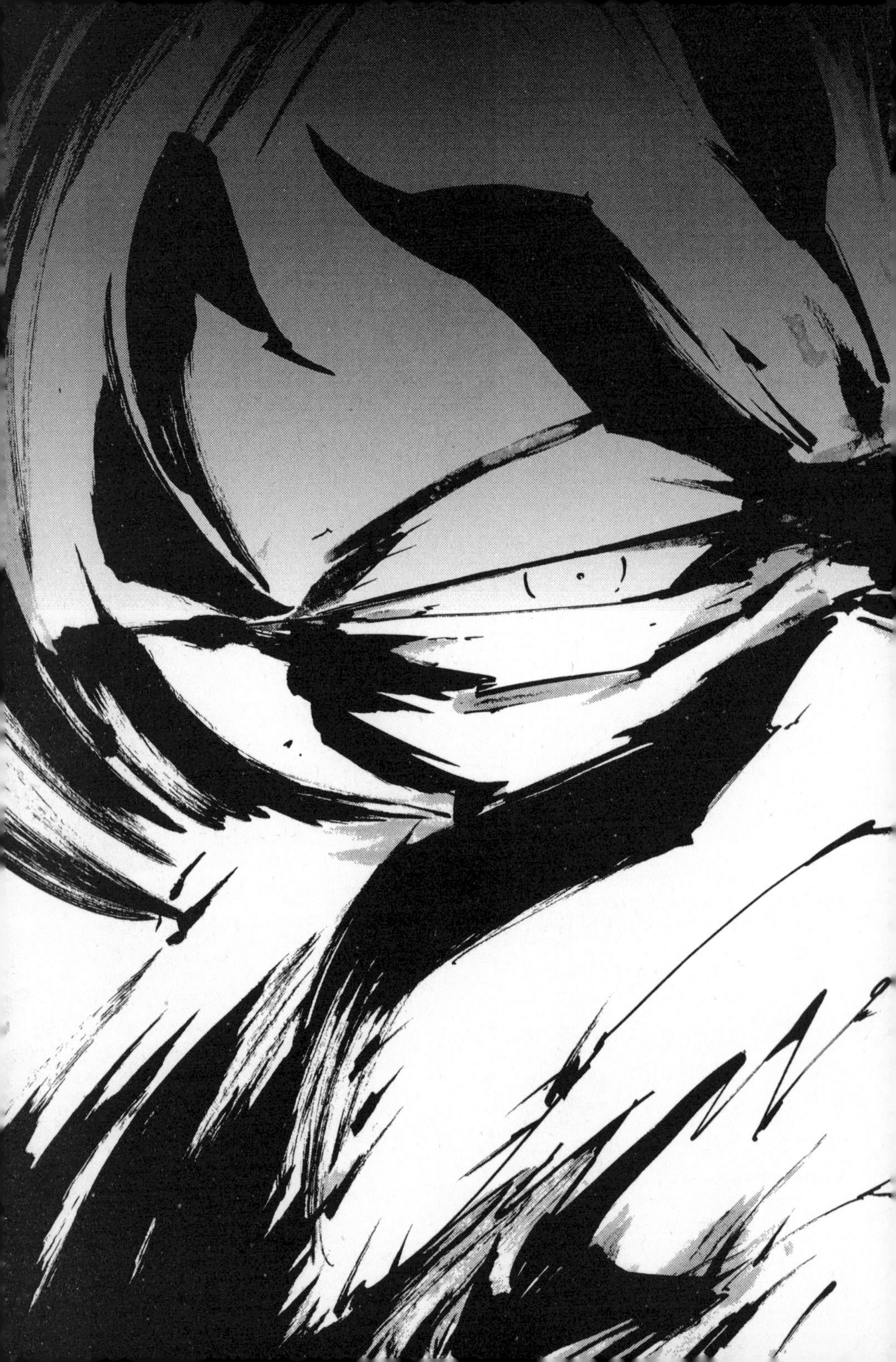

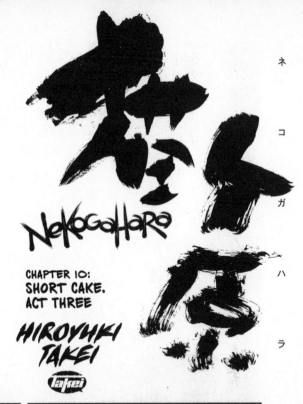

ネコガハラ

NEKOGAHARA

CHAPTER 10: SHORT CAKE. ACT THREE

HIROYUKI TAKEI

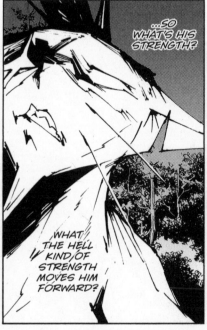

AND WOULDN'T YOU KNOW IT, I AIN'T GOT EVEN **ONE** OF THOSE.

NOPE. INSTEAD, I GO PICKING FIGHTS WITH CATS I GOT NO BUSINESS TANGLING WITH...
...AND NOW I'M ABOUT TO BE OFFED BY SOME OLD MOG WITH HIS JUNK HANGING OUT.
...SO WHAT'S HIS STRENGTH?
WHAT THE HELL KIND OF STRENGTH MOVES HIM FORWARD?

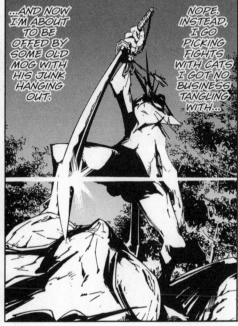

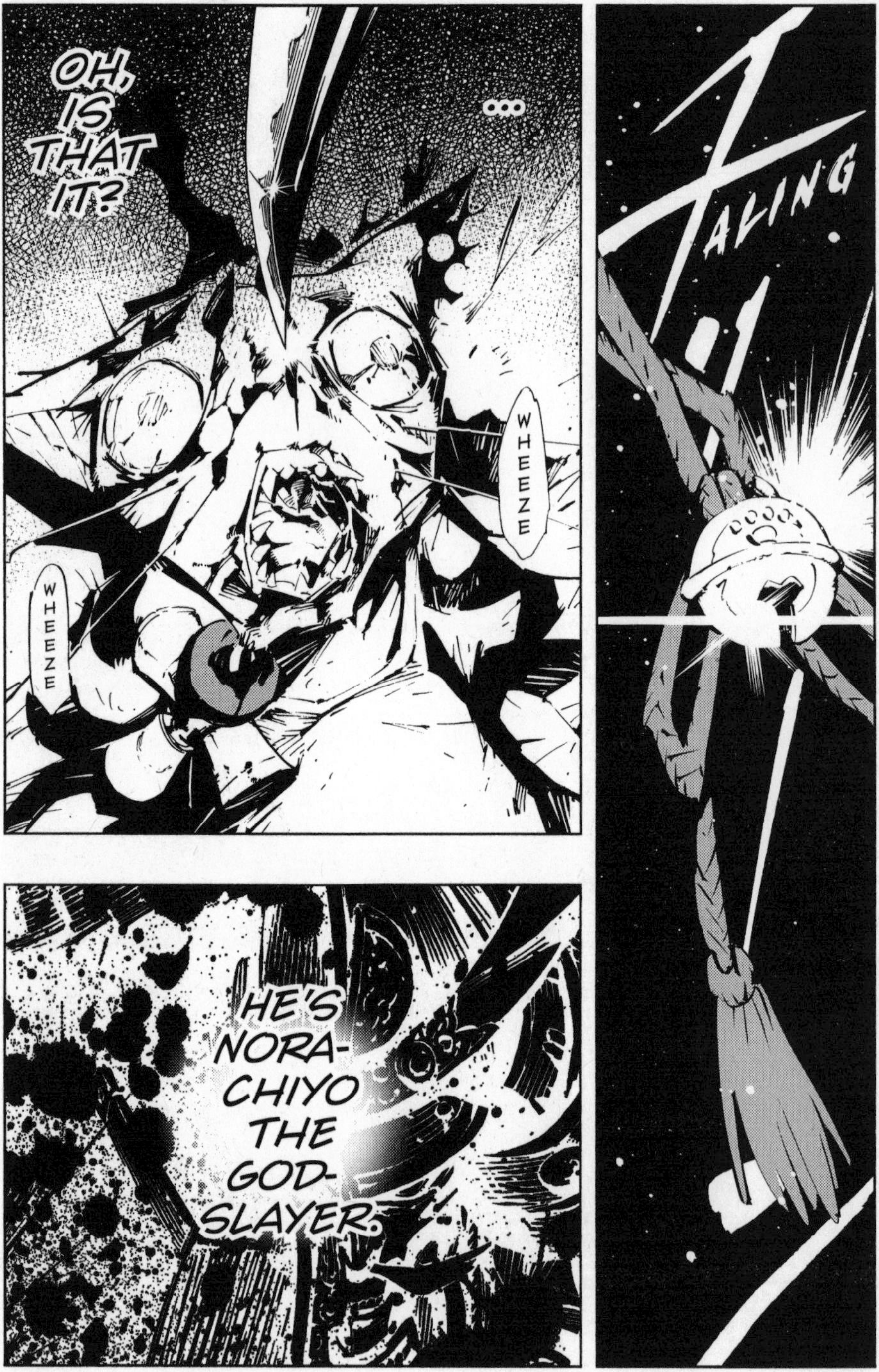
TALING
...
OH, IS THAT IT?
WHEEZE
WHEEZE
HE'S NORA-CHIYO THE GOD-SLAYER.

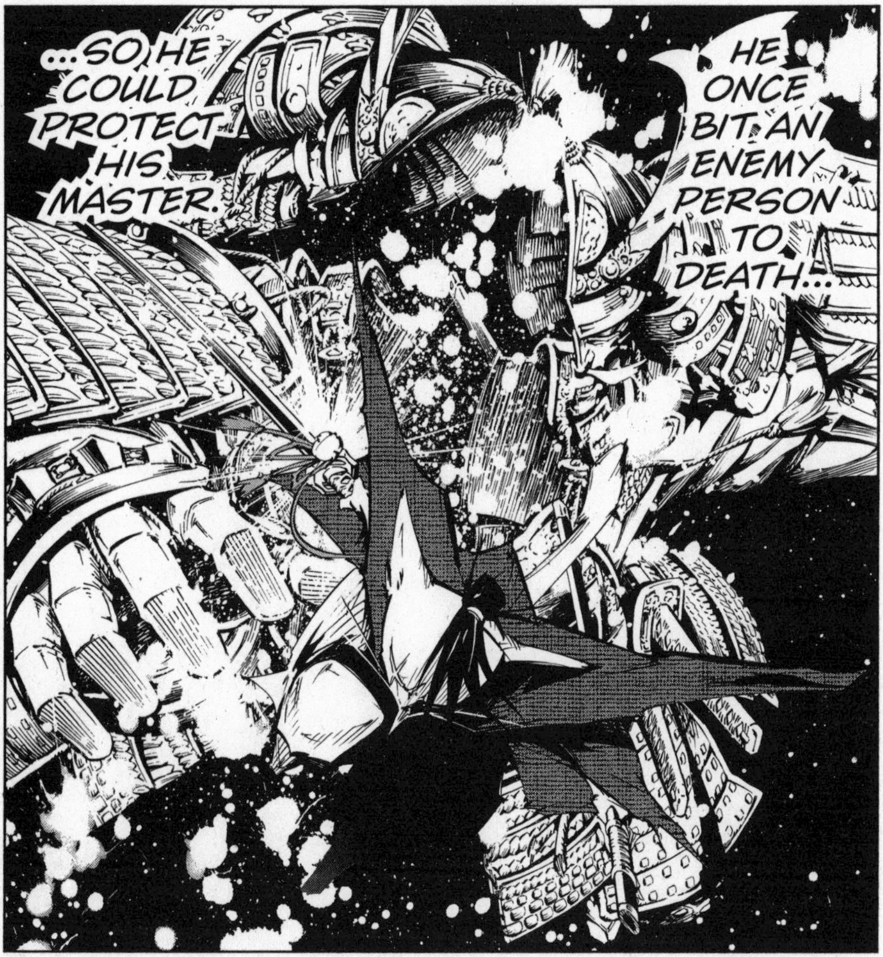
HE ONCE BIT AN ENEMY PERSON TO DEATH...
...SO HE COULD PROTECT HIS MASTER.

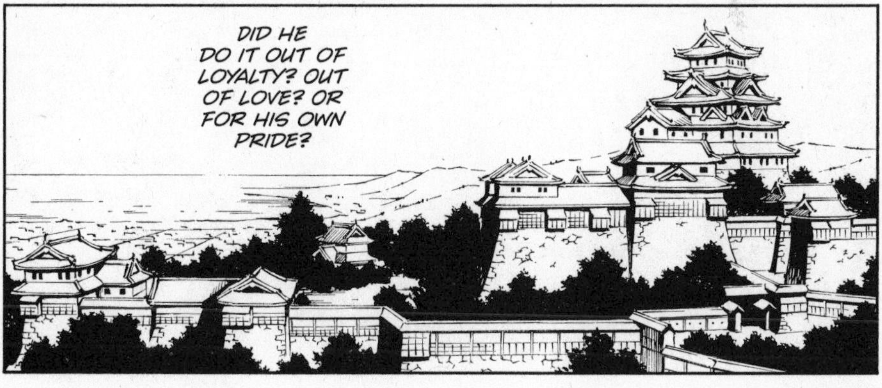
DID HE DO IT OUT OF LOYALTY? OUT OF LOVE? OR FOR HIS OWN PRIDE?

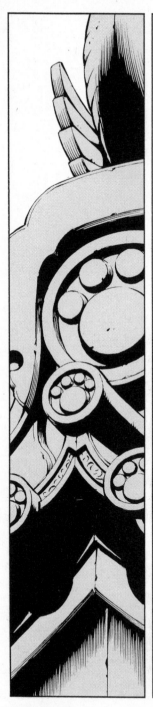

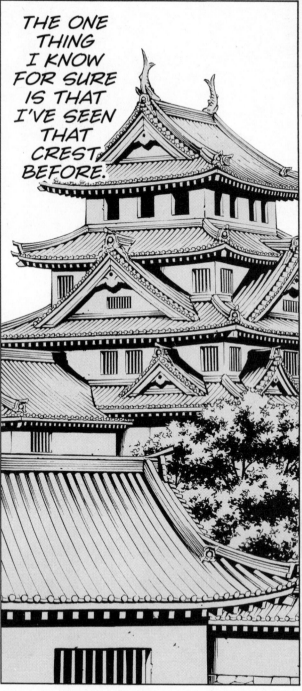

THE ONE THING I KNOW FOR SURE IS THAT I'VE SEEN THAT CREST BEFORE.

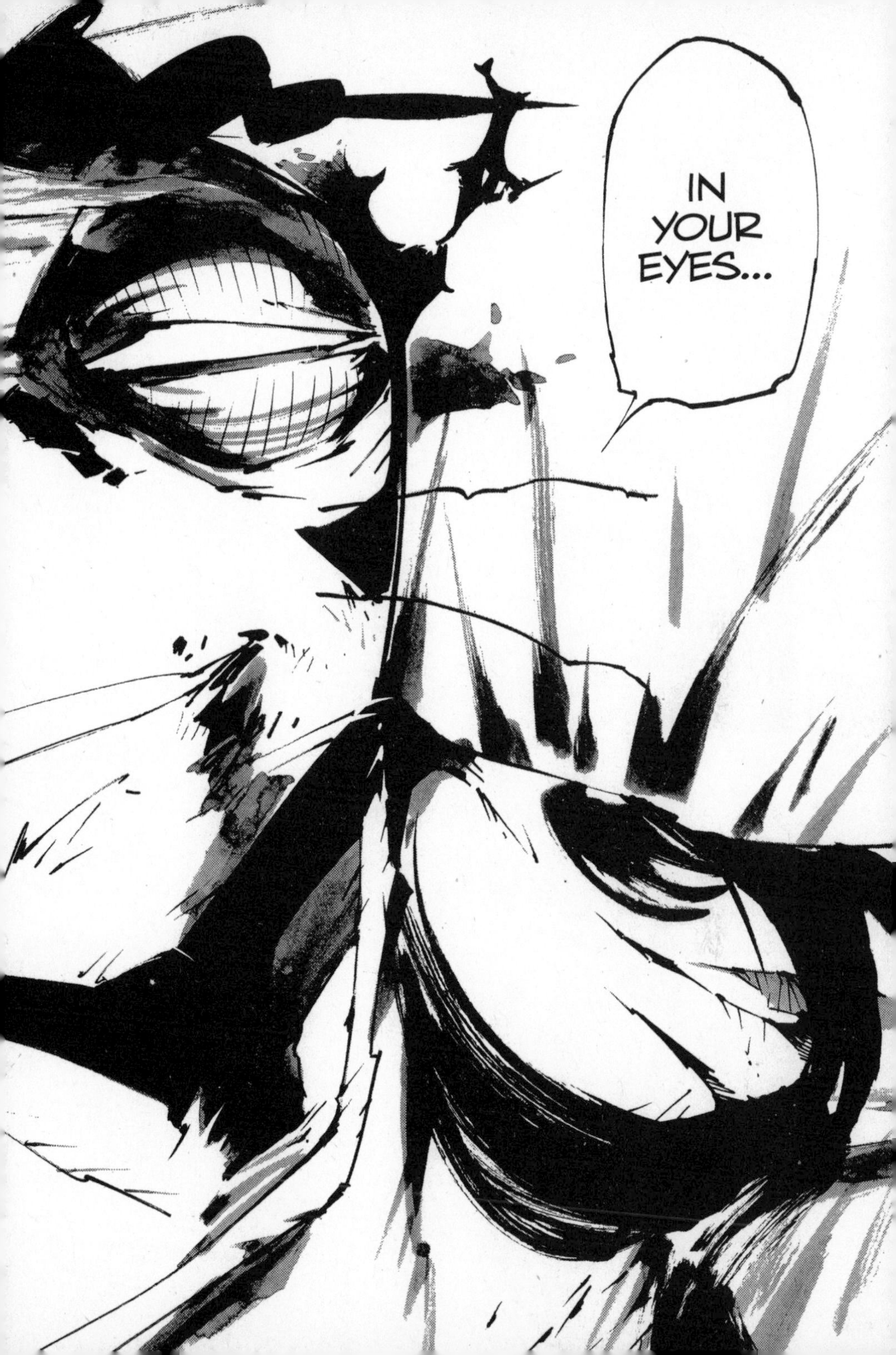
IN YOUR EYES...

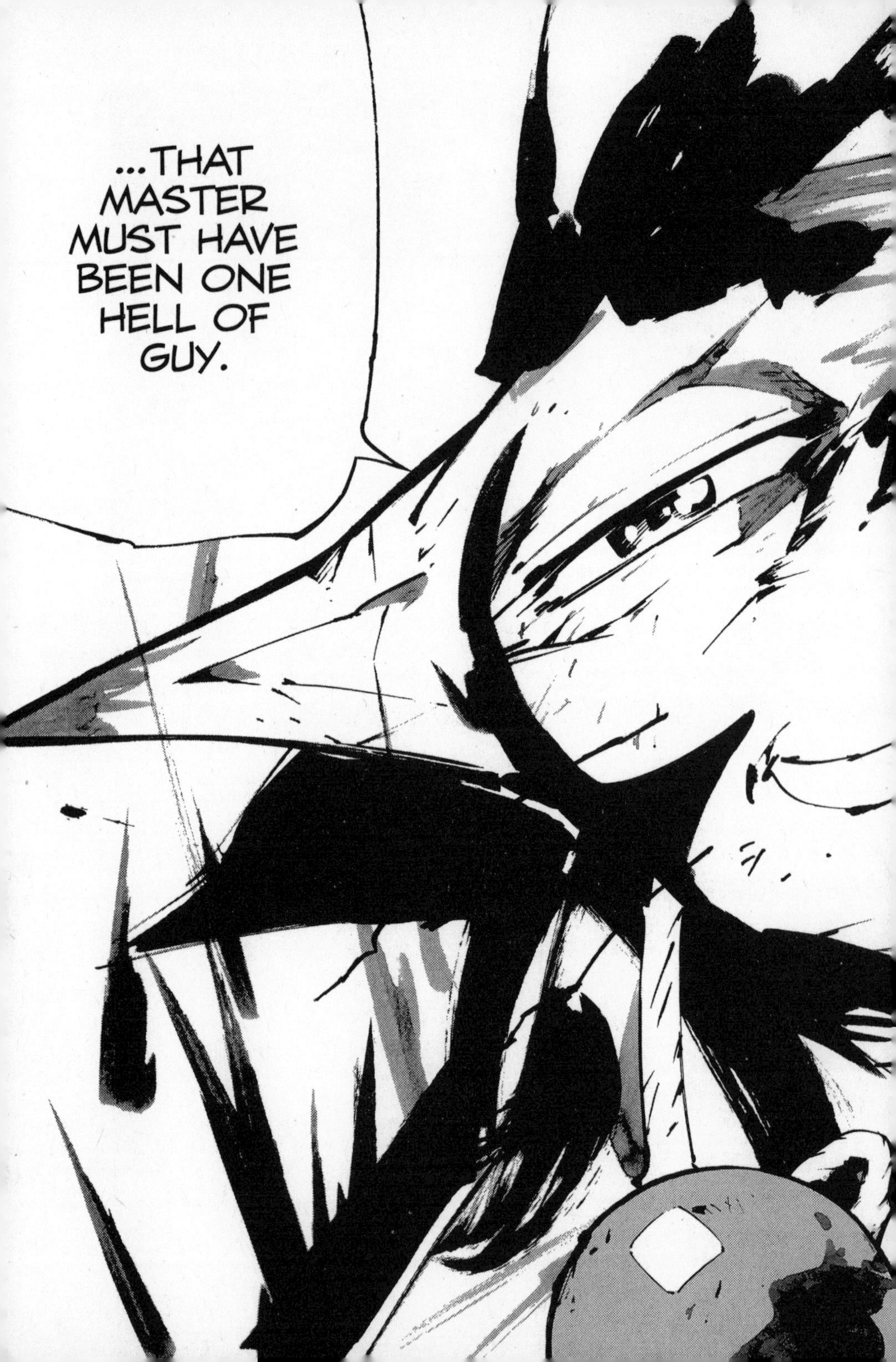
...THAT MASTER MUST HAVE BEEN ONE HELL OF GUY.

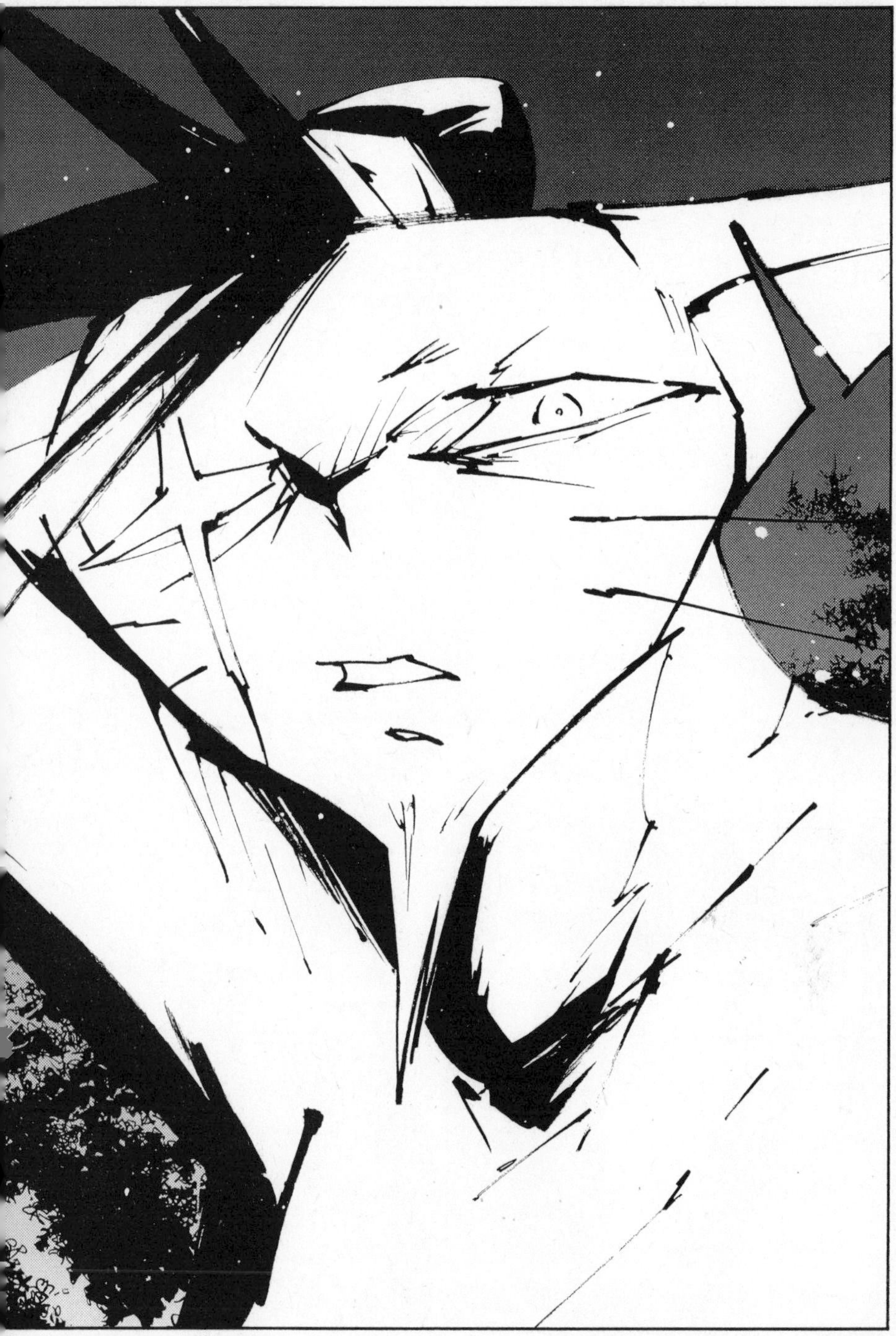

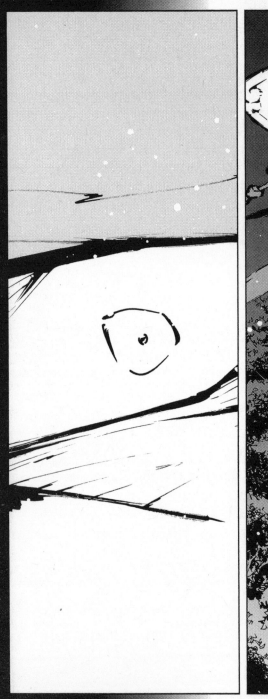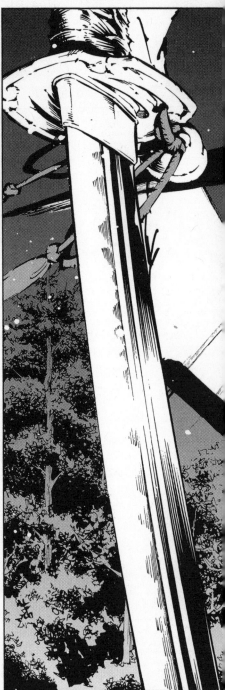

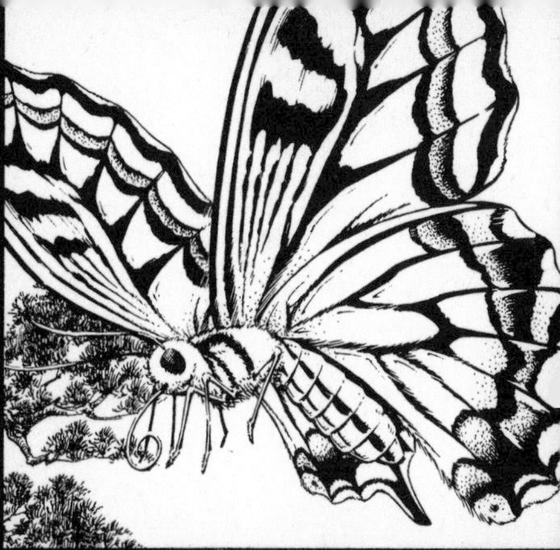
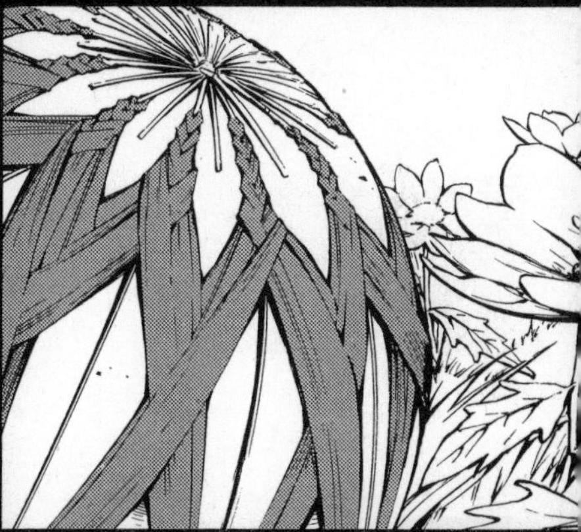
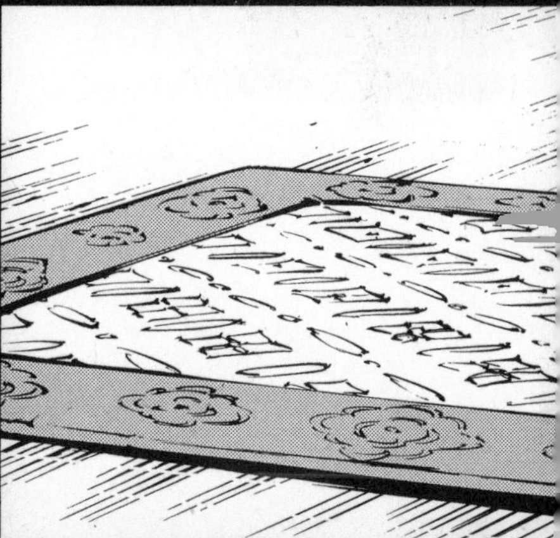
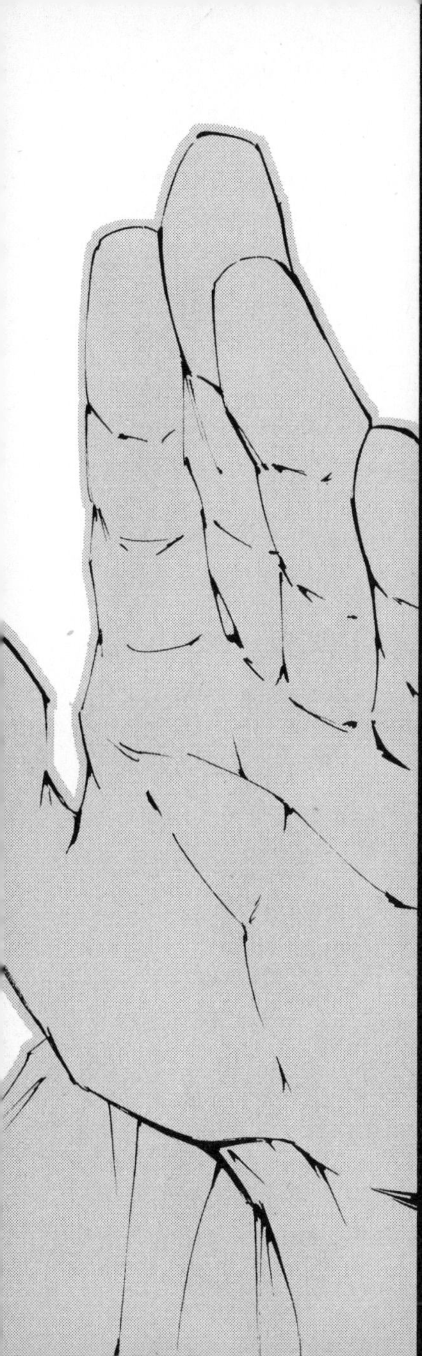

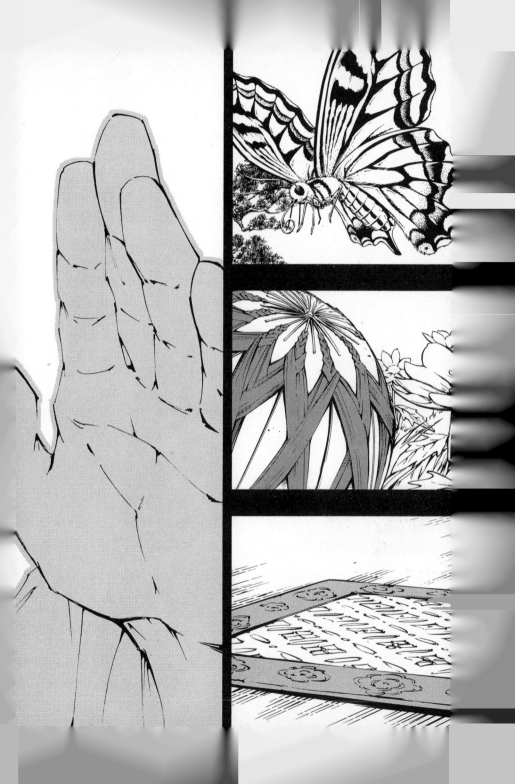

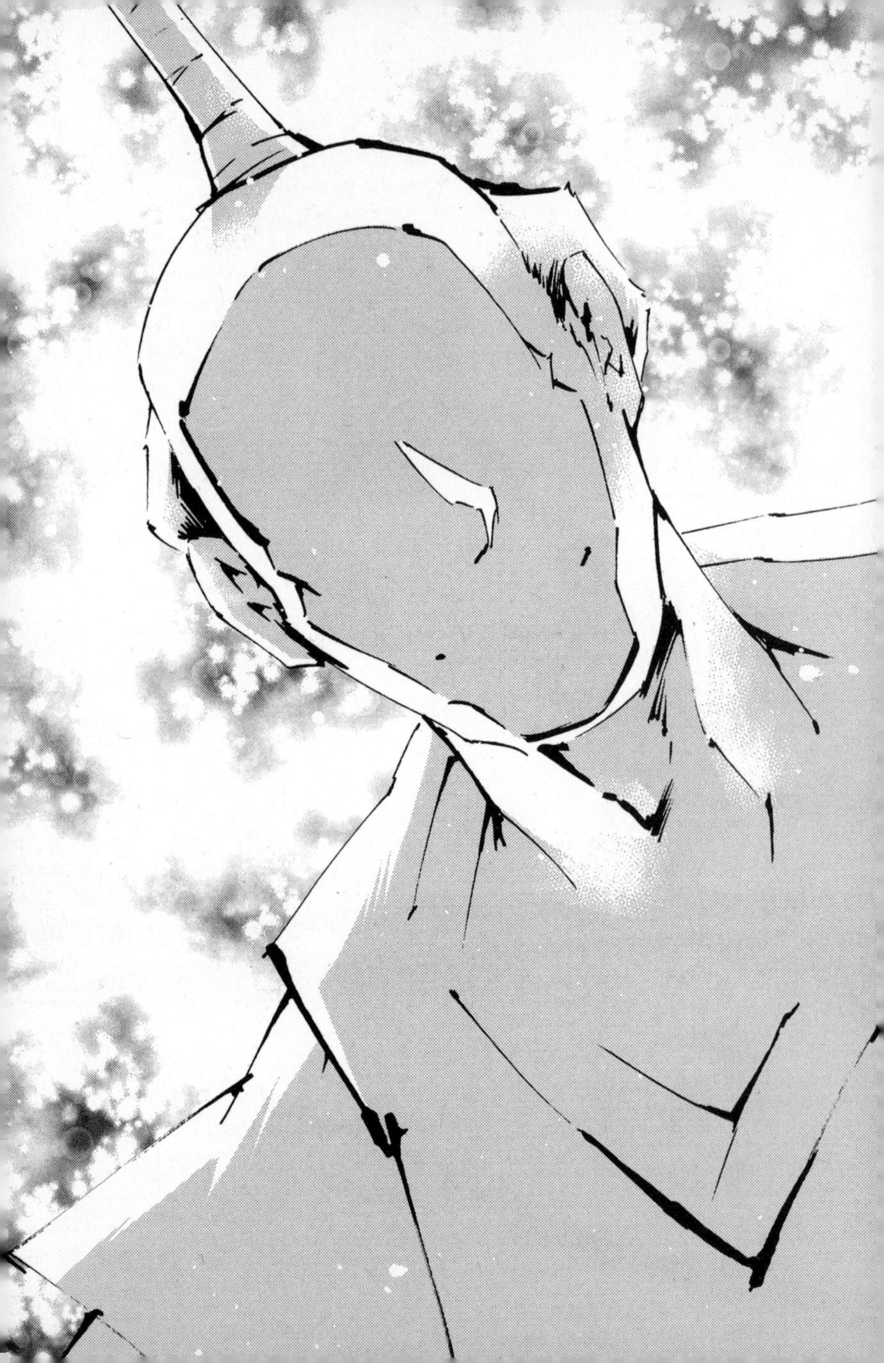

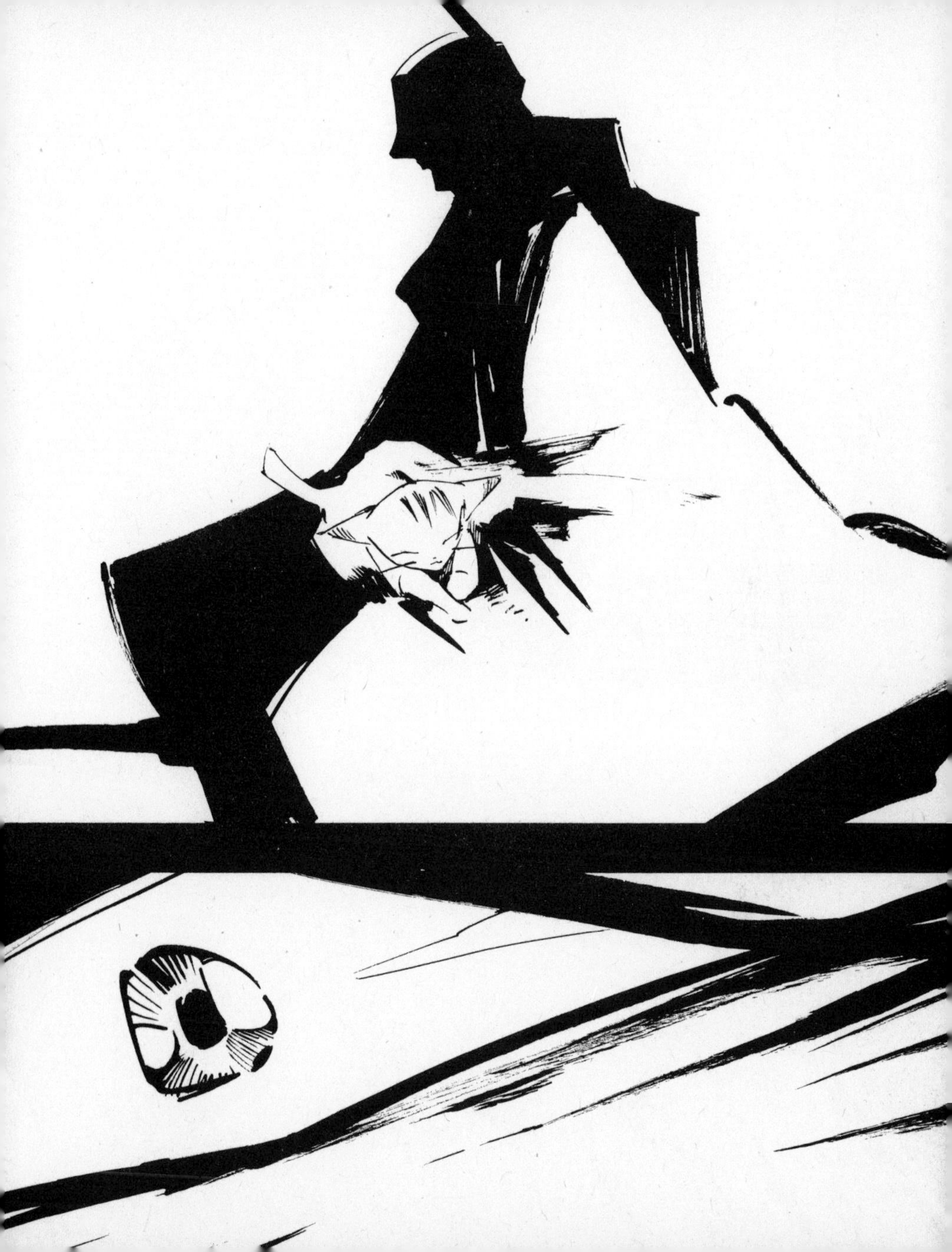

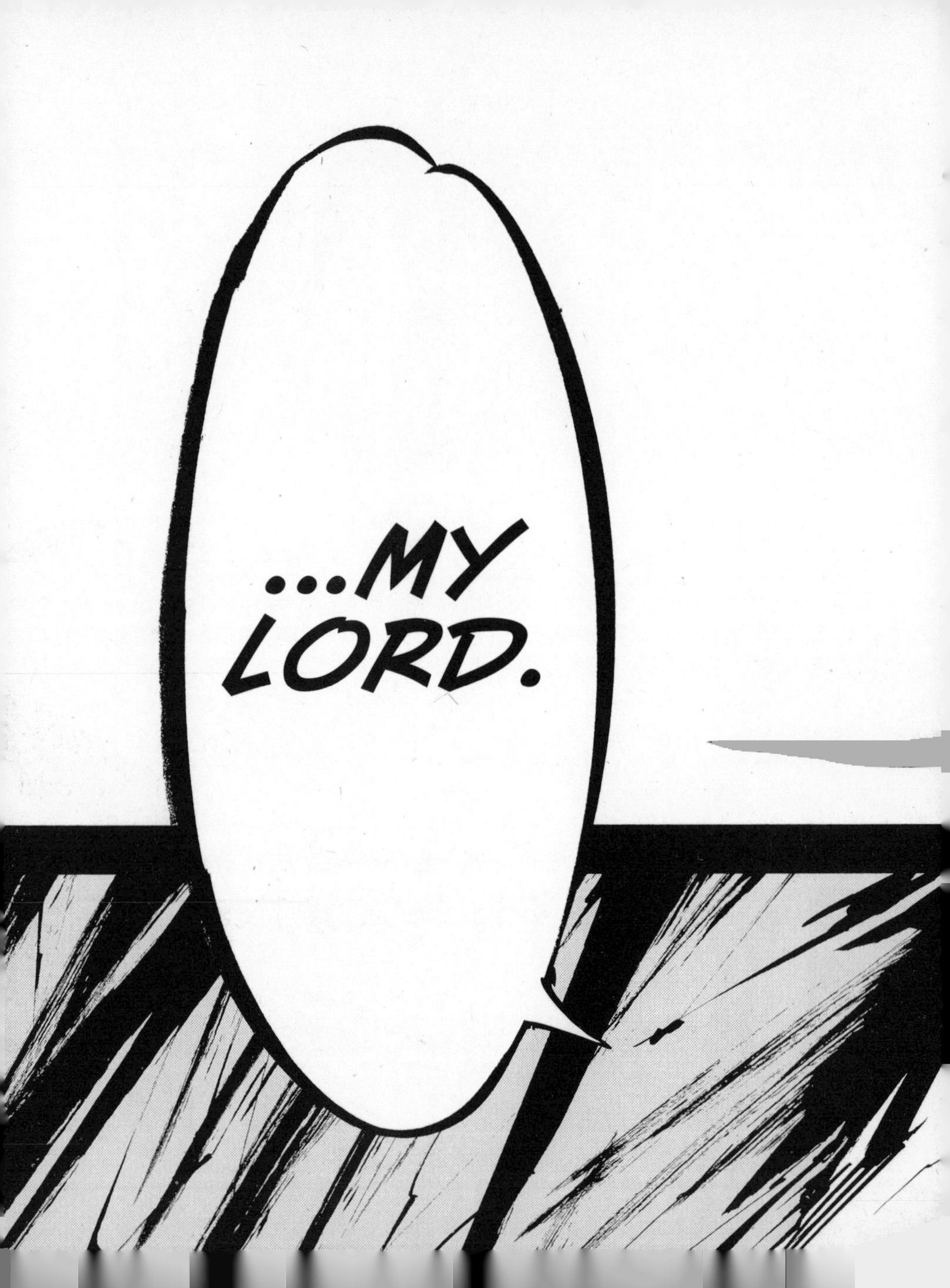
...MY LORD.

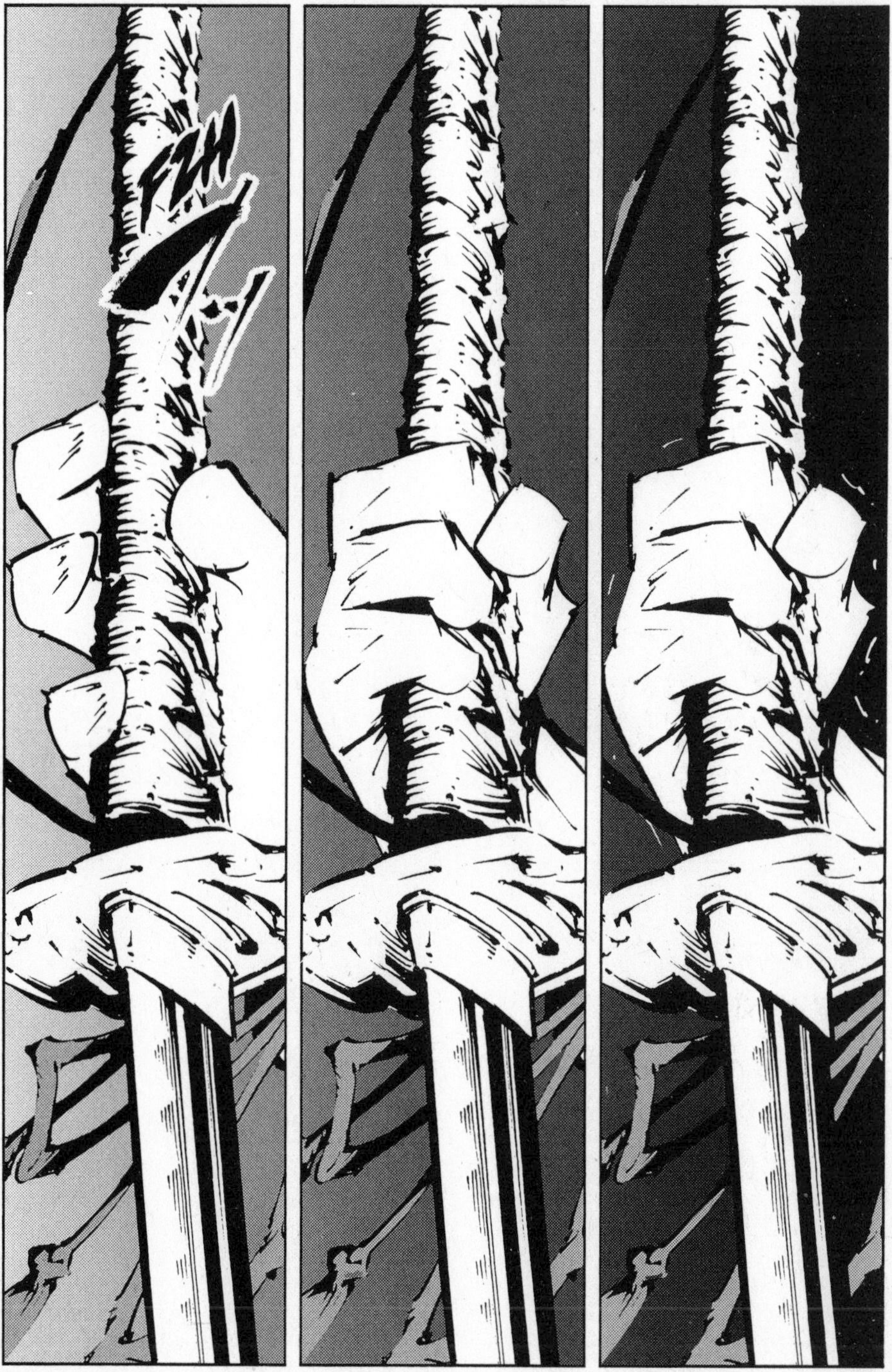
FZH

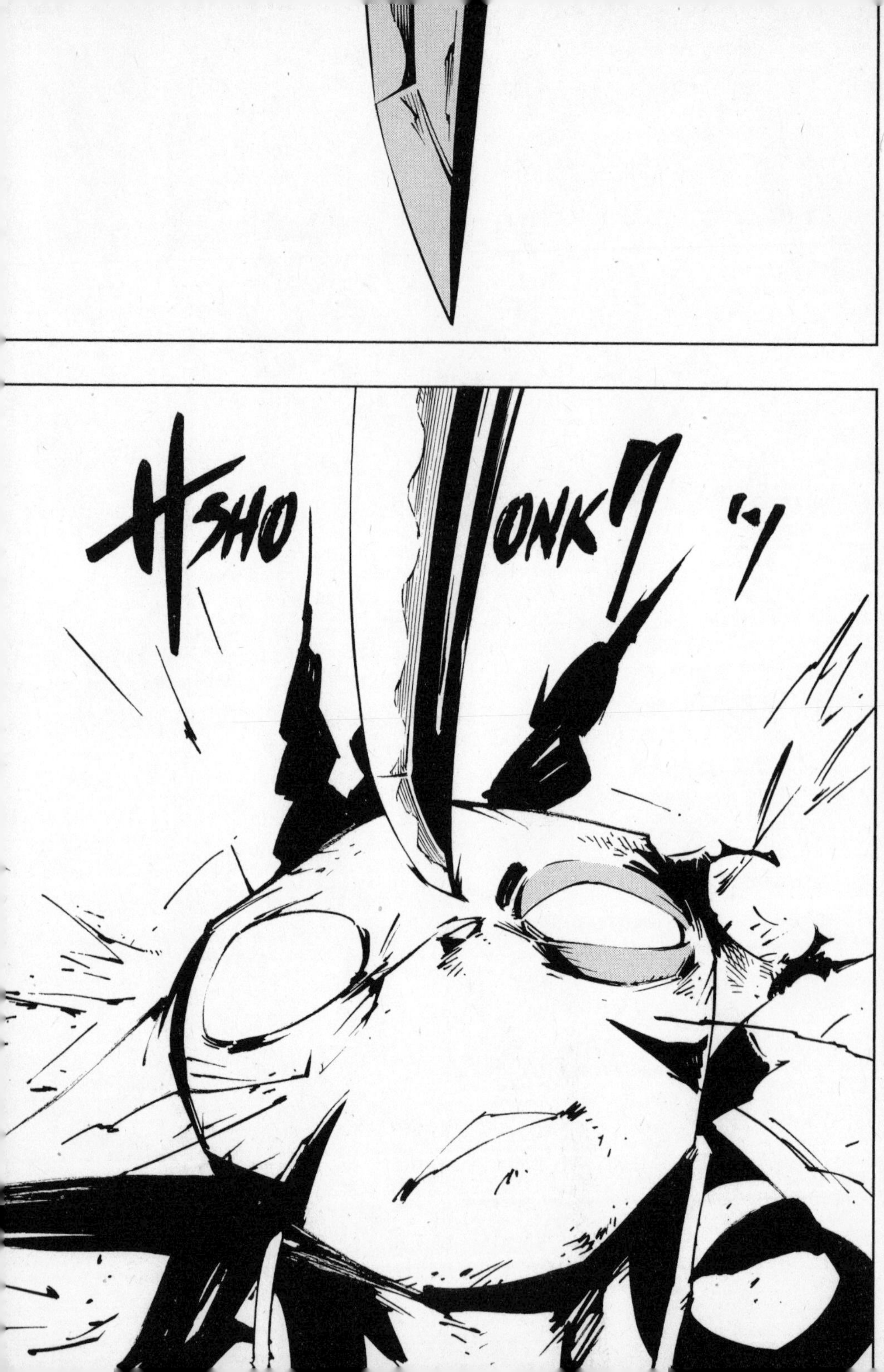
SHO ONK

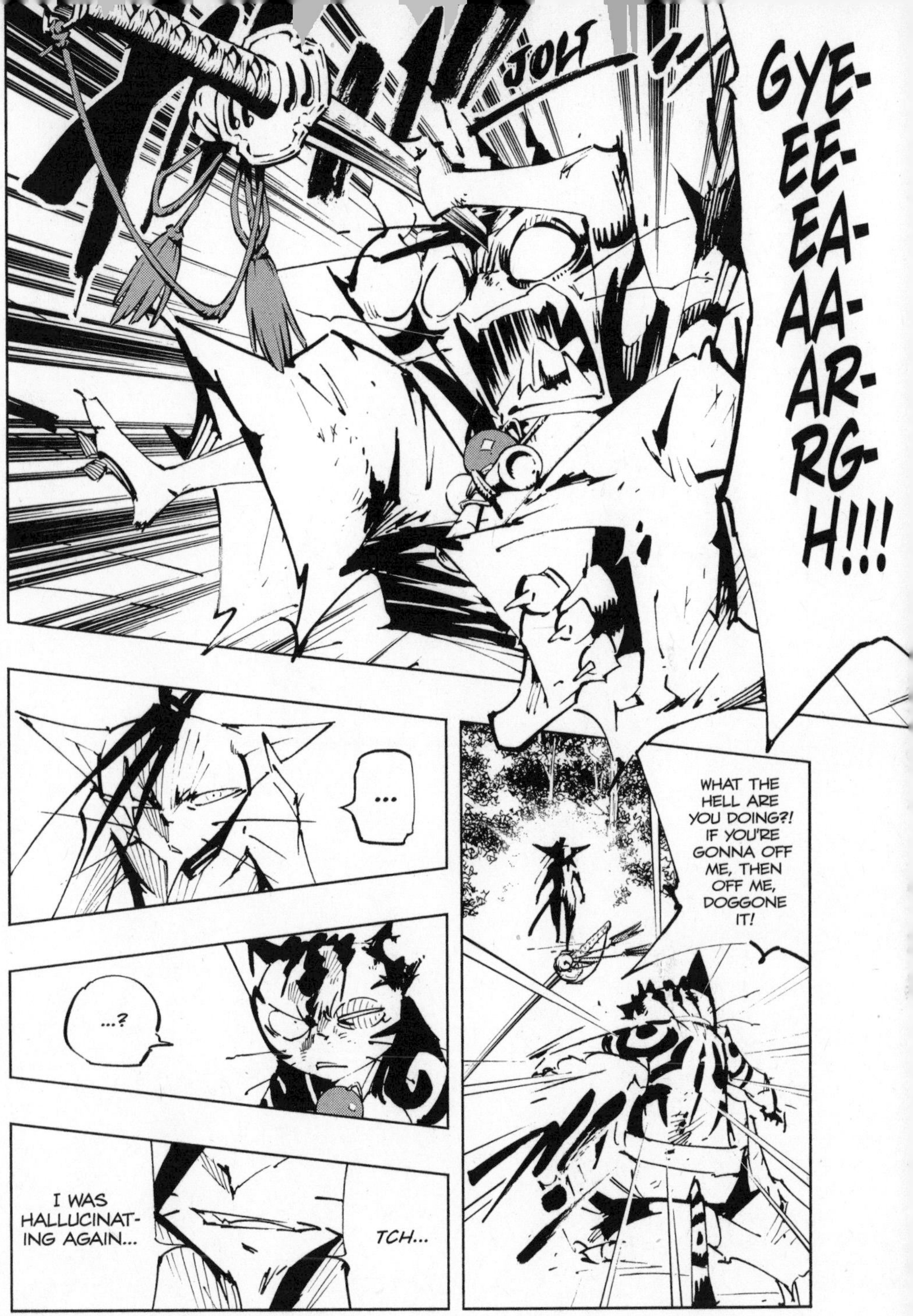
GYE-EE-EA-AA-AR-RG-H!!!
JOLT
WHAT THE HELL ARE YOU DOING?! IF YOU'RE GONNA OFF ME, THEN OFF ME, DOGGONE IT!
...
...?
TCH...
I WAS HALLUCINATING AGAIN...

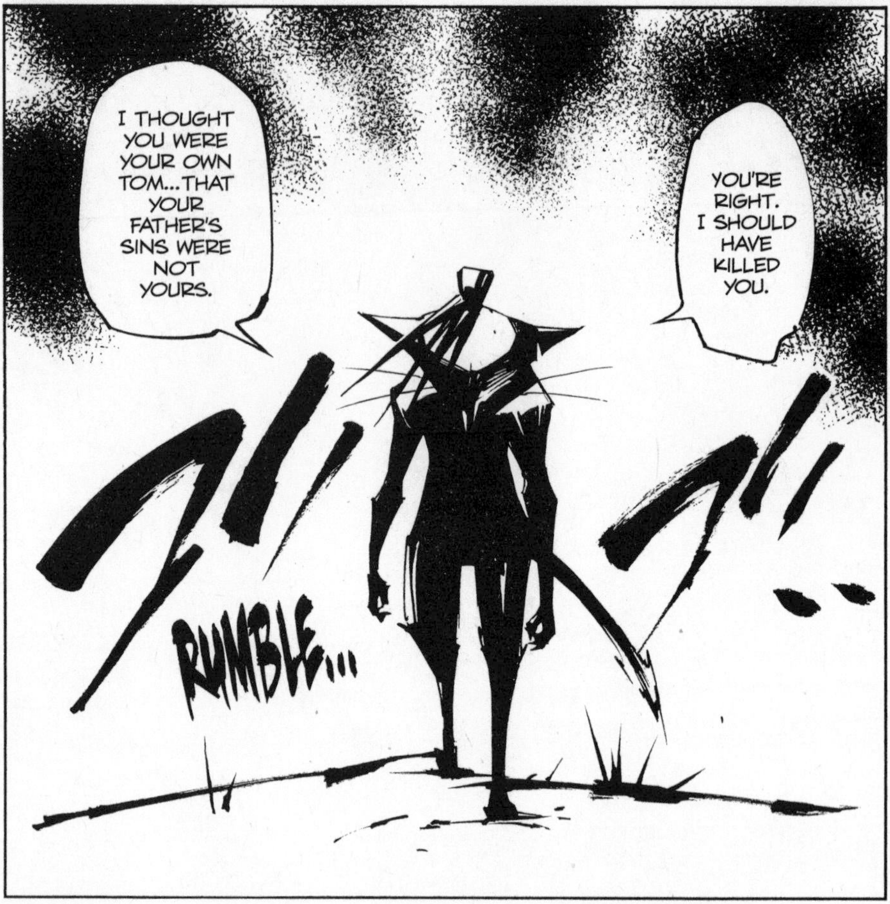
YOU'RE RIGHT. I SHOULD HAVE KILLED YOU.
I THOUGHT YOU WERE YOUR OWN TOM...THAT YOUR FATHER'S SINS WERE NOT YOURS.
RUMBLE...
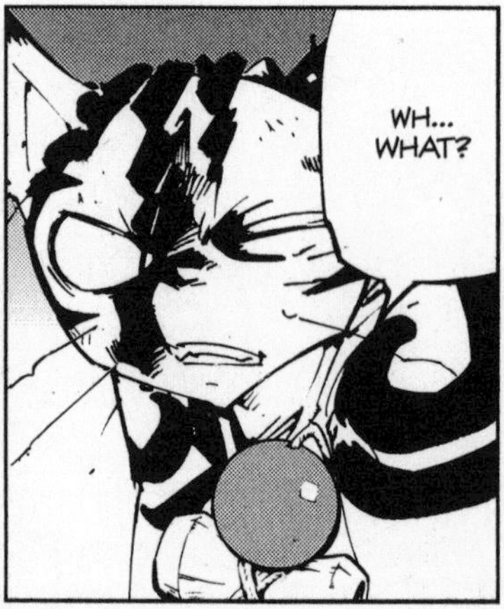
WH... WHAT?
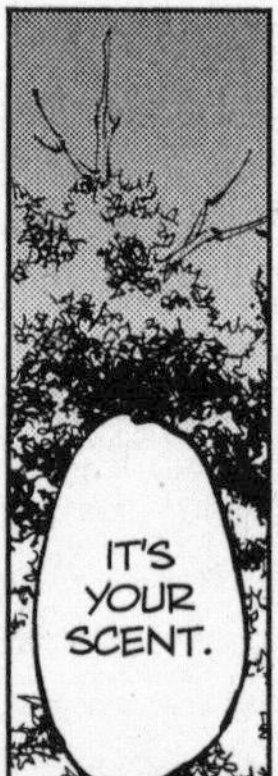
IT'S YOUR SCENT.
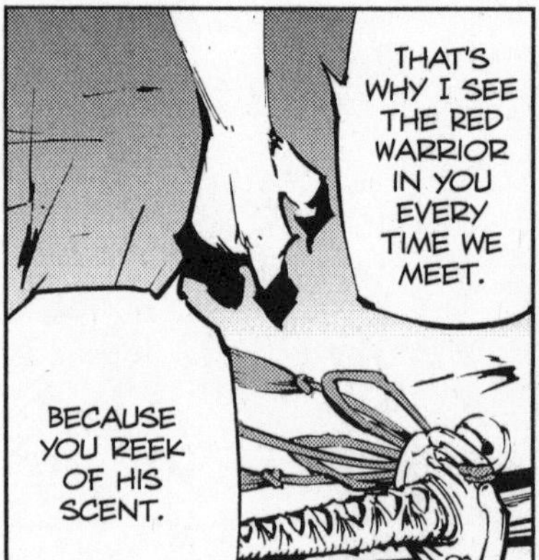
THAT'S WHY I SEE THE RED WARRIOR IN YOU EVERY TIME WE MEET.
BECAUSE YOU REEK OF HIS SCENT.

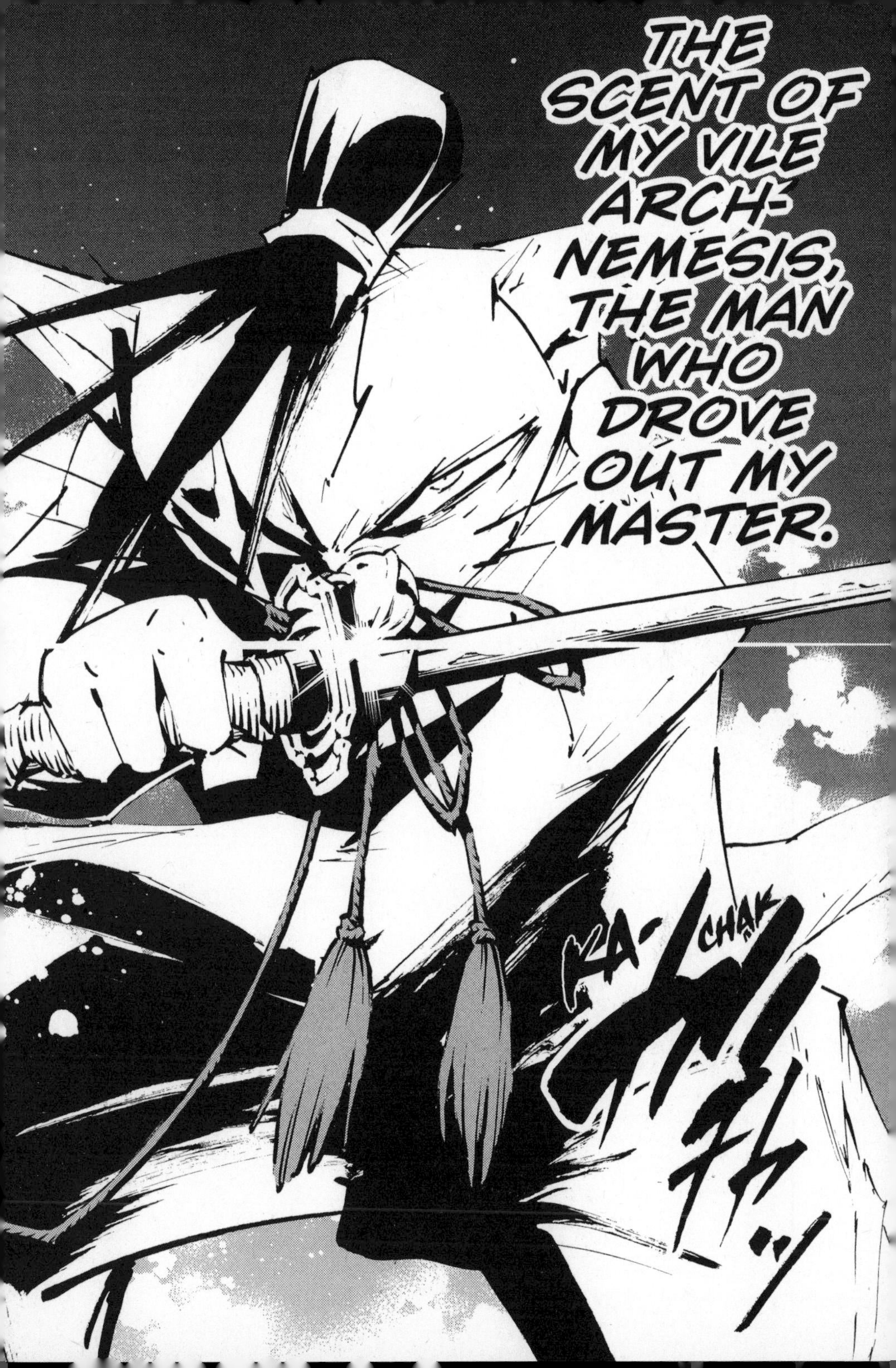
THE SCENT OF MY VILE ARCH-NEMESIS, THE MAN WHO DROVE OUT MY MASTER.
KA-CHAK

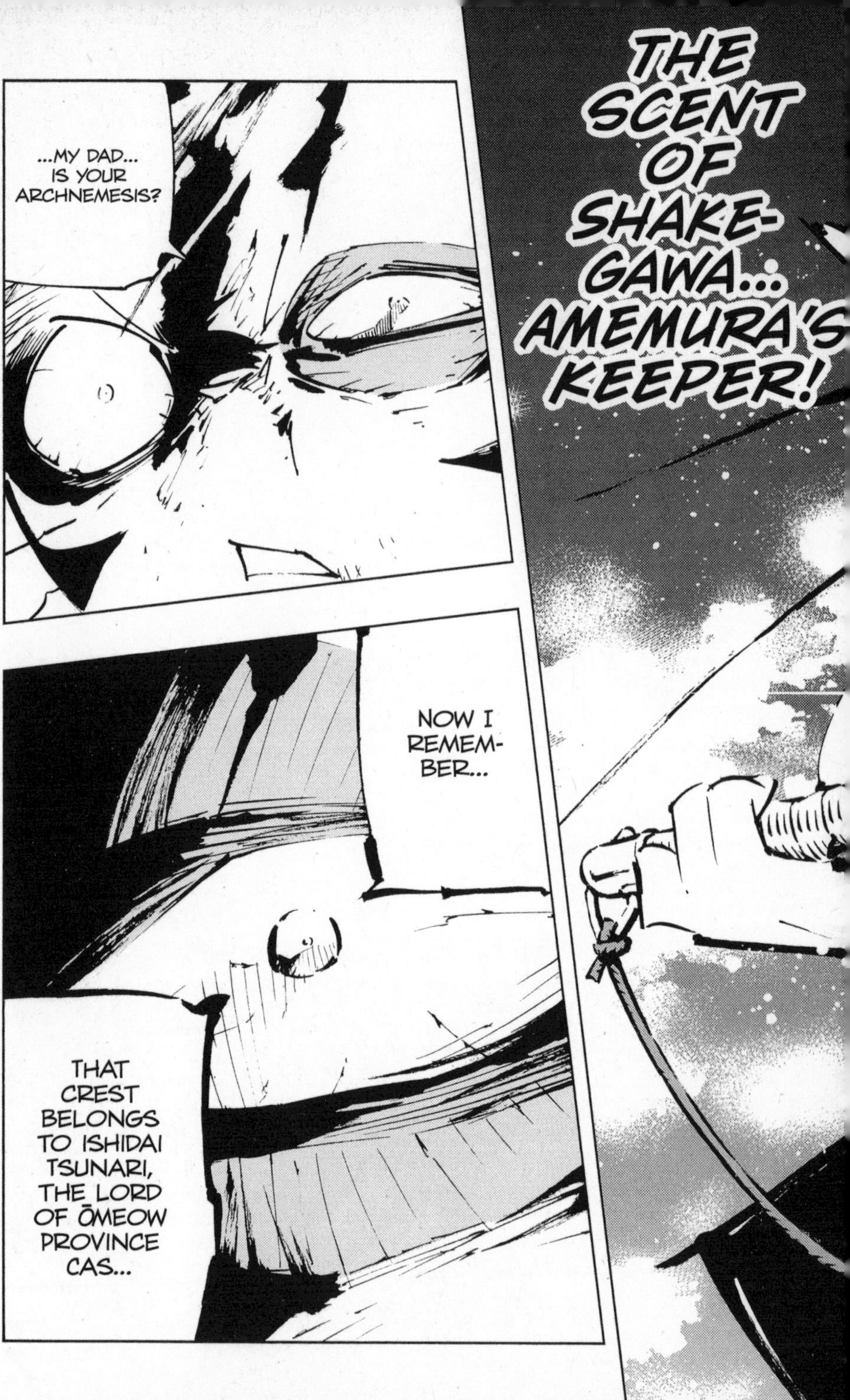
THE SCENT OF SHAKE-GAWA... AMEMURA'S KEEPER!
...MY DAD... IS YOUR ARCHNEMESIS?
NOW I REMEMBER...
THAT CREST BELONGS TO ISHIDAI TSUNARI, THE LORD OF ŌMEOW PROVINCE CAS...

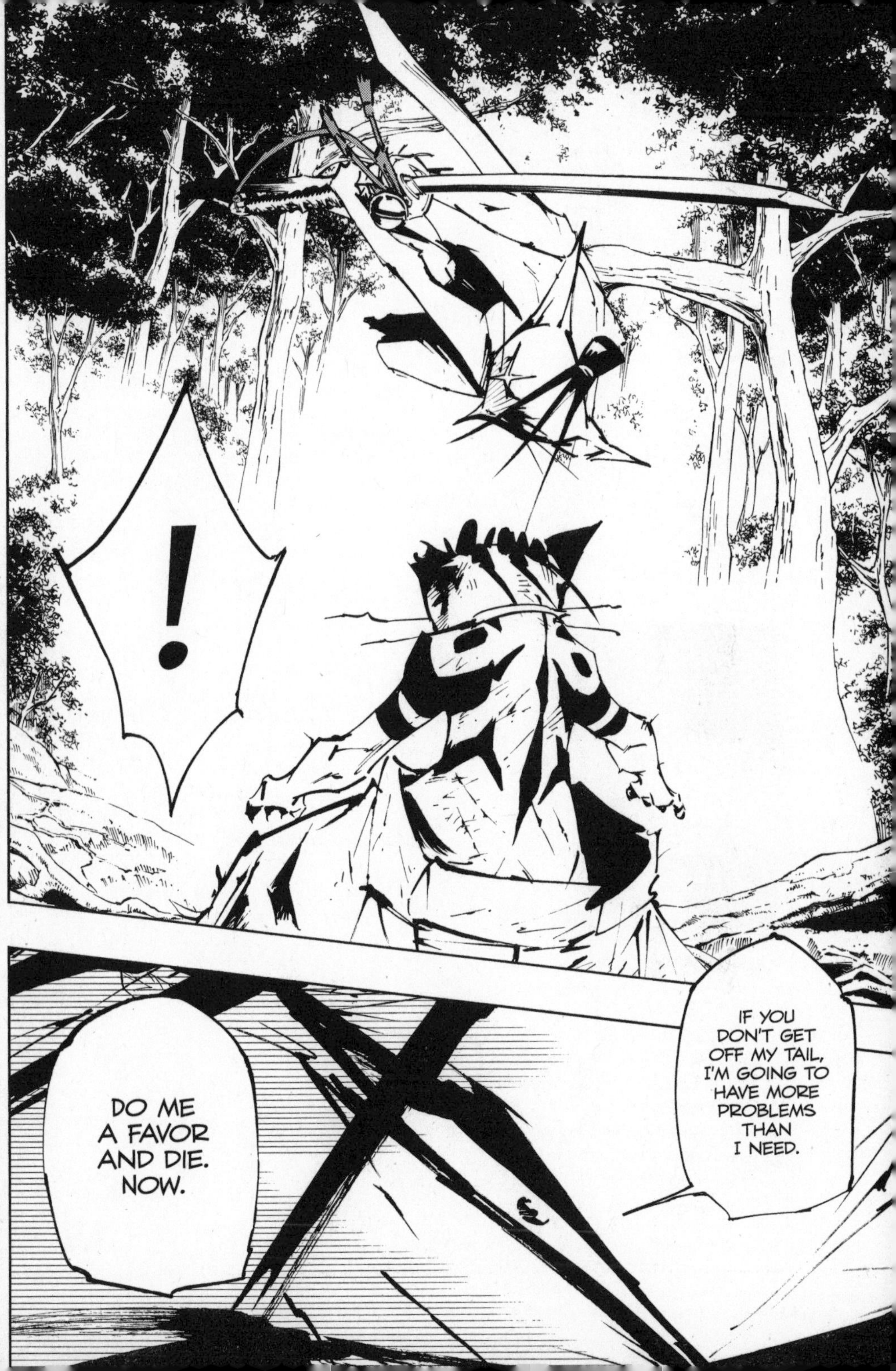
!
IF YOU DON'T GET OFF MY TAIL, I'M GOING TO HAVE MORE PROBLEMS THAN I NEED.
DO ME A FAVOR AND DIE. NOW.

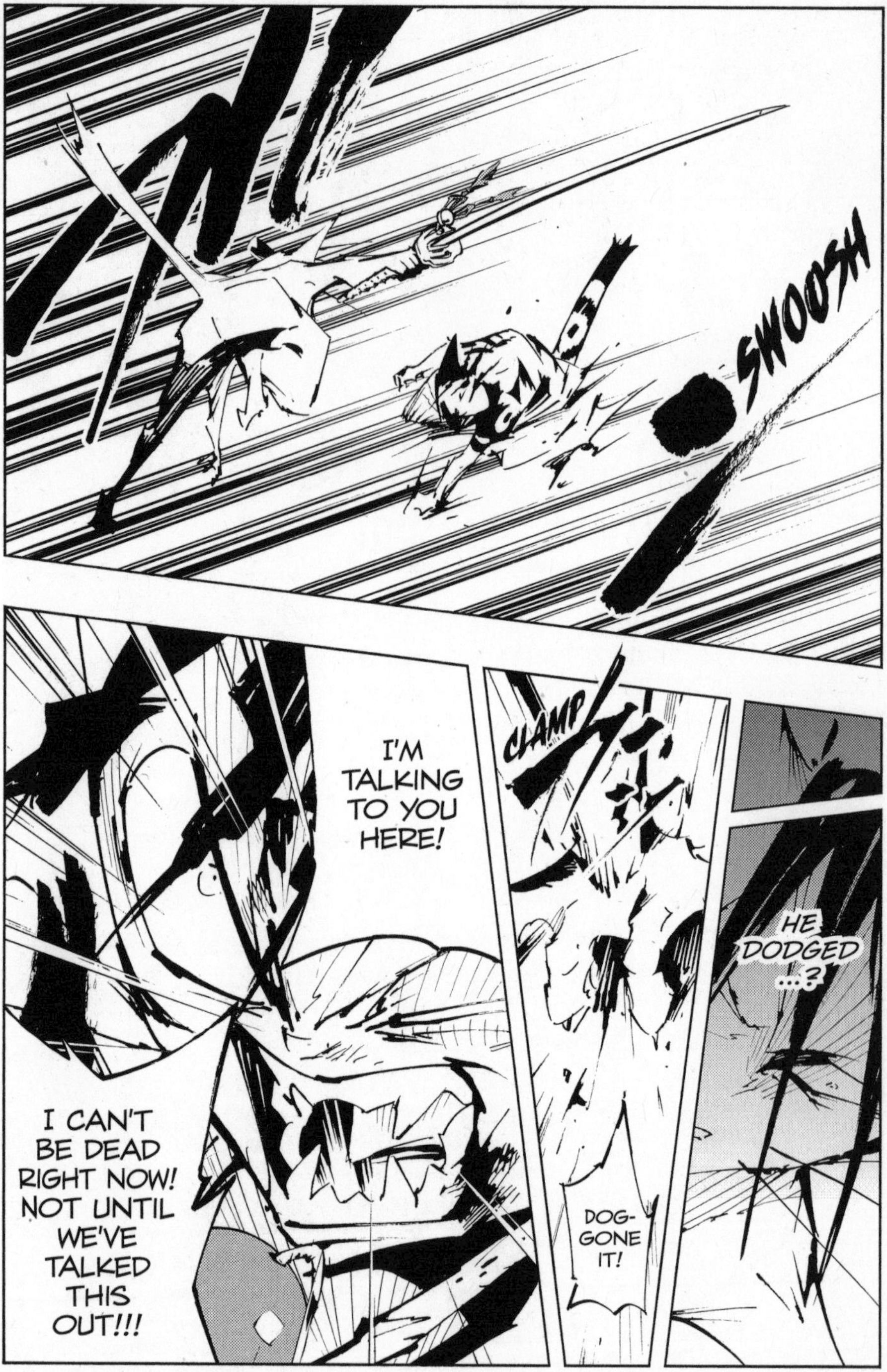
SWOOSH
HE DODGED ...?
CLAMP
DOG-GONE IT!
I'M TALKING TO YOU HERE!
I CAN'T BE DEAD RIGHT NOW! NOT UNTIL WE'VE TALKED THIS OUT!!!

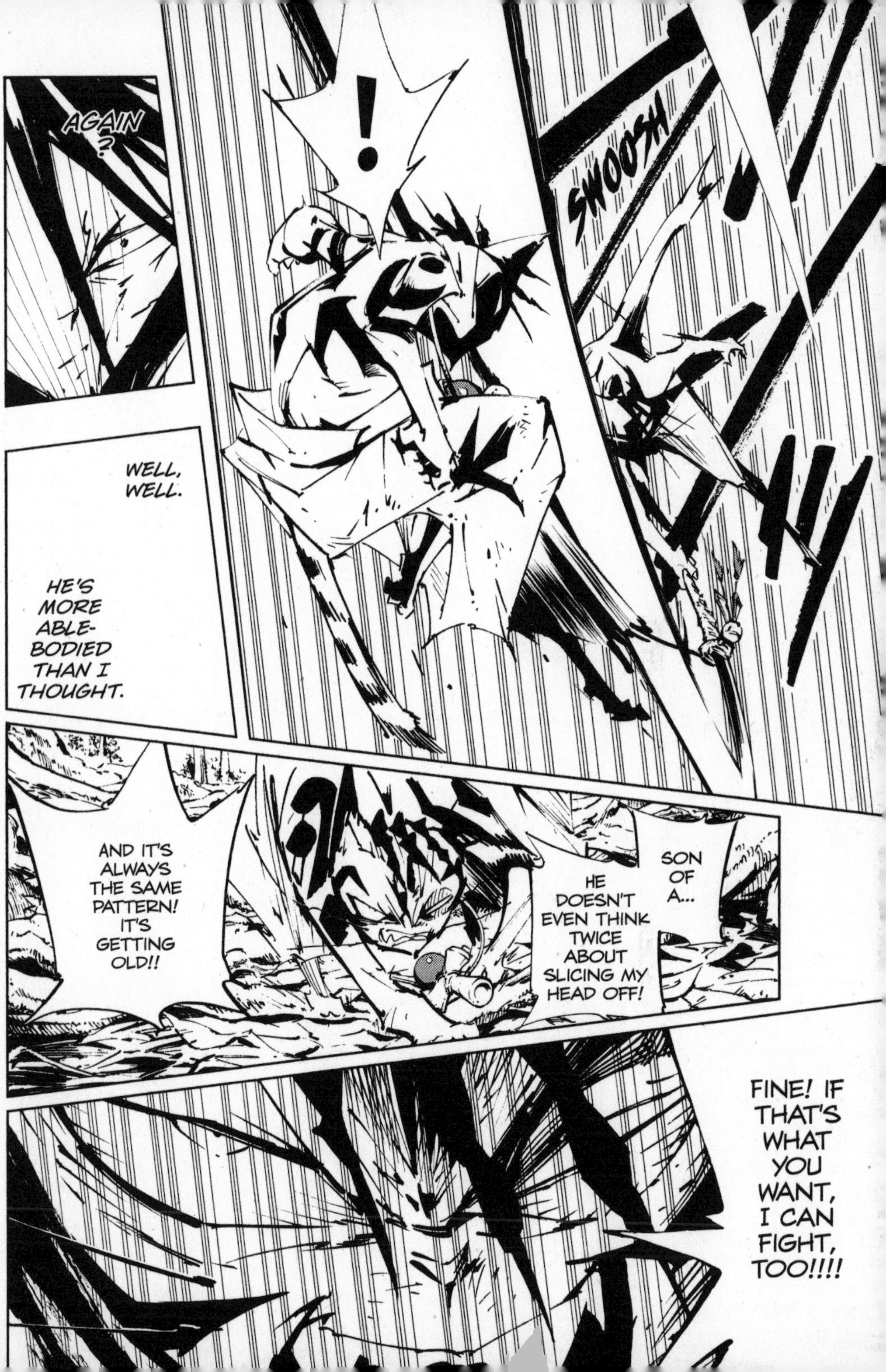
SWOOSH
!
AGAIN?
WELL, WELL.
HE'S MORE ABLE-BODIED THAN I THOUGHT.
SON OF A...
HE DOESN'T EVEN THINK TWICE ABOUT SLICING MY HEAD OFF!
AND IT'S ALWAYS THE SAME PATTERN! IT'S GETTING OLD!!
FINE! IF THAT'S WHAT YOU WANT, I CAN FIGHT, TOO!!!!

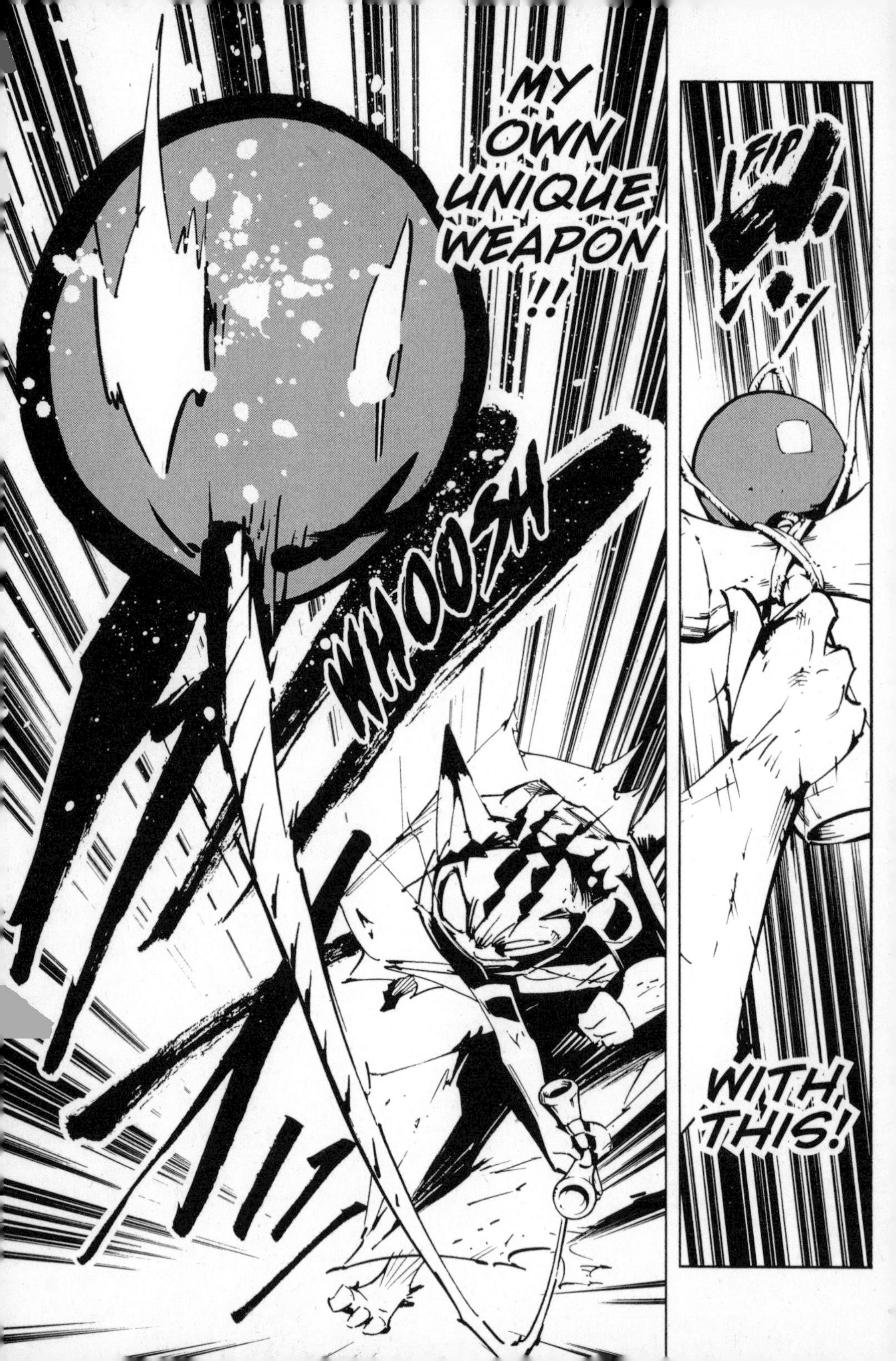
FIP
WITH THIS!
MY OWN UNIQUE WEAPON!!
WHOOSH

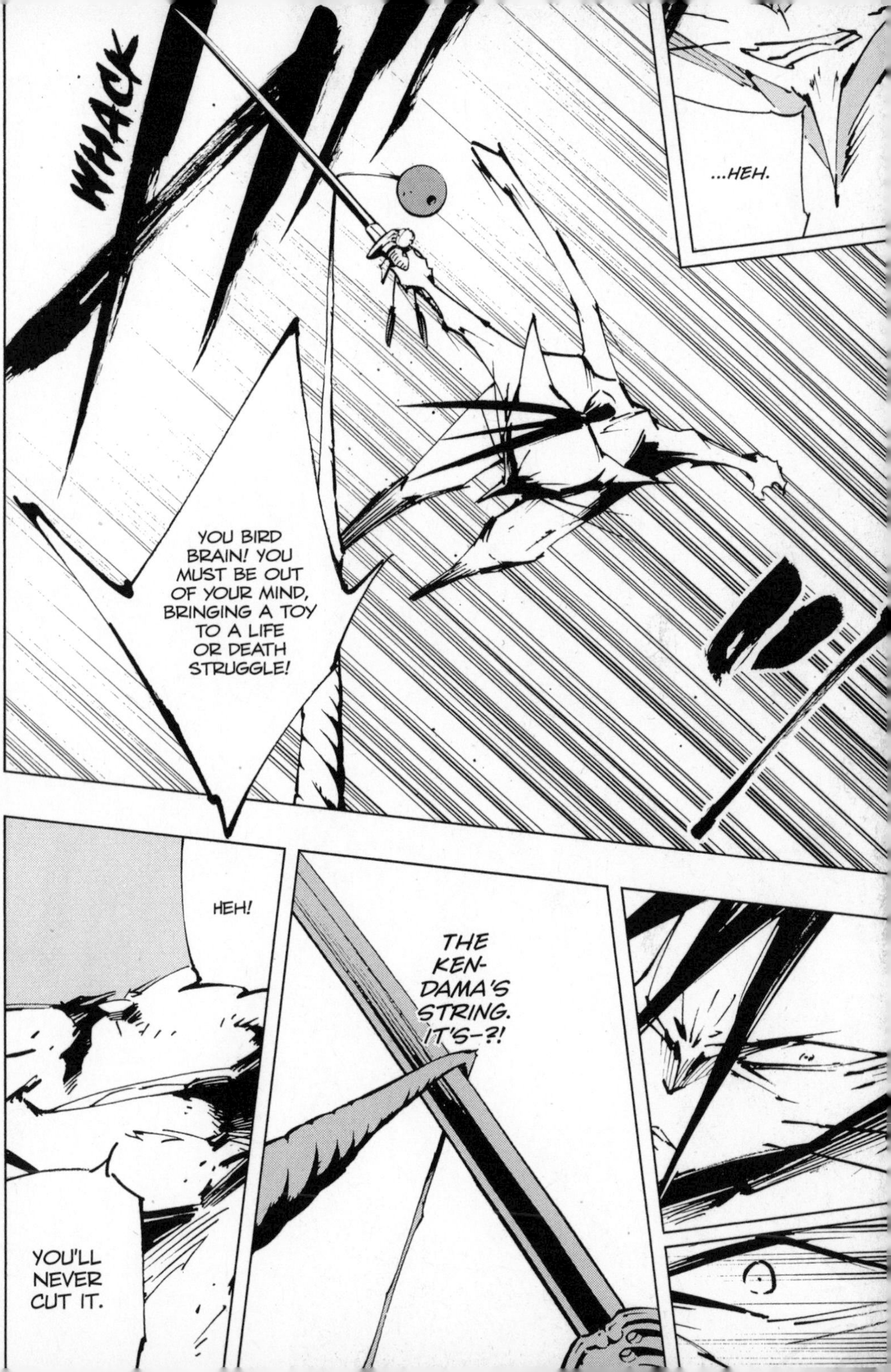
...HEH.
WHACK
YOU BIRD BRAIN! YOU MUST BE OUT OF YOUR MIND, BRINGING A TOY TO A LIFE OR DEATH STRUGGLE!
THE KEN-DAMA'S STRING. IT'S-?!
HEH!
YOU'LL NEVER CUT IT.

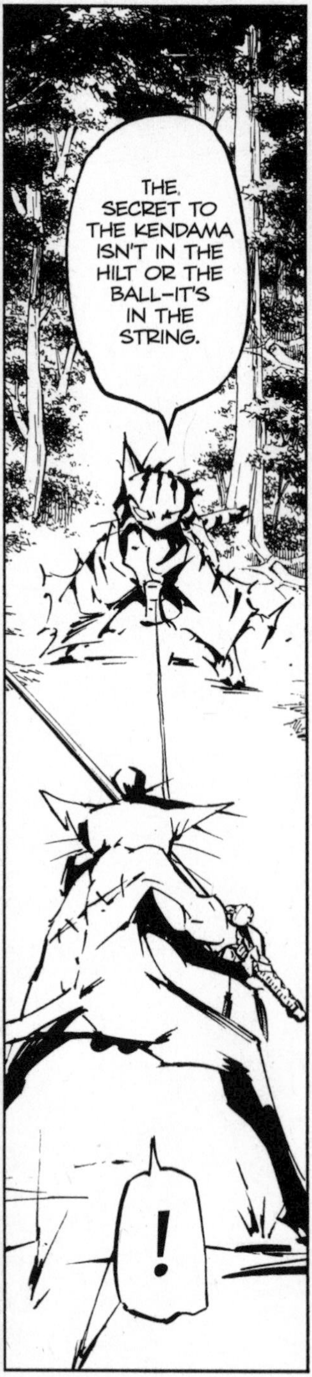
THE SECRET TO THE KENDAMA ISN'T IN THE HILT OR THE BALL–IT'S IN THE STRING.
!
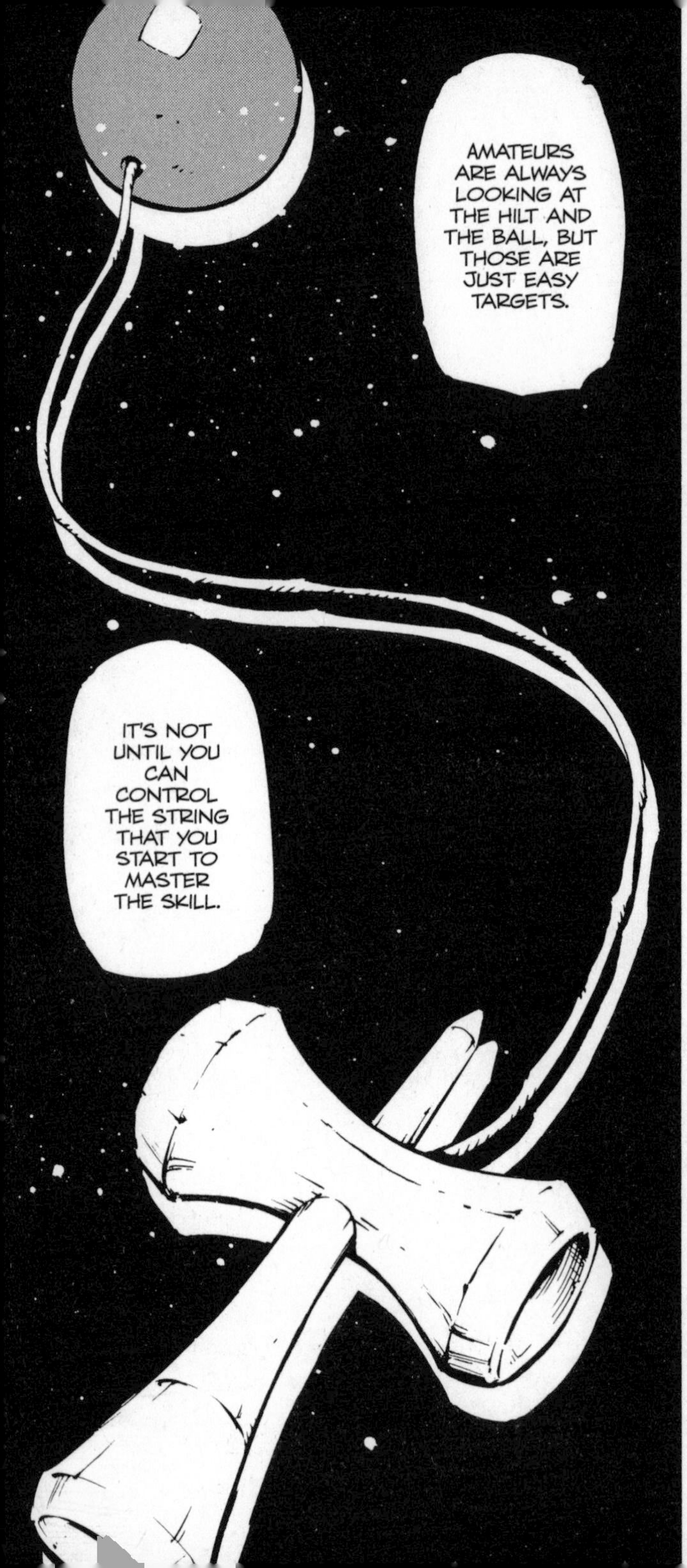
AMATEURS ARE ALWAYS LOOKING AT THE HILT AND THE BALL, BUT THOSE ARE JUST EASY TARGETS.
IT'S NOT UNTIL YOU CAN CONTROL THE STRING THAT YOU START TO MASTER THE SKILL.

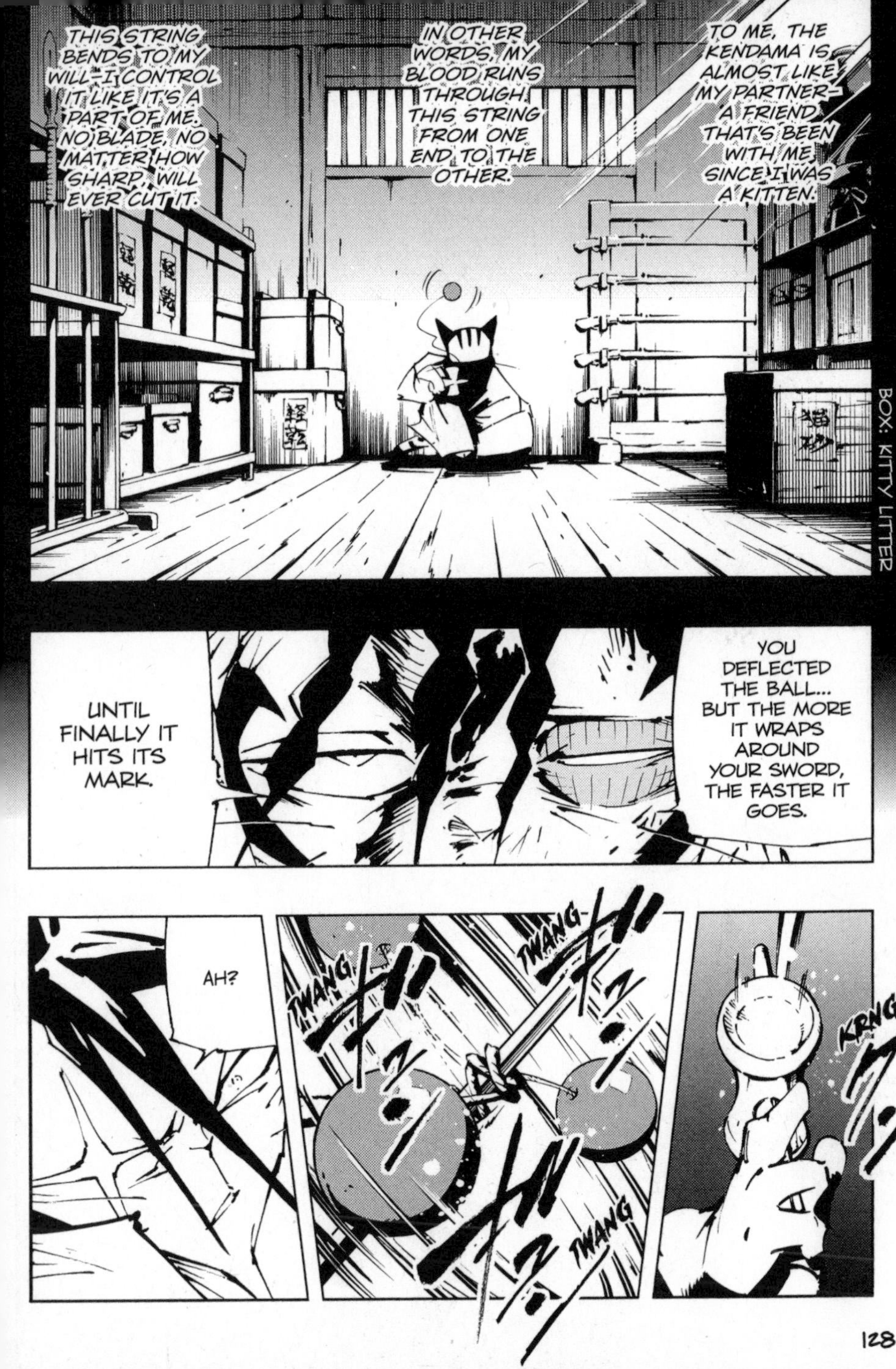
TO ME, THE KENDAMA IS ALMOST LIKE MY PARTNER— A FRIEND THAT'S BEEN WITH ME SINCE I WAS A KITTEN.
IN OTHER WORDS, MY BLOOD RUNS THROUGH THIS STRING FROM ONE END TO THE OTHER.
THIS STRING BENDS TO MY WILL—I CONTROL IT LIKE IT'S A PART OF ME. NO BLADE, NO MATTER HOW SHARP, WILL EVER CUT IT.
BOX: KITTY LITTER
YOU DEFLECTED THE BALL... BUT THE MORE IT WRAPS AROUND YOUR SWORD, THE FASTER IT GOES.
UNTIL FINALLY IT HITS ITS MARK.
KRNG
TWANG
TWANG
TWANG
AH?

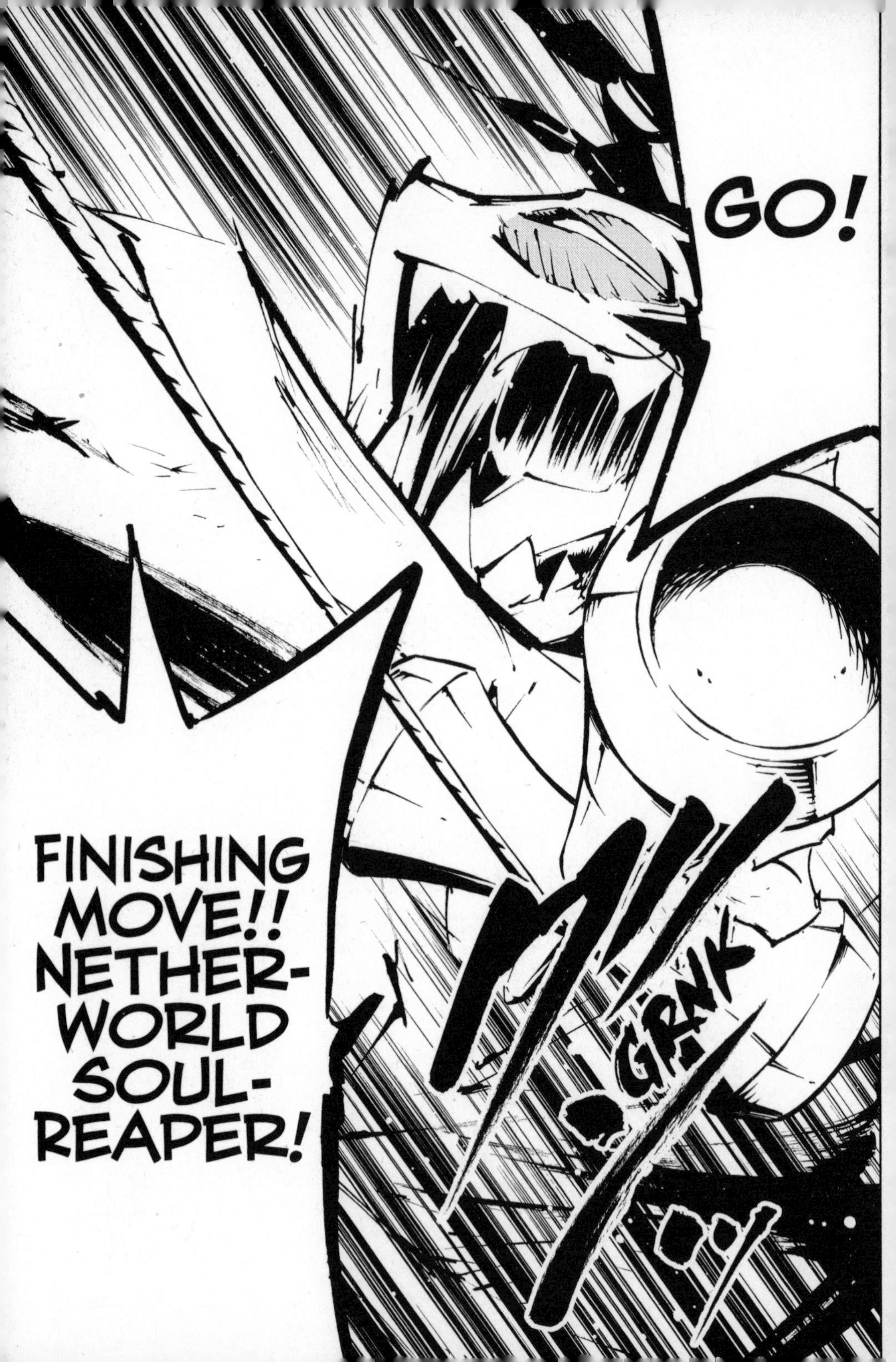
GO!
FINISHING MOVE!! NETHER-WORLD SOUL-REAPER!
GRNK

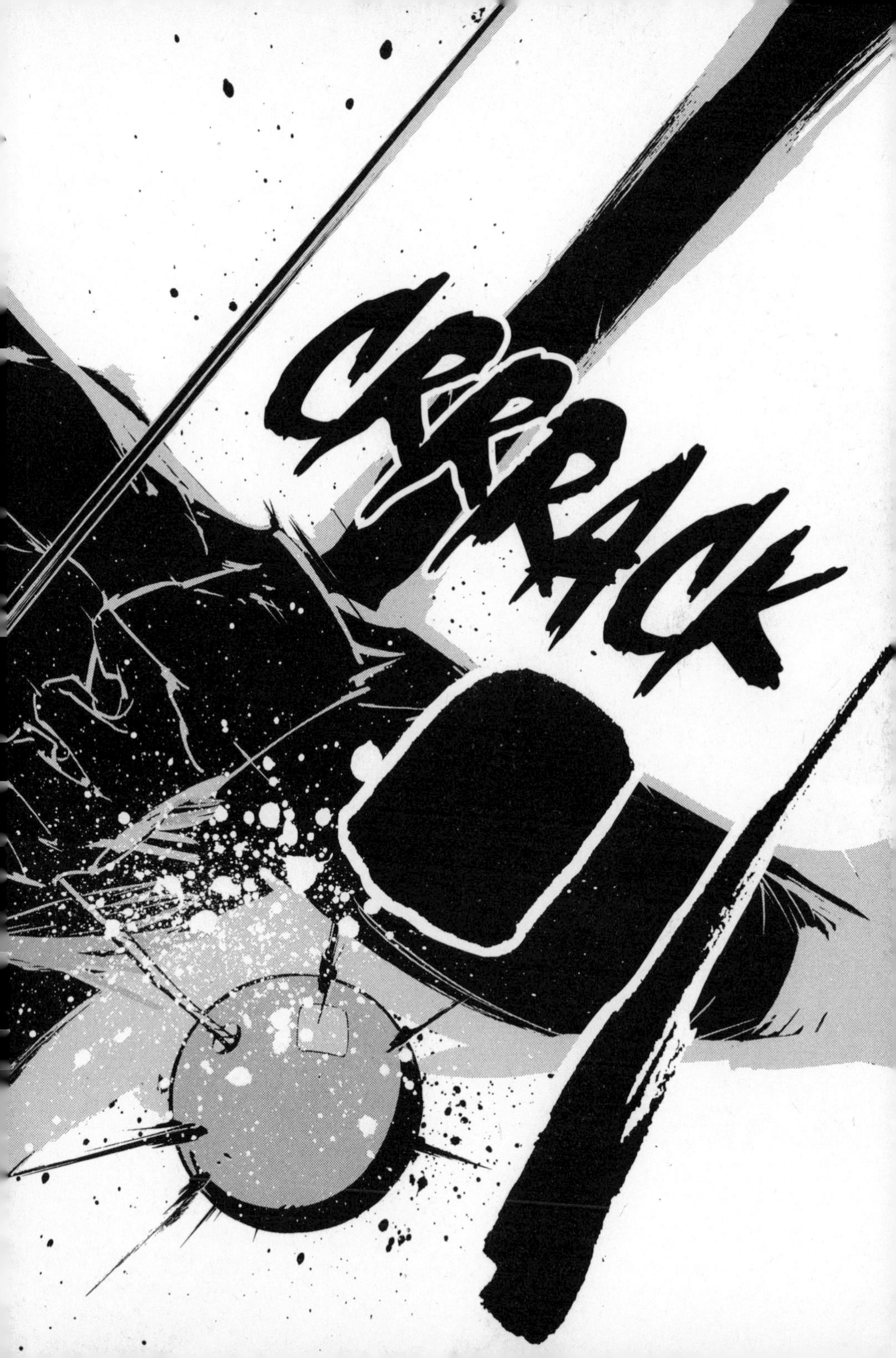
CRRRACK

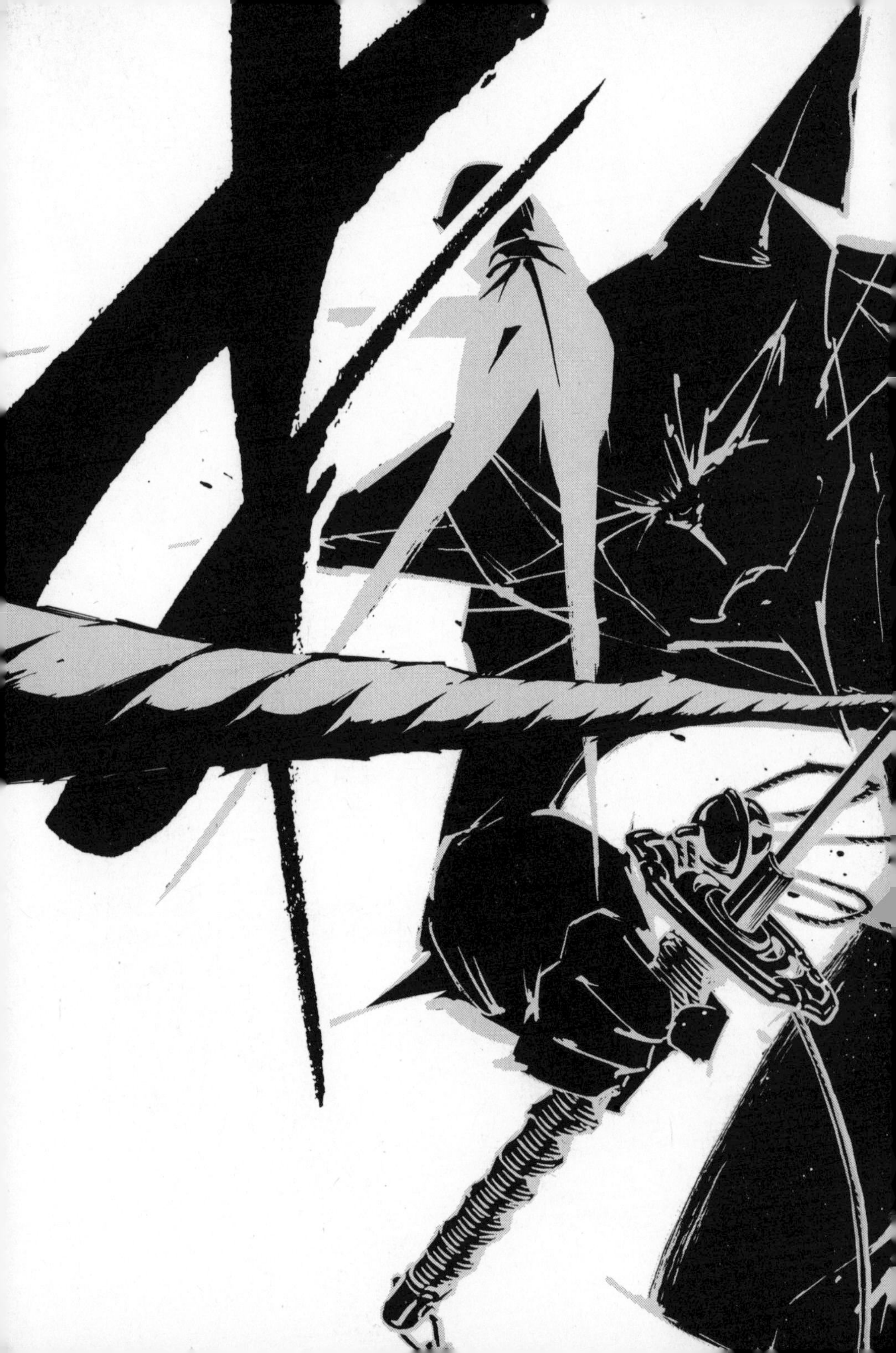

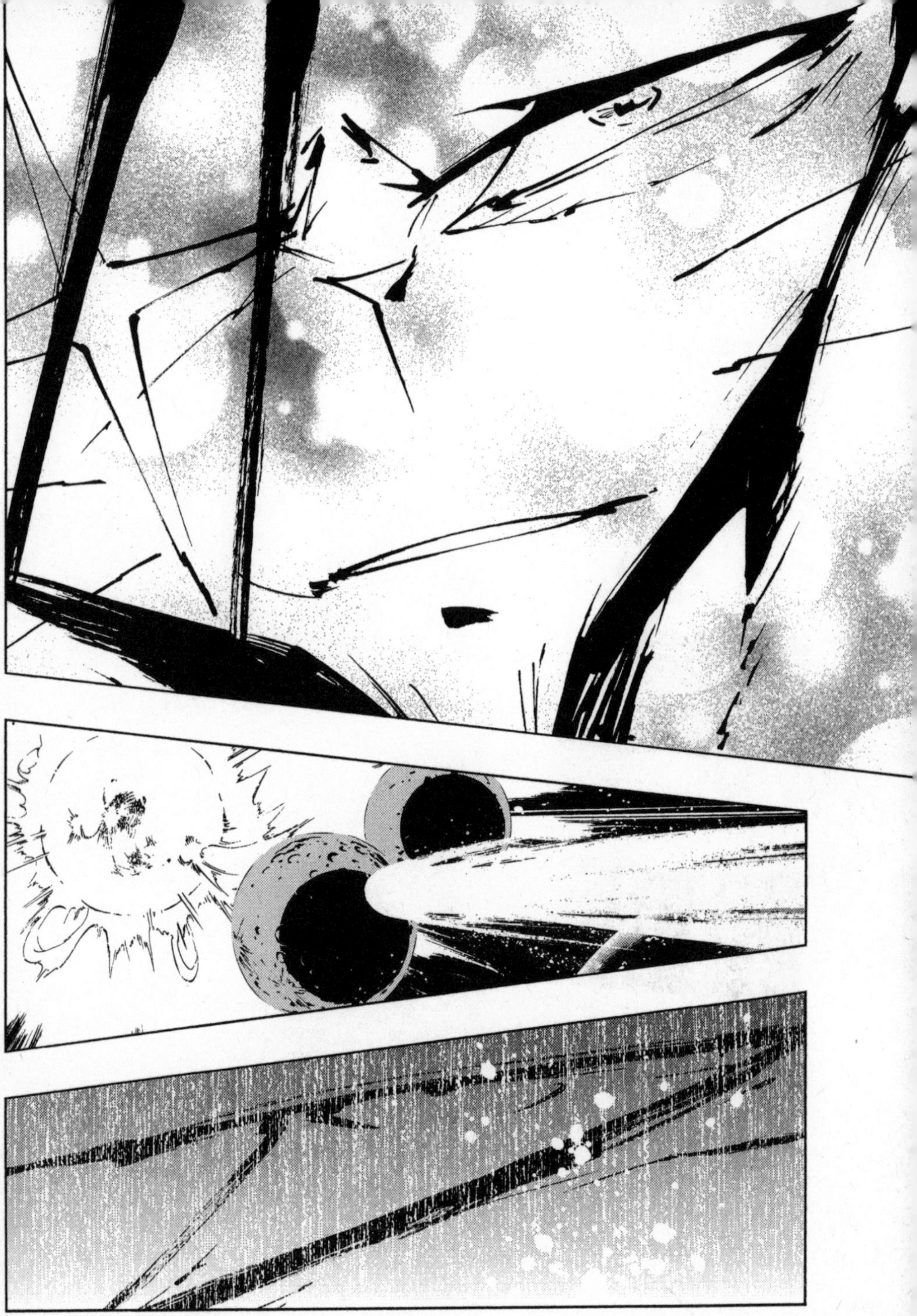

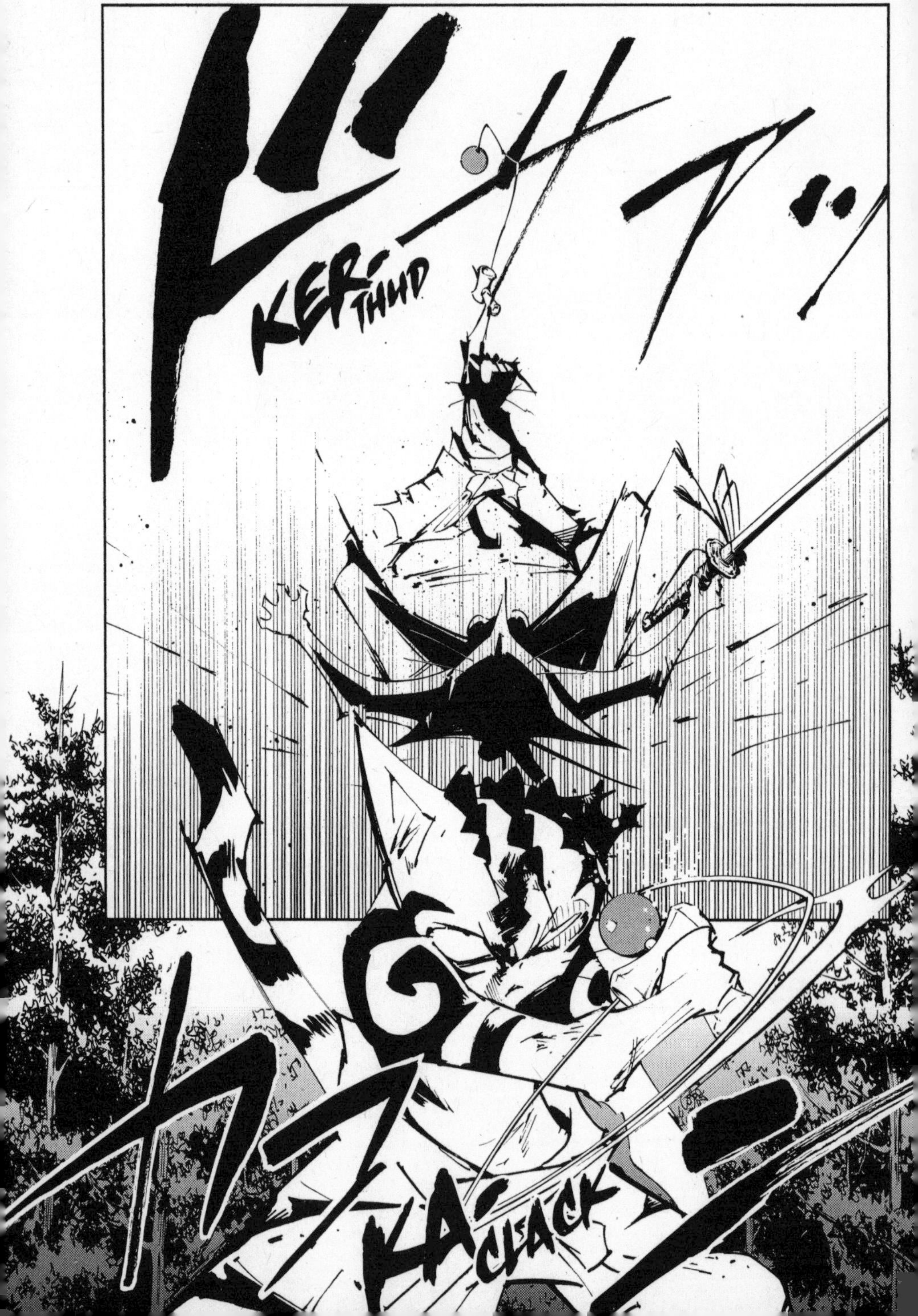
KER-THUD
KA-CLACK

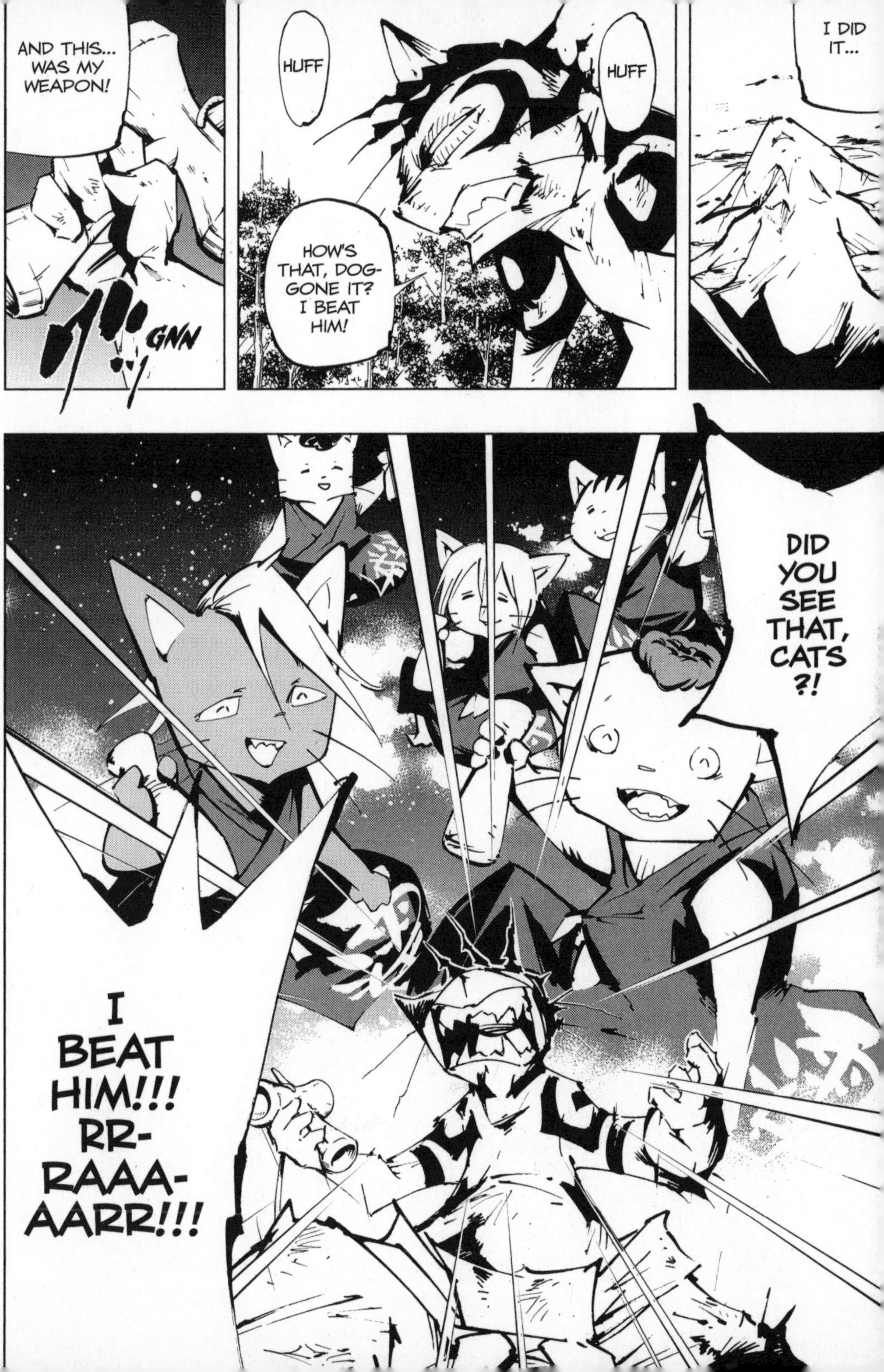
I DID IT...
HUFF
HUFF
HOW'S THAT, DOG-GONE IT? I BEAT HIM!
AND THIS... WAS MY WEAPON!
GNN
DID YOU SEE THAT, CATS?!
I BEAT HIM!!! RR-RAAAA-AARR!!!

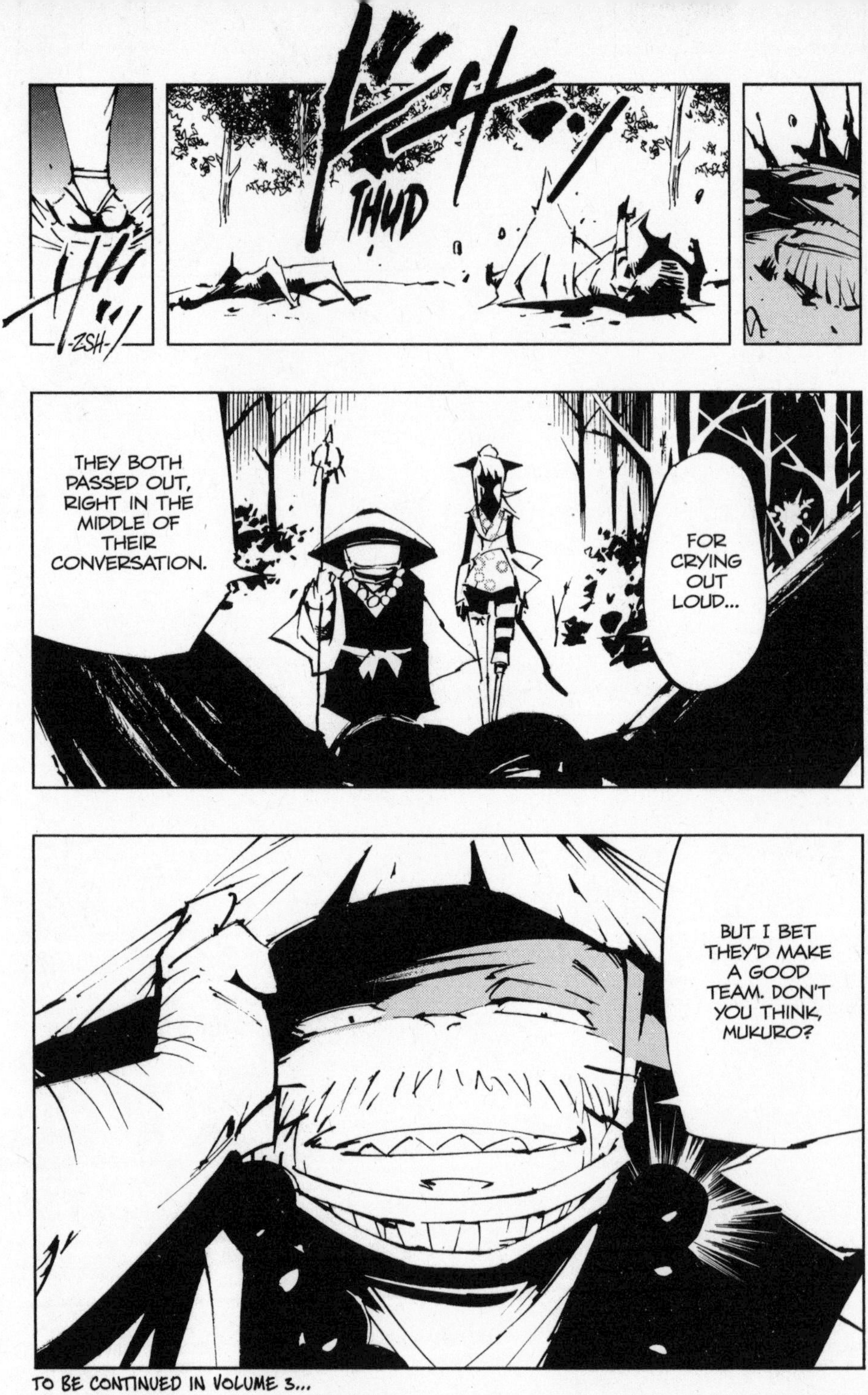
THUD
-ZSH-
FOR CRYING OUT LOUD...
THEY BOTH PASSED OUT, RIGHT IN THE MIDDLE OF THEIR CONVERSATION.
BUT I BET THEY'D MAKE A GOOD TEAM. DON'T YOU THINK, MUKURO?

TO BE CONTINUED IN VOLUME 3...

猫ヶ原

NeKoGaHaRa

ネコガハラ

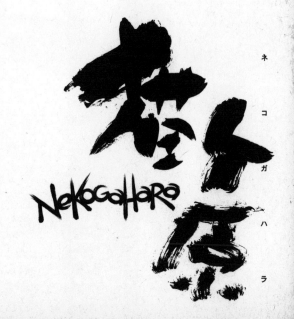

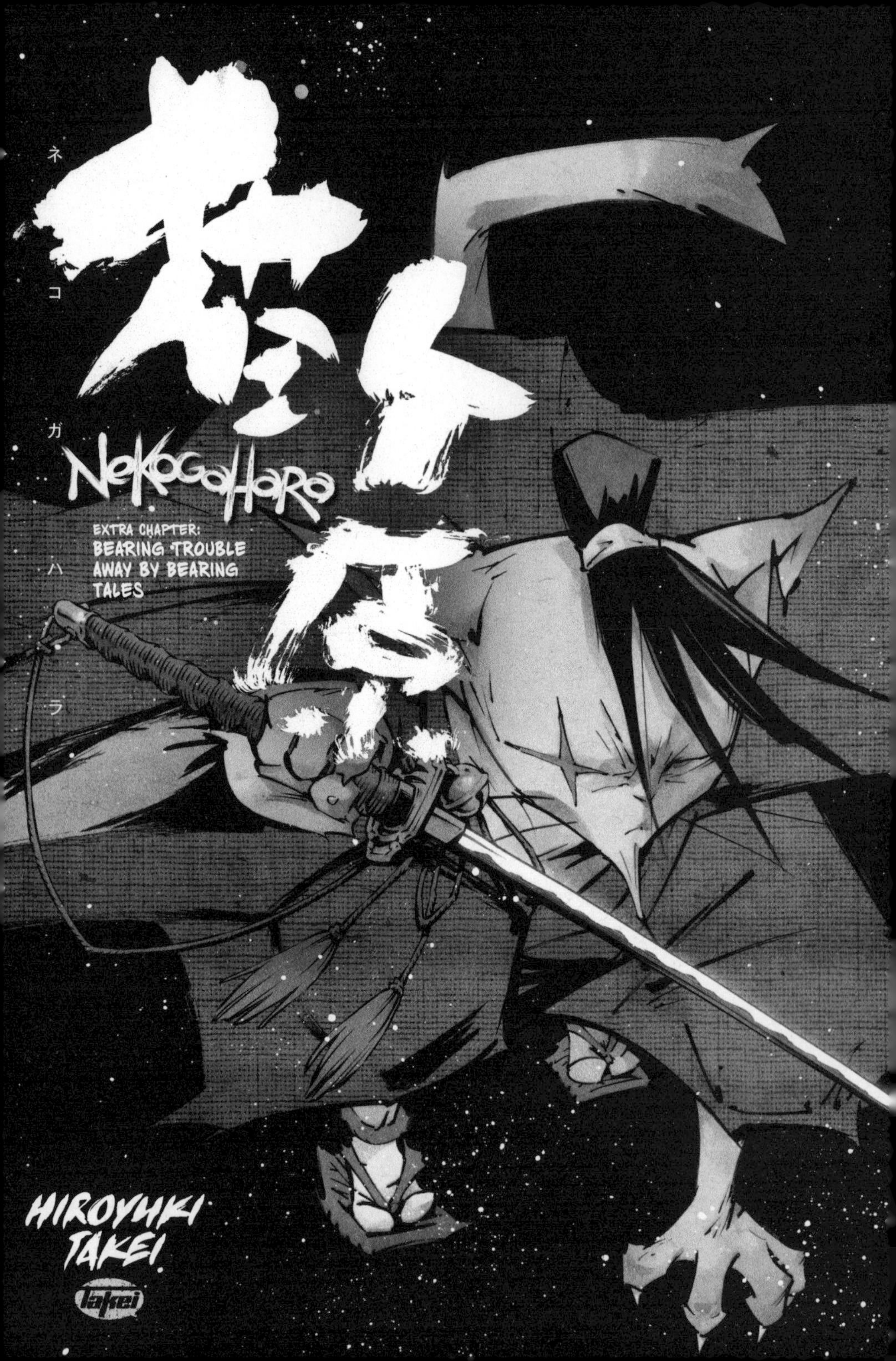
ネコガハラ
NekogaHara
EXTRA CHAPTER:
BEARING TROUBLE AWAY BY BEARING TALES
HIROYUKI TAKEI
Takei

猫ヶ原

ネコガハラ

NeKoGaHaRa

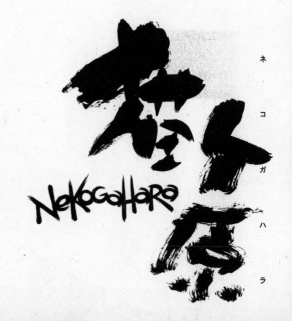

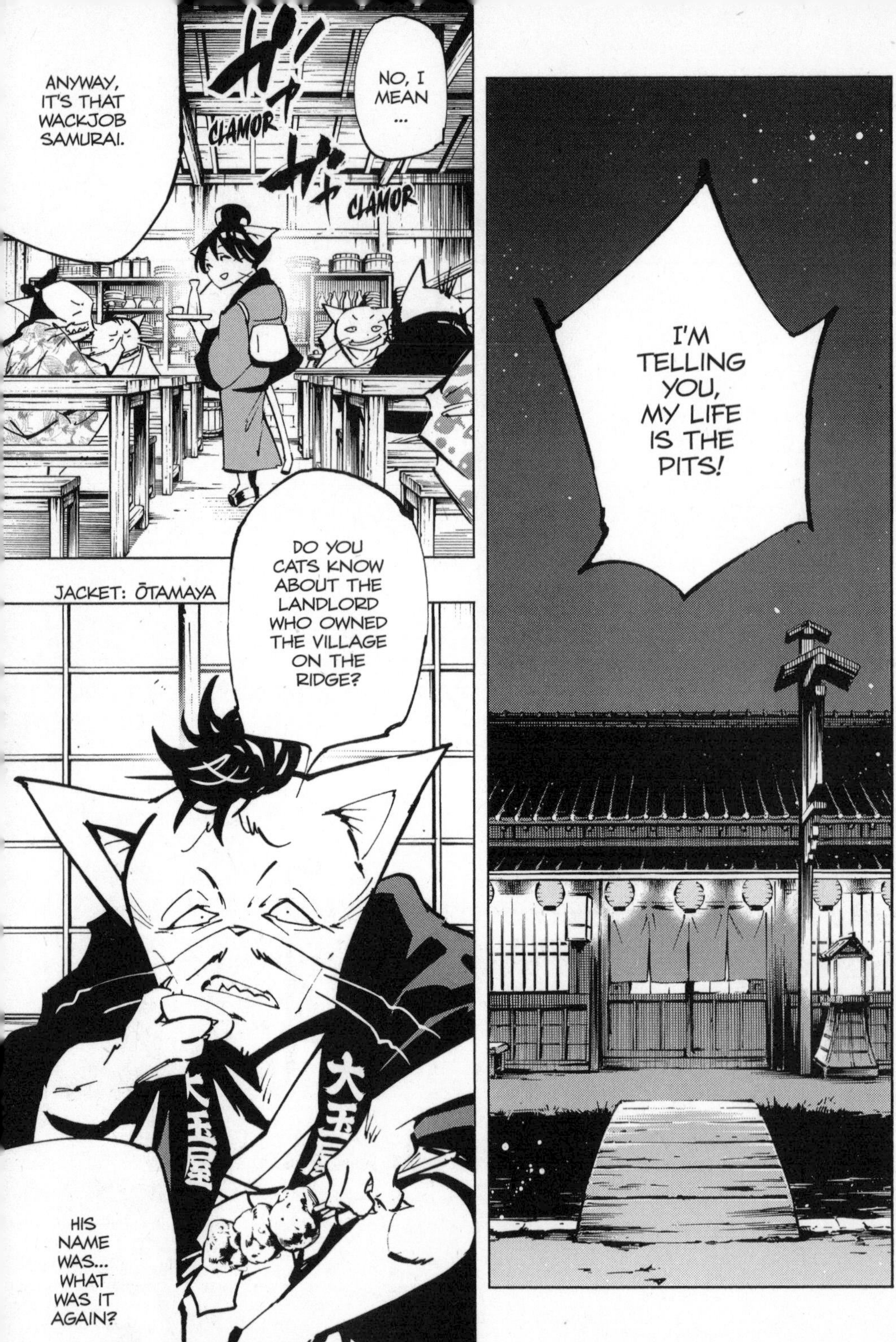
I'M TELLING YOU, MY LIFE IS THE PITS!
NO, I MEAN ...
CLAMOR
CLAMOR
ANYWAY, IT'S THAT WACKJOB SAMURAI.
DO YOU CATS KNOW ABOUT THE LANDLORD WHO OWNED THE VILLAGE ON THE RIDGE?
JACKET: ŌTAMAYA
大玉屋
大玉屋
HIS NAME WAS... WHAT WAS IT AGAIN?

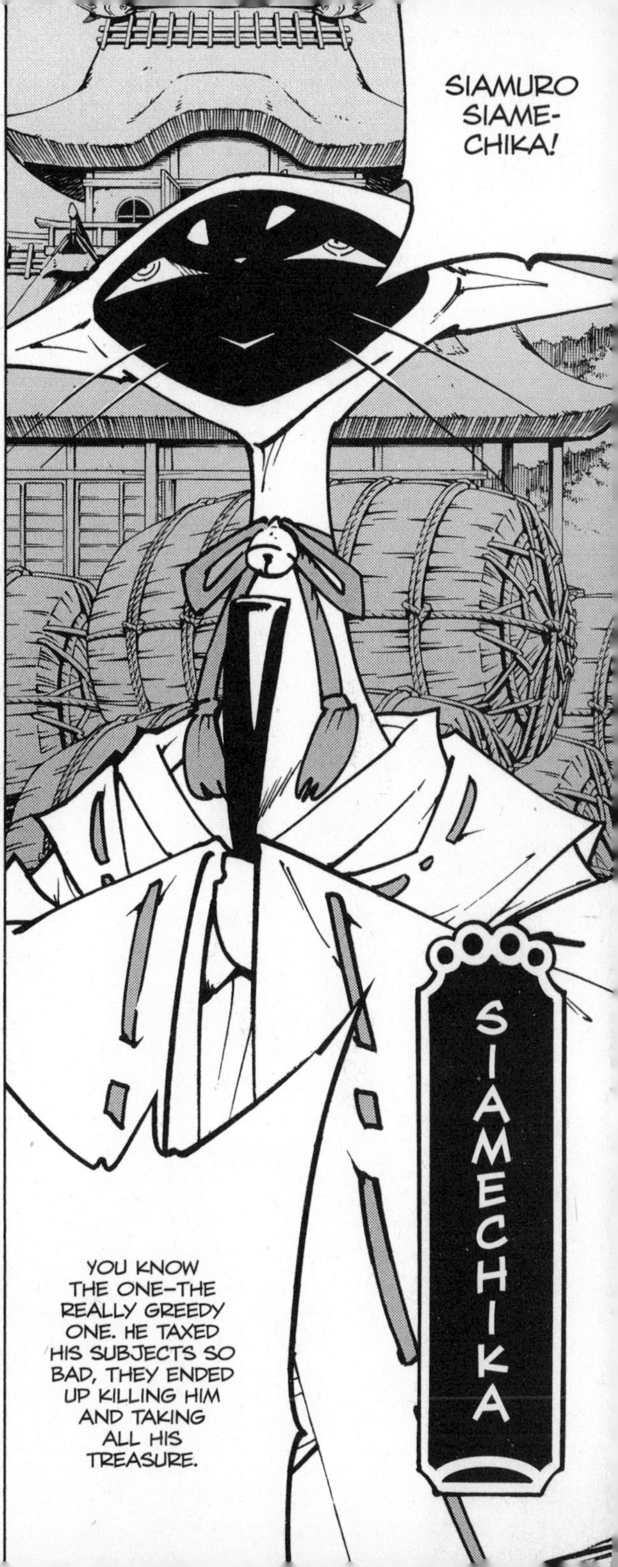
SIAMURO SIAME-CHIKA!
SIAMECHIKA
YOU KNOW THE ONE—THE REALLY GREEDY ONE. HE TAXED HIS SUBJECTS SO BAD, THEY ENDED UP KILLING HIM AND TAKING ALL HIS TREASURE.
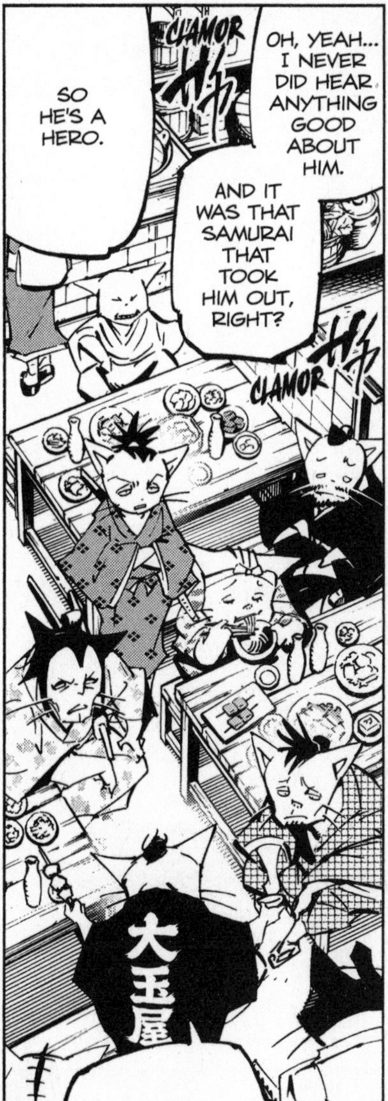
OH, YEAH... I NEVER DID HEAR ANYTHING GOOD ABOUT HIM.
CLAMOR
SO HE'S A HERO.
AND IT WAS THAT SAMURAI THAT TOOK HIM OUT, RIGHT?
CLAMOR
大玉屋
DON'T BE STUPID! I KNOW WHAT IT SOUNDS LIKE, BUT THERE'S MORE TO THIS STORY!

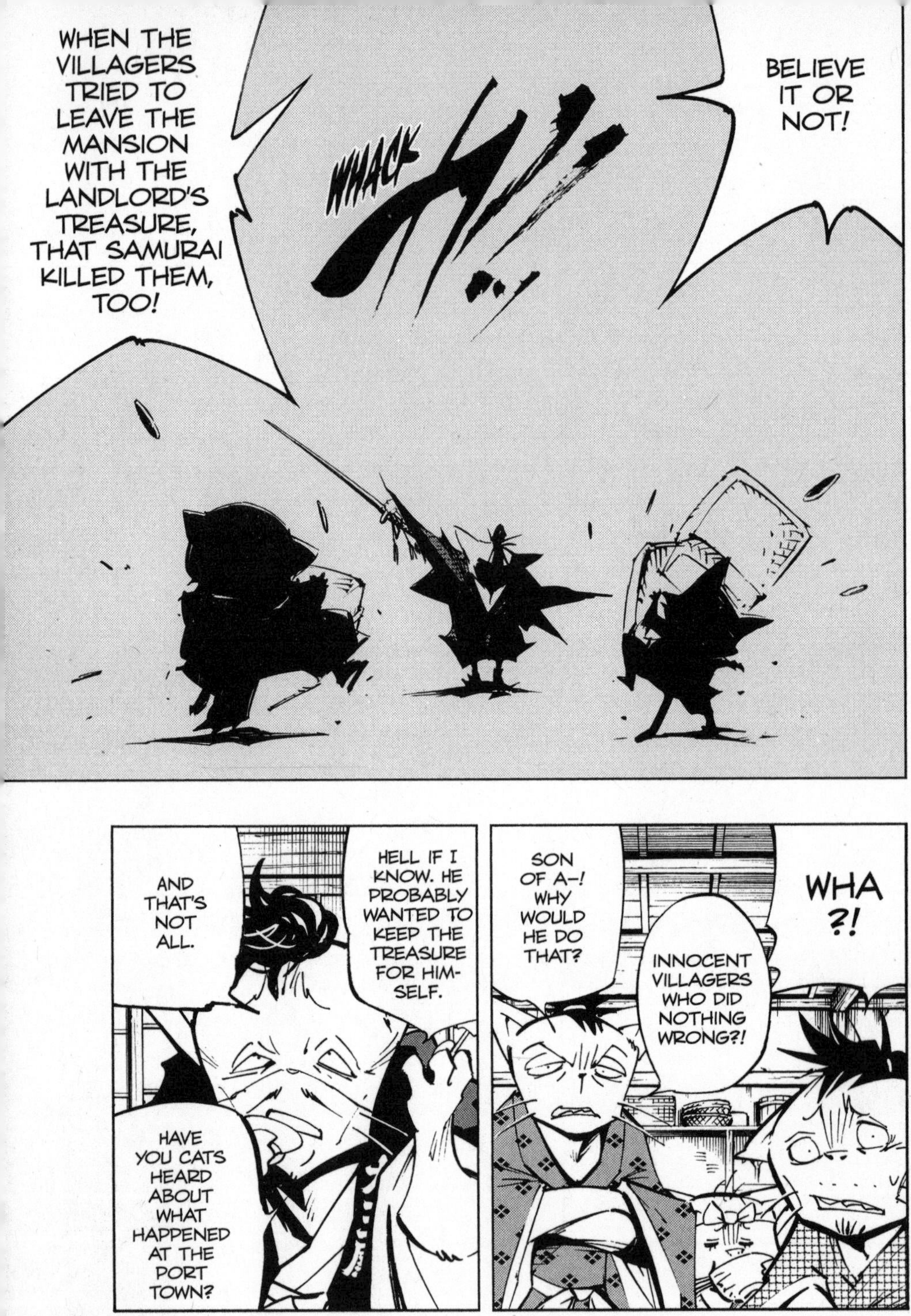
BELIEVE IT OR NOT!
WHACK
WHEN THE VILLAGERS TRIED TO LEAVE THE MANSION WITH THE LANDLORD'S TREASURE, THAT SAMURAI KILLED THEM, TOO!
WHA ?!
INNOCENT VILLAGERS WHO DID NOTHING WRONG?!
SON OF A-! WHY WOULD HE DO THAT?
HELL IF I KNOW. HE PROBABLY WANTED TO KEEP THE TREASURE FOR HIM-SELF.
AND THAT'S NOT ALL.
HAVE YOU CATS HEARD ABOUT WHAT HAPPENED AT THE PORT TOWN?

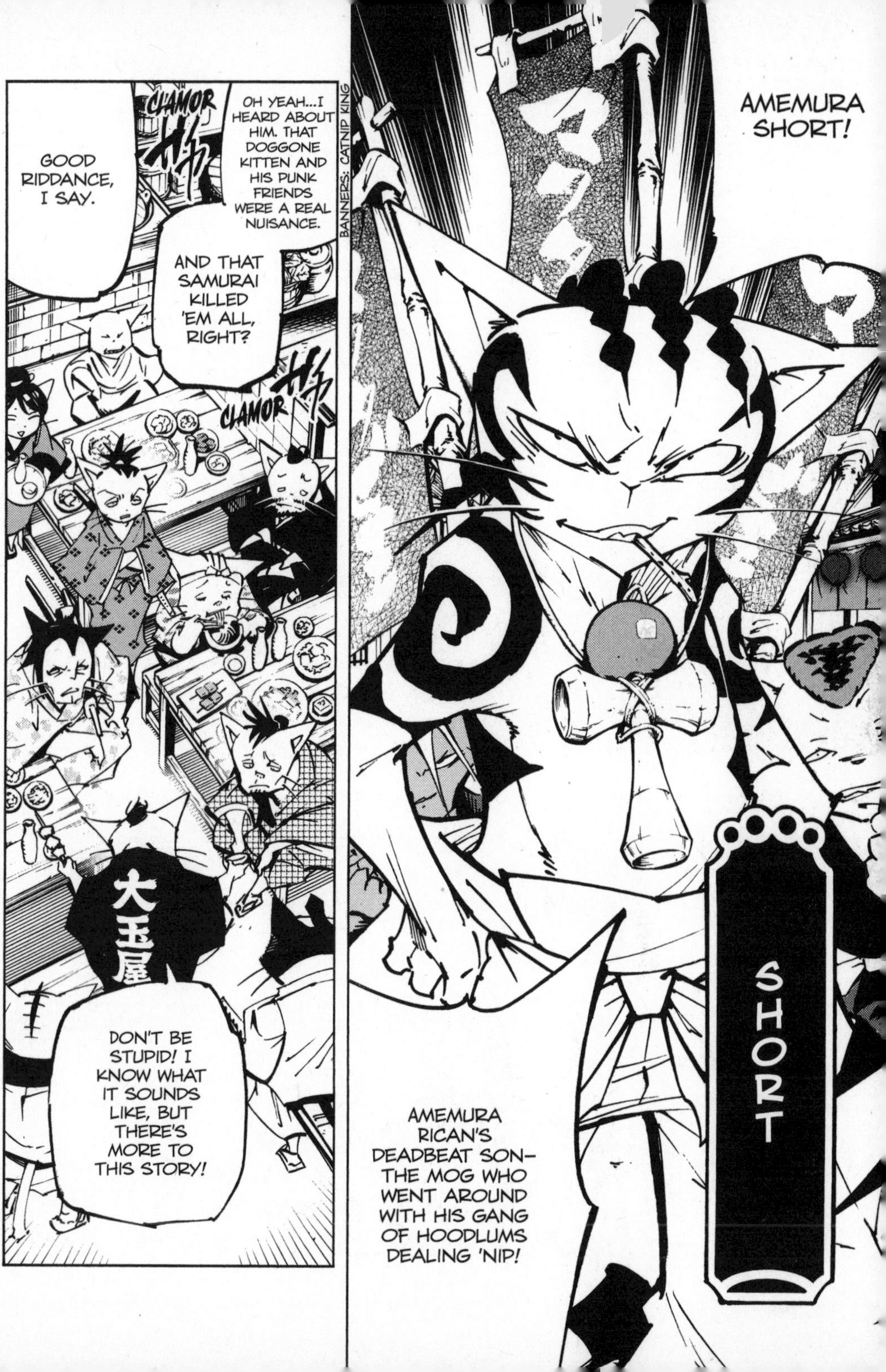
AMEMURA SHORT!
SHORT
AMEMURA RICAN'S DEADBEAT SON—THE MOG WHO WENT AROUND WITH HIS GANG OF HOODLUMS DEALING 'NIP!
BANNERS: CATNIP KING
CLAMOR
OH YEAH...I HEARD ABOUT HIM. THAT DOGGONE KITTEN AND HIS PUNK FRIENDS WERE A REAL NUISANCE.
GOOD RIDDANCE, I SAY.
AND THAT SAMURAI KILLED 'EM ALL, RIGHT?
CLAMOR
大玉屋
DON'T BE STUPID! I KNOW WHAT IT SOUNDS LIKE, BUT THERE'S MORE TO THIS STORY!

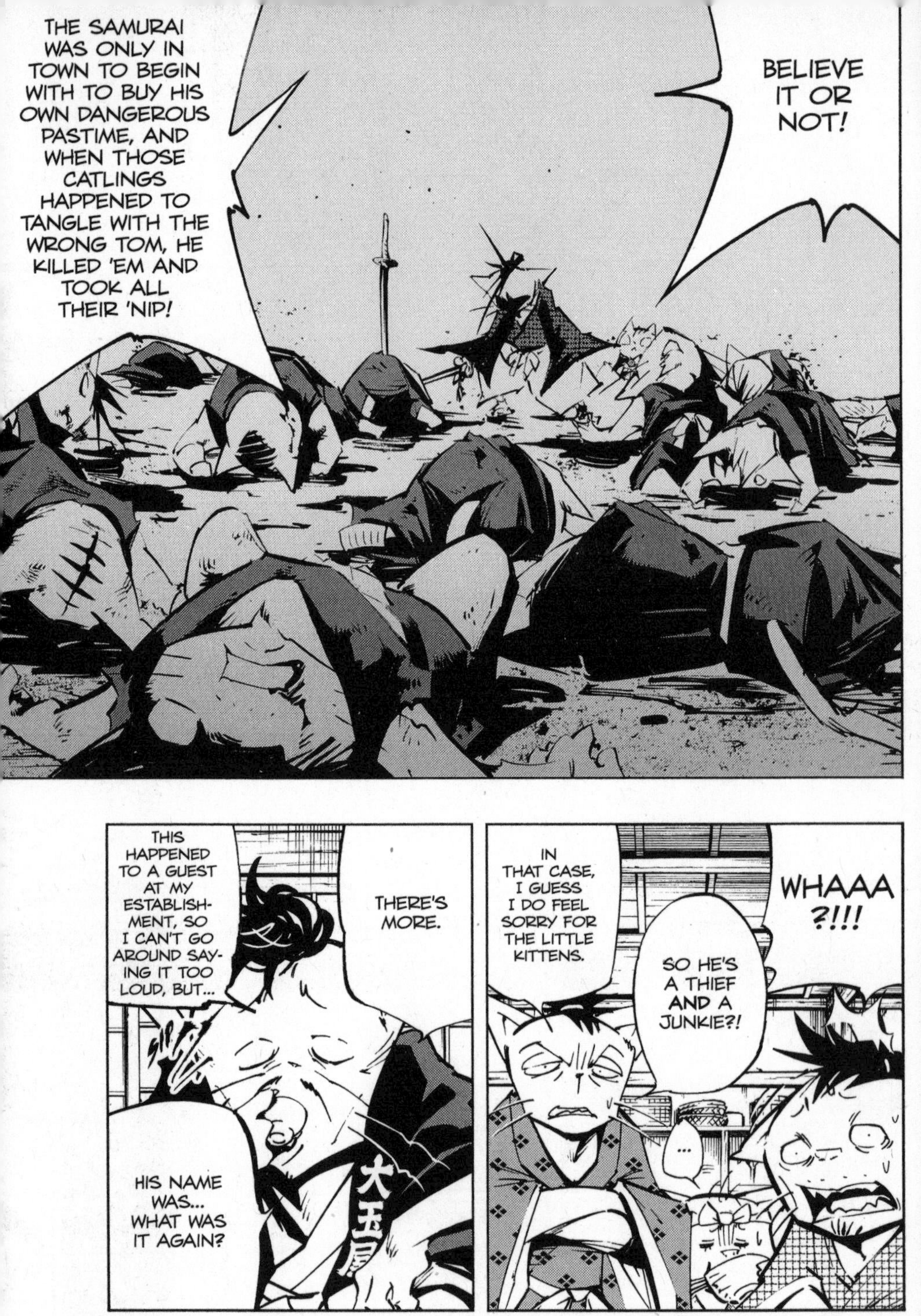
BELIEVE IT OR NOT!
THE SAMURAI WAS ONLY IN TOWN TO BEGIN WITH TO BUY HIS OWN DANGEROUS PASTIME, AND WHEN THOSE CATLINGS HAPPENED TO TANGLE WITH THE WRONG TOM, HE KILLED 'EM AND TOOK ALL THEIR 'NIP!
WHAAA ?!!!
IN THAT CASE, I GUESS I DO FEEL SORRY FOR THE LITTLE KITTENS.
SO HE'S A THIEF AND A JUNKIE?!
...
THERE'S MORE.
THIS HAPPENED TO A GUEST AT MY ESTABLISH-MENT, SO I CAN'T GO AROUND SAY-ING IT TOO LOUD, BUT...
SIP
HIS NAME WAS... WHAT WAS IT AGAIN?

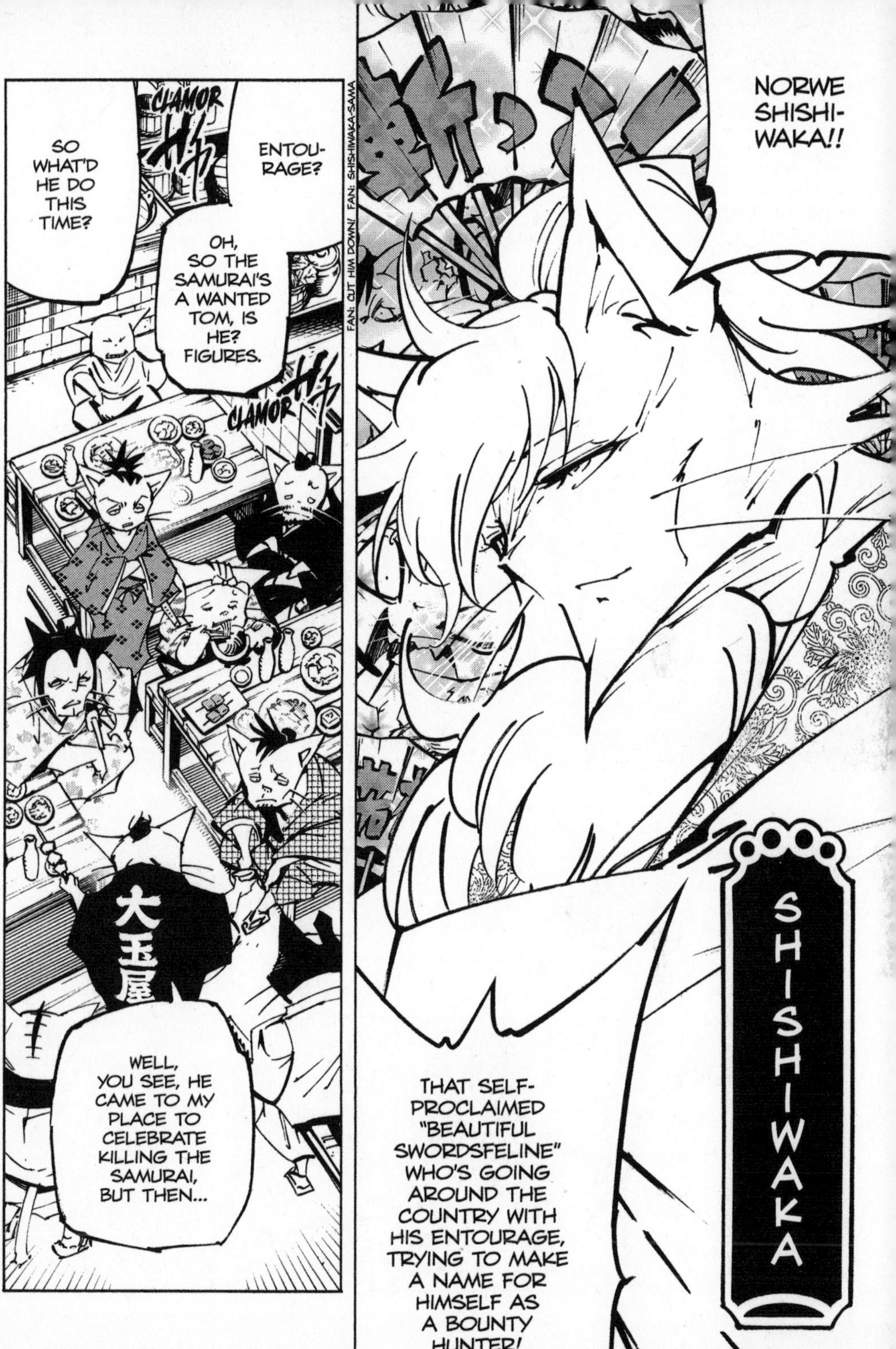
NORWE SHISHI-WAKA!!
FAN: SHISHIWAKA-SAMA
FAN: CUT HIM DOWN!
SHISHIWAKA
THAT SELF-PROCLAIMED "BEAUTIFUL SWORDSFELINE" WHO'S GOING AROUND THE COUNTRY WITH HIS ENTOURAGE, TRYING TO MAKE A NAME FOR HIMSELF AS A BOUNTY HUNTER!
ENTOU-RAGE?
CLAMOR
SO WHAT'D HE DO THIS TIME?
OH, SO THE SAMURAI'S A WANTED TOM, IS HE? FIGURES.
CLAMOR
大玉屋
WELL, YOU SEE, HE CAME TO MY PLACE TO CELEBRATE KILLING THE SAMURAI, BUT THEN...

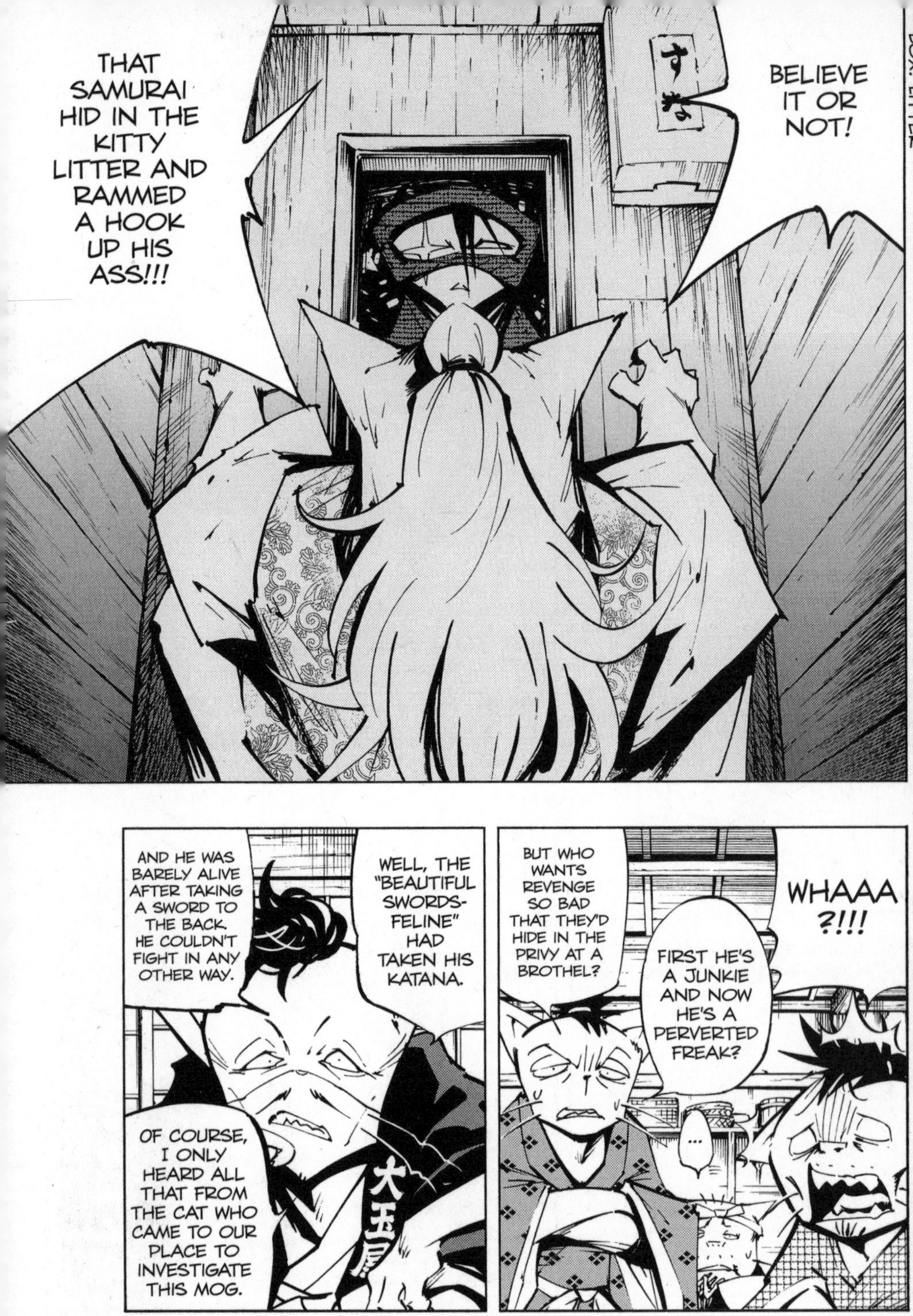
BELIEVE IT OR NOT!
THAT SAMURAI HID IN THE KITTY LITTER AND RAMMED A HOOK UP HIS ASS!!!
WHAAA ?!!!
BUT WHO WANTS REVENGE SO BAD THAT THEY'D HIDE IN THE PRIVY AT A BROTHEL?
FIRST HE'S A JUNKIE AND NOW HE'S A PERVERTED FREAK?
...
WELL, THE "BEAUTIFUL SWORDS-FELINE" HAD TAKEN HIS KATANA.
AND HE WAS BARELY ALIVE AFTER TAKING A SWORD TO THE BACK. HE COULDN'T FIGHT IN ANY OTHER WAY.
OF COURSE, I ONLY HEARD ALL THAT FROM THE CAT WHO CAME TO OUR PLACE TO INVESTIGATE THIS MOG.

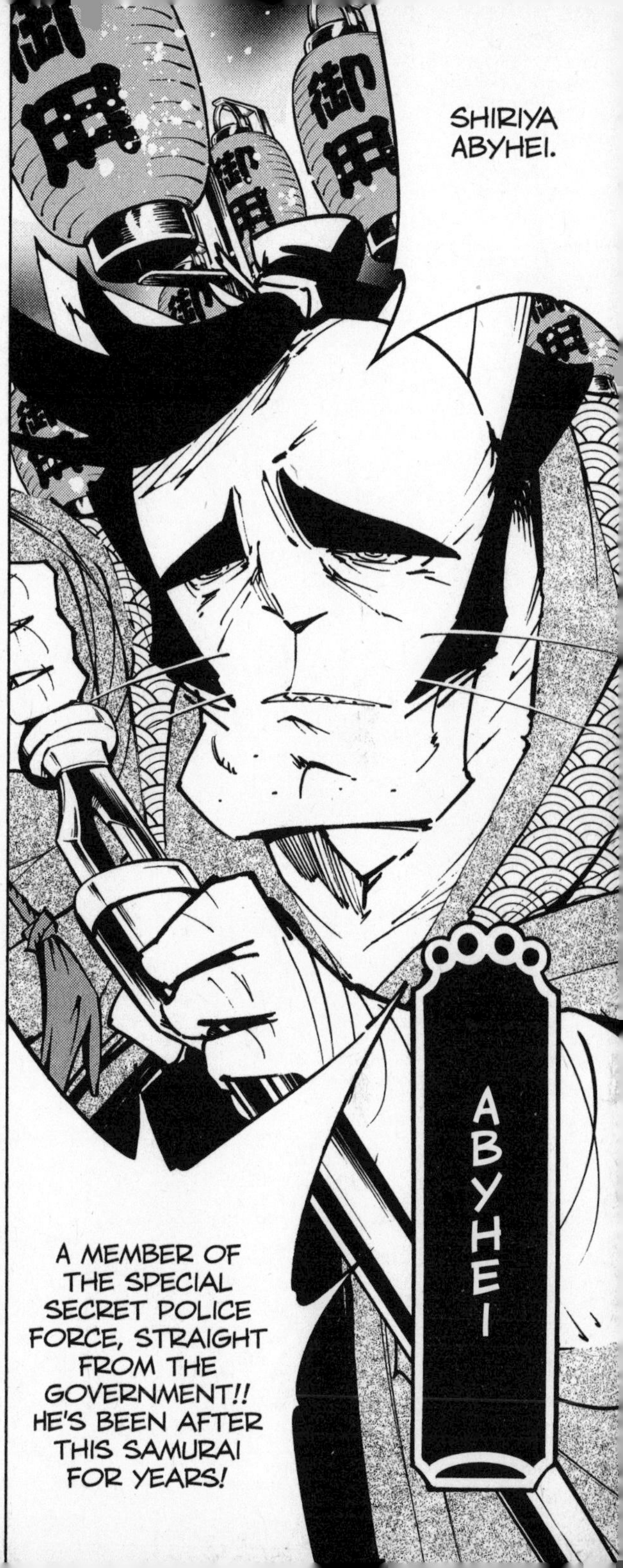
SHIRIYA ABYHEI.
ABYHEI
A MEMBER OF THE SPECIAL SECRET POLICE FORCE, STRAIGHT FROM THE GOVERNMENT!! HE'S BEEN AFTER THIS SAMURAI FOR YEARS!

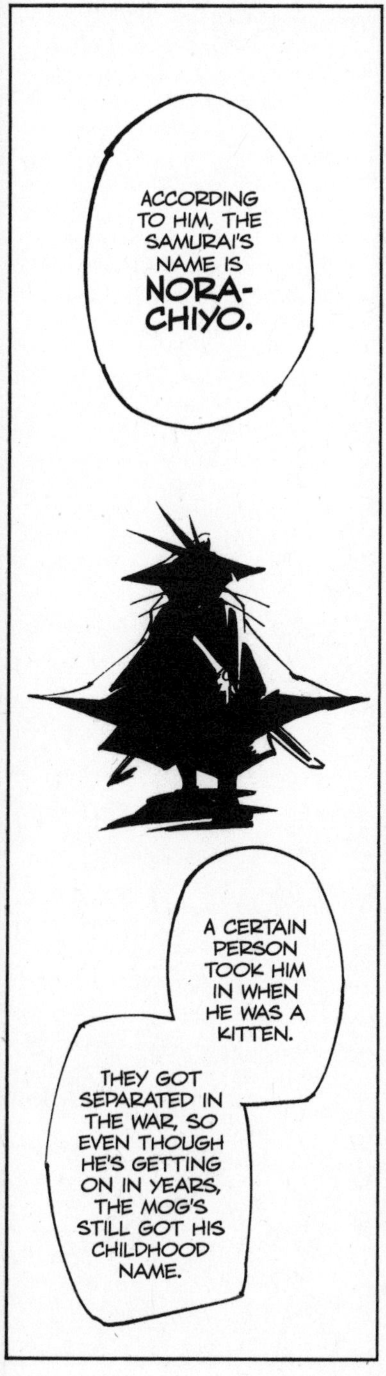
ACCORDING TO HIM, THE SAMURAI'S NAME IS **NORA-CHIYO.**
A CERTAIN PERSON TOOK HIM IN WHEN HE WAS A KITTEN.
THEY GOT SEPARATED IN THE WAR, SO EVEN THOUGH HE'S GETTING ON IN YEARS, THE MOG'S STILL GOT HIS CHILDHOOD NAME.

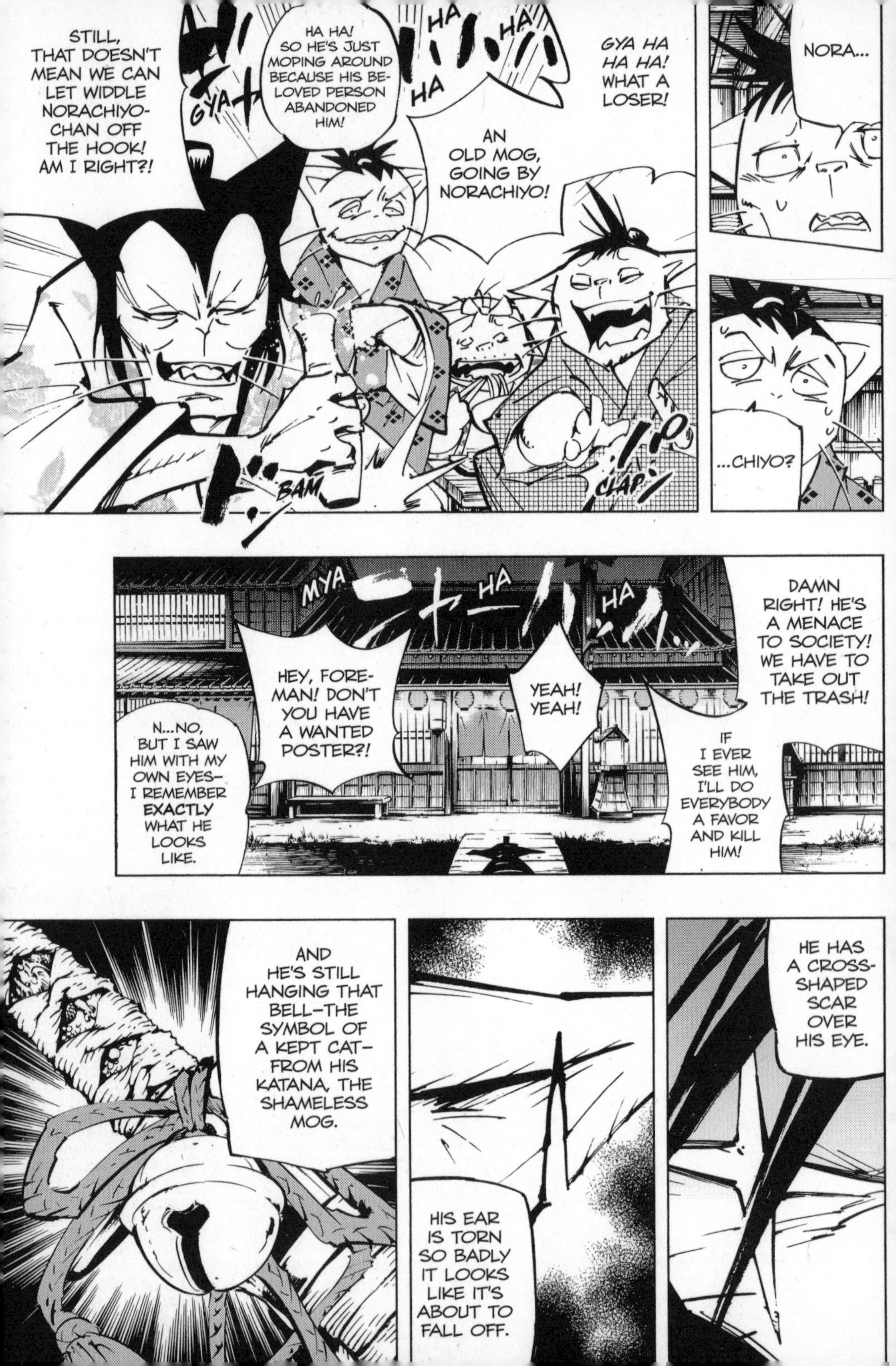
NORA...
...CHIYO?
GYA HA HA HA! WHAT A LOSER!
AN OLD MOG, GOING BY NORACHIYO!
HA HA HA HA
HA HA! SO HE'S JUST MOPING AROUND BECAUSE HIS BE-LOVED PERSON ABANDONED HIM!
STILL, THAT DOESN'T MEAN WE CAN LET WIDDLE NORACHIYO-CHAN OFF THE HOOK! AM I RIGHT?!
GYA
CLAP
BAM
DAMN RIGHT! HE'S A MENACE TO SOCIETY! WE HAVE TO TAKE OUT THE TRASH!
IF I EVER SEE HIM, I'LL DO EVERYBODY A FAVOR AND KILL HIM!
YEAH! YEAH!
MYA HA HA
HEY, FORE-MAN! DON'T YOU HAVE A WANTED POSTER?!
N...NO, BUT I SAW HIM WITH MY OWN EYES—I REMEMBER **EXACTLY** WHAT HE LOOKS LIKE.
HE HAS A CROSS-SHAPED SCAR OVER HIS EYE.
HIS EAR IS TORN SO BADLY IT LOOKS LIKE IT'S ABOUT TO FALL OFF.
AND HE'S STILL HANGING THAT BELL—THE SYMBOL OF A KEPT CAT—FROM HIS KATANA, THE SHAMELESS MOG.

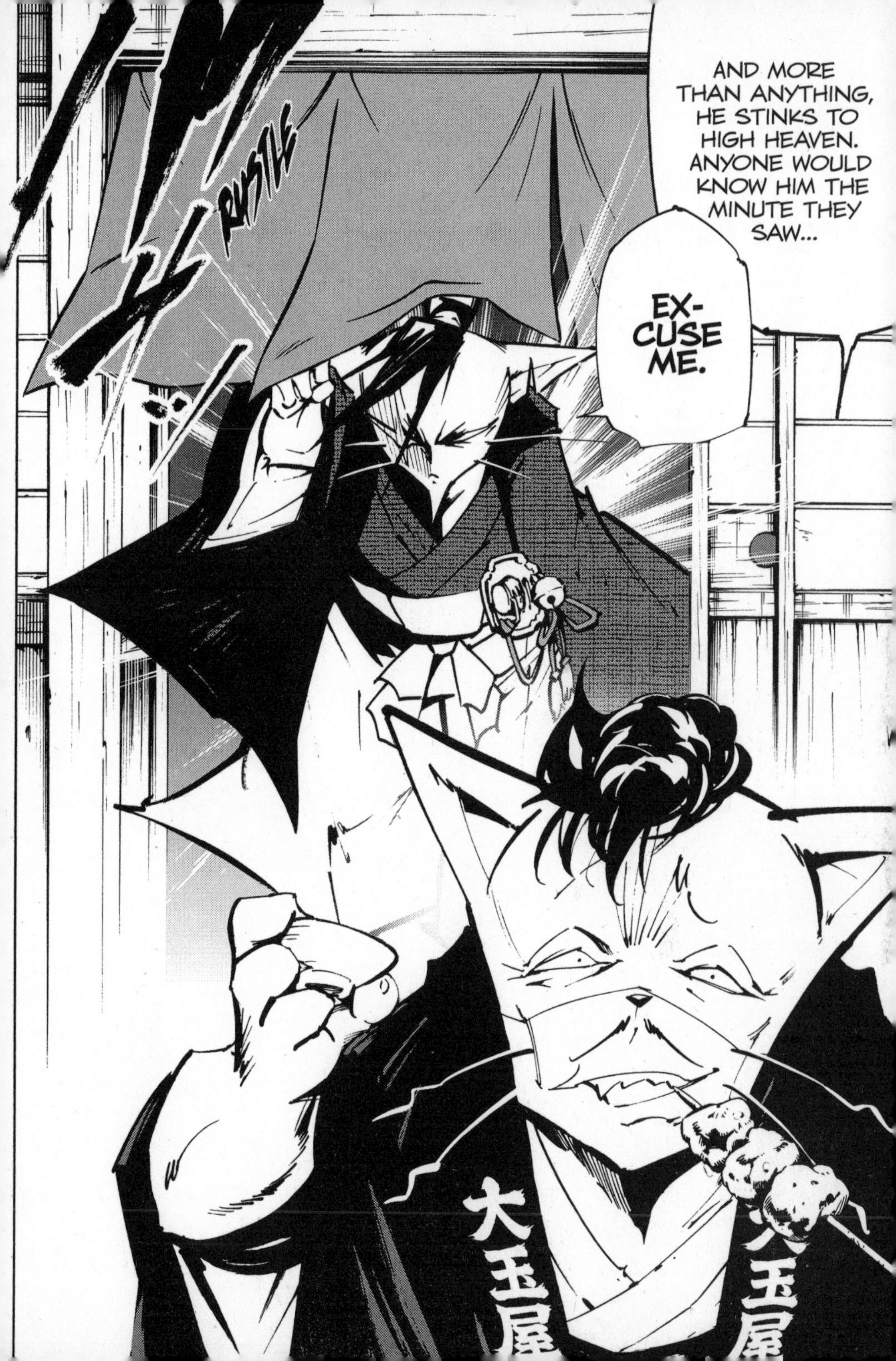
AND MORE THAN ANYTHING, HE STINKS TO HIGH HEAVEN. ANYONE WOULD KNOW HIM THE MINUTE THEY SAW...
EX-CUSE ME.
RUSTLE
大玉屋

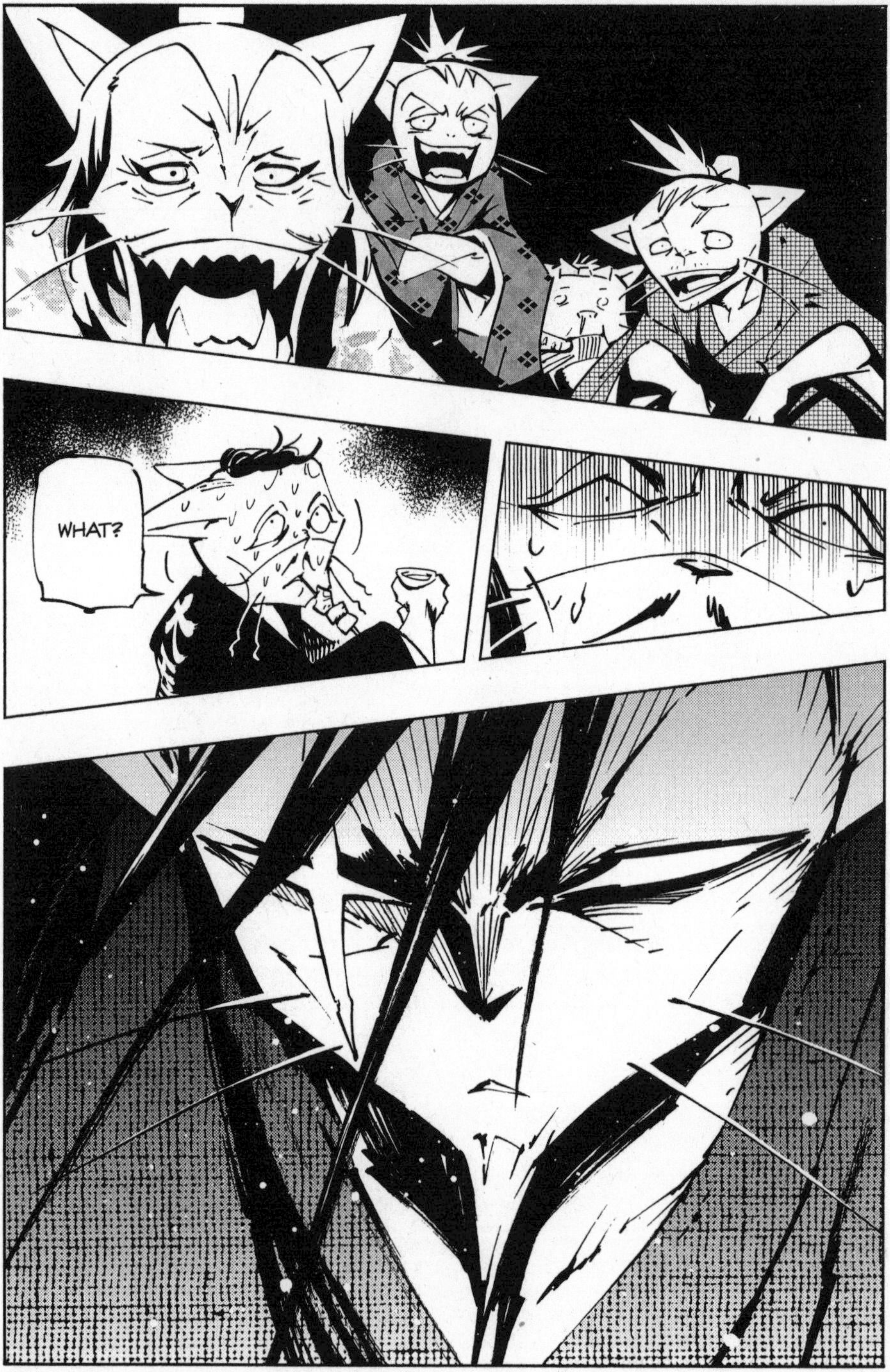
WHAT?

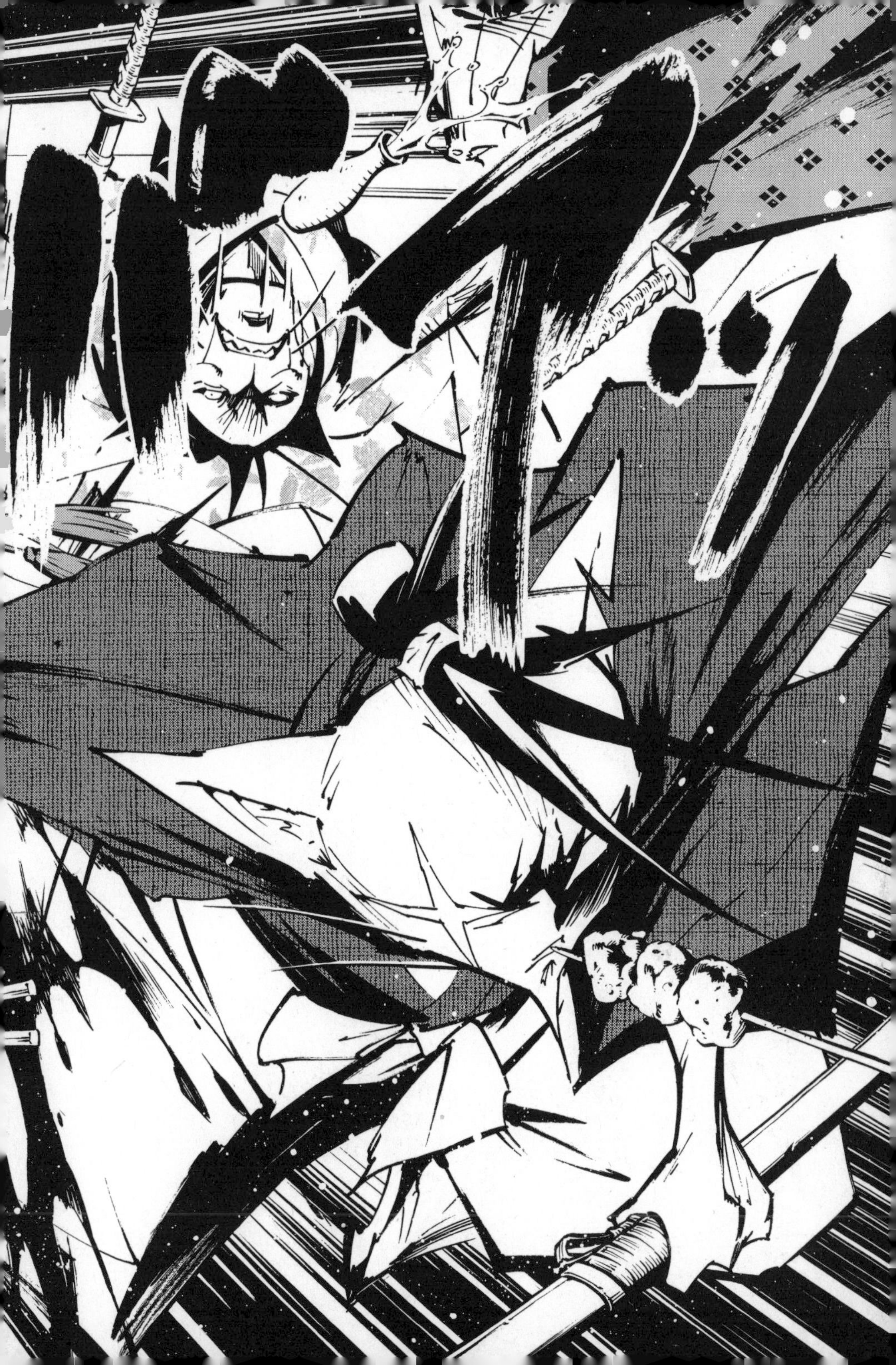

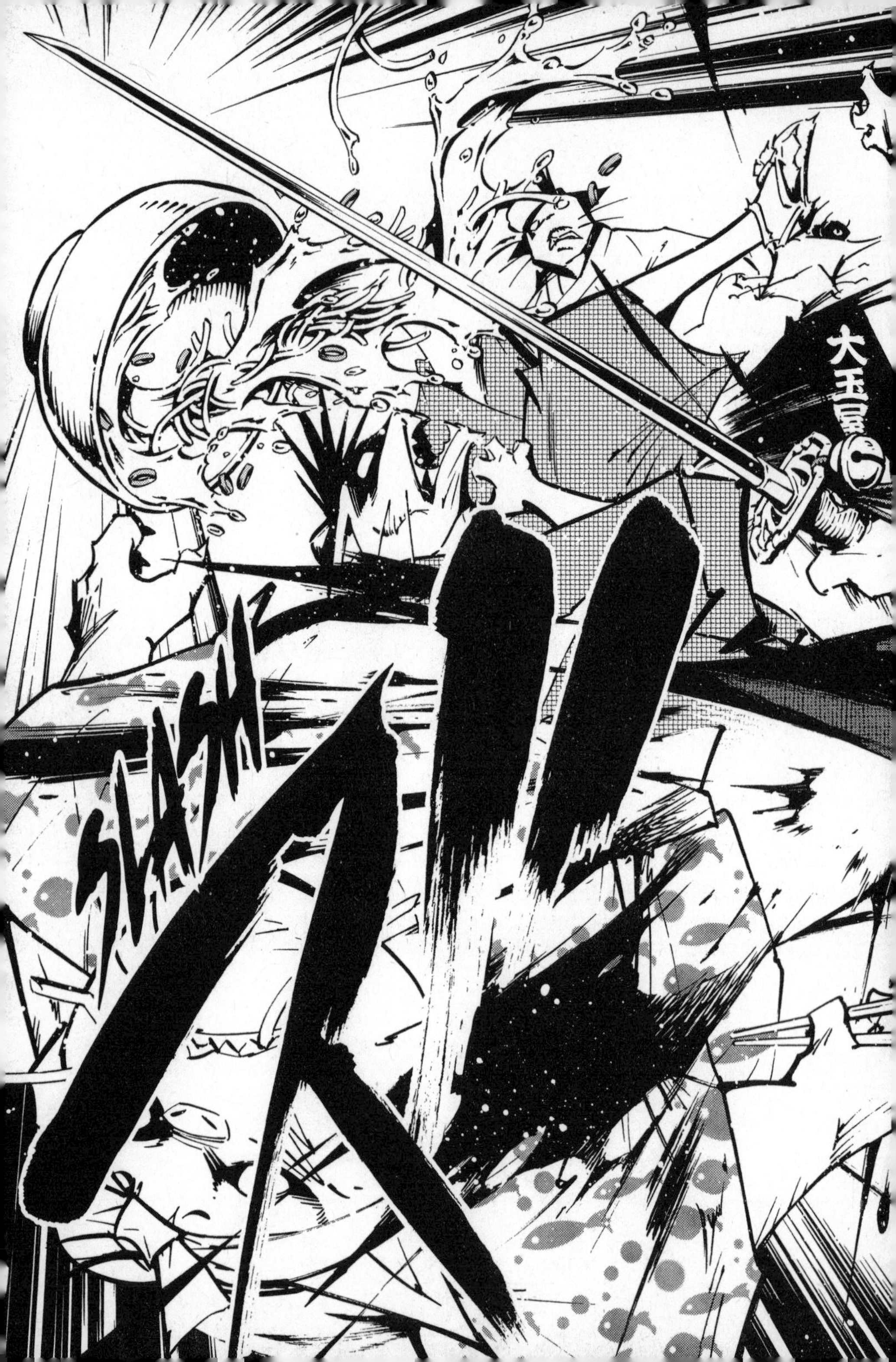
大玉屋
SLASH

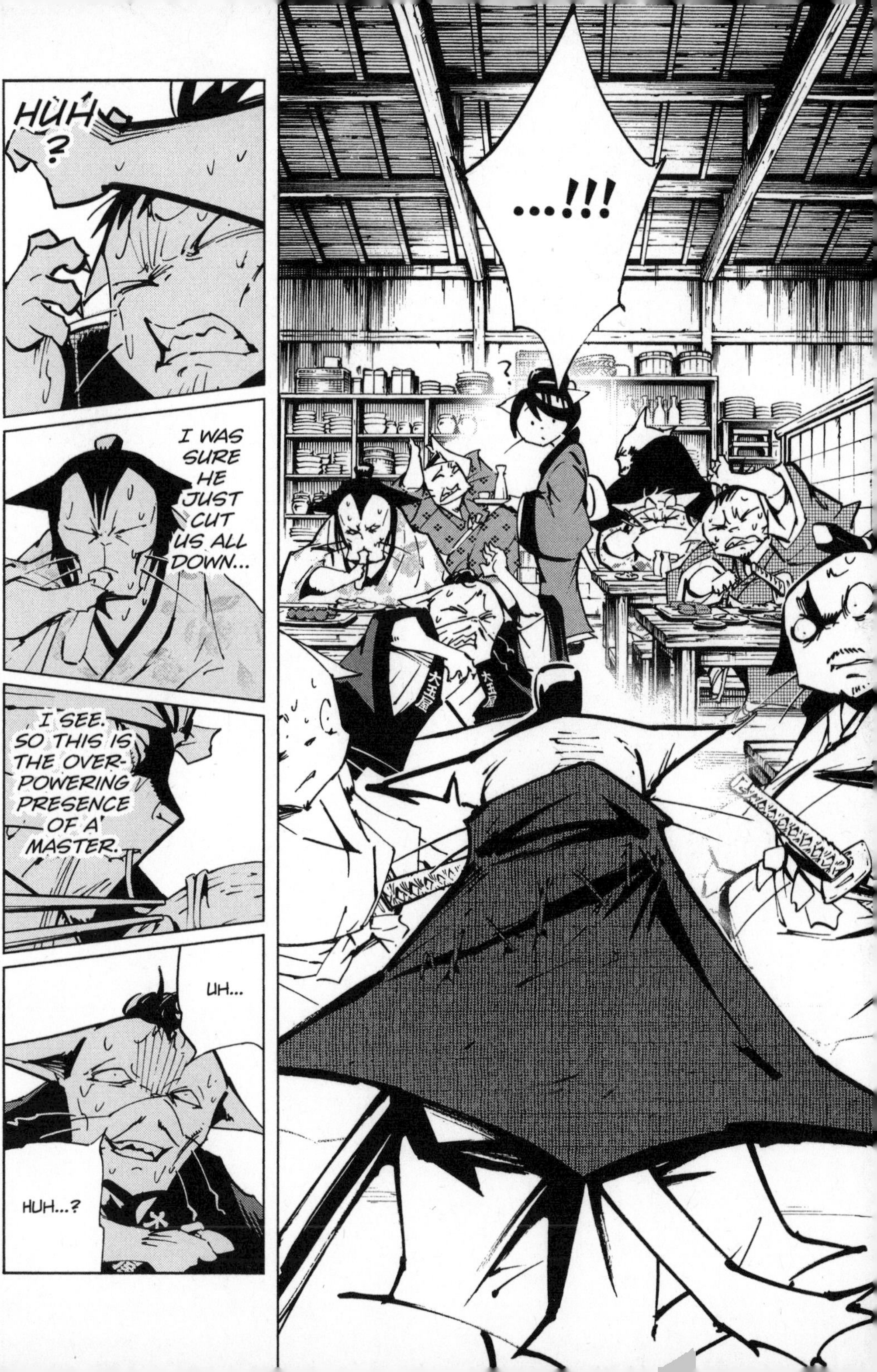
...!!!
?
HUH ?
I WAS SURE HE JUST CUT US ALL DOWN...
I SEE. SO THIS IS THE OVER-POWERING PRESENCE OF A MASTER.
UH...
HUH...?

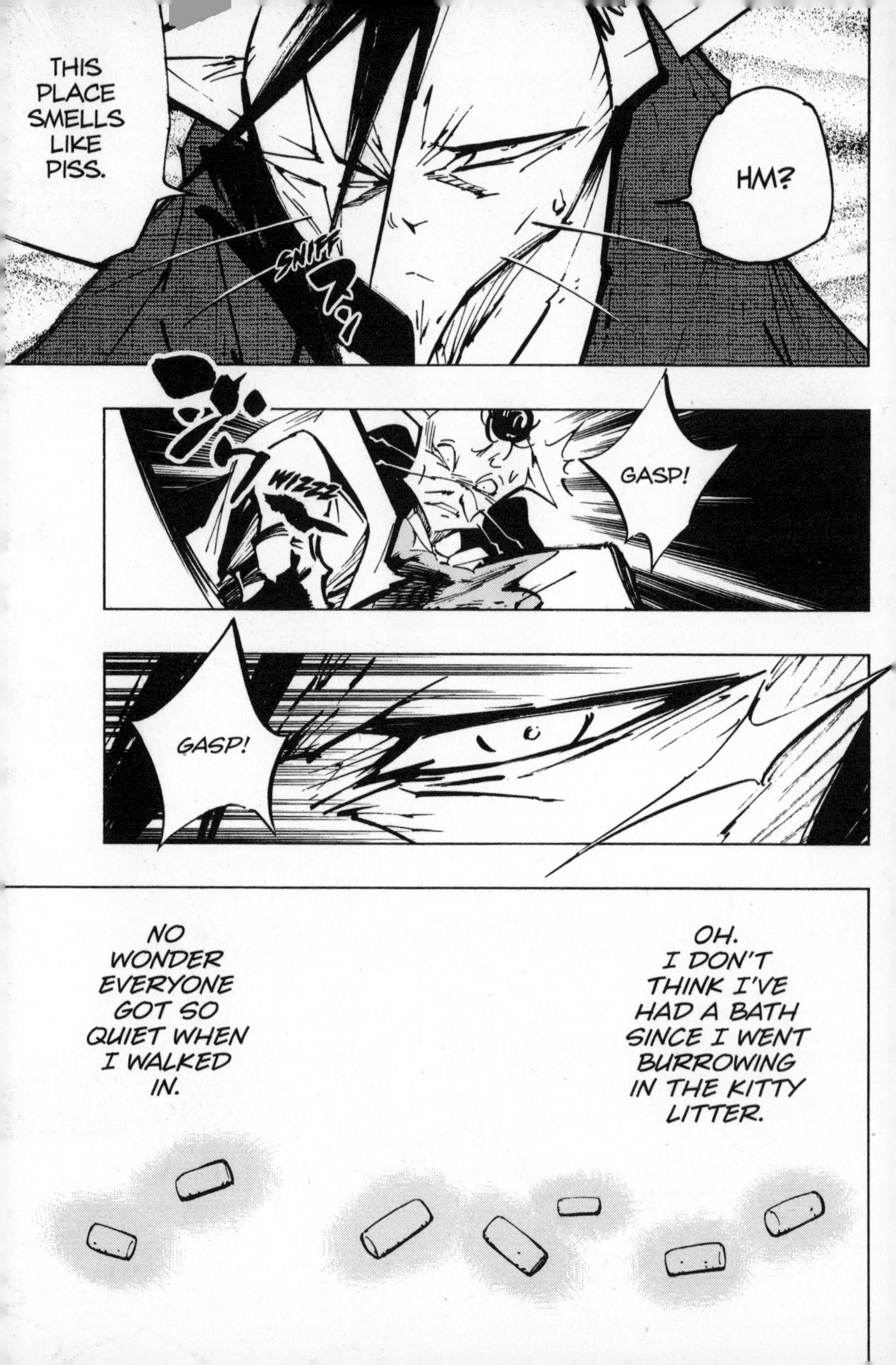
HM?
SNIFF
THIS PLACE SMELLS LIKE PISS.
GASP!
WIZZZ
GASP!
OH. I DON'T THINK I'VE HAD A BATH SINCE I WENT BURROWING IN THE KITTY LITTER.
NO WONDER EVERYONE GOT SO QUIET WHEN I WALKED IN.

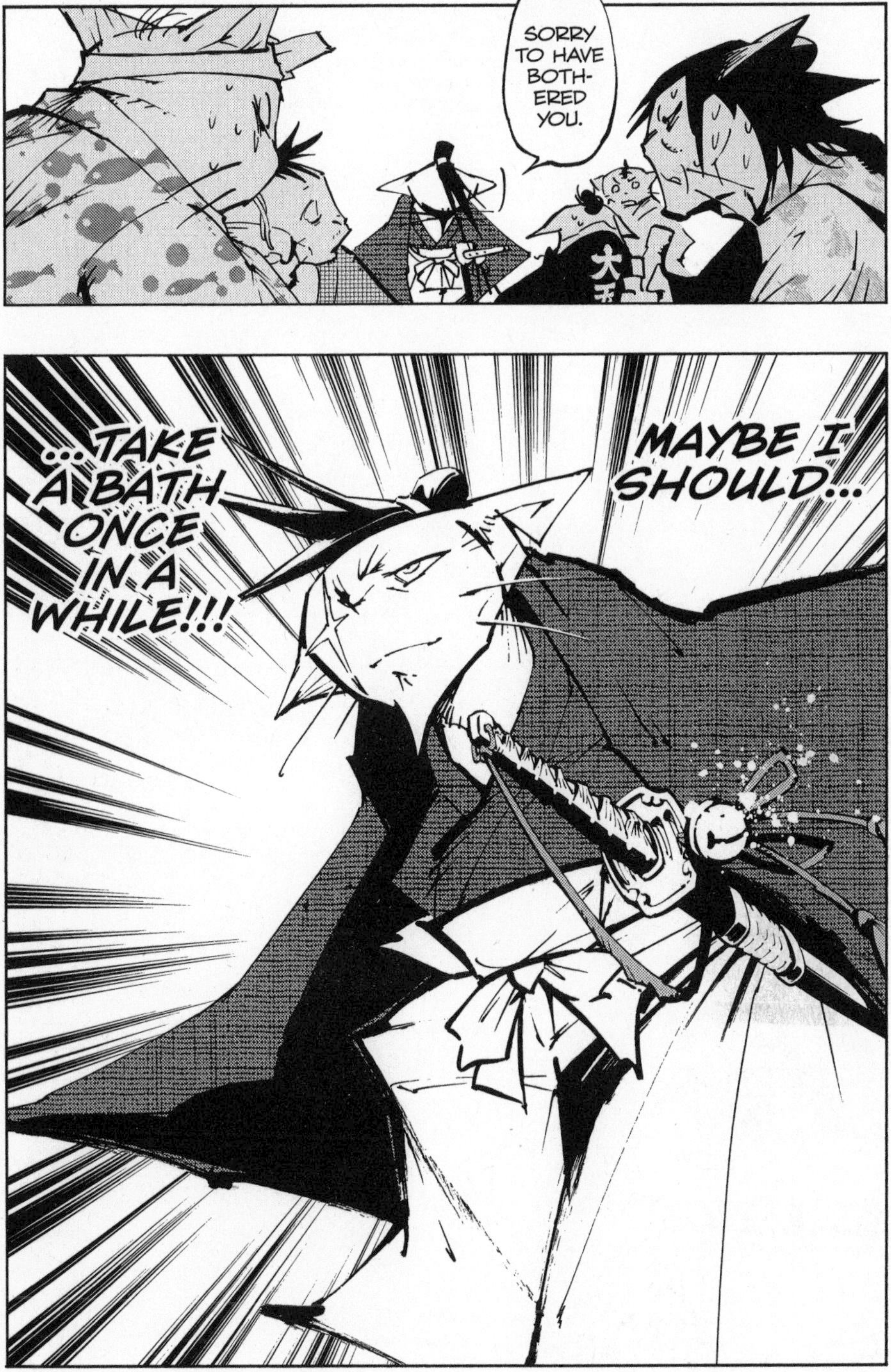
SORRY TO HAVE BOTHERED YOU.
MAYBE I SHOULD...
...TAKE A BATH ONCE IN A WHILE!!!

猫ヶ原

ネコガハラ

NeKoGaHara

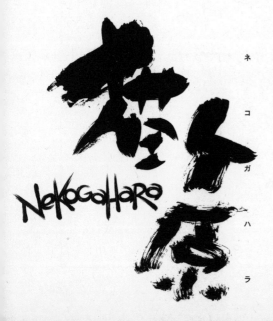

SPECIAL
MANGA
IN HONOR
OF THE
NEKOGAHARA/
NOBUNYAGA'S
AMBITION
COLLABORATION

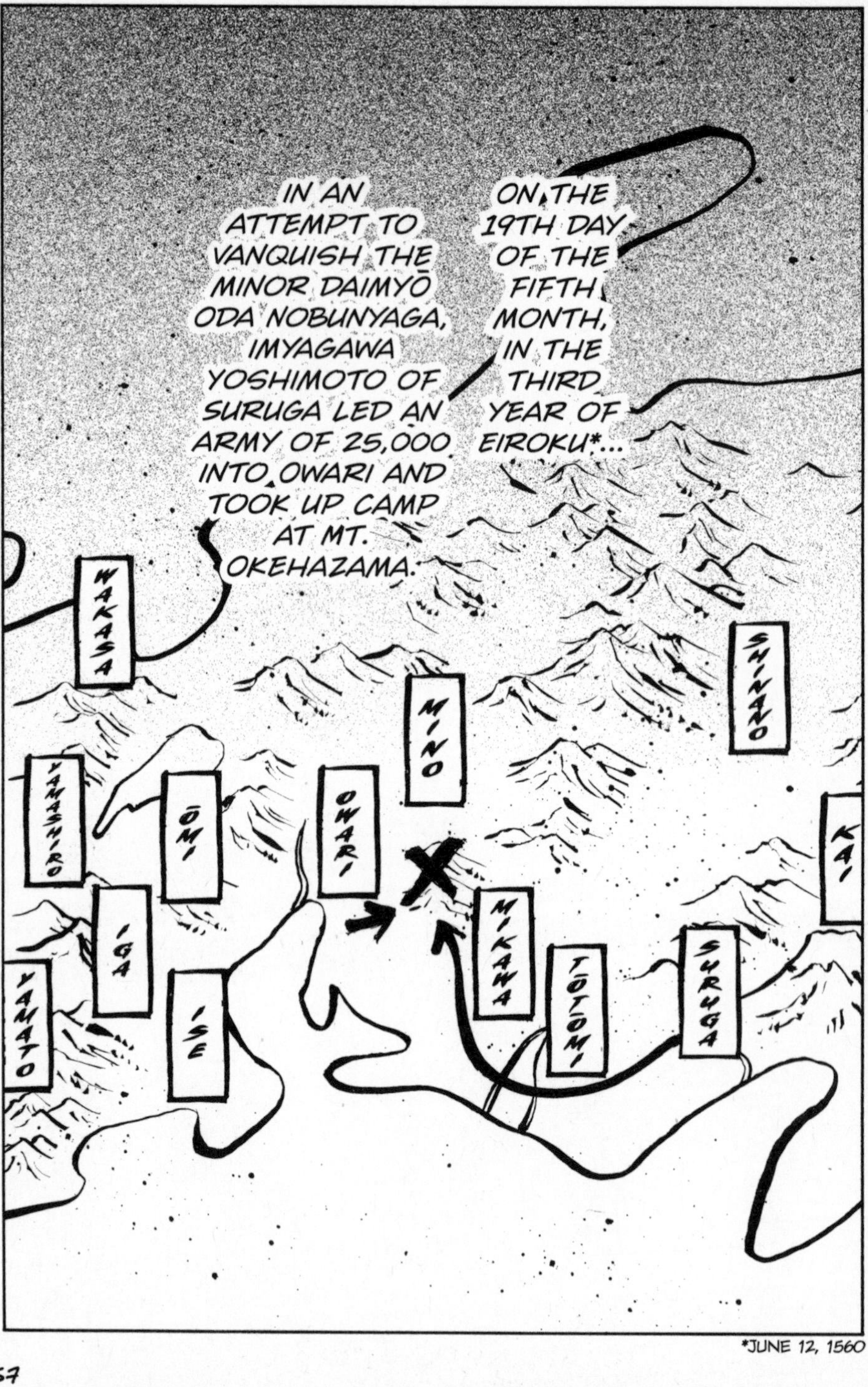
ON THE 19TH DAY OF THE FIFTH MONTH, IN THE THIRD YEAR OF EIROKU*...
IN AN ATTEMPT TO VANQUISH THE MINOR DAIMYŌ ODA NOBUNYAGA, IMYAGAWA YOSHIMOTO OF SURUGA LED AN ARMY OF 25,000 INTO OWARI AND TOOK UP CAMP AT MT. OKEHAZAMA.
SHINANO
KAI
SURUGA
TŌTŌMI
MIKAWA
MINO
OWARI
ŌMI
WAKASA
YAMASHIRO
IGA
ISE
YAMATO

*JUNE 12, 1560

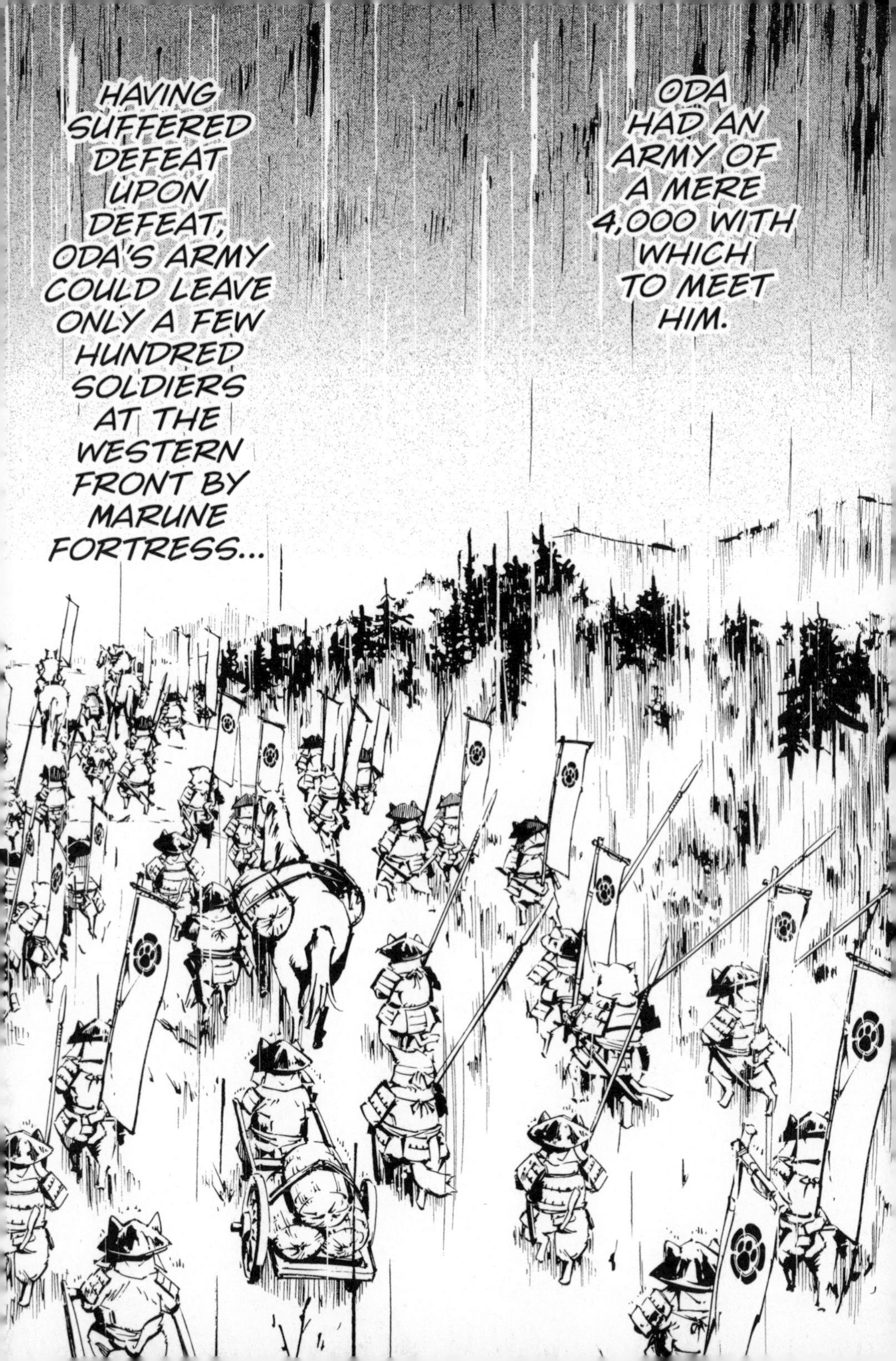
ODA HAD AN ARMY OF A MERE 4,000 WITH WHICH TO MEET HIM.
HAVING SUFFERED DEFEAT UPON DEFEAT, ODA'S ARMY COULD LEAVE ONLY A FEW HUNDRED SOLDIERS AT THE WESTERN FRONT BY MARUNE FORTRESS...

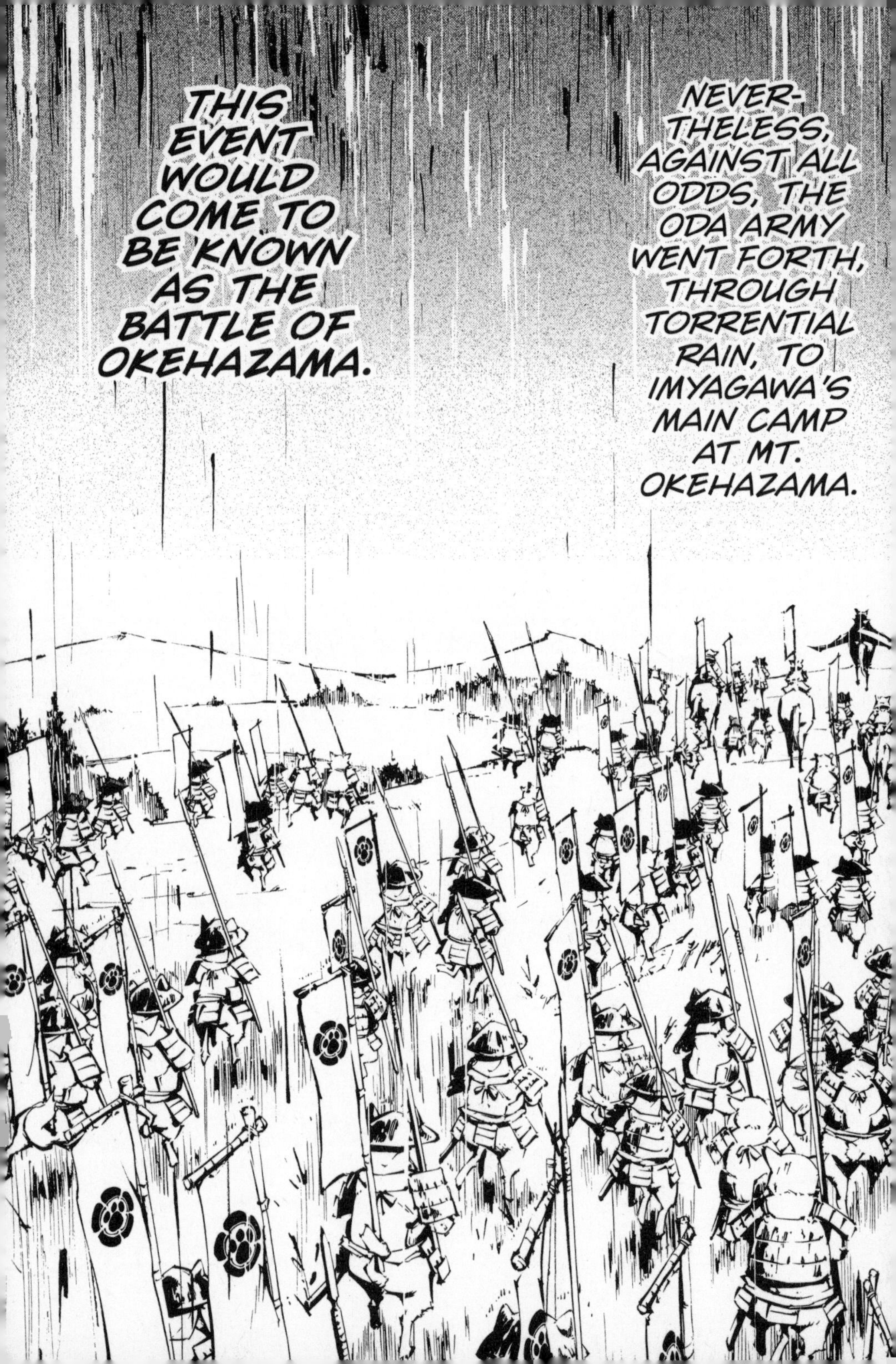
NEVER-THELESS, AGAINST ALL ODDS, THE ODA ARMY WENT FORTH, THROUGH TORRENTIAL RAIN, TO IMYAGAWA'S MAIN CAMP AT MT. OKEHAZAMA.
THIS EVENT WOULD COME TO BE KNOWN AS THE BATTLE OF OKEHAZAMA.

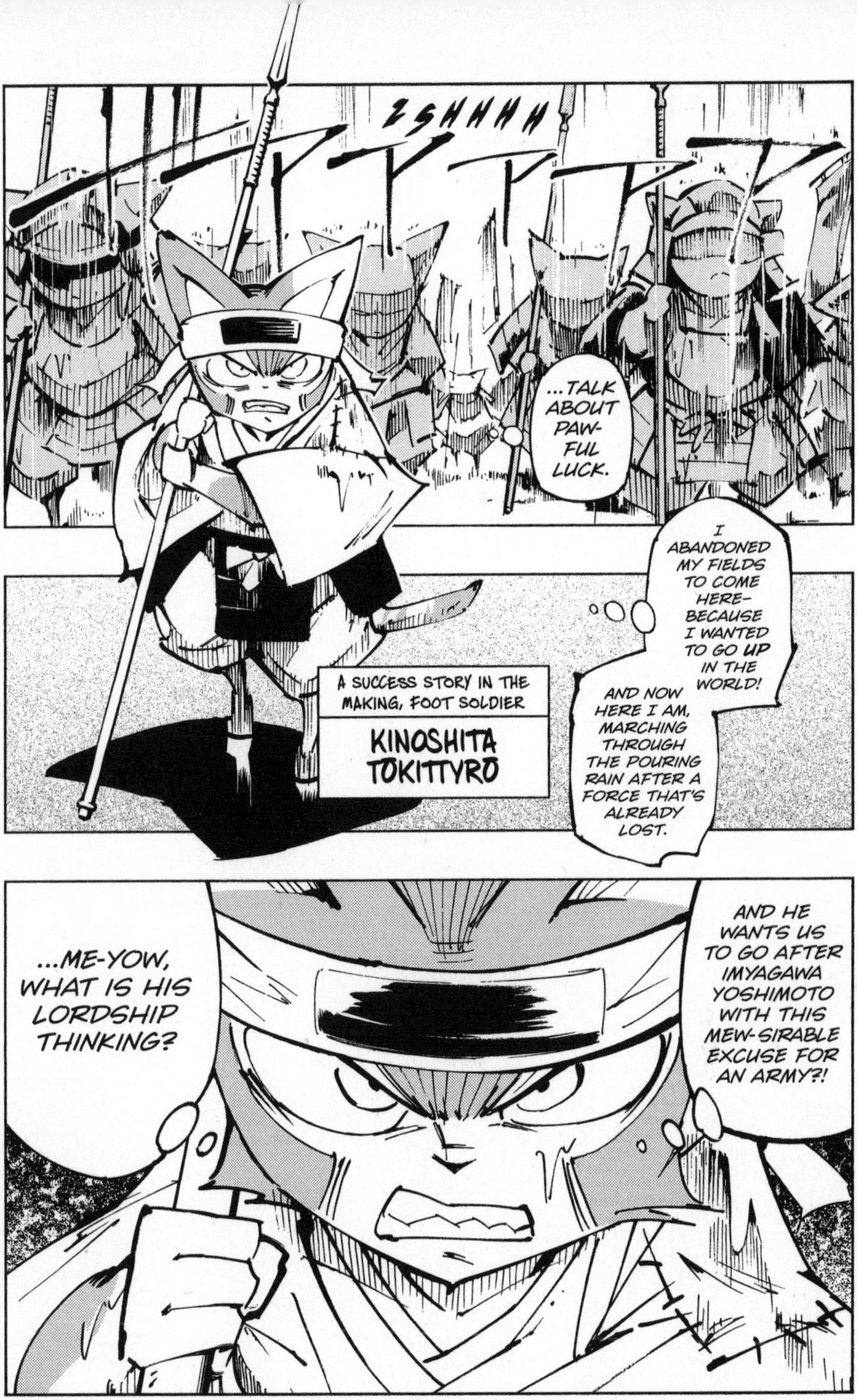
ZSHHHH
...TALK ABOUT PAW-FUL LUCK.
I ABANDONED MY FIELDS TO COME HERE- BECAUSE I WANTED TO GO UP IN THE WORLD!
AND NOW HERE I AM, MARCHING THROUGH THE POURING RAIN AFTER A FORCE THAT'S ALREADY LOST.
A SUCCESS STORY IN THE MAKING, FOOT SOLDIER
KINOSHITA TOKITTYRO
AND HE WANTS US TO GO AFTER IMYAGAWA YOSHIMOTO WITH THIS MEW-SIRABLE EXCUSE FOR AN ARMY?!
...ME-YOW, WHAT IS HIS LORDSHIP THINKING?

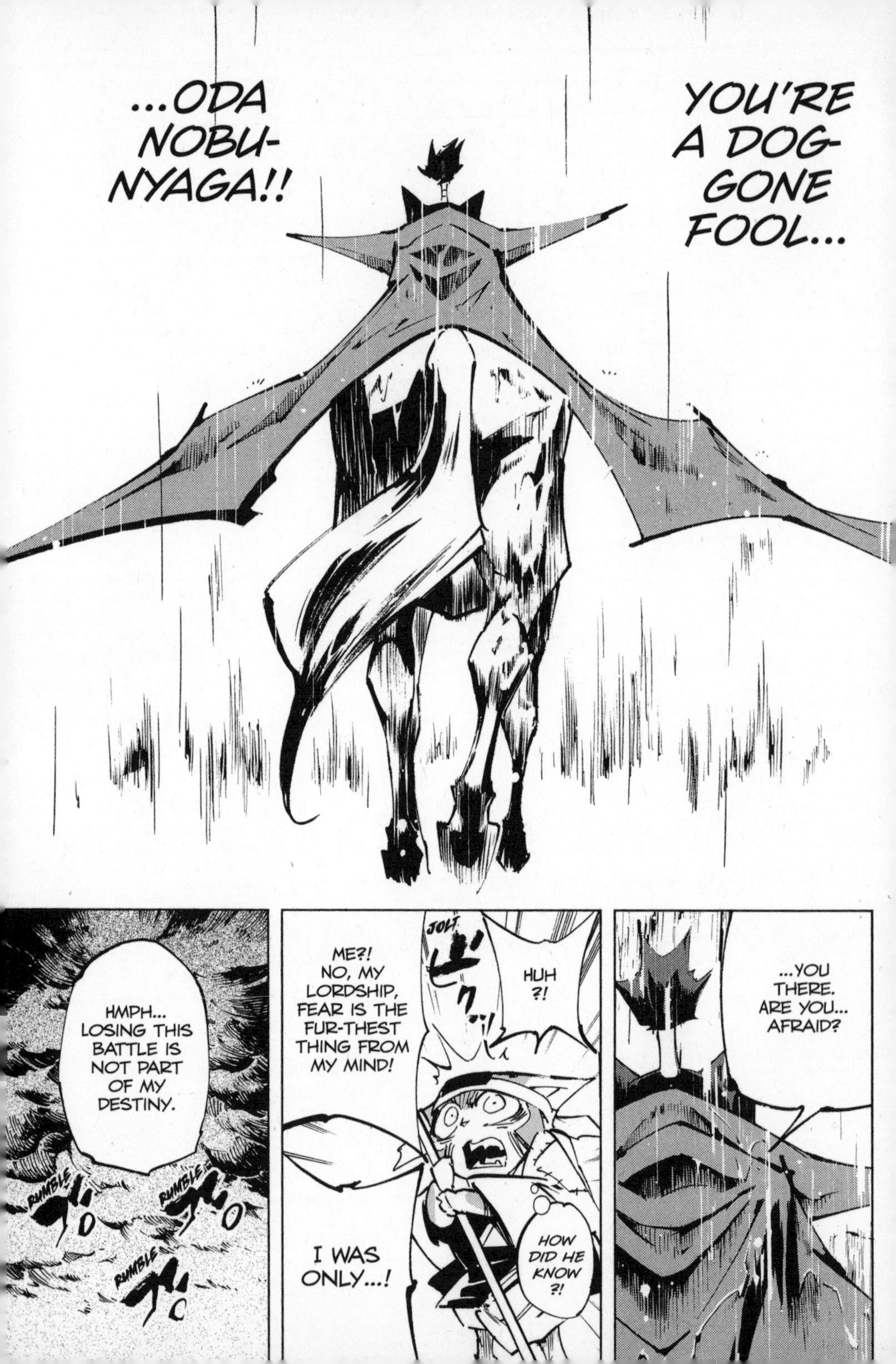
YOU'RE A DOG-GONE FOOL...
...ODA NOBU-NYAGA!!
...YOU THERE. ARE YOU... AFRAID?
JOLT
HUH ?!
ME?! NO, MY LORDSHIP, FEAR IS THE FUR-THEST THING FROM MY MIND!
HOW DID HE KNOW ?!
I WAS ONLY...!
HMPH... LOSING THIS BATTLE IS NOT PART OF MY DESTINY.
RUMBLE
RUMBLE
RUMBLE

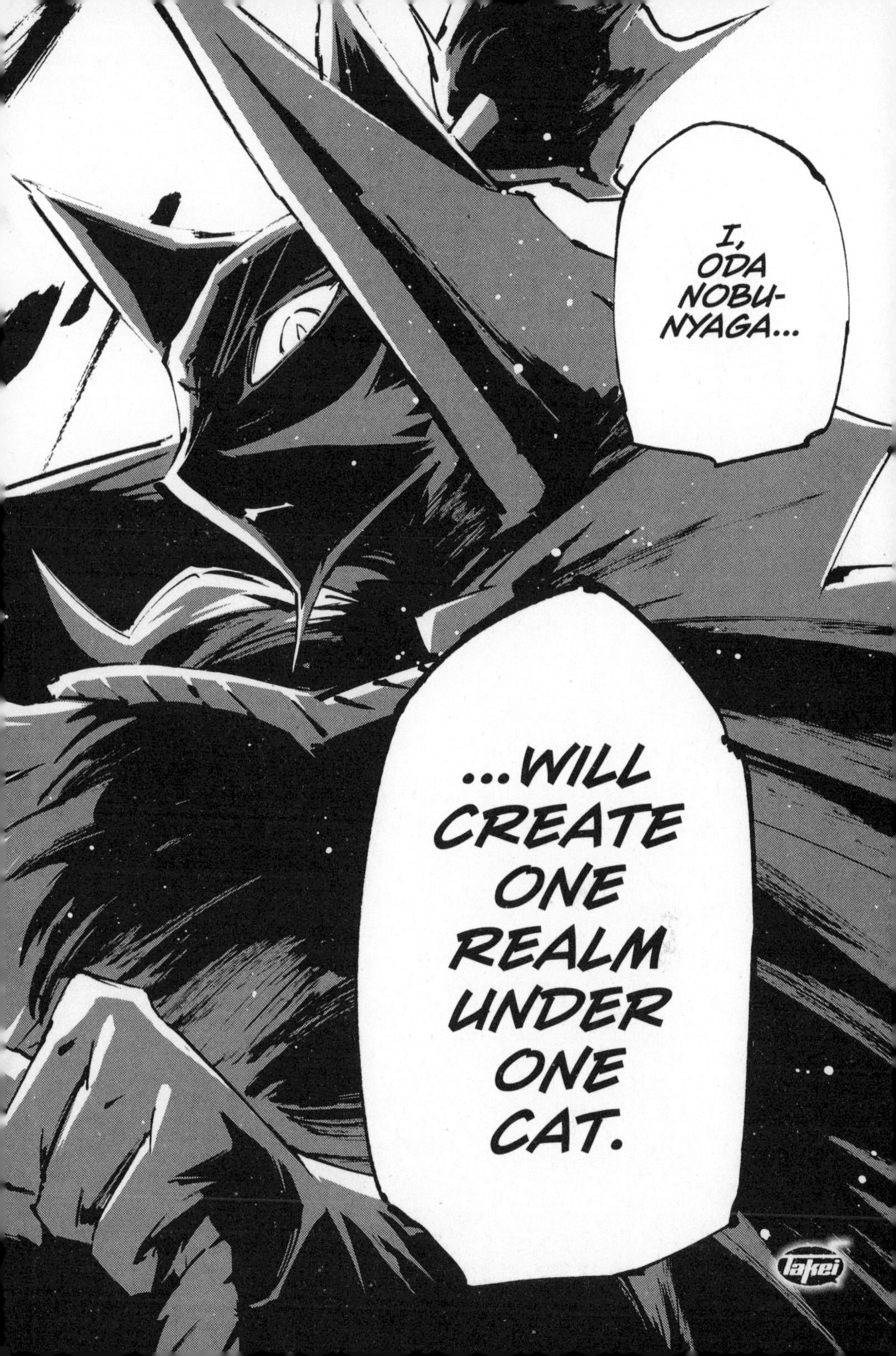
I, ODA NOBU-NYAGA...
...WILL CREATE ONE REALM UNDER ONE CAT.

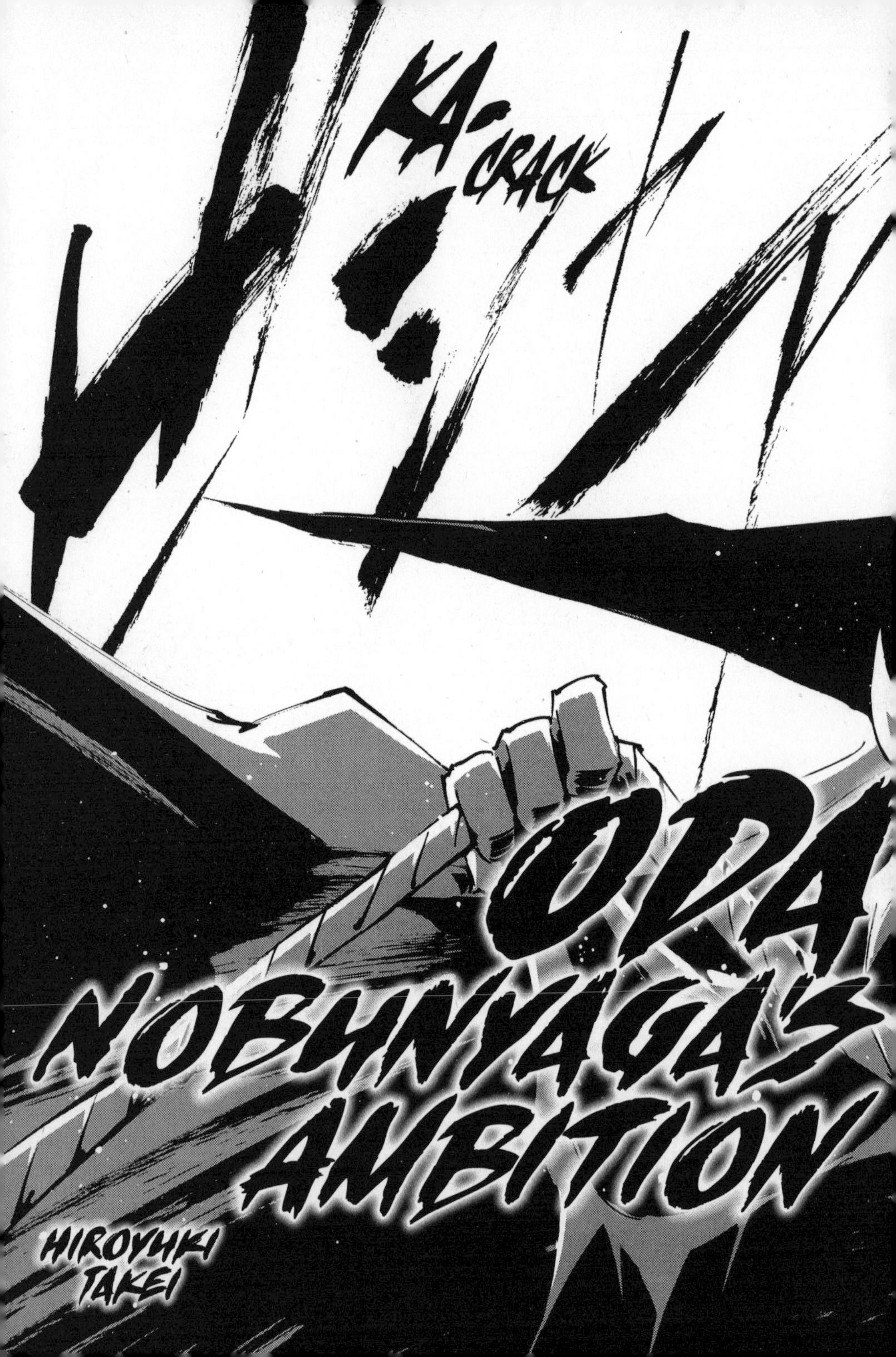
KA-CRACK
ODA NOBUNAGA'S AMBITION
HIROYUKI TAKEI

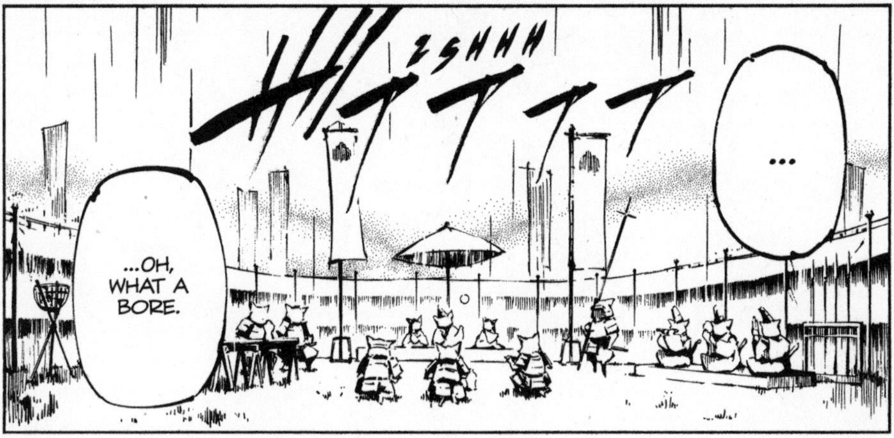
...
ZSHHH
...OH, WHAT A BORE.

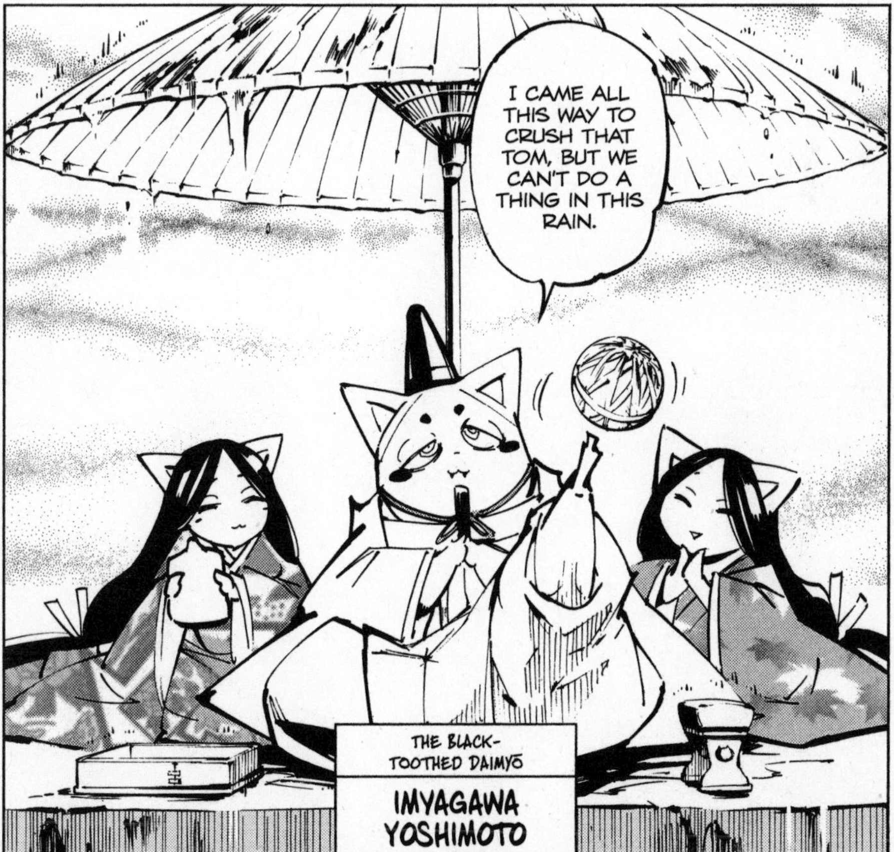
I CAME ALL THIS WAY TO CRUSH THAT TOM, BUT WE CAN'T DO A THING IN THIS RAIN.
THE BLACK-TOOTHED DAIMYŌ
IMYAGAWA YOSHIMOTO

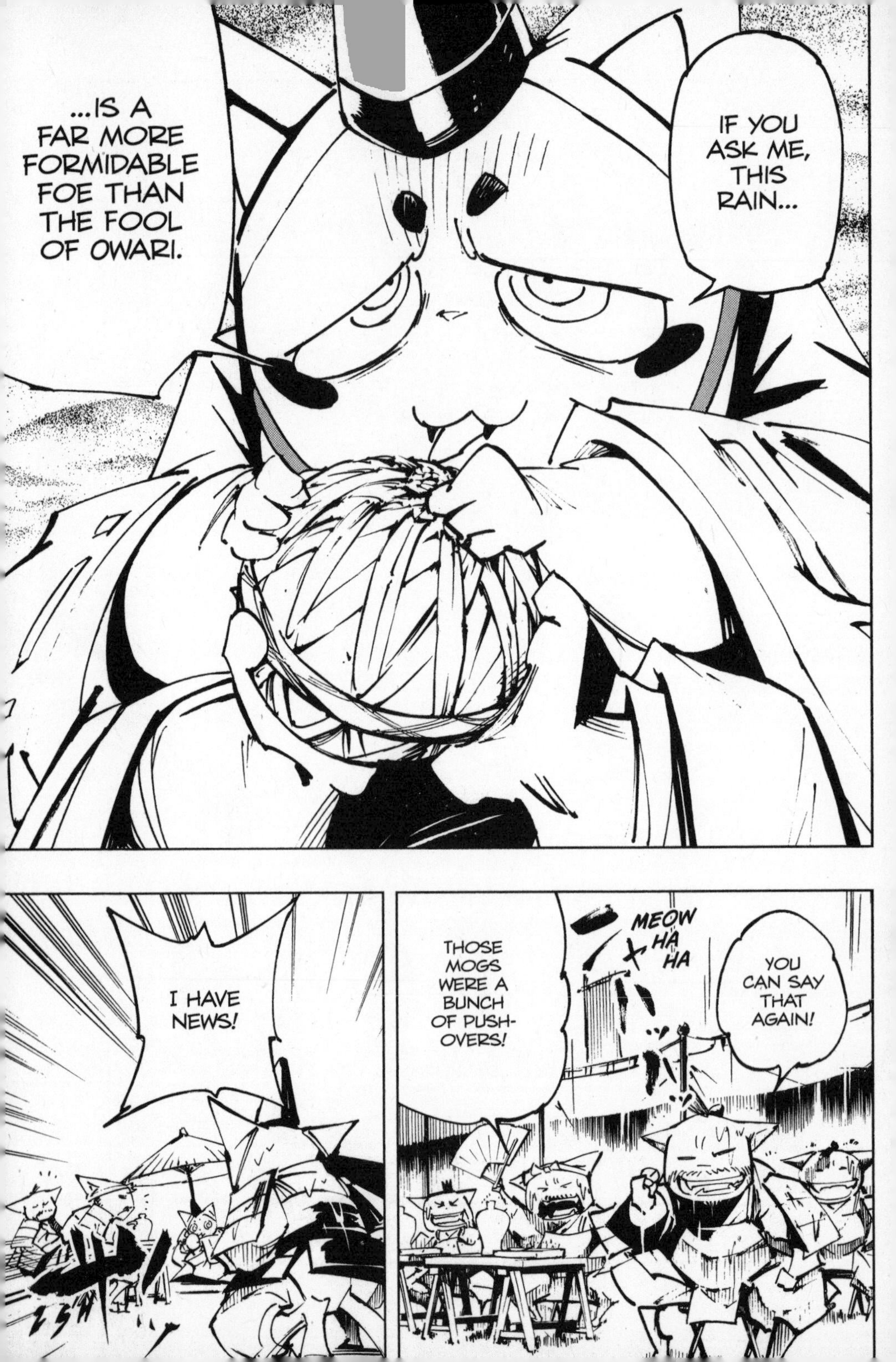
IF YOU ASK ME, THIS RAIN...
...IS A FAR MORE FORMIDABLE FOE THAN THE FOOL OF OWARI.
THOSE MOGS WERE A BUNCH OF PUSH-OVERS!
MEOW HA HA
YOU CAN SAY THAT AGAIN!
I HAVE NEWS!

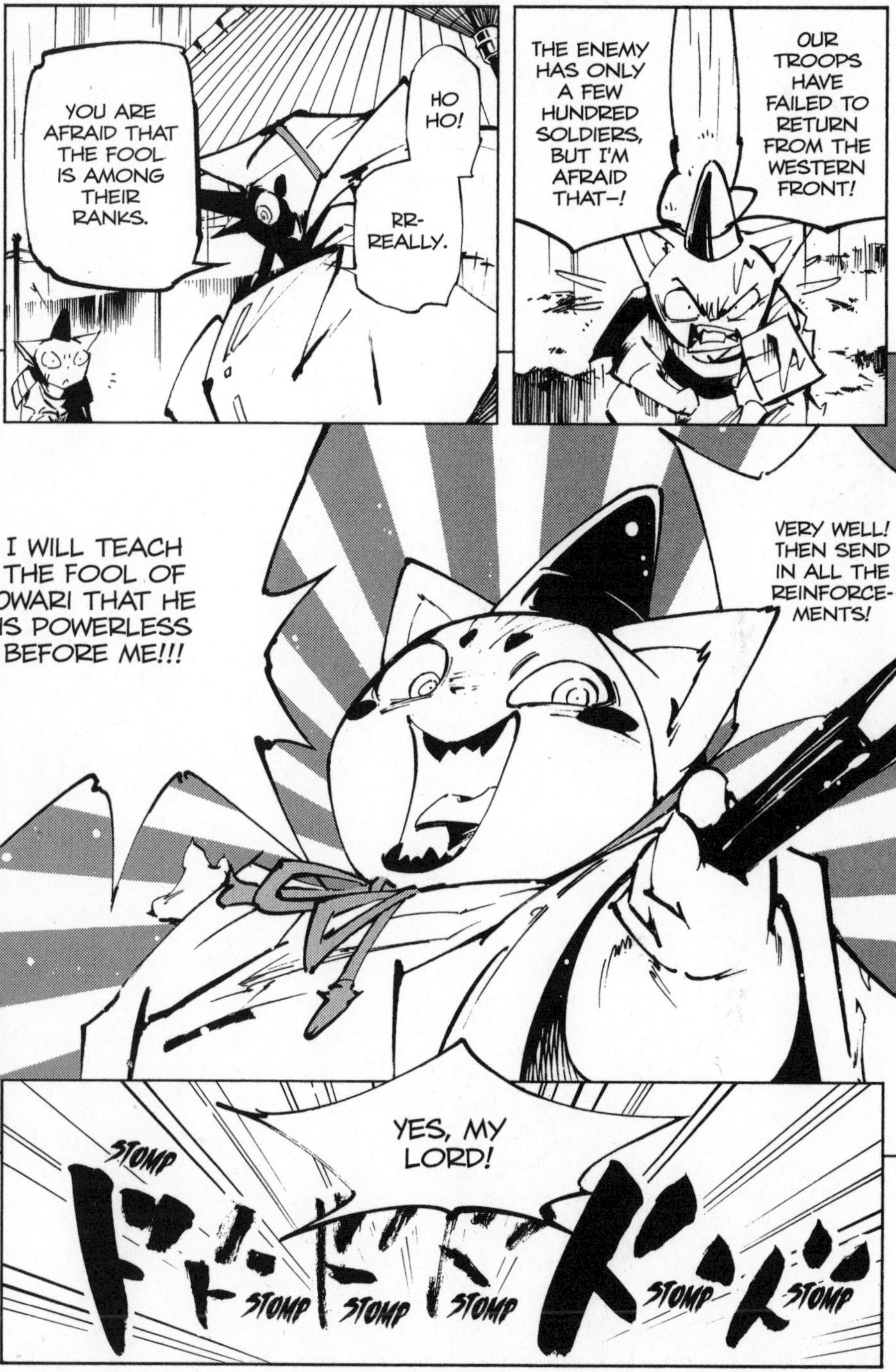
OUR TROOPS HAVE FAILED TO RETURN FROM THE WESTERN FRONT!
THE ENEMY HAS ONLY A FEW HUNDRED SOLDIERS, BUT I'M AFRAID THAT—!
HO HO!
RR-REALLY.
YOU ARE AFRAID THAT THE FOOL IS AMONG THEIR RANKS.
VERY WELL! THEN SEND IN ALL THE REINFORCE-MENTS!
I WILL TEACH THE FOOL OF OWARI THAT HE IS POWERLESS BEFORE ME!!!
YES, MY LORD!
STOMP
STOMP
STOMP
STOMP
STOMP
STOMP
STOMP

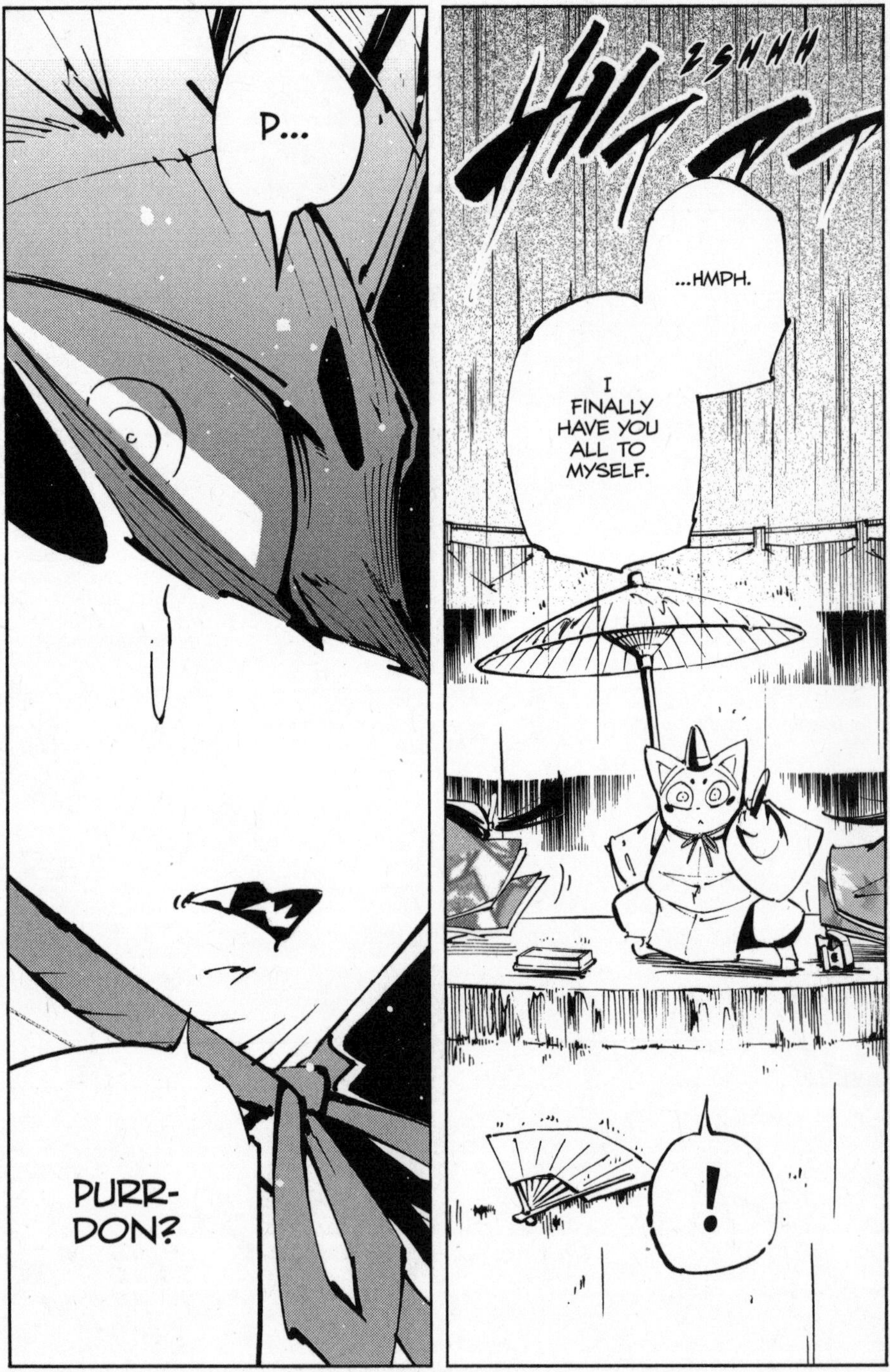
ZSHHH
...HMPH.
I FINALLY HAVE YOU ALL TO MYSELF.
!
P...
PURR-DON?

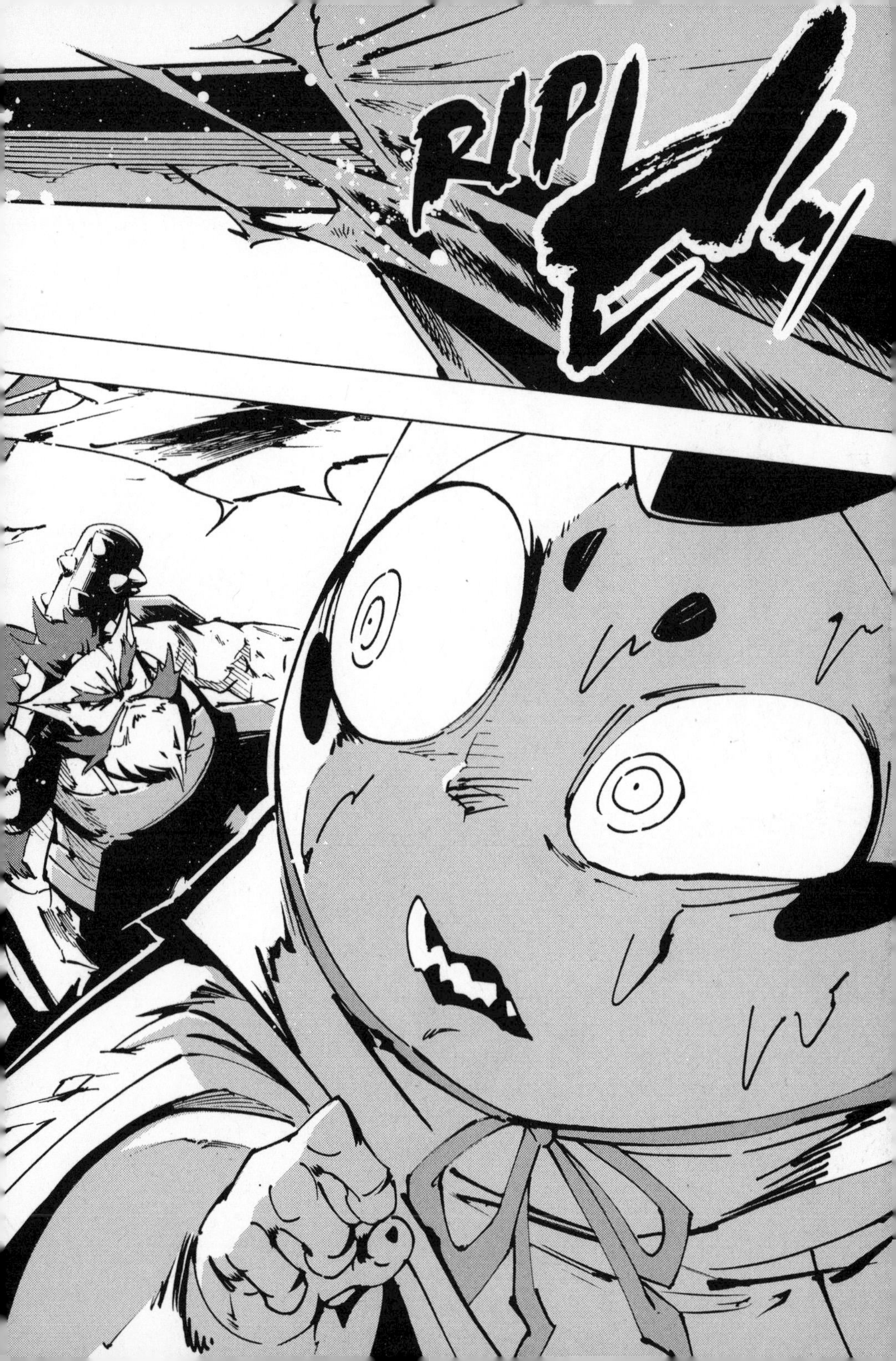
RIP!

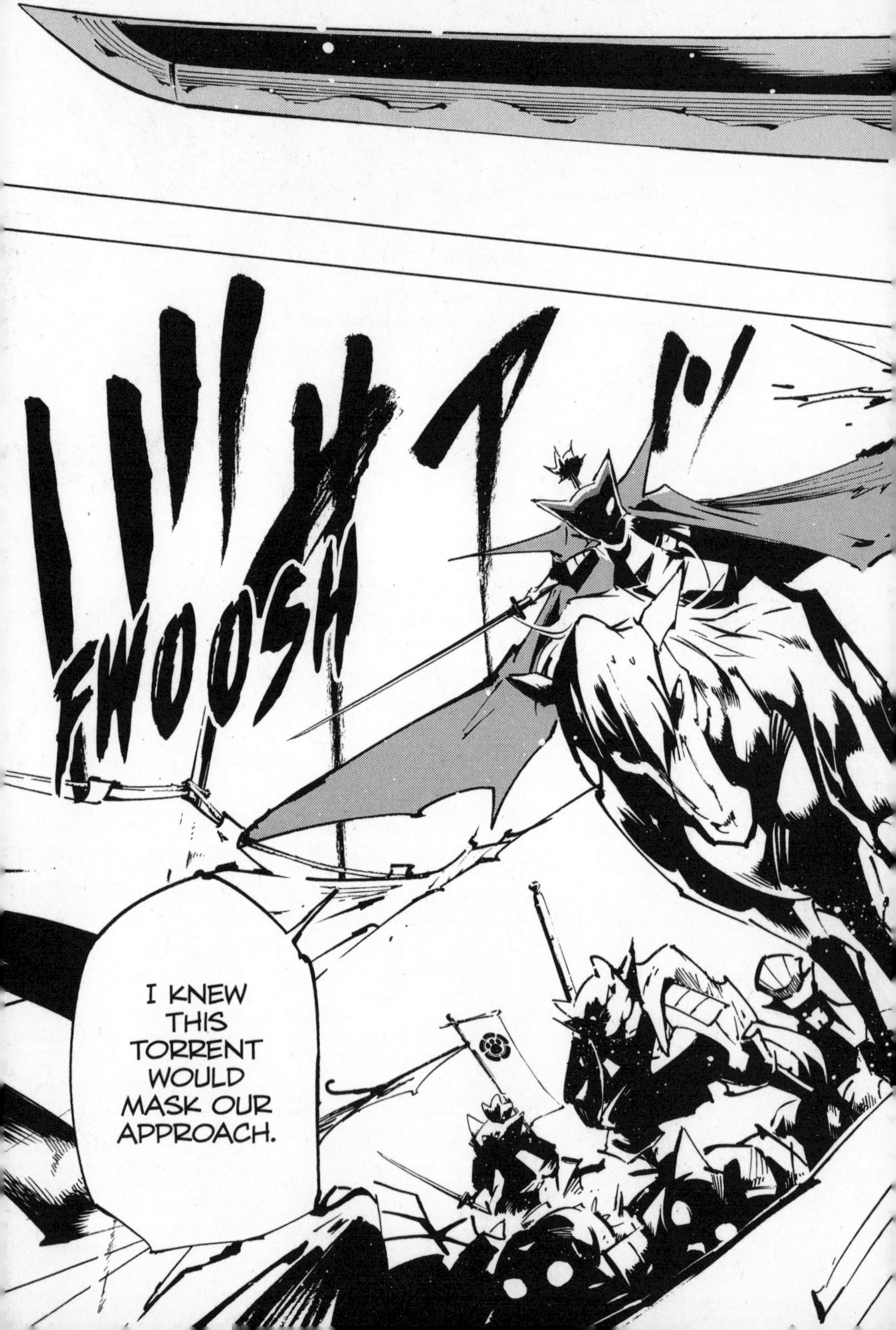
FWOOSH
I KNEW THIS TORRENT WOULD MASK OUR APPROACH.

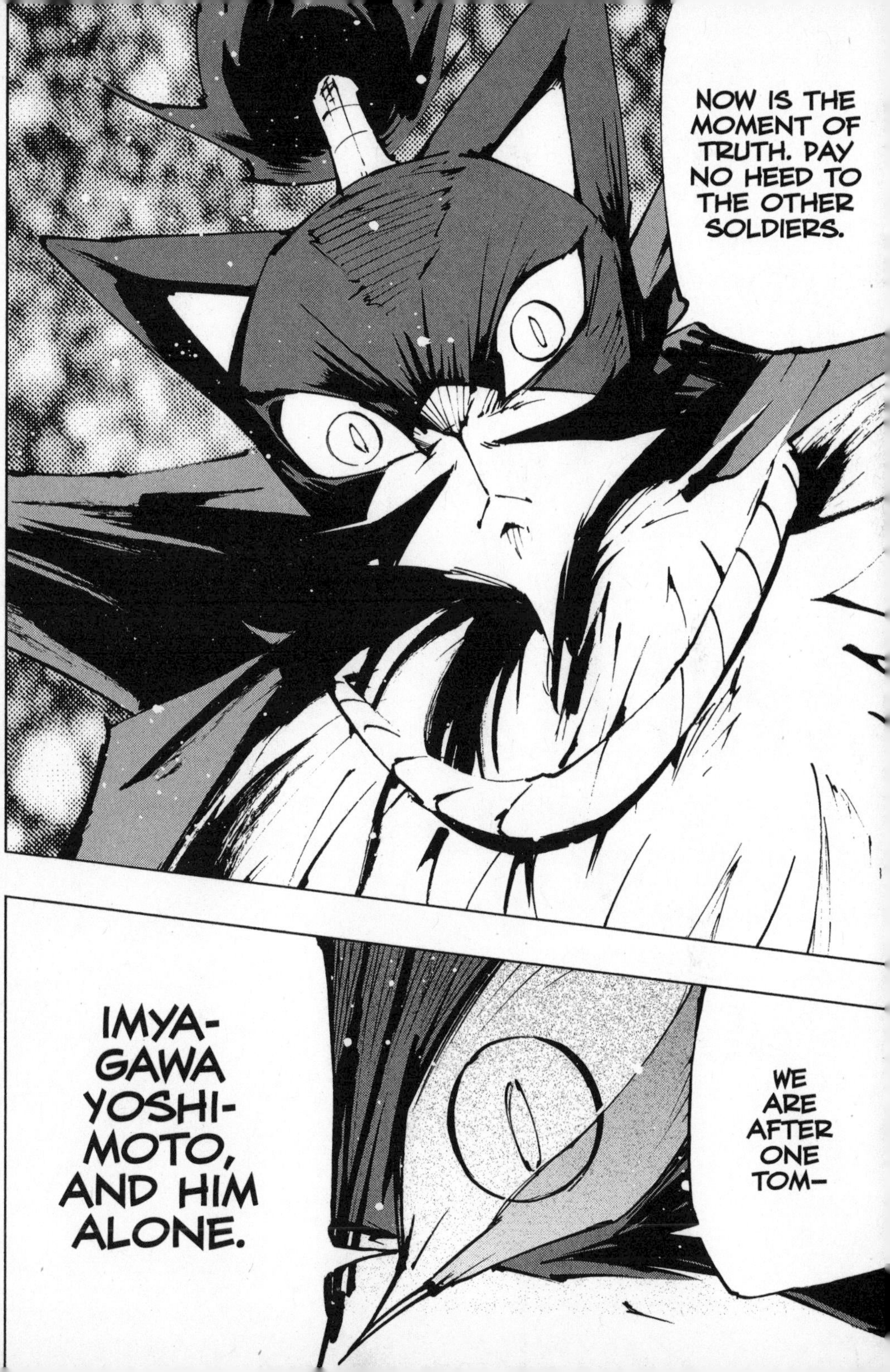
NOW IS THE MOMENT OF TRUTH. PAY NO HEED TO THE OTHER SOLDIERS.
WE ARE AFTER ONE TOM-
IMYA-GAWA YOSHI-MOTO, AND HIM ALONE.

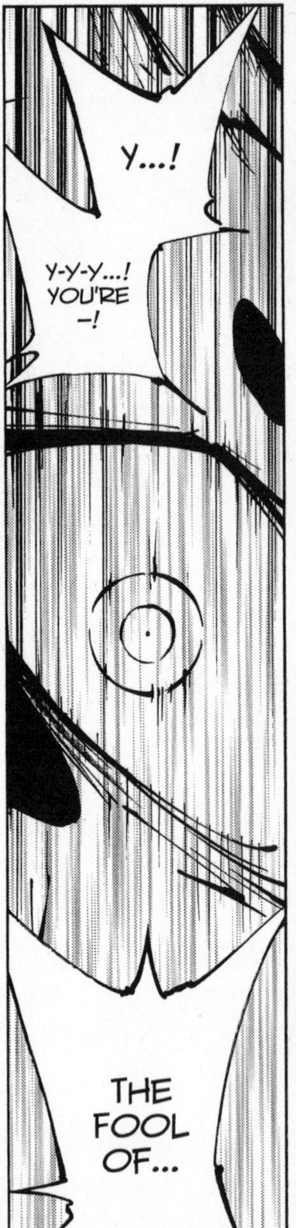
Y...!
Y-Y-Y...! YOU'RE —!
THE FOOL OF...
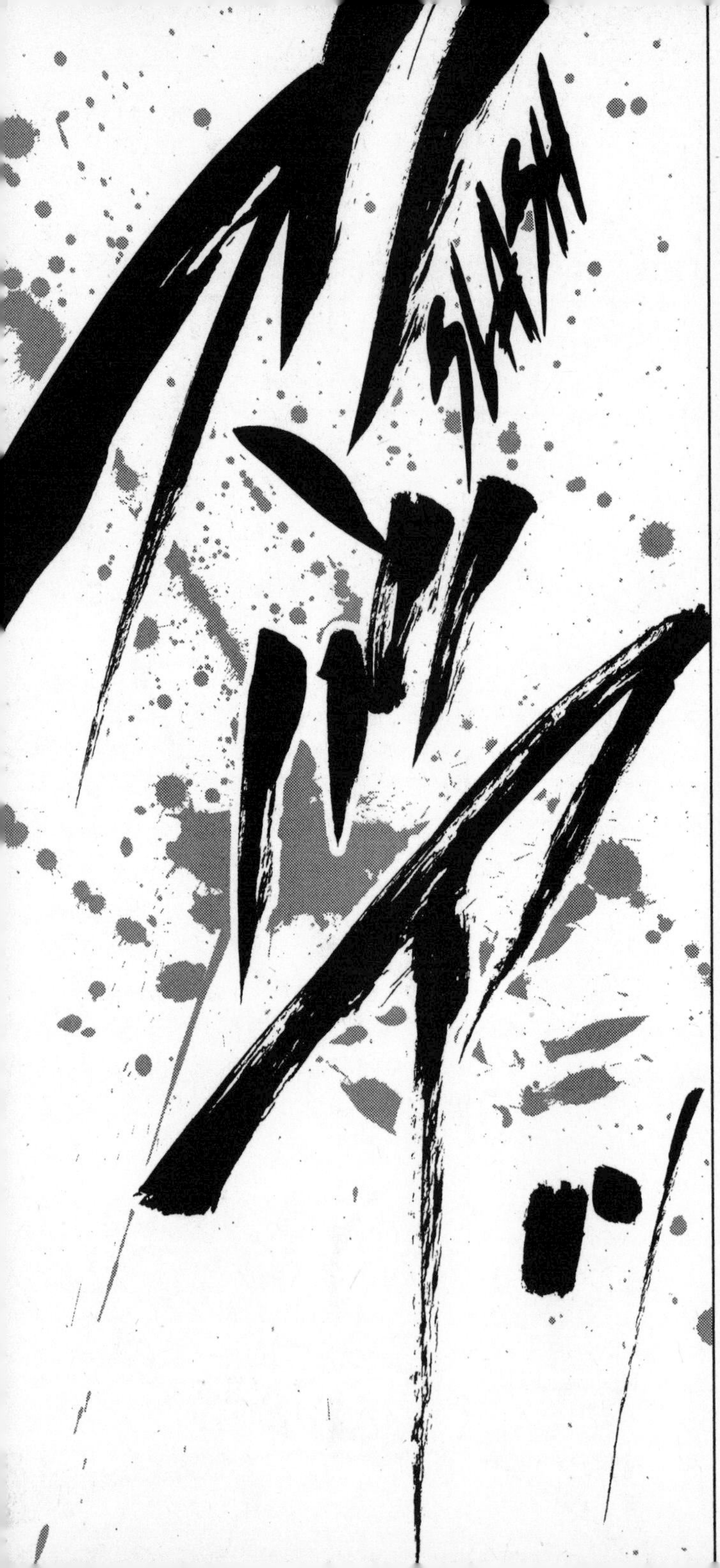
SLASH

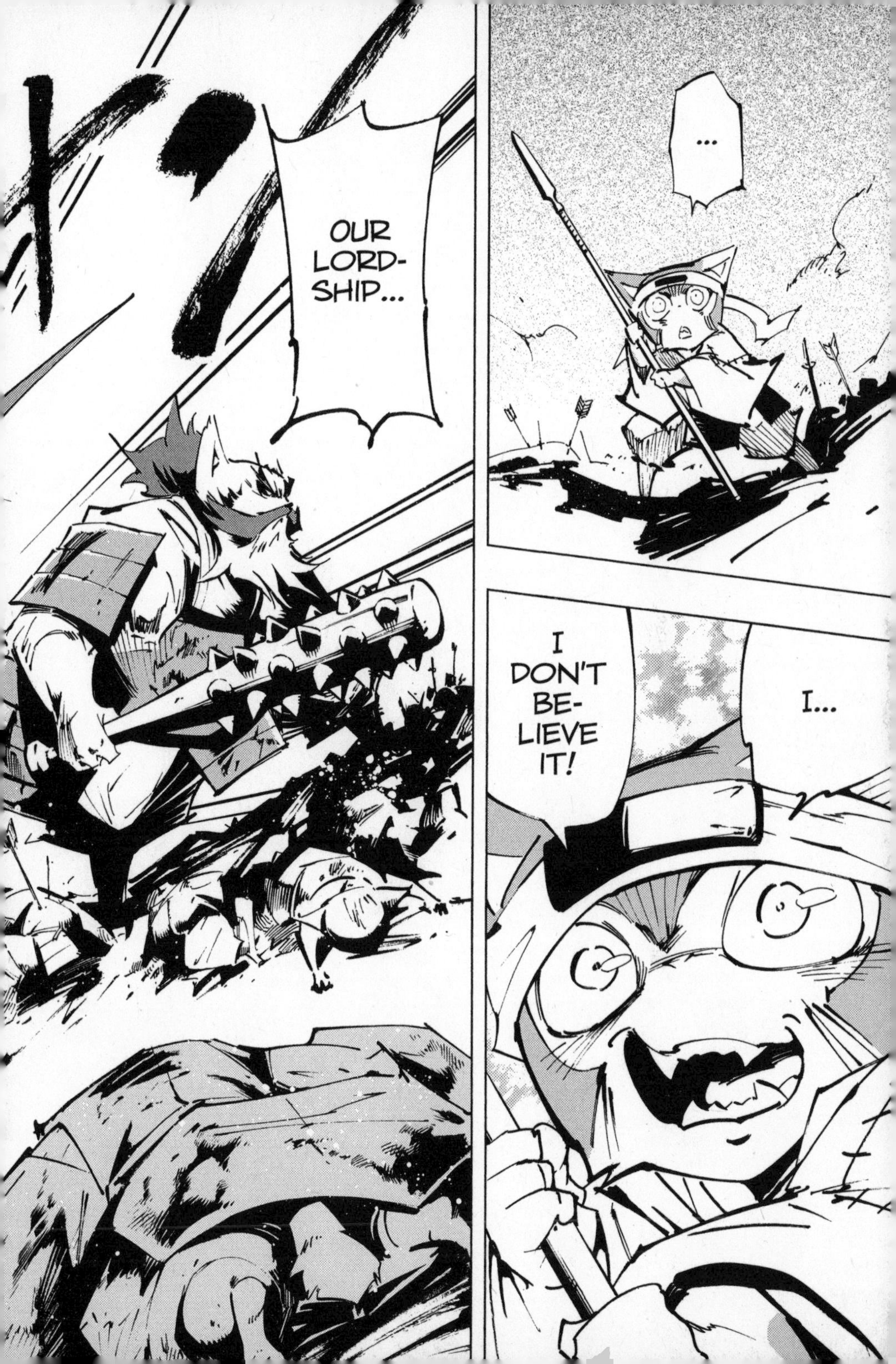
...
I...
I DON'T BE-LIEVE IT!
OUR LORD-SHIP...

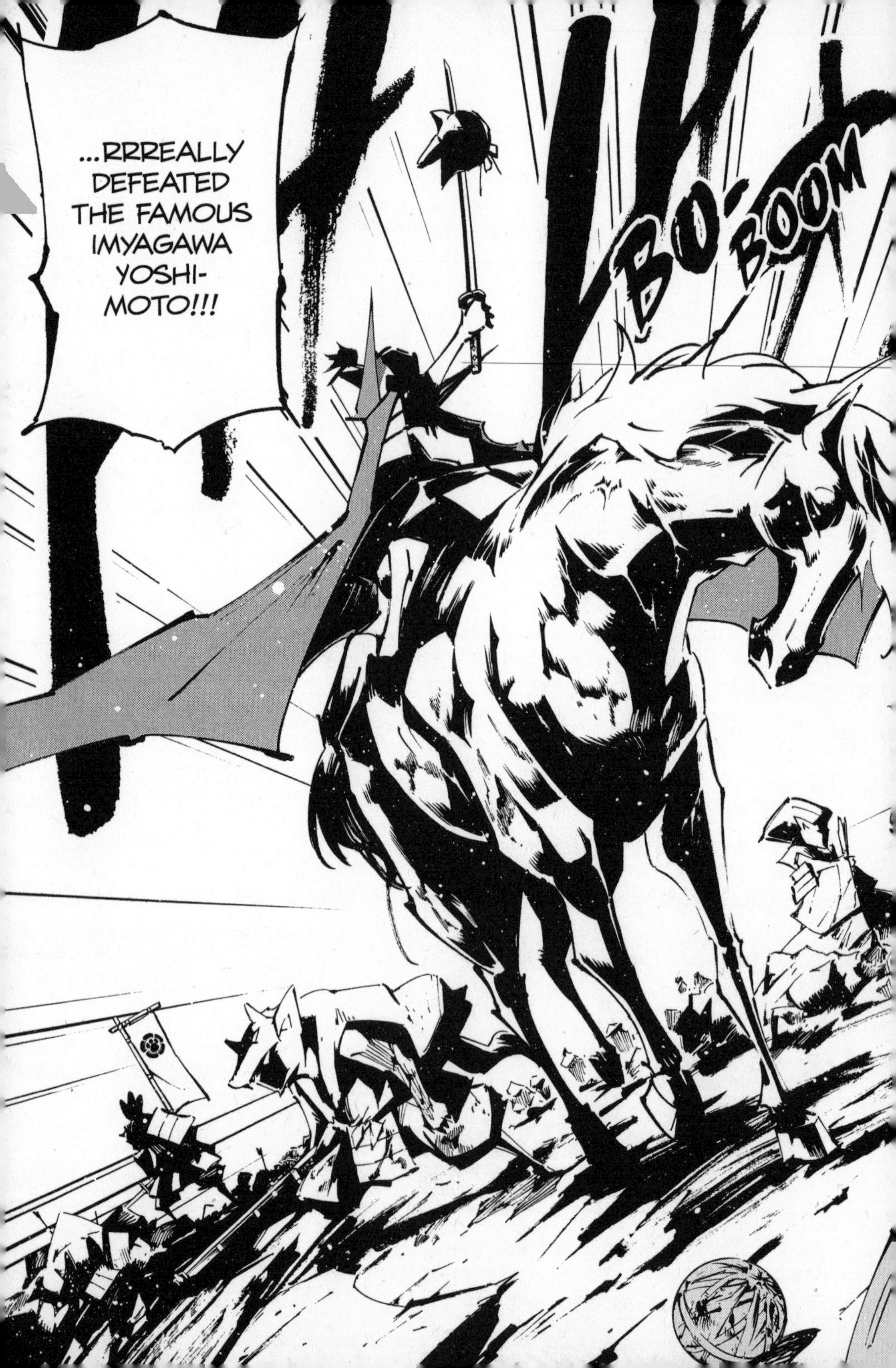
...RRREALLY DEFEATED THE FAMOUS IMYAGAWA YOSHI-MOTO!!!
BO-BOOM

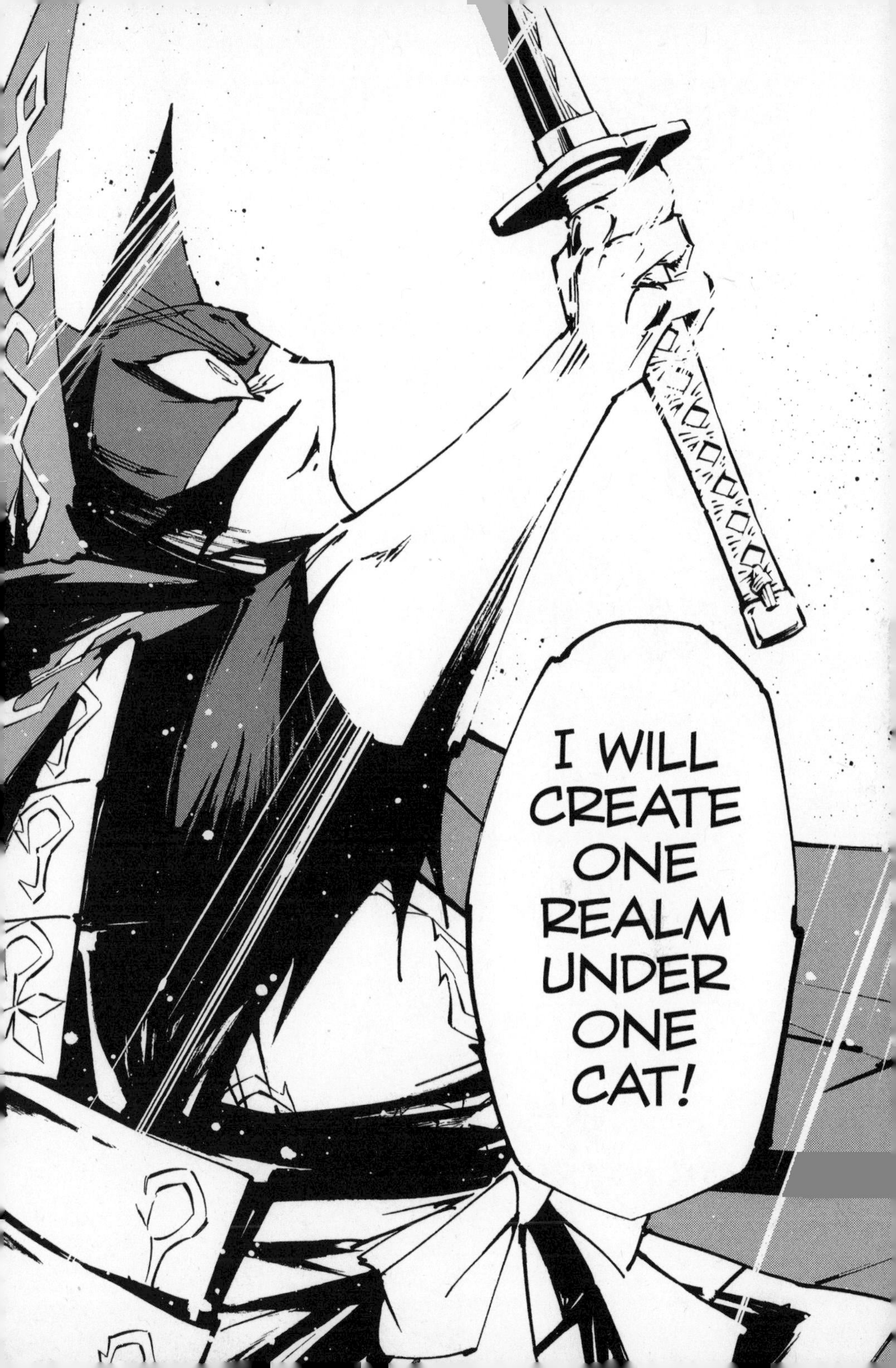
I WILL CREATE ONE REALM UNDER ONE CAT!

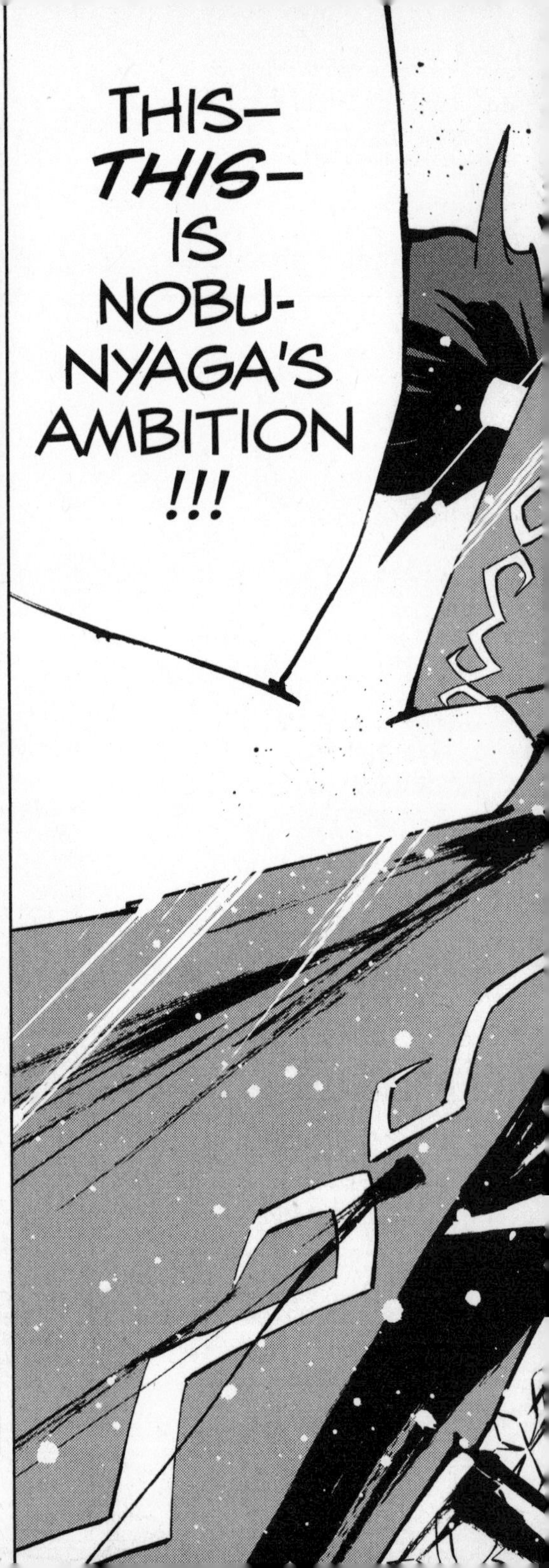
THIS- *THIS*- IS NOBU-NYAGA'S AMBITION!!!

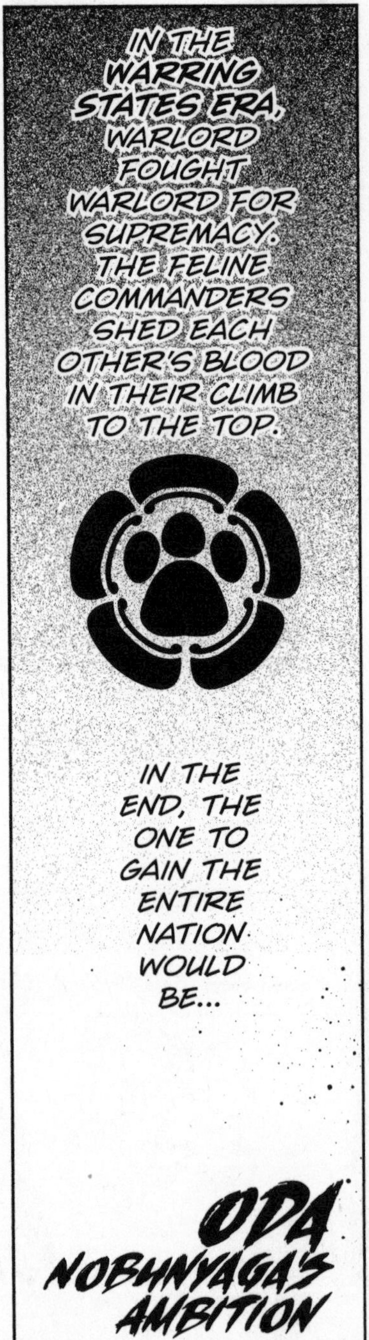
IN THE WARRING STATES ERA, WARLORD FOUGHT WARLORD FOR SUPREMACY. THE FELINE COMMANDERS SHED EACH OTHER'S BLOOD IN THEIR CLIMB TO THE TOP.
IN THE END, THE ONE TO GAIN THE ENTIRE NATION WOULD BE...
ODA NOBUNYAGA'S AMBITION

TRANSLATION NOTES

Wakizashi, page 22

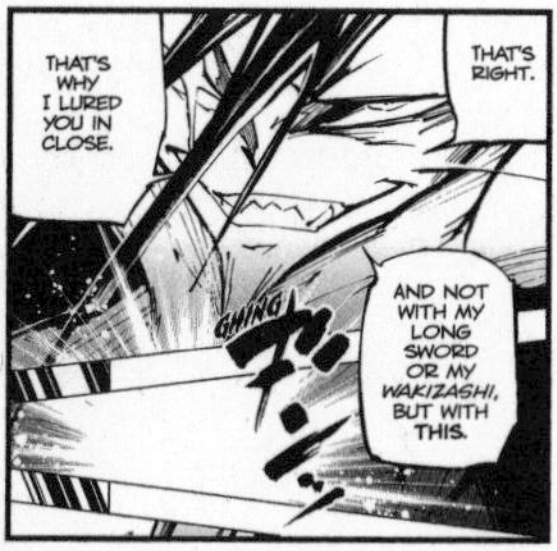
THAT'S RIGHT.
THAT'S WHY I LURED YOU IN CLOSE.
AND NOT WITH MY LONG SWORD OR MY WAKIZASHI, BUT WITH THIS.
GHING

Meaning "side insert," a *wakizashi* is a sword worn at a warrior's side along with his longer katana as a symbol of his samurai status. This blade can be used as a backup sword, or for closer combat.

Okakatō, page 23

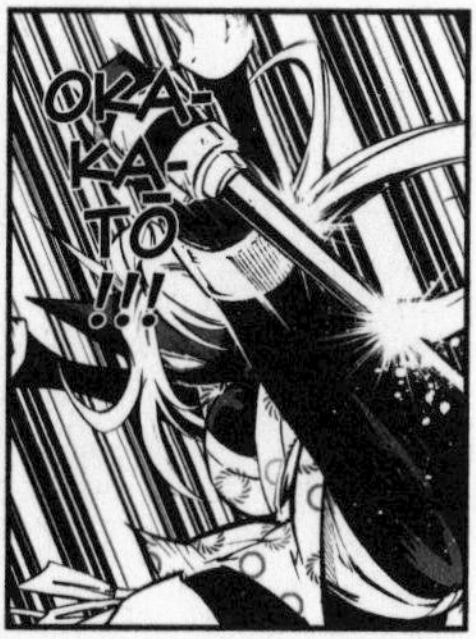
OKA-KA-TŌ!!!

The name of Mukuro's secret weapon literally means "bonito flakes blade," where bonito is a type of fish—possibly one of Mukuro's favorites. Or perhaps she named her sword after the tasty treat because together, *okakatō* means "heel," as in "the heel of the foot."

Himemasu Castle, page 32

This castle bears a striking resemblance to the real life historical fortress, Himeji Castle, which was awarded by the shogun Tokugawa Ieyasu to his son-in-law for the latter's service in the battle of Sekigahara. The name Himemasu may be more palatable to the characters of *Nekogahara*, as it is the Japanese word for the sockeye salmon, and it is ruled by the Shakegawa, whose name means "salmon skin".

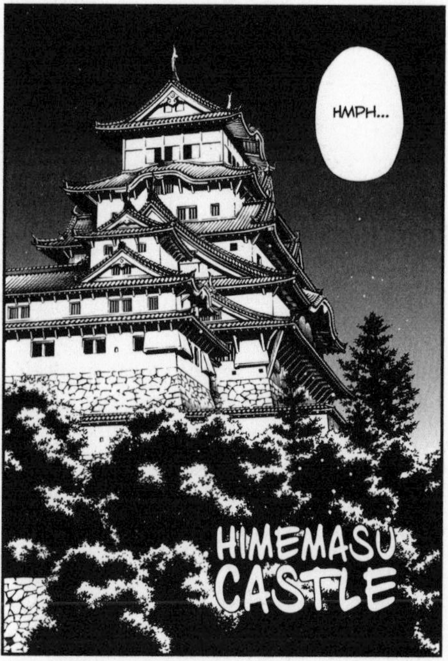
HMPH...
HIMEMASU CASTLE

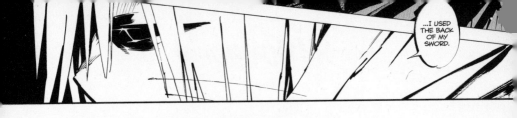

...I USED THE BACK OF MY SWORD.

I used the back of my sword, page 90

The katana used by samurai is a single-edged sword, meaning it's sharp on one side and blunt on the other. Striking one's enemy with the blunt side of the blade is a way to teach them a lesson while letting them live to remember it.

Ishidai Tsunari, page 121

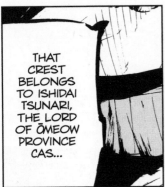

THAT CREST BELONGS TO ISHIDAI TSUNARI, THE LORD OF ŌMEOW PROVINCE CAS...

The name of the man Short is remembering will perhaps bring two things to the mind of a Japanese reader. The first is the striped beakfish, or *ishidai*. A few of these fish became famous for taking up residence in a ship that broke loose and went adrift after the Tohoku Earthquake and following tsunami in 2011, earning them the name "tsunami fish." The second thing Japanese readers will remember is the name Ishida Mitsunari, who was a military commander who fought, and lost, in the battle of Sekigahara.

Netherworld Soul-Reaper, page 129

The name of Short's special move is rife with wordplay. In Japanese, it is *jigoku no kama-otoshi*. The first part, *jigoku no*, is straightforward enough, meaning "of or relating to hell, the netherworld, etc." *Kama-otoshi* can mean "sickle drop," as in bringing a sickle down either to harvest grain or to strike an enemy. In Japan, a small sickle was often connected to a heavy weight via a chain, creating a weapon not entirely unlike Short's kendama. *Kama* is also the word for the

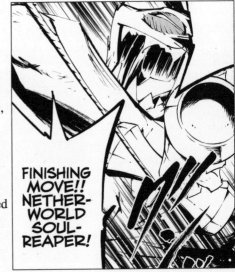

FINISHING MOVE!! NETHER-WORLD SOUL-REAPER!

head of a fish, and *kama-otoshi* is the removal of the fish's head in preparation for cooking, hence the alternate spelling for this attack name: Netherworld Sole-Reaper.

Nobunyaga's Ambition, page 156

Nobunyaga's Ambition is a spinoff of the *Nobunaga's Ambition* game series, in which all the characters—who are real Japanese historical figures—are reimagined as cats. It's a social game that can be played on mobile devices, and for a time was available in North America as *Samurai Cats*. The game had a collaboration with this manga series, in which players could obtain in-game items featuring artwork by Hiroyuki Takei.

Success story in the making, page 160

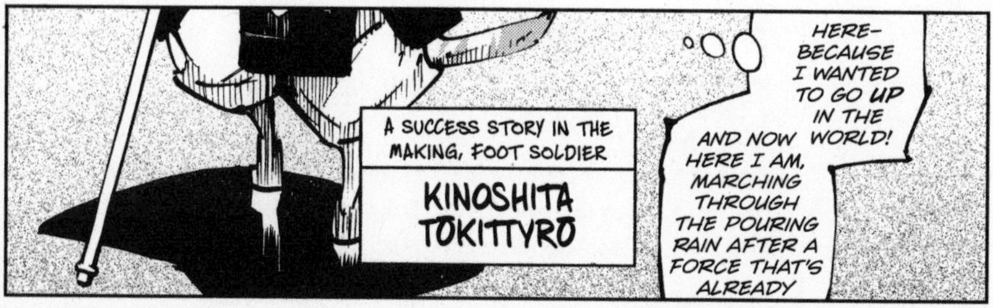
AND NOW HERE I AM, MARCHING THROUGH THE POURING RAIN AFTER A FORCE THAT'S ALREADY HERE— BECAUSE I WANTED TO GO UP IN THE WORLD!
A SUCCESS STORY IN THE MAKING, FOOT SOLDIER
KINOSHITA TŌKITTYRŌ

Kinoshita Tōkittyrō, known in human form as Kinoshita Tōkichirō, began his career as a lowly foot soldier, but eventually became the successor to Nobunaga himself and the second of Japan's unifiers, who put an end to the Warring States Period.

One realm under one cat, page 162

This is the feline version of one translation of Oda Nobunaga's historical slogan, *tenka fubu*, or "one realm under one sword." The slogan, which he used on his personal seal to sign all written correspondence, announced his intention to unify the nation, which up to that point had been in a state of constant civil war.

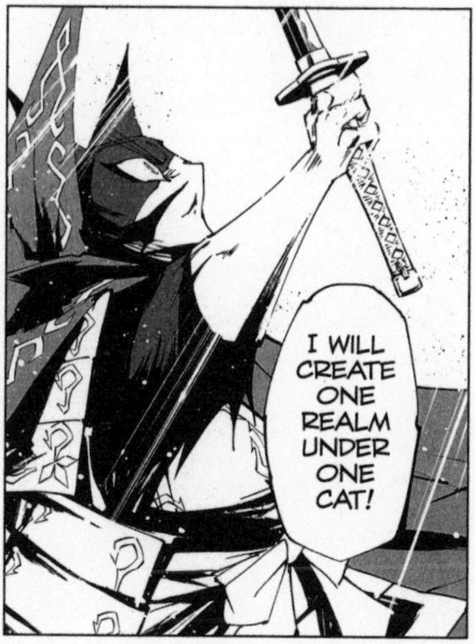
I WILL CREATE ONE REALM UNDER ONE CAT!

The Black-Toothed Daimyō, page 164

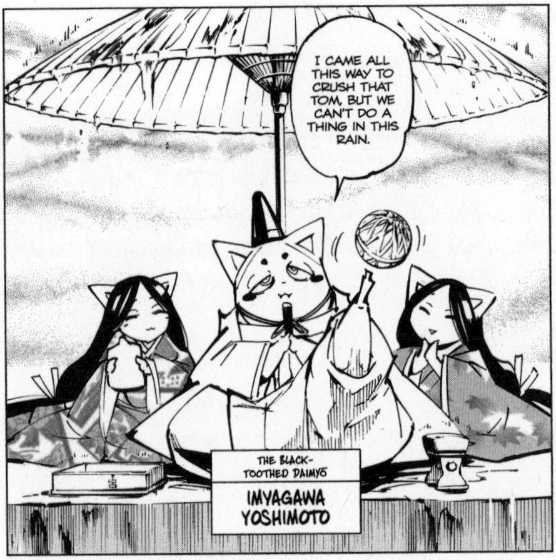
I CAME ALL THIS WAY TO CRUSH THAT TOM, BUT WE CAN'T DO A THING IN THIS RAIN.
THE BLACK-TOOTHED DAIMYŌ
IMYAGAWA YOSHIMOTO

Imyagawa is seen here wearing the traditional dress of the nobles of his time, including the black lacquer over his teeth. Even though he was busy waging war, he still took the time to apply his makeup as a sign of his courtly sensibilities.

A Kodansha Comics Trade Paperback Original.

Published in the United States by Kodansha Comics,
an imprint of Kodansha USA Publishing, LLC, New York.

Publication rights for this English edition arranged through Kodansha Ltd.,
Tokyo.

First published in Japan in 2016 by Kodansha Ltd., Tokyo, as *Nekogahara*
volume 2.

ISBN 978-1-63236-396-1

Printed in the United States of America.

www.kodanshacomics.com

9 8 7 6 5 4 3 2 1

Translation: Alethea Nibley & Athena Nibley
Lettering: Scott O. Brown
Editing: Ajani Oloye
Kodansha Comics edition cover design: Phil Balsman